THE
GLORY, GLORY
NIGHTS

THE
GLORY, GLORY
NIGHTS

The Complete History
of SPURS in
European Competition

ISBN 1 869914 00 7 (Hardback)
ISBN 1 869914 01 5 (Leatherbound)

Printed by: Toppan Printing Co (S) PTE. LPD
38 Liu Fang Road, Jurong Town, Singapore
Designed by: Osborn & Stephens Ltd
Typesetting by: Vigo Press
Origination by: Dot Gradation

IN ORDER TO PRODUCE THIS BOOK IT HAS TAKEN AN ENORMOUS AMOUNT OF HARD WORK AND SPECIAL THANKS ARE DUE TO THE FOLLOWING:

Bob Tanner and Mark Pickhard for their valuable information
John Harris . . . for access to his cuttings library.
Alex Bew . . . without whose dedication and unflagging effort, not to say organization, we would not have got past the first round.
Monte Fresco . . . who, despite being Fleet Street's number one sports photographer, advised on picture selection.

Thanks also to: The British Newspaper Library, Colindale.Syndication departments of the Daily Express, the Daily Mail and the Daily Mirror. Peter Byrne, Anita Crawley, Peter Elston, Stephanie Fincham, Harry Garett, Bob Haydon, Christine Kelly, Larry Mercieca, Jackie Mould, Diane Reeves, Andrew Spearman, Cora Weston.

THE PHOTOGRAPHS IN THIS BOOK HAVE BEEN REPRODUCED BY THE KIND PERMISSION OF THE FOLLOWING:
Associated Press, Carleton, Coloursport, Daily Express, Daily Mail, Daily Mirror, Tommy Hindley, Mark Jameson (Coleraine Chronicle), Keystone, Laurence Lustig, Popperfoto and Sport and General.

THE NEWSPAPER ARTICLES HAVE BEEN REPRODUCED WITH THE KIND PERMISSION OF THE FOLLOWING:

Daily Express, Sunday Express, Daily Herald, Daily Mail, Daily Mirror, Daily Sketch, Daily Telegraph, Evening Standard, Guardian, Manchester Evening News, News of the World, Star, Sun, Sunday Times, Times.

First published by Cockerel Books Ltd. London 1986

FRONT ENDPAPERS 1963: Spurs supporters welcome the European Winners' Cup home – Daily Mail
BACK ENDPAPERS: 1984: Spurs players stare in disbelief as Tony Parks saves a penalty – Monte Fresco

FOREWORD

Twenty-five years ago, in season 1960/61, Tottenham Hotspur became the first club this century to win the League Championship and F.A. Cup Double. To record this momentous achievement, a book entitled "Spurs Supreme" was published. It recorded every game played that season, by way of reprinting at least one newspaper match report. A copy of the book was given to me by an uncle and I must have read it at least fifty times over, never tiring of its content. I had hoped that an author might have chronicled some of Spurs' other achievements in this way over the ensuing years, but no-one has. It was therefore decided to commission Colin Gibson and Harry Harris to chart Spurs' voyage through history in European competition, a subject which I know is very close to the hearts of all Spurs' supporters. The detailed research has taken some time to complete and consists of original reports of all eighty-four matches, played, home and away, in addition to retrospective views from many of those involved.

In winning the 1961 Championship, Spurs were to join that elite band of English clubs: Manchester United, Wolves and Burnley, in competing with the finest teams in Europe for the European Cup. At that time, only Manchester United had ever survived the Quarter Finals and the Cup itself had only been lifted by two clubs – Real Madrid, five times winners, and the then holders, Benfica of Lisbon. This campaign opened new horizons for the Spurs Double Team and included some matches that their supporters will never forget. Epic encounters that will live on forever in the minds of those lucky enough to have witnessed them.

Over the last twenty-five years, White Hart Lane has been the setting for some magnificent matches involving many of Europe's leading players, including: Pohl of Gornick, Masopust of Dukla Prague, Eusebio of Benfica, Shroif of Slovan Bratislava, Rivera of A.C. Milan, Djazic of Red Star Belgrade, Bonhof of Cologne, Cruyff of Feyenoord, Ruminegge of Bayern Munich and two of the brightest stars of the future, Enzo Scifo of Anderlecht and Emilio Butragueno of Real Madrid.

Spurs too have fielded some of the finest players since the war, including Blanchflower, Mackay, Greaves, Jones, Gilzean, Chivers, Peters, Hoddle, Ardiles and Jennings.

The White Hart Lane Press box, during these years, has been graced by many of Fleet Street's most renowned scribes and characters, including Brian Glanville, Geoffrey Green, Desmond Hackett, David Lacey, Hugh McIlvanney, Jeff Powell, Victor Railton and Ian Wooldridge.

Whilst searching through the annals of Fleet Street, it quickly became apparent that journalistic style and presentation has changed quite considerably over the last twenty-five years, and whilst we have tried to give a cross section of writers and opinions, we have not necessarily chosen all of those that we believe to be the best match reports.

This book is intended to capture the atmosphere of so many unforgettable nights at White Hart Lane and overseas for the many thousands of fans who witnessed the events. It is also for the many, present day supporters, who were too young to have seen the heroes of the past and have only heard about them from family and friends.

Being a Spurs supporter is to appreciate football of a high quality whether it be from Tottenham or the opposition.

IRVING SCHOLAR
CHAIRMAN – TOTTENHAM HOTSPUR FOOTBALL CLUB
MAY, 1986

CONTENTS

PAGE 16

	P.	W.	D.	L.	F.	A.	Pts
Tottenham H. ...	39	30	4	5	111	49	64
Sheffield Wed. ...	39	22	12	5	74	41	56

TOTTENHAM CLINCH TIT

Spectacular Spurs march on Europe

From Burnley the League trophy moves to White Hart-lane. Now the super Spurs wait eagerly till Saturday, May 6, for the chance to become the first club this century to win the F.A. Cup as well. The last highest hurdle is Leicester City.

THEY SAID . . .

SPURS' manager **Billy Nicholson**: "I am very happy. Now we are going for the record number of points. But this was not one of our best displays."

Skipper **Danny Blanchflower**: "I felt we had won the championship psychologically at Easter, when we started to pull away from the others. I was amazed that Sheffield Wednesday kept going the way they did."

Chairman **Mr. Fred Bearman**: "It's a great day in my life."

Mr. Eric Taylor, Wednesday's general manager: "We gave them a good run. But I've seen them five times this season and they are certainly worthy champions. I think they'll win the Cup too."

Referee **Mr. T. W. Dawes**: "The match was certainly tough. The atmosphere was electric. I certainly knew I had refereed a match!"

And, of course, chairman of retiring champions Burnley, **Mr. Bob Lord**: "Well done."

The smile of a man who planned a victory with his head and welcomed it with his heart . . . the smile of Danny Blanchflower.

SMITH PIERCES WAL OF STEEL

By JOHN CAMKIN: Tottenham 2, Sheffield Wed. 1

THE Football League championship is triumphantly, worthily home at last—at White Hart-lane. The proud name of Tottenham Hotspur shines in the record books of British Soccer. And now on to the Cup Final and the double!

The hard work of manager Mr. Bill Nicholson and his great team has its first reward, and England has a worthy representative in next season's European Cup.

Seconds after the last victory kick against Sheffield Wednesday, the only League challengers to the idols of half London, happy crowds streamed over the brown pitch.

Command appearance

"We want Danny," they chanted in their hundreds. "Glory, glory," they sang when Tottenham's captain did not appear. Finally Blanchflower and his team bowed to popular demand, and the grimy, white-shirted, heroes filed into the director's box.

So the thousands left happily to wait hopefully for another triumph at Wembley on May 6.

The bitter acrimony
pute is forgotten for a
side ascends its throne.
good in the game; a tr
tion of great artistry an

The influence of Tc
of the football pyramid.
for the good.

A bath-towel is Les A
to a

BILL NICHOLSON

DAILY MAIL, Tuesday, April 18, 1961

DAILY EXPRESS, Tuesday, April 18, 1961

TOTTENHAM . . . 2 SHEFFIELD WEDNESDAY . . . 1

SPURS – THE SUPER CHAMPIONS!

Allen goal clinches triumph after moments

By CLIVE TOYE

Tottenham Hotspur became champions of England last night. And the grey, gaunt two-tiered stands of Tottenham can scarcely have gazed down on moments drawn so tight with nerve-tugging tension.

Or moments so filled with the magic impulse that makes Spurs THE great team THE great goal machine, THE great champions as the 120 seconds of sheer, incisive, savage Soccer which threw back the final challenge from Sheffield Wednesday.

The seconds of success started their brief life three minutes before half-time. Spurs, on their night of nights, were a goal down – scored after half an hour by Wednesday left back Don Megson when a free kick rebounded to him from Spurs' defensive wall.

And Wednesday were fighting grimly, gallantly to prove their worth as challengers in front of the 61,000 fans waiting only to hail the champions.

Then Bobby Smith hooked the ball past one England team-mate, Peter Swan, swung it viciously past another, Wednesday goalkeeper Ron Springett, and dived a whirling dance of delight into the arms of his own colleagues.

One minute later Maurice Norman leaped to head a free kick down on to the right foot of Les Allen. And the roof of the net bulged with the goal which took the title to White Hart Lane and turned the crowd's roar into a crescendo.

Those were the magic moments the crowd, the vast, demanding crowd were remembering when they raced on to the pitch, chanted: "We want Danny" and stayed on until the team came out for a proud parade of victory at the end.

Those goals . . . and the other glittering moments, when Spurs strode to triumph . . . will never be forgotten. But oh, how taut the waiting for the final, unassailable success!

The tension pulled Spurs away from their fierce flow of football. Gave a fraction's hesitation. A fractional inaccuracy.

A heart-lifting, blood-pounding period of fear for Spurs' hysterical fans as Wednesday fought and fought on, even when Springett, charged by Smith, was carried off on a stretcher and spent five minutes on the touchline until he forced his way back on to the field.

The shredded-nerve atmosphere built up by the baying-for-victory crowd, even excuses the moments of football violence which made referee Tommy Dawes note Dave Mackay's name, lecture Tony Day, Brian Hill, and Peter Johnson.

For this was the night Tottenham became champions.

DAILY EXPRESS TUESDAY APRIL 18 1961

The 39 Steps To Glory — More than two and a quarter million have watched Spurs this season . . . They have won more games than any other team in the history of the First Division. Their total of 16 away wins is a record for the League Championship. . . . Spurs started by winning 11 games in a row . . . have won the title in 39 games.

SPURS—THE SUPER CHAMPIONS!

TOTTENHAM'S TITLE

	P	W	D	L	F	A	W	D	L	F	A	Pts
TOTTENHAM	39	14	3	2	63	26	16	1	3	48	23	64
SHEFF WED	39	15	4	1	44	15	7	8	4	30	26	56
WOLVES	40	17	2	1	59	28	7	5	8	37	42	55

Allen goal clinches triumph after two magic moments

By CLIVE TOYE: Tottenham 2 Sheffield Wed. 1

TOTTENHAM HOTSPUR became champions of England last night. And the grey, gaunt two-tiered stands of Tottenham can scarcely have gazed down on moments drawn so tight with nerve-tugging tension.

Or moments so filled with the magic impulse that makes Spurs THE great team, THE great goal machine, THE great champions as the 120 seconds of sheer, incisive, savage Soccer which threw back the final challenge from Sheffield Wednesday.

The seconds of success started their brief life three minutes before half-time. Spurs, on their night of nights, were a goal down—scored after half an hour by Wednesday left back Don Megson when a free kick rebounded to him from Spurs' defensive wall.

DANCE OF DELIGHT

And Wednesday were fighting grimly, gallantly to prove their worth as challengers in front of the 61,000 fans waiting only to hail the champions.

Then Bobby Smith hooked the ball past one England team-mate, Peter Swan, swung it viciously past another, Wednesday goalkeeper Ron Springett, an ddived a whirling dance of delight into the arms of his own colleagues.

One minute later Maurice Norman leaped to head a free kick down on to the right foot of Les Allen. And the roof of the net bulged with the goal which took the title to White Hart-lane and turned the crowd's roar into a crescendo.

Those were the magic moments the crowd, the vast, demanding crowd, were remembering when they raced on to the pitch, chanted "We want Danny" and stayed on until the team came out for a proud parade of victory at the end.

Those goals . . . and the other glittering moments, when Spurs strode to triumph . . . will never be forgotten. But oh, how taut the waiting for final, unassailable success!

The tension pulled Spurs away from their fierce flow of football. Gave a fraction's hesitation. A fractional inaccuracy.

MACKAY 'BOOKED'

A heart-lifting, blood-pounding period of fear for Spurs' hysterical fans as Wednesday fought and fought on, even when Springett, charged by Smith was carried off on a stretcher and spent five minutes on the touchline until he forced his way back on to the field.

The shredded-nerve atmosphere built up by the baying-for-victory crowd, even excuses the moments of football violence which made referee Tommy Dawes note Dave Mackay's name, lecture Tony Kay, Brian Hill, and Peter Johnson.

For this was the night Tottenham became champions.

SPURS.—Brown; Baker, Henry; Blanchflower, Norman, Mackay; Jones, White, Smith, Allen, Dyson.
SHEFFIELD WEDNESDAY.—Springett; Johnson, Megson; Hill, Swan, Kay; Finney, Craig, Ellis, Fantham, Wilkinson.

THE GOALS THAT DID IT

THE FIRST: Bobby Smith, extreme right, beats Springett

THE CLINCHER: Scored by Allen and Smith jumps for joy

THE GOOD—AND BAD BY SMITH

BOBBY SMITH of Spurs and England went in against Sheffield Wednesday last night with his left leg strapped up.

He still suffered from the injury received in the England-Scotland match.

But, last night was the most unforgettable night of Smith's life.

He said "There were moments I shall always remember—and one I should like to forget."

★

His first great moment was three minutes from half-time with Spurs a goal down.

Smith, in a brilliant double-juggle, beat his England international team mate centre half Peter Swan to score one of the best goals I have ever seen.

The moment he wants to forget was midway through the second half when he charged England goalkeeper Ron Springett.

Smith covered his face in anguish when he saw an ambulance chief signal for a stretcher.

★

Springett was laid out for five minutes. He looked badly hurt. Peter Johnson, Wednesday right back, had gone into goal when Springett got up, shook himself, and walked into position.

It was an act that brought one of the greatest and most moving bursts of spontaneous cheering I ever heard. Every one of the 60,000 crowd cheered and clapped for a full two minutes.

At the end Smith dashed over to Springett and the two walked off with arms round each other's shoulders.

DESMOND HACKETT

2,334,489 cheers!

WHEN Spurs clinched the First Division title at White Hart-lane last night they achieved it with. . . .

THE MOST wins (30) in First Division history.

THE MOST away wins (16).

THE MOST League goals (111) in a season in the club's history.

THE MOST wins to start a season . . . 11 in a row.

Spurs also set a record in the race to 50 points. It took them just 29 games.

This is their second League Championship (previous—1951).

They are F.A. Cup Finalists for the third time . . . But when they meet Leicester on May 6 it will be their first visit to Wembley.

★

They have used only 17 players to win the championship. Four—Blanchflower, Henry, White, and Allen—have played in every match.

There remains for Spurs to beat. . . .

Arsenal's record of 66 points in season 1930-31 (Spurs need another three).

There remains for Spurs to equal. . . .

The League and Cup double previously achieved by Aston Villa (1897) and Preston (1889). . . .

There remains to record. . . .

Super Spurs have been watched this season by this impressive number of people—

2,334,489

SPORTS OPINION

GIBSON 'RETIRES'

THE TITLE ROAD

HERE are the figures that add up to success, the match by match record of Spurs' march to the First Division title:—

HOME

			Goals F–A
Aug.	20	Everton	2—0
Aug.	31	Blackpool	3—1
Sep.	3	Man. Utd.	4—1
Sep.	14	Bolton	3—1
Sep.	24	Aston Villa	6—2
Oct.	10	Man. City	1—1
Nov.	2	Cardiff City	3—2
Nov.	5	Fulham	5—1
Nov.	19	Birmingham	6—0
Dec.	3	Burnley	4—4
Dec.	24	West Ham	2—0
Dec.	31	Blackburn	5—2
Jan.	21	Arsenal	4—2
[illegible]	[illegible]	[illegible]	2—3

AWAY

			Goals F–A
Aug.	22	Blackpool	3—1
Aug.	27	Blackburn	4—1
Sep.	7	Bolton	2—1
Sep.	10	Arsenal	3—2
Sep.	17	Leicester	2—1
Oct.	1	Wolves	4—0
Oct.	15	Nottm. Forest	4—0
Oct.	29	Newcastle	4—3
Nov.	12	Sheff. Wed.	1—2
Nov.	26	West Brom.	3—1
Dec.	10	Preston	1—0
Dec.	17	Everton	3—1
Dec.	26	West Ham	3—0
Jan.	16	Man. Utd.	0—2
[illegible]	11	Aston Villa	2—1

'Treble' soon

SUNDAY EXPRESS, May 7, 1961

TOTTENHAM HOTSPUR . . . 2 LEICESTER CITY . . . 0

A WONDER GOAL – AND SPURS TAKE CUP AND DOUBLE

Injury hoodoo shakes the Leicester rhythm

By ALAN HOBY

At exactly 4.45 yesterday afternoon an ear-splitting racket of sound rose from the giant grey bowl of Wembley Stadium. It was a roar full of triumph and joy and it came from the mighty host of Tottenham fans in the 100,000 crowd. For at that moment – as Referee Jack Kelly's whistle shrilled "Time" – Tottenham Hotspur became the first club of the century to win the fabulous Cup and League double.

Aston Villa in the misty gaslit days of 1897, 64 long years ago, were the last team to achieve the feat.

But what a fearful fright these not-so-super Spurs – the magnificient exception was left back Ron Henry – were given before they clinched the club record unparalleled throughout the world!

It took them 69 minutes of frustration before Tottenham could prise open Leicester's drum-tight defence.

Time and again Leicester's cool Scottish centre half Ian King, as craggily tough as a highland peak, flung back the challenge of the League champions.

Time and again, playing only 10 men – the Wembley curse struck once more in the first half when right back Len Chalmers fell writhing to the green turf after a clash with Spurs' inside left Les Allen – Leicester's magnificently drilled defenders brushed aside Tottenham's stuttering raids with almost nonchalant insolence.

Then, with exhaustion and the heavy green carpet of Wembley taking their roll of flagging limbs, Spurs at last produced an irresistible surge of genius.

The goal roar from the Tottenham thousands packed into the stands and terraces rushed up and clutched us by the throat as left winger Terry Dyson, who had moved into the middle, suddenly sent a glorious through-ball into the Leicester goalmouth.

There, lurking like a confidence man about to make his kill, was Spurs' rugged, broad-shouldered centre forward, Bobby Smith.

With the nerves of Leicester's heavily tried supporters jangling like alarm bells Smith, for only the second time in the match, beat King.

Smith dummied the centre half, feinted and swivelled to hit the ball on the turn.

The ball – a brown blur – rose at an acute angle and crashed into the net with Leicester's superb young goalkeeper Gordon Banks diving in vain.

As the ball lodged in the back of the net their earlier fears, when the shadow Spurs with left half Dave Mackay temporarily out of touch and right half Danny Blanchflower strained and tense, fell from the Tottenham fans like dead skins.

It was a magnificent solo goal and it was scored, to my delight, by the one man I predicted last week could turn this crucial match for Tottenham – that underrated Yorkshireman with the lion heart, Bobby Smith.

Now with Leicester's defence falling apart like a burst bag of grain Spurs, for the first time, reached their true stature.

In the brief moments left the blinding cheetah speed of Cliff Jones, the sly positioning and passing of John White, the sudden surges of left winger Terry Dyson had the crowd gasping and enthralled.

Seven minutes later unlucky Leicester succumbed again when their injured right back Len Chalmers, hobbling painfully at outside left, pushed a pass inside that went astray.

Les Allen, the man who had accidentally crippled him earlier in the game, pounced and pushed a gem of a pass forward to Scotland's John White.

The Spurs' pale and artistic inside right slid a lovely ball to Bobby Smith who had moved out to the right.

Smith with infinite poise looked up and saw Dyson unmarked 15 yards from the far post. Over sailed the ball and in stormed Dyson.

You could almost see the muscles bulging in the little man's neck as he headed a bullet of a ball into the Leicester net, 2-0.

It was all over and the fans danced and pranced with delight.

But what would have happened – I wonder – had Len Chalmers not been one more victim of the Wembley hoodoo 18 minutes from the start?

At that point Tottenham were looking anything but the pride of London or the team of the century. Bedraggled and faltering, leaving large gaps in the middle, they looked at this point artisan; blue-shirted Leicester the artists.

With Leicester's Scottish skipper and inside right Jimmy Walsh inspiring his men . . .

With young Hugh McIlmoyle, the former Glasgow painter, twisting and turning exuberantly in eel-like darts . . .

With raking three-man moves often piercing Tottenham's defence, the day looked black for the champions.

Indeed, three times before tragedy intervened Leicester might have scored.

A dazzling dribble from Walsh which beat both Mackay and Blanchflower left the canny McIlmoyle with a glorious chance.

Alas! for Leicester his shot taken first time whipped across goal.

Another spreadeagling Leicester move with Scotland's Frank McLintock sweeping a wonderful cross ball over to their right winger box-of-tricks Howard Riley, again had Tottenham reeling.

Riley centred straight to McIlmoyle playing in his first Cup game with the assurance of a veteran but it was a difficult, swirling ball – the wind was blowing high – and the Scots' centre forward scooped over the bar. I doubt if Ken Leek could have done better.

Again Walsh knived through and slid the ball to Riley. Over came another pinpoint centre and there was Albert Cheesebrough, Leicester's left winger, hurtling in like a

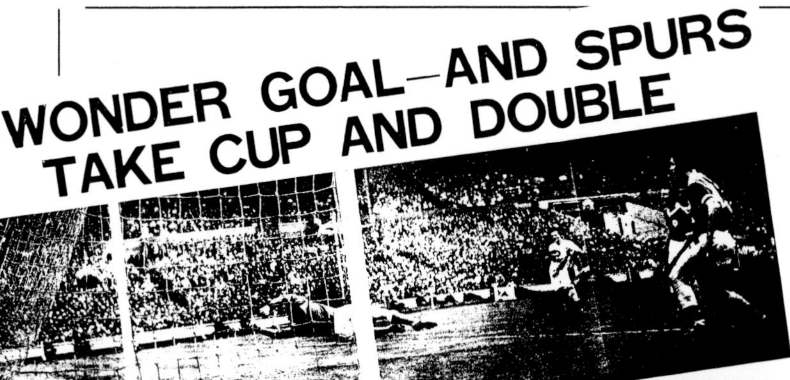

WONDER GOAL—AND SPURS TAKE CUP AND DOUBLE

● Here it is . . . Bobby Smith's shot flashes into the net for Spurs' first goal as Gordon Banks flings himself despairingly at the ball

THE CUP IN PICTURES PAGE 22

Injury hoodoo shakes the Leicester rhythm

TOTTENHAM HOTSPUR 2 (Smith, Dyson) LEICESTER CITY 0

H.T. 0–0 Attendance 100,000 Receipts £49,813

by ALAN HOBY

AT exactly 4.45 yesterday afternoon an ear-splitting racket of sound rose from the giant grey bowl of Wembley Stadium. It was a roar full of triumph and joy and it came from the mighty host of Tottenham fans in the 100,000 crowd. For at that moment—as Referee Jack Kelly's whistle shrilled "Time"—Tottenham Hotspur became the first club of the century to win the fabulous Cup and League double.

Aston Villa in the misty gaslit days of 1897, 64 long years ago, were the last team to achieve the feat.

QUOTES

as told to JAMES CONNOLLY

LINE-UP

TOTTENHAM HOTSPUR

Brown

Baker Henry

Blanchflower Norman Mackay

White Allen Dyson

Jones Smith

Cheesebrough McIlmoyle Riley

Keyworth Walsh

Appleton King McLintock

Norman Chalmers

Banks

LEICESTER CITY

SILENCE

SYMPATHY

THE CURSE

ENTHRALLED

rocket for what seemed a certain goal.

But up, almost out of the ground, popped Tottenham's ice-cube of a right back Peter Baker to get Cheesebrough's boot flush in the face as he bravely headed clear.

Baker recovered but two minutes later a groan rose from the thousands of Leicester fans.

Right back Chalmers coming through with the ball on the right was tackled by Bobby Smith.

The ball slipped through Smith's feet and over came Spurs' Les Allen to finish the job.

There was a crack of legs, a split-second mingling of blue and white shirts and then a silence spread round the stadium.

For there, writhing on the grass, was Chalmers. His face creased in agony, his right leg threshing in pain.

For what seemed endless minutes he was attended by the Leicester and Spurs trainers.

They fussed over him. They tried to get him to his feet. He collapsed, and the silence grew even more ominous.

For the seventh time in nine years the Wembley hoodoo – the dreaded injury jinx – had struck.

And now Len Chalmers . . .

He rose gallantly and limped a painful few yards. Then he stopped, made as if to go off the pitch, changed his mind, and hobbled, a sad, lame figure, to the left wing.

His injury was twofold. He had a four inch bruise on his shinbone. He also had a wrenched knee. Later the doctor said there might be a cracked bone.

There was a dramatic moment when Chalmers upset and unhappy looked up and caught sight of Allen. The Leicester right back pointed an accusing finger at the Spurs inside left.

Some of the crowd also booed Allen for several minutes – but it was not his fault. It was the black hoodoo of Wembley which year after year claims its Cup final sacrifice.

One day the rulers of the Football Association will decide to have substitutes in the one match which season after season is ruined in this manner.

They will decide that the Cup final is a show spectacle between two equal teams – not an exhibition of pluck and guts by one hopelessly crippled side.

When . . . ?

Leicester did their best. They put Chalmers on the left wing, where he was out of harm. They pulled back right half McLintock to right back.

They put inside left Ken Keyworth in a roving commission at inside right and they called Albert Cheesebrough in from the left

Les Allen scores for Spurs in the Charity Shield of 1961. Spurs beat an England XI 3-2. Left to right: Les Allen, Ron Springett, Bobby Robson, Ron Flowers, Bobby Smith, Jimmy Armfield, 12 August 1961

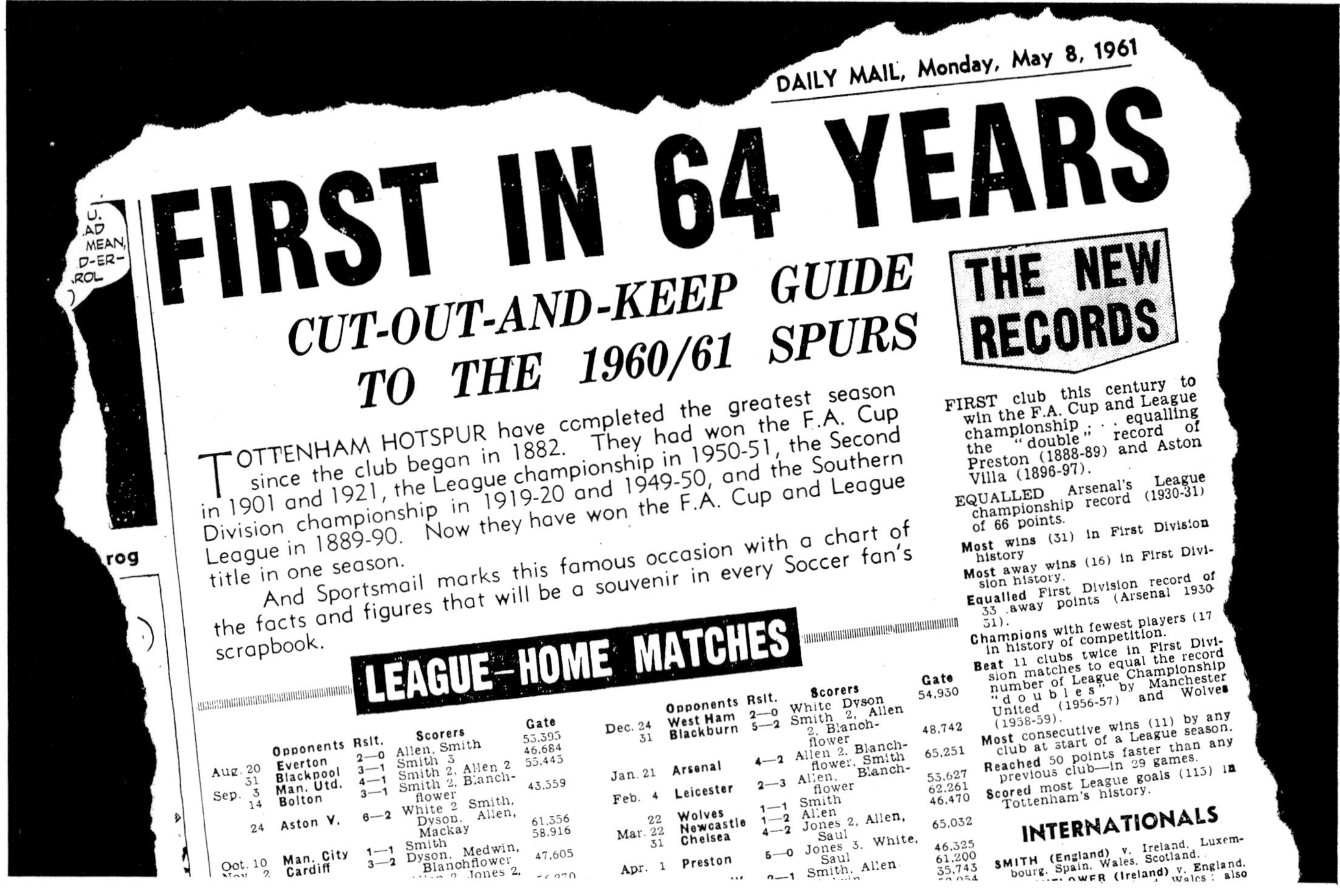

DAILY MAIL, Monday, May 8, 1961

FIRST IN 64 YEARS

CUT-OUT-AND-KEEP GUIDE TO THE 1960/61 SPURS

TOTTENHAM HOTSPUR have completed the greatest season since the club began in 1882. They had won the F.A. Cup in 1901 and 1921, the League championship in 1950-51, the Second Division championship in 1919-20 and 1949-50, and the Southern League in 1889-90. Now they have won the F.A. Cup and League title in one season.

And Sportsmail marks this famous occasion with a chart of the facts and figures that will be a souvenir in every Soccer fan's scrapbook.

LEAGUE—HOME MATCHES

	Opponents	Rslt.	Scorers	Gate
Aug. 20	Everton	2—0	Allen, Smith	53,395
31	Blackpool	3—1	Smith 3	46,684
Sep. 3	Man. Utd.	4—1	Smith 2, Allen 2	55,445
14	Bolton	3—1	Smith 2, Blanchflower	43,559
24	Aston V.	6—2	White 2 Smith, Dyson, Allen, Mackay	61,356
Oct. 10	Man. City	1—1	Smith	58,916
	Cardiff	3—2	Dyson, Medwin, Blanchflower	47,605

	Opponents	Rslt.	Scorers	Gate
Dec. 24	West Ham	2—0	White Dyson	54,930
31	Blackburn	5—2	Smith 2, Allen 2, Blanchflower	48,742
Jan. 21	Arsenal	4—2	Allen 2, Blanchflower, Smith	65,251
Feb. 4	Leicester	2—3	Allen, Blanchflower	53,627
22	Wolves	1—1	Smith	62,261
Mar. 22	Newcastle	1—2	Allen	46,470
31	Chelsea	4—2	Jones 2, Allen, Saul	65,032
Apr. 1	Preston	5—0	Jones 3, White, Saul	46,325

THE NEW RECORDS

FIRST club this century to win the F.A. Cup and League championship ; . . equalling the "double" record of Preston (1888-89) and Aston Villa (1896-97).

EQUALLED Arsenal's League championship record (1930-31) of 66 points.

Most wins (31) in First Division history

Most away wins (16) in First Division history.

Equalled First Division record of 33 away points (Arsenal 1930-31).

Champions with fewest players (17 in history of competition.

Beat 11 clubs twice in First Division matches to equal the record number of League Championship "doubles" by Manchester United (1956-57) and Wolves (1958-59).

Most consecutive wins (11) by any club at start of a League season.

Reached 50 points faster than any previous club—in 29 games.

Scored most League goals (115) in Tottenham's history.

INTERNATIONALS

SMITH (England) v. Ireland, Luxembourg, Spain, Wales, Scotland.

wing to inside left.

Leicester, to their eternal fame, fought all the way, until their limbs were buckling and their knees were sagging against a Tottenham side desperately struggling to find its old flowing rhythm, its famous mid-field expertise and magical passing.

True, Leicester had some chilling moments. John White skied over from eight yards in the third minute. Then, just before half-time, Cliff Jones had a goal disallowed for offside.

But in the end they had to capitulate to superior numbers – not superior skill.

At the end of the match Billy Nicholson, the Spurs manager, waited for his team to come off the field so that he could shake them by the hand one by one.

It may have been my imagination, but he seemed to linger a moment longer with man of the match Ron Henry who tamed Leicester's ace winger, Howard Riley.

But that final unanswered question will always remain:-

What would have happened if Leicester had been able to field 11 fit men for the start to the end?

We can only applaud Tottenham for writing an imperishable page in the fabled book of Soccer and sympathise with Leicester for being one more victim of the Wembley hoodoo.

DANNY BLANCHFLOWER: (Spurs right half and captain): "I don't think we played particularly well but I think that was due to the conditions. Wembley is soft and luxurious and it slows up the ball sometimes.

"We always believed the double could be achieved and now we have done it."

LES ALLEN (inside left):

"Len Chalmers had his back to me as he turned to play the ball inside. He caught my foot. He was slipping as he tried to turn and I am sure he never saw me coming.

"I heard someone call for the ball and I went in to cut out the pass. But the incident spoiled my game too. I was quite upset."

CLIFF JONES (outside right):

"I thought I had scored in the first half. That was why I appealed to a linesman against being given offside. I passed right half Frank McLintock, who had taken up a full back position, as I went for the ball."

MATT GILLIES (Leicester manager):

"I thought we were getting on top. Everything was going to plan until that injury to Len Chalmers. Even so, we were still very much in it until we ran out of puff. The injury completely upset our plans. It meant we had to bring Frank McLintock out of the half back line. Hugh McIlmoyle justified himself at centre forward. I was quite happy."

HUGH McILMOYLE (centre forward):

"I was excited but never nervous. Once the preliminaries were over and the game started I enjoyed it tremendously."

LEN CHALMERS (right back):

"I tried to put the ball away as Les Allen came, but we clashed and I got a crack on the shin. My knee was wrenched at the same time. I know I wagged my finger at Allen later on but that was in the heat of the moment. It was an accident.

"Alec Dowdells, our trainer, wanted me to come off, but I stayed and was told to play at outside left. He eventually called me off 10 minutes from the end.

"Les Allen came in after the game to say how sorry he was. The right leg was very painful. I could only drag it along, but I always felt I had some nuisance value. If I was out there somebody had to watch me."

So Spurs, now champions of England and FA Cup holders, had qualified to make their first assault on Europe in the European Cup.

Team line-up, October 1984. Back row from the left: Ron Henry, Peter Baker, Maurice Norman, Bill Brown, Bobby Smith, Tony Marchi. Front row from the left: Cliff Jones, Terry Medwin, Danny Blanchflower, Les Allen, Terry Dyson

LOOKING BACK WITH DANNY BLANCHFLOWER

It was the late summer of 1958. A British European Airways plane lifted into the sky above Sweden and Danny Blanchflower turned to Joe Mercer.

He said simply: "Tottenham are going to win the double within the next few years."

Blanchflower recalls: "Joe was sat alongside Stan Cullis who had seen the double dream vanish. Neither of them believed me I could tell."

But that summer in the World Cup finals Blanchflower believed that he had learnt so much that could help the Tottenham side develop.

He said: "We had qualified for the World Cup finals with Northern Ireland when we were not expected to. That World Cup gave me the experience that was to be invaluable in the years to come.

"I was given total authority on the field by Northern Ireland to run the show. It was not the greatest team in the world but this worked for us."

The tricks that the great sides launched on the world in those finals were to be used by Spurs later in their development in the domestic game.

Blanchflower remembers: "In the build up to those finals we had beaten both Portugal and Italy. We used to do things that nobody else thought of. We had to, because they were better sides.

"In Italy in 1957 we put up the first wall at a free kick. The Italians could not believe their eyes. We just stood 10 yards from the kick.

"The Italians seemed to be frightened by this tactic. It had taken them long enough to get out of their own half. It did have its teething problems though.

"The referee had never seen it before either. So when the Italian picked up the ball and moved it five yards away from the wall and shot into the net he gave a goal."

But the thinking behind that free kick play was the sort that was to inspire Spurs in the years to come. Blanchflower had to think of how to tackle the problems the tactics threw up as well.

He said: "We qualified for the second phase of the competition and that was an outstanding achievement. But then we came up against the French.

"They curled the ball round the wall so we had to make sure that it was lined up properly. Jimmy McIlroy did the job.

"As the inside forward he would stand behind the kick and line the wall up but he got booked for holding the game up.

"We then used the full back and that led to everyone being played onside. Finally we ended up with the last man on the wall lining it up. Thirty years on teams have not got round to that.

"It sounds a simple thing but it showed the planning and the work that went into everything. That was the sort of thinking that we took back to our clubs. It is now commonplace. At the time though it was revolutionary."

McIlroy took the word back to Burnley and the club enjoyed a glorious period. Blanchflower went back to Spurs but found it hard to get the new school of thought accepted.

"We used to call our ploys moving plays – not set pieces. It showed though what sort of damage and dangers could be created. The Tottenham team were just starting to get together and I realised what we could achieve.

"I knew that Tottenham had better players than Northern Ireland. They were really a bit like a Great Britain side and with the right direction would be outstanding."

But Blanchflower's attempts at a tactical revolution were to be frustrated. Arthur Rowe was to be replaced as manager not by his coach Bill Nicholson but by his chief scout Jimmy Anderson.

Blanchflower said: "Jimmy was a great scout but there was a vast difference between spotting good players and being able to handle them on a day to day basis.

"He was very unsure of these new tactics. He even went as far as telling the players to ignore them. I could not believe it.

"I kept wanting to go up for corners and Jimmy kept ordering me back. He said it was safer. So in one match Tommy Harmer was taking a throw-in in front of the directors' box.

"I told him to throw it so I could volley it. I did. Straight into the directors' box. Jimmy was furious. He screamed: 'Why did you do that?' 'It was safe,' I replied.

"When Bill Nicholson took over he left me out for a few games and I started to think about my future. One day he came to me. He said: 'I am giving you the authority on the field, but I want it off the field.'

"We started at Wolves with a 1-1 draw which was like winning the League in those days. The party started then . . ."

Blanchflower said: "Even now when I see Joe Mercer he says that he remembers that day on the way back from Sweden."

DAILY MAIL, Wednesday, September 13, 1961

Plane, train to Katowice for their first European Cup-tie

PAGE 16 Sport

1,100 miles ... to the loneliest match they'll ever play

60,000 to 1 AGAINST SPURS!

Lone British student will cheer them on

From IAN WOOLDRIDGE
Katowice, Tuesday

JON'S SPORTING TYPES

'COME BACK' PLEA TO FANS

Players back Watford in Holton row

MISS!

RADFORD RETURNS AGAINST FRANCE

MISSED 'ER!

MERRICK AXES TOP-SCORER JIMMY HARRIS

Manager runs on pitch

Rangers first into last sixteen

Day-trip Charlton win at last

Liz Long is first choice for England

Shade, Carr —Christmas

DAILY MAIL, Wednesday, September 13, 1961

60,000 TO 1 AGAINST SPURS!

1,100 miles . . . to the loneliest match they'll ever play
Lone British student will cheer them on

From IAN WOOLDRIDGE
KATOWICE, TUESDAY

Tottenham Hotspur kick off their European Cup crusade here tomorrow with the loneliest match in their history.

Eleven hundred miles from their 50,000 roaring Londoners, they are certain of only one, solitary supporter – a nomadic Southampton student named David Mummery.

The European Cup exhortation of this David will be drowned by the Goliath gathering of at least 60,000 impassioned Poles.

How Spurs react to the one-sided sound-effects in the Slazki stadium remains to be seen. But I believe they need only to draw to be through to the second round.

For Gornik, their mineworker opponents, admit they do not relish the thought of the second leg excursion to London.

I have seen Gornik show their paces only in a practice match, but these certain facts emerged:

They have a forward line reinforced by four internationals, Wilchek, Pohl, Jankowski, and Lentner, which looks as good as anything I saw in England last season.

They have a defence, with three further internationals in Gawlik, Oslizko, and Kowalski, which shows its age and could be cracked open by the speed of Jones and Dyson.

They have a goalkeeper, Kostka, who on the form he showed in practice would not hold his place in any English First Division team.

They have a playing pattern which is the conventional European: their centre forward lies deep and their centre half almost permanently resides in his own penalty box.

Any preconceived plans that Danny Blanchflower may have had to contain the powerful Ernest Pohl may well be shattered without being put to the test.

For Augusta Dziwisz, said to be the possessor of the finest tactical brain for football in Poland, undoubtedly proved it by announcing today two separate teams which baffled the Polish Press almost as much as the British. In one, Pohl was named as inside left, in the other as inside right.

One positive piece of information is that Kusialek has recovered from his back injury. The services of Kulanek, the 16½-year old who was standing by, will not therefore be required.

This should be welcome news to Dave Mackay, for infanticide is said to be a serious charge in the People's Republic.

LOOKING BACK WITH BILL NICHOLSON

Bill Nicholson knew that life in European football was not the same the moment that he arrived in the magnificent Gornik Stadium in the Polish mining town of Katowice.

Nicholson flew to Warsaw three weeks before Tottenham's first adventure into European football to look at what the famous double team could expect.

Even the experienced Nicholson who had taken his Spurs side to Eastern Europe before on friendly encounters was surprised at the differences he discovered.

"There were no quick spying missions to that part of the world in those days," said Nicholson. "I remember flying into Warsaw and the train journey down to Katowice took four hours.

"It was a very depressed place. You had to feel sympathy for the people. It was a cold mining area. Everything was grey. They tried their best for us.

"I remember going to the stadium and seeing women on their hands and knees with scissors cutting every blade of grass. The pitch was in immaculate condition.

"There was a pattern running from corner to corner of the ground. It was an example of how they were determined to put on their best face.

"However it was obvious in some cases that the best in Poland was just not good enough. The hotel standards were a prime example.

"It was supposed to be one of the best in that part of Poland. I was not happy though, and we had a bit of an 'up and downer' about it.

"But to show how wonderful those people were, when we returned with the team the whole hotel had been given a face lift.

"The whole place had been painted, the restaurant area had been vastly improved, there had been a general spring cleaning of all the rooms and the curtains were replaced.

"It was not exactly the Ritz, but it was still a great deal better than before."

It was not only the off the pitch factors that were a great surprise to those Tottenham pioneers. The playing style of the Europeans was very different.

Nicholson actually had a League game

of Gornik's watched and said: "We knew nothing of them. The League game did not tell us anything that was remotely useful either.

"We knew that they had a good player in Pohl but we were not expecting anything more unusual than a normal English League game.

"What a shock we got. We had practised normally. We worked very hard and we were convinced that our European preparation was as thorough as it could be.

"We had decided that we would adopt the same sort of principles and philosophies that had helped us to win the double.

"We were convinced that we had nothing to worry about unduly. We were a very good side and we knew it. What we did not know was how to play in Europe.

"We did not know how to play games over two legs. We had to learn quickly though. At 4-0 down in the first leg we were in danger of being tossed out of the competition at the first time of asking.

"We had tried to play our normal attacking football. We threw caution to the wind and we paid the price. They hit us hard.

"It made us realise that some teams on the continent prepare for the European ties very differently. They played a much more containing game.

"We had to learn to eradicate the other teams' strengths without losing our own strengths. Gornik did it to perfection and, but for our ability to play oustanding football, we would have been out."

Nicholson had feared watching the game from the Gornik dugout that his side would be caught in the 'whirlwind' effect. He said: "It is so easy when goals are going in to be swept away.

"It happened to Gornik at White Hart Lane. They were crushed 8-1. They were not that bad but they were caught in a domino effect. When one goal goes in it is difficult to halt the flood.

"It was an amazing start to a period that has covered 25 years. Maybe we learnt more in that 90 minutes than we had learnt in 90 years before. Europe was certainly a different place."

DAILY EXPRESS, Thursday, September 14, 1961

GORNIK ZABRE . . . 4 SPURS . . . 2

POLAND MINERS SHAME SPURS

Fans rage after Mackay tackle

From DESMOND HACKETT

Zabre, Poland, Wednesday. – Tottenham Hotspur, the pride of British Soccer, were booed and whistled off the field by a threatening 90,000 crowd here last night after losing the first leg of their first round European Cup match with Gornik Zabre.

It was a match not far removed from being an evening of Soccer shame for Tottenham. Spurs came back from 4-0 down to a slightly more respectable 4-2, but their goals were scored after left half Kowalski was so badly crippled he had to leave the game.

Even in the last 12 minutes, when 18-year old wonder boy centre forward Musialek crawled out of the game, nine Zabre men were sufficient to keep this fumbling Tottenham in check.

Manager Bill Nicholson says he is confident Spurs can overhaul the Zabre miners in the second leg at Tottenham next Wednesday, but I give you that merely as Mr Nicholson's own opinion. The crowd came near to rioting when vigorous Dave Mackay went into a tackle which left Kowalski grovelling in pain.

The wildly roaring fans rose, shaking their fists, growling. It was a grim and terrifying situation.

Nor did Tottenham attempt to seek forgiveness. Some of their petulant tactics were as ill-mannered as their game was ill-planned.

When the game ended the whole arena rose howling, booing, and whistling.

This was Super Spurs reduced from champs to chumps in 90 uneasy minutes.

The polished, highly-skilled Zabre team attacked with a seven-power forward line and took command of the game within seconds.

Ernest Pohl, a player of rare talents, so graceful and menacing this stormy evening, beat Bill Brown with a shot which crashed against the bar.

Zabre, who were in no need at all of outside assistance, were gifted a goal by Tottenham after eight minutes.

A blunder, one of the many committed by Spurs, between Cliff Jones and Peter Baker, gave Lentner the freedom of the field to make his cross. Musialek touched the ball against

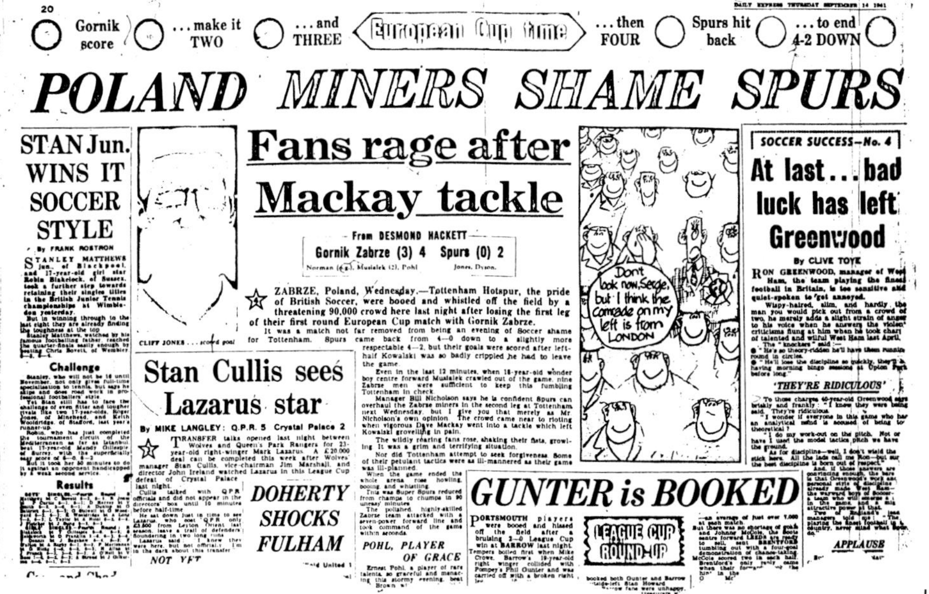

Gornik score ... make it TWO ... and THREE European Cup time ... then FOUR Spurs hit back ... to end 4-2 DOWN

POLAND MINERS SHAME SPURS

STAN Jun. WINS IT SOCCER STYLE

Fans rage after Mackay tackle

From DESMOND HACKETT

Gornik Zabrze (3) 4 Spurs (0) 2

SOCCER SUCCESS—No. 4

At last... bad luck has left Greenwood

By CLIVE TOYE

Stan Cullis sees Lazarus star

By MIKE LANGLEY: Q.P.R. 5 Crystal Palace 2

DOHERTY SHOCKS FULHAM

POHL, PLAYER OF GRACE

GUNTER is BOOKED

LEAGUE CUP ROUND-UP

'THEY'RE RIDICULOUS'

Danny Blanchflower leads the team onto the coach on their way to the airport for their first leg tie in Poland against Gornik. Left to right: Danny Blanchflower, Cliff Jones, Dave Mackay, Terry Dyson, Bill Brown, Tony Medwin, John Hollowbread, Maurice Norman, Ron Henry

Maurice Norman who turned it into his own goal.

The second goal after 20 minutes, came when Baker headed out. Musialek volleyed and although Brown touched this searing shot he could not save it.

It was 3-0 to Zabre after 40 minutes when Tottenham's gasping defence was sagged again.

Terry Dyson, who tried to upset corner kickers, was hit by the ball from a corner. It spun out to Musialek, who briskly headed the ball past Brown.

The misery of Tottenham continued into the second half when after two minutes an error by Mackay let Ernest Pohl go strolling through to pick his own spot.

After 16 minutes of the second half the tackle by Mackay on Kowalski started a storm of rebuke which never ceased.

The shame of Tottenham was eased 20 minutes from time when Mackay, battling courageously, started a great run which ended with Jones heading into goal.

Four minutes later it was 4-2 and Mackay again was the man behind the goal. He centred for Smith to head down and give Dyson a complete gift of a goal.

After the match the Zabre coach Augustyn Dziwisz told me: "We have had many foreign teams to play, but this Tottenham side was the hardest I have ever known."

DAILY EXPRESS, Thursday, September 21, 1961

TOTTENHAM HOTSPUR . . . 8 GORNIK . . . 1

EUROPEAN CUP FIRST ROUND, SECOND LEG. SPURS WIN 10-5 ON AGGREGATE

8-1 SPURS MARVELS MARCH ON

Jones slams 3 and the Poles are destroyed

By CLIVE TOYE

Spurs, the marvels of British Soccer, stand straight and proud after the savage destruction of the brave Polish miners from Gornik Zabre, men who stood shamelessly in awe at the wonder of Tottenham Hotspur.

This European Cup battle was won in the first ferocious 45 minutes of a night of emotion at White Hart Lane.

They were minutes that had the huge, bawling crowd screaming with joy as Spurs wiped out Gornik's 4-2 first leg lead, went ahead, were pulled back again – and then pulled away from the floundering Poles to march into round two.

Eleven heroes were Spurs on last night. Eleven men playing flawless football, with the determination of giants who will not be beaten.

But the man who petrified the Polish defence was Cliff Jones, the jet-paced Welsh winger whose 17-minute first half hat-trick had Gornik shrugging their shoulders and wondering what had changed this team they had whipped in Poland last week.

The drama, the supercharged sensations, began in the first half-minute when Spurs, playing with an intensity that became almost frightening, rocked Gornik with a move of pure skill which ended in Les Allen jabbing the ball against the bar.

And the first goal, the one which started Spurs on their way to their incredible success, came in the ninth minute.

Danny Blanchflower, nervous as never before, stepped up to score from the penalty spot as the fans cheered till lungs were near bursting – just one of the partisan roars which helped in the shattering of Gornik.

Ten minutes later Blanchflower dazzled Gornik on the right and Terry Dyson's left-foot lob was headed past helpless Hubert Kostka by Cliff Jones. Now Spurs were level on aggregate, 4-4.

Jones struck again with two glorious efforts in the 24th and 35th minutes – a left-footed drive after Dave Mackay's long throw-in, and a flick when Allen pulled the ball back from the goal-line.

Between these goals came the one, sad Polish score, a fine 25-yard volley from skipper Ernest Pohl.

Spurs'sixth goal from Bobby Smith (out of picture) whilst Terry Dyson looks on

Bill Brown and Maurice Norman combine to stop Gornik scoring

From Gornik Zabre to commemorate their 1961 European Cup match against Spurs

That little flurry left Spurs ahead 6-5. And they never looked back for an instant.

By half-time Bobby Smith, bulky and with the strength of 10, had headed his first goal. He pulled Spurs out of temporary rest with his second goal, another magnificent header in the 72nd minute.

One more minute of magic and Terry Dyson darted on to a Blanchflower return pass to slam No. 7.

And it was left to John White, in this match the master of inside forwards, to score the eighth one minute from the end.

On a night like this are memories engraved – engraved with the emotion that surged from the dedicated 11 of Tottenham to the amazed crowd.

And marked for ever by the tension which hung like a thick London fog over every move.

It could have been a vicious match. There were moments in the first 20 minutes when you held your breath as the no-quarter tackles shuddered in.

But after that Tottenham blitz the tough tackles were not necessary. Spurs knew it, the crowd knew it, and Gornik knew.

20

'The wonders of British Soccer stand straight and proud'

8-1 SPURS MARVELS MARCH ON

Jones slams 3 and the Poles are destroyed

By CLIVE TOYE

Tottenham Hotspur 8 Gornik 1

European Cup first round, second leg. Spurs win 10—5 on aggregate.

SPURS, the marvels of British Soccer, stand straight and proud after the savage destruction of the brave Polish miners from Gornik Zabrze, men who stood shamelessly in awe at the wonder of Tottenham Hotspur.

This European Cup battle was won in the first ferocious 45 minutes of a night of emotion at White Hart-lane.

They were minutes that had the huge, bawling crowd screaming with joy as Spurs wiped out Gornik's 4—2 first-leg lead, went ahead, were pulled back again—and then pulled away from the floundering Poles to march into Round Two.

Eleven heroes were Spurs on last night. Eleven men playing flawless football, with the determination of giants who will not be beaten.

Super! HERE ARE EIGHT REASONS WHY

HOW LONDON'S OTHER CLUBS FARED...

Arsenal on spot

IT WAS BRUTAL GROANS Mr. D

By MIKE LANGLEY

BURSTING

HEADING

CERTIFIED DIVIDENDS OF MEMBERS OF THE POOL PROMOTERS ASSOCIATION FOR 16th SEPTEMBER 1961

Punter's late goal

STORY OF THE NIGHT: goalkeeper Kostka lies in vain having been beaten eight times on the night

SPURS PROGRAMME, Saturday, September 30, 1961; page 5

The European Cup

. . . Harking back to our match with KS Gornik, it was thrilling to hear the old-time "Tottenham Roar" at full blast, but though our supporters were obviously out to do their best to help the team "wipe the slate clean" as soon as possible, their vocal enthusiasm seems to have worried some members of the Press.

"Hate" and "fanaticism" have been suggested as the reasons for such prolonged enthusiasm, but those who know the true Spurs' supporters know fans who appreciate good football, as was witnessed by the spontaneous ovation given to Gornik when Pohl hit that tremendous goal.

But what's the use of supporters if they do not support, the more so in such an important game when support is even more necessary? We, at any rate, were proud of our supporters, and of our players who made it such a memorable evening.

Feyenoord

Gifts and pennants from some of Spurs' European opponents

Dukla Prague

Glasgow Rangers

DAILY MAIL Thursday November 2 1961

Sport

IN ROTTERDAM

Saul's two wipe out Dutch resistance

IN BELFAST

League hit Irish for five in half-hour

IN GLASGOW

Gerry Hitchens goal shakes the Scots

BLACK MARKS, SPURS!

Nicholson says 'we muddled through'

Feyenoord . . 1 Spurs . . . 3

TWO black scars on a crossbar in the towering Feyenoord stadium stand witness tonight to Tottenham's luck in this second round of the European Cup.

Those marks were made in the last three impassioned minutes by two shots from inside-right Rinus Bennaers, a tiny 31-year-old car salesman who plays Soccer for pocket money.

Both shots whipped through Spurs' defence. Both whipped past a limping Bill Brown. Both struck the bar. Both ricocheted to safety as 64,000 Dutchmen raised imploring hands.

Had either gone in Spurs would still have a great fight on their trembling hands in the second leg in London in 13 days' time.

For Bennaers and the other Feyenoord men revealed new dimensions of Dutch resistance to the 1,000 British fans who like me expected a flood of Spurs goals against the same men who played so poorly only last Sunday.

I can only quote the words of Bill Nicholson, Spurs mana

IAN WOOLDRIDGE

SUCH A SHABBY TRICK, FUMES SACKED HILL

By JOHN ROSS

ANGRY Frank Hill, sacked as manager of Notts County and replaced by Tim Coleman, former ... and third-team coach, last night accused chair... and his directors of "the shabbiest

Rochdale of Rotterdam . . . this gesture can have only

Rotha[illegible]—by the pale

DAILY MAIL, Thursday, November 2, 1961

FEYENOORD . . . 1 SPURS . . . 3

BLACK MARKS, SPURS!

Nicholson says 'we muddled through'

IAN WOOLDRIDGE

REPORTS FROM ROTTERDAM

Two black scars on a crossbar in the towering Feyenoord stadium stand witness tonight to Tottenham's luck in this second round of the European Cup.

Those marks were made in the last three impassioned minutes by two shots from inside right Rinus Bennaers, a tiny 31-year old car salesman who plays Soccer for pocket money.

Both shots whipped through Spurs' defence. Both whipped past a limping Bill Brown. Both struck the bar. Both ricocheted to safety as 64,000 Dutchmen raised imploring hands.

Had either gone in, Spurs would still have a great fight on their trembling hands in the second leg in London in 13 days' time.

For Bennaers and the other Feyenoord men revealed new dimensions of Dutch resistance to the 1,000 British fans who, like me, expected a flood of Spurs goals against the same men who played so poorly only last Sunday.

I can only quote the words of Mr Bill Nicholson, Spurs' manager:

"We muddled through. That's all you can say. Our mistake? There were so many, I don't know where to start."

My own criticism of Spurs is tempered by the fact that I prefer to pour credit on the 11 men who tonight might so easily have been heroes of Holland.

For 30 minutes up to half-time they ran a fetch-and-carry shuttle service through Spurs' defence.

Twice in the 30th and 32nd minutes, Spurs' goal had escapes as lucky as those in the last few minutes.

Twice Peter Baker had to up-end Coen Moulijn to stop the flying left winger.

Dutchmen watched in silent disbelief. And who can blame them if there was little acclaim for Spurs as they quietly accumulated the goals that are now destined to take them to the next round.

For Spurs, despite the criticism of their own boss, achieved an efficient victory, even if it lacked genius.

John White, their one constant forward was the most cultured attacker on the field.

Blanchflower in the first half, and Marchi in the second, were always there, striving to reassert authority.

And, for me, the greatest success of all must be Frank Saul, the 18-year old centre forward from Canvey Island.

After a nervous first 30 minutes he triumphed over the tension, the earsplitting chaos of a European Cup occasion, to score two goals that were elegant, maturely taken, and a financial fortune to his club.

It was Terry Dyson, following a Cliff Jones header, who first shocked the Dutch two minues from half-time with goal No. 1.

It was Saul, soaring up to nod in a White cross in the 48th minute, then running on to a Jones pass in the 71st, who took over the job of scoring.

But it was Feyenoord – fighting to the background of the fans' roars and 10,000 klaxons – who warmed the heart.

They matched Spurs in efficiency and power in defence. They equalled them in elegant mid-field pattern.

And Spurs had no man to match the fighting spirit of Bennaers, a tiny, bustling fellow who flung himself into battle for 90 minutes and was then cheated of two goals in the last three minutes.

Feyenoord's goal, a blinding 35-yard shot, came from right half Reiner Kreijermaat, in the 61st minute.

Terry Dyson heads the first goal for Spurs in Rotterdam watched by Frank Saul

DAILY EXPRESS, Thursday, November 16, 1961
EUROPEAN CUP 2ND ROUND, SECOND LEG

SPURS WIN 4-2 ON AGGREGATE

MACKAY . . . KNOCKED-OUT HERO

Iron-man Dave shocks doctors and fights on

By DESMOND HACKETT

Dave Mackay, Mr Iron Man of Soccer, was the hero of Spurs' unhappy progress in the European Cup test against Dutch champions Feyenoord at crowd-packed Tottenham last night.

And this match required a hero as desperately as Tottenham appear to want the Greaves boy.

Having watched these brawling, mauling Dutchmen strongman their way through a depressing second half I came to the firm decision that if this is the Common Market of European football, we are better out of it.

The drab action of the second half brought disgrace to the European Cup, which rates second only to the World Cup.

It was not surprising that Tottenham did not appear over-anxious to score in the second half. They were fully occupied in surviving against some of the most alarming tackling I have ever seen.

In the end, Norwegian referee B. Nilson,

who had been so neutral and tolerant was compelled to take the name of mighty-chested Feyenoord right back, Kerkum, whose lunging tackles had the fans almost as alarmed as the players.

After the first leg in Holland, when Spurs won 3-1, manager Billy Nicholson commented: "I am bitterly disappointed."

Last night 61,957 fans and an international Press box fully agreed with him.

The moment of Mackay durability came after eight minutes when he went hurtling into a heading duel with craggy centre half Kraay during a brisk Tottenham chase for a goal.

When the attack was beaten off, the roaring crowd hushed, Kraay and Mackay were lying motionless face downwards in the Dutch penalty area.

After two minutes Kraay tottered to his feet. Mackay did not move. He was carried off on a stretcher with his head swathed in a bloodstained towel.

It was reported from the dressing room that he had concussion and a suspected fractured eardrum. Two doctors who attended him were shaken when after 10 minutes Mackay recovered consciousness, shook his head and said:–

"What am I doing here? Let me get back in the game."

When it was seen he was quite aware of what was going on he was permitted to go back.

It was a dramatic moment when Mackay, in the all-white rig of Tottenham, suddenly appeared on the touchine with his shorts splashed with blood.

A lively enough first half brought a shock goal for the part-timers of Holland after eight minutes. A long, hopeful shot from centre forward Gyp was inexpertly prodded out for Bennaers to move in alertly and score from around eight yards.

Three minutes later, the black night was full of jubilant noise when Tottenham scored with a move straight from the Soccer planners' drawing board.

Taking part were Danny Blanchflower, Cliff Jones, Mackay, with an impudent overhead kick, and a diving head from wee Terry Dyson.

The match was delayed seven minutes because the Dutch team were held up in a traffic jam. After that appalling stuff in the second half I am only sorry they ever arrived.

GUARDIAN, Thursday, November 16, 1961

TOTTENHAM HOTSPUR . . . 1 FEYENOORD . . . 1

TOTTENHAM MAKE PROGRESS IN EUROPEAN CUP

Mackay injured, but second leg drawn

By ERIC TODD

Tottenham Hotspur drew 1-1 in the second leg of the European Cup second round tie against Feyenoord at White Hart Lane last night and they enter the quarter-finals of the competition with an aggregate of 4-2. The overall performance rather than this second result may provide Tottenham supporters if not the club itself with some compensation for the news received earlier of a breakdown in the negotiations for the transfer of Greaves.

The quality of the match was far below that in the game in Rotterdam and if Mr W Nicholson, Tottenham's manager, was disappointed then, what must he have felt like last night? The first half-hour, dominated by Blanchflower, was rich in promise, which was never fulfilled. Mackay was miscast hopelessly at inside left, although he may have been affected by a head injury in the first half.

Saul was mastered completely, and the rest of the forwards were only fitful, and not at all dangerous in front of goal. The defence played adequately after early carelessness, and Baker was particularly good. But, on the whole, this was nothing like the Tottenham one sees usually.

Feyenoord upset the crowd, late on, with their over-robust tackling, but not even the most ardent partisan could deny them a generous share of the few honours. Kraay was in magnificent form and inspired a defensive resolution the like of which Tottenham are unlikely to meet every week. He not only controlled the centre of the field but often joined in attacks and caused Brown as much anxiety as anybody.

Graafland was an alert goalkeeper behind two strong backs, and they saw to it that Tottenham's scoring efforts were kept down to a minimum. In spite of the absence of Bouwmeester, the Feyenoord forwards always looked more methodical than those of Tottenham and if the Dutch champions surprisingly had not fallen back on the defensive – quite unnecessarily – for much of the second half, they might well have brought off a surprise.

Feynoord were delayed by the traffic on their way from the West End and this caused

4 THE GUARDIAN Sport Thursday November 16 1961

Association Football

Tottenham make progress in European Cup

Mackay injured, but second leg drawn

BY ERIC TODD

Tottenham Hotspur 1, Feyenoord 1

Tottenham Hotspur drew 1-1 in the second leg of the European Cup second-round tie against Feyenoord at White Hart Lane last night and they enter the quarter-finals of the competition with an aggregate of 4-2. The overall performance rather than this second result may provide Tottenham supporters if not the club itself with some compensation for the news received earlier of a breakdown in the negotiations for the transfer of Greaves.

The quality of the match was far below that in the game in Rotterdam

another move started by Blanchflower. Mackay hooked the ball cleverly into the Feyenoord goalmouth and Dyson's header gave Graafland no chance.

Play was fast and entertaining until, in the fifteenth minute, Mackay and Kraay collided, in mid-air as it were, as they went up for the ball, and although the Dutchman was able to resume almost at once, poor Mackay was removed, unconscious, on a stretcher. It must have been a severe knock to lay low one of the game's seeming indestructibles. Feyenoord, it is almost superfluous to add, had a spell of superiority, and Bergholtz lobbed the ball over the bar from a good position.

Tottenham nevertheless fought hard.

Terry Dyson watches as a final defender clears off the line

the start to be 10 minutes late, but they were not given much time either to change or to settle down, and Saul should have done better than head the ball straight at Graafland when White centred perfectly from the left. Then Mackay, receiving a pass from Jones, aimed deliberately from 20 yards but his shot was charged down. Feyenoord took up the attack against a somewhat leisurely defence and Bergholtz was just wide with a powerful drive. Jones replied for Tottenham with a characteristic run which took him past three opponents, but he showed no better finish than Mackay, a few minutes later, when Blanchflower set his attack in motion with a superb pass.

But Feyenoord, as at Rotterdam, were not to be taken too lightly and in the ninth minute they went ahead. Once again Tottenham were slow to appreciate the danger and, when it arrived, to deal with it. Van Der Gyp ran through, and Marchi, in trying to clear, only deflected the ball to Bennaers who beat Brown from close in. This was not according to plan – not Tottenham's plan anyway – and with Mackay seemingly not sure whether to play at inside left or in the half backs, Tottenham's attack did not look at all happy in spite of Blanchflower's promptings. However, all was well again in the twelfth minute and Mackay had reason to share in the jubilations. At the end of yet another move started by Blanchflower, Mackay hooked the ball cleverly into the Feyenoord goalmouth and Dyson's header gave Graafland no chance.

Play was fast and entertaining until, in the fifteenth minute, Mackay and Kraay collided, in mid-air as it were, as they went up for the ball, and although the Dutchman was able to resume almost at once, poor Mackay was removed, unconscious, on a stretcher. It must have been a severe knock to lay low one of the game's seeming indestructibles. Feyenoord, it is almost superfluous to add, had a spell of superiority, and Bergholtz lobbed the ball over the bar from a good position.

Tottenham nevertheless fought hard, none doing better than Baker, who frequently could be found in the Feyenoord penalty area hoping for even half a chance. And Tottenham should have had a free kick when Jones, having beaten three men, was bowled over by Schouten. The referee, however, ignored the incident.

Feynoord created a diversion by winning two corners, both of which were cleared with some difficulty, and it appeared that weight of numbers alone might weigh down Tottenham, whose forwards, clever enough in individual approaches, seldom were allowed to come to grips with Graafland. Time after time Kraay and his men cleared their lines, frequently from a horizontal position, although Kraay once was a very lucky man to clear off the line from Dyson. Ten minutes before the interval Mackay came back – they must have heard the cheers half way down the Seven Sisters Road – just in time to see Graafland make a brilliant save from a header by Saul. With only one or two minutes remaining, Saul, receiving the ball from Mackay, hesitated, and was lost on Graafland's threshold.

Feyenoord resumed confidently. After a clever move on the right, Bennaers put in a sharp low centre – a favourite trick of his – and Brown saved from Van Der Gyp at the second attempt. Immediately afterwards it took three men to stop Kraay who is a great believer in disregarding the number on his back, and with Klaasens and Bennaers opening up the game with passes that made even Blanchflower and Mackay look envious, Feyenoord had more of the game than Tottenham, who must have been grateful for the advantage they gained in the first leg. It is possible, of course, they would have played differently if they had not had it.

The longer the game lasted the more did interest decline, and prospects of another goal to either side were remote. There also was more fouling than there had been in the game in Rotterdam – Tottenham invariably on the receiving end – and after White had been up-ended quite violently Kerkum had his name taken. Shortly afterwards Baker and Schouten had a few unfriendly words and the referee joined in and settled the conversation.

All this was unfortunate and unsightly; so much so that in quite appreciable time there were only two genuine scoring efforts, one from Saul saved finely by Graafland, and at the other end a speculative shot by Schouten had Brown grovelling at the foot of a post. This one very nearly crept in although nobody appeared to care much now. Feyenoord finished strongly and after Kreyermaat had hit the crossbar with one of the few good shots of the match, Brown saved from the same player and Van Der Gyp hit one over the bar from 10 yards.

The fearless warrior, Dave Mackay, grounded by Feyenoord defender, Kraay. He suffered a hairline fracture and left the field on a strecher, only to return to play on

AUGUST 1961: Jimmy Hill, president of the British Footballers' Association, arriving in Milan with Greaves and his wife

NOVEMBER 18, 1961: MISSION COMPLETED. Speculation had been rife for months as to whether Greaves would return to his old club Chelsea or sign for Tottenham. This photograph shows Bill Nicholson welcoming Spurs' new inside forward to the club after it was announced that Greaves had signed for the Lilly Whites

DAILY MIRROR, Monday, November 20, 1961 PAGE 23

£180-A-WEEK GREAVES!

He comes back to Super Tax Soccer—if League give the 'OK' tomorrow

By KEN JONES

WHEN Jimmy Greaves finally lines up in Spurs' attack, it will be for Soccer in the Super Tax bracket. A staggering income, from club and outside "perks," of at least £180 a week, awaits the goal-getting ace they signed from Milan on Saturday.

Greaves, 21, for whom the Spurs paid almost £100,000, will step straight into the top-wage level at wealthy White Hart-lane, where even unknown reserves collect more than £30 a week.

His "perks"—from advertising and articles—and his fees for international appearances will rocket this to an annual "take" of almost £10,000.

Before he left Chelsea for Milan in May, his maximum basic wage was pegged to £20 a week.

As his trouble-torn stay in Italy drew to a close last night, there was only one cloud on the horizon for the England forward who will become one of sport's best-paid young men.

'Nothing to Fear'

Both Greaves and Spurs know that the Football League hold the key to his British Soccer come-back.

When the League's management committee meet in London tomorrow they must decide either to accept his registration as a Spurs player, or order an inquiry.

When I telephoned Greaves in his Milan hotel last night, he told me:

"I have nothing to fear if the League decide they want to look into the whole business. Everything has been done straight. Everything has been above board."

'It Will Be Great'

PALACE TO GET AN APOLOGY

NO CLAIMS

● £100,000 grin—Jimmy Greaves, bought by Spurs, is glad his Italian days are over.

CARDIFF SUITS ME, SAYS MEL

By TOM LYONS

TALKING SOCCER

Is Ted No 1 thunderboot?

By JOHN BROMLEY

Fantastic

Tremendous

England are saved by Creek's plan

Five Caps

TODAY'S DIARY

ORIENT CALL OFF BID

CROSSWORD

Saturday's Solution

★ SPORTS SUMMARY ★

DAILY MIRROR, Monday, November 20, 1961

£180-A-WEEK GREAVES!

He comes back to Super Tax Soccer – if League give the 'OK' tomorrow

by KEN JONES

When Jimmy Greaves finally lines up in Spurs' attack, it will be for Soccer in the Super Tax bracket. A staggering income, from club and outside "perks", of at least £180 per week, awaits the goal-getting ace they signed from Milan on Saturday.

Greaves, 21, for whom the Spurs paid almost £100,000, will step straight into the top-wage level at wealthy White Hart Lane, where even unknown reserves collect more than £30 a week.

His "perks" – from advertising and articles – and his fees for international appearances will rocket this to an annual "take" of almost £10,000.

Before he left Chelsea for Milan in May, his maximum basic wage was pegged to £20 a week.

As his trouble-torn stay in Italy drew to a close last night, there was only one cloud on the horizon for the England forward who will become of one of sport's best-paid young men.

Both Greaves and Spurs know that the Football League hold the key to his British Soccer come back.

When the League's management committee meet in London tomorrow they must decide either to accept his registration as a Spurs player, or order an inquiry.

When I telephoned Greaves in his Milan

SPURS' CHRISTMAS PARTY, 1961. Left to right: Dave Mackay, Danny Blanchflower, Jimmy Greaves

The sight all the Spurs supporters had waited for: Jimmy Greaves in his new club colours

hotel last night, he told me:

"I have nothing to fear if the League decide they want to look into the whole business. Everything has been done straight. Everything has been above board."

The League, despite their threat to probe the Greaves case, will find themselves in a spot.

One of their own vice-presidents is Joe Mears, chairman of Chelsea, the No. 1 rival to Spurs' manager Billy Nicholson in the transfer case that ended in Milan on Saturday.

They gave both Spurs and Chelsea permission to step in with bids when, if they had wished, they could have blocked negotiations.

And they know that Greaves, a fully paid-up member of the Professional Footballers' Association, can ask for his union's defence if he finds himself banned.

I feel the League will allow the registration to go through – and finally end a story that has sickened Soccer.

Greaves was happily hoping for this decision when he told me:

"It will be great to line up in a Spurs shirt. There are so many good players in the side that it will be a treat to play with them.

"And you can forget any rubbish about my wanting to have warm-up games in the reserves."

Then he added: "It's unfortunate for Les Allen. But he's too good a player to be out of the limelight for long."

For Greaves knows that his arrival will make Allen his "shadow" again.

Allen was a reserve goal-snatcher to Greaves at Chelsea when Spurs bought him.

Now he is almost certain to become a transfer target again.

Bobby Smith and Jimmy Greaves still inseparable at the Bill Nicholson testimonial in August 1983

SPURS IN DEFENCE. Bill Brown punches clear in a Dukla attack

DAILY SKETCH, Thursday, February 15, 1962

DUKLA . . . 1 SPURS . . . 0

SPURS KEEP IT TO ONE DOWN

Defence plan holds Czechs

By LAURIE PIGNON

PRAGUE, WEDNESDAY

Spurs, playing a strange but magnificent tactical defensive game, held the tough Czech champions to a single goal here at the snow blanketed Dynamo Stadium this afternoon.

SHED NO TEARS! This one goal lead will not be enough for the Czechs when they visit White Hart Lane on Monday week. I expect Spurs to revert to their normal attacking football, and score at least three against these tough Czechs.

"I am well satisfied the plan worked as I expected, especially in the first half, although it wilted a little in the second half," said a smiling Bill Nicholson immediately after the game.

Bill helped plan England's tactics when we held Brazil to a goalless draw in the last World Cup. He tried the same idea today, playing three forwards, three half backs, three full backs, and Tony Marchi acting as an extra centre half.

Blanchflower played in Jimmy Greaves' No. 10 shirt, but normal positions meant little in this all defensive Tottenham line-up. One Spurs director remarked: "It worked, but I wouldn't like to see it every week."

NOR WOULD I, but Tottenham didn't come here to put on a spectacle for the 40,000 crowd. They came with hopes of becoming the first English team since Manchester United to reach the semi-final of the European Cup.

Cheering on Spurs were 100 of their own supporters, who brought an island of colour into the grim grey stands.

DUKLA STARTED ON THIS SNOW-COVERED PITCH, WITH ITS BLOOD RED LINES, AT A TREMENDOUS TEMPO, OBVIOUSLY TRYING TO BUILD UP A BIG LEAD.

The Spurs defence, as cool as the ice around the ground, frustrated them into making impossibly long shots at goal.

The Czech goal came in the 59th minute from inside right Rudolf Kucera, a beautifully taken ball which followed a bout of passing between the always dangerous Adamec and Masopust.

SKETCH SPORT Thursday

SPURS KEEP IT TO ONE DOWN

By LAURIE PIGNON

PRAGUE, Wednesday

SPURS, playing a strange but magnificent tactical defensive game, held the tough Czech champions to a single goal here at the snow blanketed Dynamo Stadium this afternoon.

SHED NO TEARS! This one goal lead will not be enough for the Czechs when they visit White Hart Lane on Monday week. I expect Spurs to revert to their normal attacking football, and score at least three against these tough Czechs.

"I am well satisfied the plan worked as I expected, especially in the first half, although it wilted a little in the second half," said a smiling Bill Nicholson immediately after the game.

Bill helped plan England's tactics when we held Brazil to a goalless draw in the last World Cup. He tried the same idea today, playing three forwards, three half-backs, three full-backs, and Tony Marchi acting as an extra centre-half.

Defence plan holds Czechs

DUKLA (0) 1, SPURS (0) 0
(Kucera)

BOBBY CRAIG.—Hi! There's one date missing.

Eleven mugs

Worked

Adamec's shot was blocked by Henry, but the inside right picked up the ball, slipped past Marchi, and in it went, not giving Brown the slightest chance.

Bobby Smith, bravely battling to win back his England place, was always trying hard at centre forward.

IN THE 68TH MINUTE HE WAS EXTREMELY UNLUCKY TO HAVE A HEADED GOAL DISALLOWED FOR OFFSIDE – THERE COULDN'T HAVE BEEN MORE THAN INCHES IN IT.

The Austrian referee, Herr Stoll, had plenty to do, especially in the second half when the snow again began to fall and blood began to rise.

Time and again on the odd breakaways, especially by Jones and Smith, the Spurs attackers were sent crashing to the snow by foul tackles.

This led to reprisals. Smith and Jones, as well as Dukla centre half Cadek, had their names taken by the referee.

After being brought down on the edge of the penalty area Smith was so annoyed that he picked up a handful of snow and threw it at his assailant. Later Bobby crashed into goalkeeper Kouba, who was sent spinning down.

He had hardly reached the ground before a party of stretcher bearers and doctors rushed on to the pitch, but within seconds the 'keeper was up, kicking the ball as if nothing had happened.

Realising that one goal was not enough Dukla hurled everything at Tottenham in the last storming ten minutes, but even when the defence began to falter BROWN WAS THERE MAKING MAGNIFICENT SAVES.

DAILY HERALD, Tuesday, February 27, 1962

TOTTENHAM 4 DUKLA 1

SPURS WIN ON AGGREGATE 4-2

YES, IT WAS WORTH IT!

All glory for Spurs as Smith and Mackay bounce those Czechs

By PETER LORENZO

Spurs, the ice-age magnificents, are through to the semi-finals of the European Cup. And after this superb display on the White Hart Lane skating rink, they surely rate as Britain's finest all-weather club side.

Dukla, the powerful, unemotional Czech champions, were shattered and demoralised by the physical might and skill of our double champions.

Super Spurs have proved their merit in perfect conditions, in mud, and in slush.

Now they've done it again under possibly the most treacherous conditions of all – a rock-hard ground, windswept by snow, where skis rather than football boots should have been the order of the night.

Bobby Smith and Dave Mackay each scored two goals, one in each half, that so fittingly send Spurs into the last four of the greatest Soccer show in Europe.

What a success night it was for burly Smith, the buccaneering Yorkshireman who started off the season by losing his club and international place.

Now he seems destined to crash himself back into the heights again.

It was the sheer physical fury of Smith and Mackay almost as much as their scoring power, that demoralised the Czechs. Every time these two white-shirted demons got the ball it was almost possible to see the Dukla defence shudder with fright.

The match was virtually decided after 15 minutes when Smith and Mackay had scored to wipe out the 1-0 first leg deficit.

YES, IT WAS WORTH IT!

All glory for Spurs as Smith and Mackay bounce those Czechs

SPURS, the ice-age magnificents, are through to the semi-finals of the European Cup. And after this superb display on the White Hart Lane skating rink, they surely rate as Britain's finest all-weather club side.

Dukla, the powerful, unemotional Czech champions, were shattered and demoralised by the physical might and skill of our double champions.

PETER LORENZO reports
TOTTENHAM 4, DUKLA 1
Spurs win on aggregate 4-2

Behind a mound of snow, muffled against the bitter wind, the loyal fans of Tottenham forsook fireside TV for the real thing last night. And as Spurs sailed into the European Cup semi-final, the fans decided that the long, long wait and cold, were well worth putting up with.

PRESENT

CHANTING

AGGRESSIVE

NEVER MOVED

RESULTS

Cooper's left has American licked

TOM PHILLIPS at the ringside

WARNING

Adjei challenge

This was Bobby Smith's first goal for Spurs . . . perhaps the most important goal of the match. You can see him just about to score it.

On the right is one Smith DIDN'T get. The Dukla goalkeeper, Kouba, made this magnificent save.

They're at 15-8 now

'ONE LEG' THOMPSON SETTLES IT

Swim records go

GREYHOUND GUIDE

Bobby Smith scoring Spurs' first goal to bring the tie level on aggregate

In the opening seconds of the second half an amazing blunder by Tony Marchi cost a gift goal to Dukla outside left Josef Jelinek – but nothing, certainly not these slow moving Czechs could stop Spurs on this memorable night.

Five minutes after Jelinek's shock goal which levelled the aggregate score to 2-2, the mighty Smith struck again with a super header from John White's perfectly-floated cross.

Within a minute, from Peter Baker's free kick, man of the match Smith skilfully back-headed to send Mackay racing through.

The inside left swept into the penalty area and cracked in a tremendous left foot cross-shot which whizzed past Pavel Kouba, a sad man in black in the Dukla goal.

Long before the end, the 60,000 crowd who had played such a roaring part in cheering their side on to success, relaxed and began to chant their victory hymn "Hallelujah – the Spurs go marching on".

It was one of the coldest nights of the year – but for these delighted fans it was one of the warmest, most satisfying nights of the decade.

Spurs' magnificent, controlled football, sustained at a breathtaking pace, was enough to make anyone forget the arctic chills.

An indication of Spurs' complete domination is that apart from Jelinek's goal, 'keeper Bill Brown had to save only twice.

Though Smith and Mackay were the formidable spearhead in this rampaging Spurs, there was so much talent and method all round them.

John White flitted like a ghost, maintaining amazing control. He had a talented foot in three of the goals and was always moving in unnoticed to the empty space.

In defence, Maurice Norman, Peter Baker and Ron Henry never lost control. They were always too aggressive and quick for a Dukla attack that was never allowed to show the football they obviously can produce.

Spies from Real Madrid, Juventus, Benfica and Liege, the other clubs left in the competition, saw this crushing Spurs performance.

They now know what a task faces them if they have the misfortune to be pitched against Spurs in the draw in today's semi-final draw in Paris.

GOALS: Ten minutes: White flicked a Blanchflower free kick straight on to Smith who cracked home from close range.

15 minutes: another White pass to Mackay, who brilliantly brought the ball down with his

left and smashed it in with his right.

46 minutes: Marchi misjudged a pass back to Bill Brown and pushed the ball straight to Jelinek, who ran on for a simple goal.

55 minutes: another splendid White cross for Smith to leap high and head into the corner of the net. The ball hurtled in at such speed Kouba never moved a muscle.

56 minutes: Mackay, with that whizz-bang shot from Smith's back-header.

READY TO POUNCE. Smith and Mackay hoping for a mistake from Kouba, the Dukla goalkeeper

DAILY EXPRESS, Thursday, March 22, 1962

BENFICA . . . 3 TOTTENHAM HOTSPUR . . . 1

EUROPEAN CUP SEMI-FINALS FIRST LEG

SPURS . . . THE SPLENDID LOSERS

Tough Guys of Benfica lead 3-1

From DESMOND HACKETT

Tottenham Hotspur elbowed their way through a gloating, howling crowd who invaded the pitch here tonight after Benfica, the European Cup champions, had beaten them in the first leg of this European Cup semi-final.

But for Spurs it was heads high and shoulders proudly back after their fighting show in the second half. Spurs go into the record as being two goals down, but I will always insist that Bobby Smith made it 3-2 in the last minute of the match.

Spurs, who have become hardened to this toughest-ever world Soccer contest, were shaken and alarmed by the fury and noise of the first half. The fast, skilled and so needlessly ruthless football of Benfica was enough to test any team.

But the 70,000 crowd who soared in mighty tiers 120 feet in the black skies were the most terrifying audience I have ever heard. They snarled, roared, screamed and whistled in an endless Niagara of noise.

But I feel Spurs can still fight back to new football fame.

In face of this barrage, any team that picks itself off the floor as did Spurs after the mauling they took in the first half can still win through to the final in the second leg at White Hart Lane on April 5.

Much as I admired the courageous way some of Spurs' players risked injury by hurling themselves into the pitched battle of the second half, it must be emphasised they did not play well.

Jimmy Greaves, in his first European Cup match, appeared at outside right, Tony Marchi at left half and Danny Blanchflower as a roaming inside left. But this combination did not click.

In the first half in particular, Blanchflower failed to find his old skilled and competent command.

It was Dave Mackay who roused the Spurs and roused this savage crowd even more. Mackay's brusque handling of the pride of Portugal, the black panther Eusebio, had his fans snarling like a French Revolution mob.

In the midst of this wild and often frightening football, men like Maurice Norman and Tony Marchi looked calm and superbly efficient players.

Before Spurs had become accustomed to the pace and fury, Benfica struck. These men in livid scarlet who were on £175 bonus, streaked into action.

Within five minutes they were a goal up. Spurs' goalkeeper Bill Brown looked startled as he punched away a shot from Benfica's dark, bulky Coluna.

The ball went spinning to the babe of the match and the only non-international in the Benfica team, 18-year old Simoes.

This skilled youngster sent the ball back into goal and centre forward Aguas wriggled his way through the tangled Spurs and eased the ball into the few inches in between the desperately-grasping Brown and the post.

A minute after Benfica's goal, the 500 Londoners who had come to cheer for Spurs were roaring their delight as Greaves soared through for a typical, alertly-taken goal – which was disallowed for offside by the Swiss referee.

But I thought it was a very close thing.

Then Benfica's slim, elusive outside right Augusto eeled his way through in the 19th minute and it was Benfica two up.

Spurs missed a superb chance after 35 minutes when John White crossed and

Danny Blanchflower scratches his head whilst Peter Baker picks the ball out of the net after Jose Augusto had scored Benfica's second goal

OFFSIDE. Jimmy Greaves fires the ball into the back of the net – unfortunately for Spurs, the referee ruled it offside

Greaves could not get his head to the kind of goal he scores with such ease back in England.

A minute later Mackay put Jones clean through, but Jones, without any opposition at all, incredibly put the ball wide. At half-time then, it was 2-0 to Benfica.

Benfica, who had been rough and tough in action, were even more bad-mannered at half-time which lasted 18 minutes.

While Tottenham came on to the field at the correct time, they were left waiting for seven minutes until the referee sent instructions to order the Benfica players back on to the field.

They were quickly menacing Tottenham and in the first four minutes Aguas had a shot inches wide and Brown made a wonderful save from Eusebio.

But the gallant band of British supporters made themeselves heard all right when Spurs scored in the 54th minute. Bobby Smith headed in a splendid Blanchflower centre.

Spurs had their dander up. Smith was through again with a glorious chance and just failed. Greaves was inches short, White went close and Jones headed just wide of goal.

But Spurs' defence again sagged and broke and Augusto got up to nod the ball in after 19 minutes of the second half.

It was Benfica 3-1 and again raging forward.

In the end Spurs were desperately unlucky not to have made it 3-2 in the last fighting minutes.

Greaves crossed the ball when he might have scored and Smith charged up to put the ball over the line. There were two Benfica players on the line and it is difficult to see why the referee could have decided that Smith was offside.

BILL NICHOLSON:

"The lads played very hard, but badly. We must play better at White Hart Lane."

DAVE MACKAY:

"We shall do them at Tottenham, just wait and see."

COSTA PEREIRA (Benfica goalkeeper):

"Bobby Smith and Jimmy Greaves are not gentlemen. They played very rough."

BELA GUTTMAN (Benfica manager):

"Tottenham played too hard, but they are a very good team. Two goals might not be good enough."

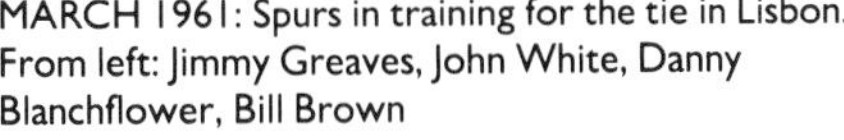

MARCH 1961: Spurs in training for the tie in Lisbon. From left: Jimmy Greaves, John White, Danny Blanchflower, Bill Brown

DAILY MAIL, Friday, April 6, 1962

SPURS . . . 2 BENFICA . . . 1

BENFICA WIN 4-3 ON AGGREGATE

ONE GOAL FROM GLORY

Benfica stagger off after 90-min blitz

By IAN WOOLDRIDGE

20 Sport

Referee says 'Yes,' linesman says 'No'—so ends European Cup crusade

ONE GOAL FROM GLORY

Benfica stagger off after 90-min blitz

By IAN WOOLDRIDGE: Spurs 2, Benfica 1

JON'S SPORTING TYPES

Glory, glory, Benfica

SPURS

BENFICA

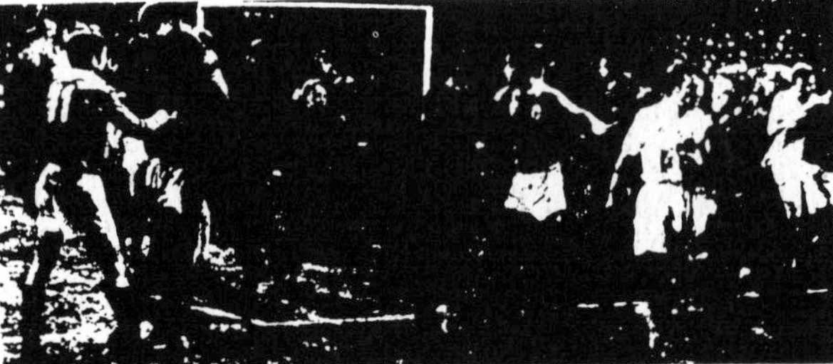

The end . . . Spurs 2, Benfica 1. But this was the night when one goal and 11 magnificent fighters were not enough.

GREAVES CALLS IT CUP ROBBERY No. 2

By ROY PESKETT

They tried to upset me—but it failed!

Blanchflower

A goal? Scorer Jimmy Greaves thought it was. So did Cliff Jones, seen turning away here. But the verdict was offside.

Real? No

Masters

And this was the sequel to the Greaves "goal"—a fan running on to the field to protest and being taken off.

Recklessly

Desperately

Look what Spurs miss

INDIA 61-5 CHASING 444

First 50

Time for hope—Danny Blanchflower slips in a penalty, and Spurs are 2-1 up.

Ingber soon shot out

Cap completes Smith's day

The seven-month crusade is over. But in the emptiness of the morning after let us pay tribute to the team that finally triumphed over Tottenham. Benfica, champions of Portugal, survived 90 minutes of football hell that would have destroyed almost any other team on earth.

For 65 of those minutes they withdrew into a red fortress round their own penalty area and withstood the greatest pounding that Spurs have ever mounted.

In the end, staggering with weariness and mottled with bruises, they were too exhausted to do more than fall on the necks of their opponents.

This to me is the true picture of the most exciting finale I have ever seen to a football match, truer indeed than to try to make an international incident of the fact that a Danish linesman named Hensen will be blamed forever by Tottenham's fans.

But that man probably robbed Spurs of the chance of a replay in neutral Brussels.

In the 23rd minute Jimmy Greaves waltzed on to a flicked pass from Bobby Smith and slid it past the careering body of Costa Pereira. It looked a perfect goal.

The referee, tubby Aage Poulsen, seemed satisfied. As 65,000 hysterical Londoners unleashed the greatest roar of this ear-shattering night, he went striding back to the centre spot.

But Hensen, a slim, erect, isolated figure on the far touchlines, had his magenta flag pointed skywards. This was fortune's vengeance on Spurs.

Poulsen strode back, listened intently, thrust his way out from a bouncing encirclement of wildly protesting Tottenham men and ruled Greaves offside.

That was the turning point.

Tottenham had started with the seemingly impossible burden of a two-goal deficit from Lisbon. Their fate seemed certain when, in a 15th minute of sudden shock, Jose Aguas, the

Bobby Smith (out of picture) scores Spurs' first goal

great clear-brained captain of these 11 Portuguese men o'war, strode through a great gap to score the first goal of the night.

It was from that even worse position that Spurs broke out to set seige to Benfica's goal in the most thrilling and heart-aching hour's football I have seen.

They simply forced their way through flesh and blood and bone to hammer on the great door that Benfica had slammed in their faces.

In the 35th minute came their first reward. Bobby Smith, flinging his huge frame recklessly at anybody who dared to block his path, drove in a superb White cross.

Now it was at half-time. For Spurs it was a battle more to beat the clock than to beat Benfica. Instead of 90 there were only 45 minutes left to score three goals for victory, two for survival.

Just two minutes into the second half the nerves of 65,000 were truly on the tightrope. Danny Blanchflower had cut that deficit again.

Coluna, nominally inside left but now withdrawn almost on to his own goal-line in desperate defence, backed into the advancing John White. As Blanchflower moved up to take the penalty, I would not have been in his boots.

Yet he did it as if he had been set to prove

Costa Pereira saving a shot from Jimmy Greaves

some theoretical point. He moved in with a corkscrew run, and as Pereira flung himself far to the right of his goal, Blanchflower's penalty burst into the net six yards wide of his falling body.

And so the scene was set for the finale. For 35 of the remaining 43 minutes Spurs stormed on and on. Chances came. Jones, for the second time, blazed a preciously carved chance over the bar.

Greaves, his sharpshooting blunted on a night when it was never more desperately needed, missed two slim openings.

And all the while the clock ticked on.

In the end, perhaps appropriately, it was Mackay who drew the last great gasp from a crowd now silenced by tension.

From 20 yards he unleashed a shot that climbed towards the roof of Benfica's net – glanced the top of the bar and pitched into the crowd.

The match was over. Tottenham turned

OFFSIDE – ONSIDE? Jimmy Greaves, seen looking onside, beating the Benfica goalkeeper after 23 minutes, but the linesman (seen extreme left) had his flag raised and the goal was disallowed

and embraced their enemies.

A magnificent gesture – for during 180 minutes in two countries Benfica, holders of the European Cup, had proved themselves only fractionally a greater football team than Tottenham Hotspur.

DAILY MAIL, Friday April 6, 1962

GREAVES CALLS IT CUP ROBBERY No. 2

By ROY PESKETT

Jimmy Greaves, whose "goal" for Spurs in the 23rd minute was disallowed for offside, protested after the match: "I thought it was a good one. I ran between two Benfica players before shooting."

Then the England inside forward added ruefully: "This is twice I have been 'done' in the European Cup."

Spurs' manager Bill Nicholson also thought it was a good goal. But he gave this verdict on the game:

"My men played too quickly. They were too hurried. Their enthusiasm ran away with them. They lacked a little control, and one or two players did not quite do what we had hoped.

Jimmy Greaves denied again by the Benfica goalkeeper

"If we had kept our heads the result might have been different. Losing that first goal was vital, but we had our chances."

Nicholson's summing-up of the European Cup final: "I think Benfica will beat Real Madrid."

Benfica coach Bela Guttman admitted he had been very worried. He said:

"It was the hardest game of my life. I thought Spurs would equalise in the last ten minutes."

The Danish referee, Aage Pulsen, said of that last, all-attack spell by Spurs, when they always looked likely to equalise: "I allowed

SPURS STUNNED. Jose Aguas puts Benfica 1-0 ahead on the night and 4-1 on aggregate

one minute extra because of time-wasting by Benfica."

But Guttman also criticised the referee. He said: "I blame him that we gave away more free kicks than Spurs. How many fouls didn't he give against Tottenham?"

Guttman ended with ths tribute: "Spurs played better here than in Lisbon. They attacked more. They are one of the best teams in Europe. One day soon, with one or two changes, they will win the European Cup."

Sir Stanley Rous, president of FIFA, praised Benfica. "Every one is a ball artist. They can play the ball from any angle. They are masters of the game."

Last word from Alan Hardaker, secretary of the Football League, who are very worried about falling gates in England: "It was a wonderful game. It was the best advertisement for League football for a long time."

Gifts and pennants from some of Spurs' European opponents

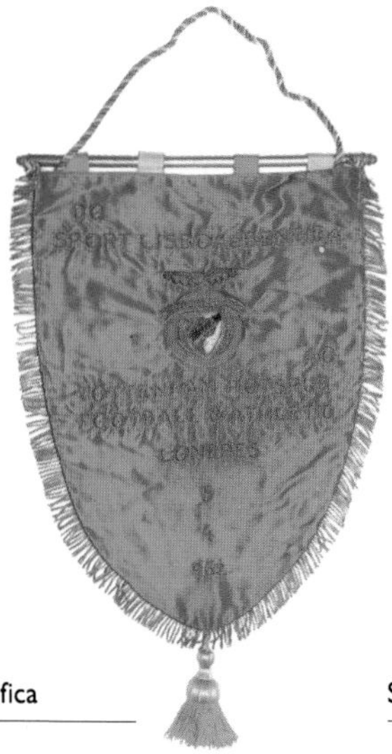

Benfica

Slovan Bratislava

OFK Belgrade

Real Madrid

Manchester United

FC Nantes

Olympiakos Piraeus

Vitoria Setubal

Liverpool

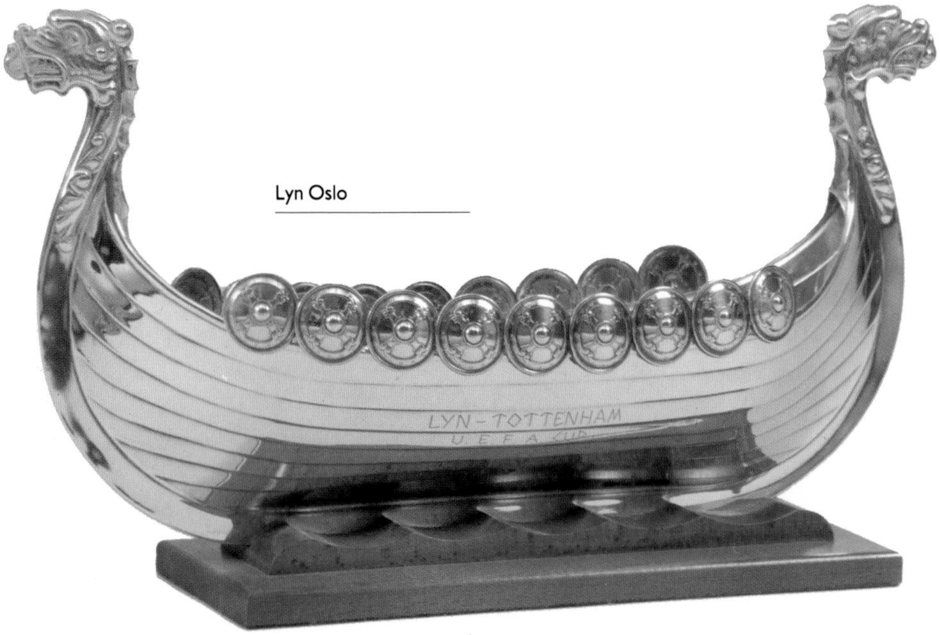

Lyn Oslo

FORTY-THREE MINUTES TO GO. Danny Blanchflower scores from the penalty spot after John White had been floored

LOOKING BACK WITH JIMMY GREAVES

It is more than 24 years since the night that Tottenham's glorious double winning side was beaten in the first European crusade – but for Jimmy Greaves the memories are as clear as if it were yesterday.

He was convinced then in the heat of the night that Tottenham had been robbed. The passing of the years has done nothing to detract from that view.

Tottenham were 3-1 down from the first leg in the Stadium of Light in Lisbon, but they believed that in the 23rd minute their real chance of reaching the final was shattered.

Greaves remembers it all. A Danish referee called Aage Pulsen. A pass from Bobby Smith and a clinical finish. The ball was in the net.

He also remembers the anger. "I was sure then that it was a good goal. I don't think that anyone will ever be able to change my view of that. There were defenders all around me.

"Bobby slotted the ball through and I went between at least two defenders before shooting past Costa Pereiera, the Benfica goalkeeper. I really thought that goal would be the one that would put us through to the final.

"The disappontment of that defeat was immense. I felt a little guilty because I missed some great chances after that, but I don't think it was meant to be my year.

"We were done a couple of times in the European Cup that season. It was a great education for us though. It helped us in the years to come. We learned to handle defeat and disappointment.

"Maybe it made us into a better side. We had learned the differences between playing in England and playing in Europe. We were no longer the innocents abroad."

It was a night of disappointment for Spurs' manager Bill Nicholson who described Benfica as one of the best sides that he had come across in Europe.

"They were a team of artists. They were the masters that season. They had the great players. They had Coluna and Eusebio. They were an outstanding collection. They proved to be the base for Portugal's best years in European football. They were the backbone too of the 1966 World Cup team."

The full greatness of the Benfica side was to be revealed less than a month after their triumph against Tottenham in front of 60,600 fans in the Olympic stadium in Amsterdam.

The 20-year old Eusebio, who was to develop into the greatest footballer that Portugal ever produced, destroyed Real Madrid and ended the most glorious era in European Soccer history.

It was the final nail in the coffin of a Madrid side of the Puskas, Gento and Di Stefano age. An age that had captured the imagination of fans across the world. An age that ensured the future of European football.

But the Spanish masters had been upstaged finally by their Portuguese rivals. For five years Real Madrid had been the undisputed kings.

Then in 1960/61, the reign was ended. Madrid's most fierce rivals Barcelona knocked them out of the European Cup and Benfica took over the mantle.

Under the management of Bela Guttman they beat Barcelona 3-2 in Berne in 1961 and then completed the ultimate triumph over Madrid themselves in Amsterdam.

It was a personal triumph for the young Eusebio. He scored twice in the 5-3 victory with all Madrid's goals coming from the great Hungarian Ferenc Puskas.

Benfica were the new kings . . . but Tottenham came so close.

Bobby Smith turns to receive the congratulations of his team mates having just scored. Eusebio doesn't show the same enthusiasm

THE AGONY AND THE ECSTASY. Benfica players being hugged by their supporters at the end of the match whilst Jimmy Greaves and Terry Medwin are seen leaving the field

DAILY MAIL, Friday, April 6, 1962

They Tried To Upset Me – But It Failed!

Blanchflower

DANNY BLANCHFLOWER (Spurs captain):

"I thought Benfica were trying to worry me when I went to take the penalty. That was why there was so much fuss. There was a time when they might have worried me – not now.

"It was a hectic sort of game and we did not get any of the breaks after giving away a goal that could have been offside.

"My impression was that one linesman kept his flag up all the time and the other fellow did not raise his.

"Benfica's goalkeeper saved them. He grabbed balls on the 18-yard line I thought we were going to get. I think Real Madrid will beat them six times out of ten."

CLIFF JONES (Spurs outside left):

"You cannot give a team like this four goals – you could not do it to Crewe Alexandra. Benfica played better here than in Lisbon."

EUSEBIO (20-year old Benfica inside right, who cried with joy after the match): "I am so happy to be in the final for the first time that I don't know what to say. I hope that in this year against Real Madrid I can win the same medal as all my colleagues."

COLUNA (Benfica inside left):

"We only tried to defend ourselves. That was our main idea.

"Tottenham fought very well. The half-line is one of the best I ever played against in the world. Mackay is an extraordinary player.

"The penalty against me was never a foul. I went for the ball and the charge was fair."

PEREIRA (Benfica goalkeeper):

"Tottenham are one of the best teams in Europe. This was the hardest game we have ever played.

"The penalty was never a foul. White just threw himself to the ground and Coluna charged in very fairly and correctly.

"Bobby Smith is a real gentleman – after the game he came over to congratulate me. I must correct my opinion. After seeing Crawford play in the England attack, I say Smith deserves a place in Chile."

JOHN WHITE (Spurs inside right):

"I don't think we found our feet as we did in previous rounds. I am terribly disappointed. Benfica had very good forwards but a suspect defence and if we had used the right tactics in front of goal we might have scored more."

Before the match, Guttman said he was resigning as Benfica coach at the end of the season . . . "They have won two championships and the European Cup. What more is there for me to do with them?"

DAILY MAIL, Friday, April 6, 1962

Look What Spurs Miss

Spurs have failed the final hurdle to the European Cup final. But they were in it long enough to prove what a fantastic money-spinner it is.

Their eight ties brought them about £80,000. If they had reached the final they would have got a further £20,000 for winning, or £10,000 as runners-up.

The players drew about £40 last night, bringing their European Cup bonuses to £200.

The Benfica team were on a £700 semi-final bonus.

Last night's 65,000 crowd raised the total attendance for Spurs' eight ties to 508,087 – 244, 087 of them at the four White Hart Lane matches.

All tickets for the European Cup final at the Olympic Stadium, Amsterdam, on May 2 have been disposed of.

The stadium holds 60,600, with seats for 44,600 at 35s., 25s., and 15s. It costs 6s. to stand.

Despite losing to Benfica in the semi-finals of the European Cup, Spurs once more won the FA Cup and so were able to march into Europe again.

SUNDAY TIMES, May 6, 1962

TOTTENHAM HOTSPUR . . . 3 BURNLEY . . . 1

TOTTENHAM SO DESERVEDLY HOLD ON TO THE FA CUP

Greaves the architect of a fine victory

By BRIAN GLANVILLE

WEMBLEY, SATURDAY

Tottenham So Deservedly Hold on to the F.A. Cup

GREAVES THE ARCHITECT OF A FINE VICTORY

By BRIAN GLANVILLE—Wembley, Saturday

How They Got There

Tottenham again: and altogether more emphatically than last year! They are only the second team to win it two years running, Newcastle United having achieved this distinction in 1951 and 1952. In a Cup final graced by the Queen, the Duke of Edinburgh and the Duke of Gloucester, unblemished, thank goodness, by injury, and full of good things, the Spurs defence was simply too well organised, too hermetic, for Burnley's striving forwards. Brown, Norman, Henry and the rest positioned cunningly, and tackled strongly, forcing Burnley to jib, tack, manoeuvre; do anything, in a word, but go straight for goal.

Burnley, by contrast, were altogether less watertight, and a Tottenham attack of this quality, with three inside forwards so eager for the kill, does not pardon vulgar error. Moreover, when Burnley's attack did produce a punch, Spurs produced a counter-punch so lethal and immediate, that it was clearly all over.

The first goal came after a mere three and a half minutes. Smith headed the ball down perfectly to Greaves, a move which has already brought copious rewards. Greaves set off with his customary acceleration, but this time, it seemed, he wasn't quick enough; a posse of Burnley defenders was with him.

Greaves stopped dead, as though he himself had realised the futility of the enterprise; then all at once, when everybody had rushed past him, he turned on the ball, left footed, and trickled a gentle, insidious shot along the ground, out of Blacklaw's reach. What an anti-climax; but what a devastating goal!

Burnley quickly showed their defiance through Miller, though perhaps it was significant and ominous that the shot should be a long one from outside the area, rather than the inevitable climax of a move. Nevertheless, it was a fine shot, which brought Brown flying across goal, to turn over the bar.

Greaves, at his most explosive, very nearly increased the lead after 19 minutes, erupting like some force of nature into the middle of a pretty, defensive duet between Cummings and Miller, snatching up the ball, and hitting a ferocious shot on the turn, which Blacklaw leaped, superbly, to turn over the bar. Clearly this was to be one of those days when Greaves felt personally involved; how one hopes they will all be such days in Chile!

There was a poise and fluency, now, about Tottenham's football, which made Burnley seem almost pedestrian. Even a Burnley attack was liable to be turned into a Tottenham counter-attack, as once when Medwin, a prolific worker, came back deep, to clear to Blanchflower, took a return, gave it back, and the ball flowed on to White, to Jones galloping down the middle, to Smith whose powerful shot wasn't appreciably wide of the post.

The broad dimensions of Tottenham strategy were now plain. Wisely, they were using Blanchflower deep in defence, so that he was playing within his diminished physical capacities, leaving Mackay to range up-field.

But there was nothing faint-hearted or inferior about Burnley, who, if they attacked with less illumination, less economy, a greater profusion of detail, were still having as much of the game as Spurs. McIlroy, closely and keenly watched by the Sampdoria general manager, Signor Giachetti, as a potential lion of Genoa, was quietly and cleverly prodding Burnley on.

Miller (thank goodness) had forsaken the defensive obsession of recent weeks, while Robson was playing better than he had played for ages, taking a part not only near goal (he shot narrowly wide of a post just before half-time) but even, uncharacteristically, in the build up.

Five minutes after half-time, it was Robson who scored a splendid equaliser. Pointer was at the back of it, that snapper-up of unconsidered trifles, toiling away with all that marvellous energy which belies his meagre physique.

It was he who snapped the ball up, passing beautifully across field to Harris. The centre was low, hard and close to the near post. Robson, anticipating perfectly, ran in and let it rebound off his shins into goal, the 100th goal in 34 Wembley FA Cup finals since they were first played there in 1923.

The game seemed open again; instead, back came the Spurs with an immediate goal. Burnley, perhaps, were relaxing a moment on their new laurels; certainly the defence seemed in repose when White crossed from the left wing, and Smith, trapping the ball, was unpardonably given time to turn on it and smash his shot past Blacklaw.

Once more, Burnley refused to lie down. Robson, taking a long pass from Elder, glided the ball deftly past Brown, but was offside. Then Harris flicked Miller's cross on to Connelly (McIlroy again was at the bottom of it) only for Connelly, largely and disappointingly invisible, to shoot with nervous haste past a post.

If there was a difference between the teams, it lay, as much as anywhere, at centre half, for while Norman was still mobile and immensely resourceful, Cummings had caught a Tartar in Smith, who played, flamboyantly, without benefit of shin-pads.

With ten minutes left, Blacklaw sadly mishandled a high cross, Medwin shot, and Cummings handled on the line to keep it out. The ball was placed on the disc, McIlroy and Cummings exchanged a wry, philosophical word, then Blanchflower strolled up, and impeccably slid the penalty kick wide of Blacklaw's left leg, into goal.

The Cup was Tottenham's: on goals, and on clear merit.

FA CUP WINNING LINE-UP, 1962. Front row from left: Medwin, White, Blanchflower, Smith, Greaves, Jones. Back row from left: Baker, Norman, Brown, manager Bill Nicholson, Henry, Mackay

SPURS WIN THE CHARITY SHIELD. FA Cup winners, Spurs, defeated League champions Ipswich Town 5-1 at Portman Road, to win the Charity Shield for the second successive year. Foreground from left: Bill Brown, Peter Baker, Dave Mackay. Back row from left: Maurice Norman, Ron Henry, Bobby Smith, Terry Medwin, Danny Blanchflower, John White, Cliff Jones, Jimmy Greaves

CHARITY SHIELD. Jimmy Greaves races through to score Spurs' third goal

ALLEN HEADS NUMBER THREE. Les Allen seen heading Spurs 3-1 ahead in London. From left: Bobby Shearer, Jim Baxter, Les Allen, Billy Ritchie

DAILY EXPRESS, Thursday, November 1, 1962

SPURS . . . 5 RANGERS . . . 2

YES, THEY'RE MARCHING ON!

Super White makes Rangers reel

By DESMOND HACKETT

Salute the Summit Soccer men of Spurs and the mighty Glasgow Rangers.

In a finery and fury of football at White Hart Lane last night the elegant Spurs flashed into a three-goal lead.

And that, in my humble opinion, will be sufficient to defy all the roars of Ibrox in the second leg of this match on December 5 which will decide the club championship of Britain.

The fact that this was also a round in the European Cup Winners Cup tournament was forgotten.

This was the greatest of England lined up against the greatest of Scotland and there were two sets of fans roaring, singing, lamenting through a night of exquisite torture.

But for all the wildness in this whirlpool of savage noise that battered down on White Hart Lane, this game possessed a moving spirit of nobility and pride.

During what was little less than raging, skilled Soccer warfare there was scarcely a boo-raising foul, and neither side would do anything but play football at its proudest peak.

And the summit Soccer belonged to Spurs.

Bold Dave Mackay, the man who had thrown down the gauntlet at the feet of the invading Scots, was the first to strike.

Mackay almost had the Scots sounding off a lament when he went into a goal bid that ignored any thought that he might break his leg in the attempt.

Mackay made himself a one-man raiding party, a lone chieftain seeking to leave behind him a line of wrecked enemies.

Rangers, equally prepared to do battle, would have been shattered by a fourth-minute goal from Spurs had they not been hardened by the affairs of world football.

Jimmy Greaves, who was to be the hammer of the Scots in the first half, curled over a corner. Three men of Rangers, suspecting the massive threat of Maurice Norman, moved his way.

John White, the slim grey wraith who never ceased to haunt his fellow Scots on this Hallowe'en, so delicately headed the ball into goal to sound off a bombardment of almost barbaric joy.

Rangers, rather than going into alarmed panic, sought to soothe down the pace to their more deliberate game.

In nine minutes Rangers were level. A too leisurely Spurs defence appeared to look on with only faint interest as Dave Wilson streaked away, crossed and up came wee Willie Henderson to score from five yards.

As this fascinating duel moved with grace and speed, the Greaves-White corner act was on parade again.

Greaves conjured the ball into a mystifying curve. The dazed Rangers appeared to freeze.

I say the ball would have gone in but White, a take-no-chance Scot, made certain with a nod.

Danny Blanchflower, a skilled, unruffled captain, designed the move that made it a surging 3-1 for Spurs.

From his pass White rainbowed the ball into goal for a move which ended in peak-form Les Allen heading into goal and dashing in after the ball as though to caress it in gratitude.

Even the stout-hearted Rangers were left gasping, wondering, bemused against a Tottenham football force that made Spurs a commanding 4-1.

So panicky were Rangers that when Terry Medwin – a master player this tremendous night – and Allen shot, Rangers captain Bob Shearer put the ball into his own goal when the shot was edging wide.

Before Spurs could fully savour this goal Henderson had put the ball across and a Jimmy Millar header made it a Spurs 4 Rangers 2 half-time breather.

There seemed no time to ease the suspense in the second half as these splendid teams fiercely fought on and on.

Ten minutes from the end of this agony of action, mighty Maurice Norman, who had

John White heading in the first goal after four minutes

GOAL NUMBER TWO. Rangers goalkeeper, Ritchie, cannot stop Spurs going ahead 2-1

come charging up for corners, got the goal that could so well prove the killer score.

Again, man-of-menace Greaves pulled off the curling, weaving corner kicks.

It came to Norman, who smashed the ball into goal with a power that would have taken with it any Ranger who had been in the way.

I salute both sides for skill, for effort that shone with pride of club and for conduct that brought nothing but honour to British football.

I am only thankful these matches come once in a lifetime.

This heady stuff, even once a month, would add to the missing millions – they just couldn't take it!

HARRY EVANS (Assistant manager and father-in-law of match winner John White):

> "You can have all your foreign stars – give me Johnny White any time."

DAVE MACKAY:

> "I don't think Rangers are good enough to give us a three-goal start. It was hard but never rough and I was delighted with the way Rangers chose to play aggressive football."

DAILY MIRROR, Wednesday, December 12, 1962

RANGERS . . . 2 SPURS . . . 3

AGGREGATE 4-8

TWO-GOAL COMEBACK BY BOBBY

By KEN JONES

It took ace goal-grabber Jimmy Greaves just eight minutes to wrap up this European Cup Winners Cup tie for Spurs last night.

Spurs, leading 5-2 after the first leg at White Hart Lane, went flat out from the start for a vital early goal to put the result beyond all doubt.

And Greaves broke the heart of every Rangers fan in the 80,000 crowd that packed Glasgow's Ibrox Park when he whipped Spurs into an impregnable four-goal aggregate lead.

Centre forward Bobby Smith, making his first team comeback in this tension-packed game started the move in mid-field.

He switched the ball to Greaves, and the little inside left out-paced three Rangers defenders to hammer home a brilliant right foot goal.

Spurs held on to their lead until half-time, but two minutes after the break inside left Ralph Brand pulled a goal back for Rangers.

Outside right Billy Henderson snaked over a cross and Brand rammed the ball into the net with a dynamic header.

But within three minutes Spurs' hit back with the dramatic counter-punch that has characterised so much of their success.

The Rangers fans hardly had time to find their breath when inside right John White "ghosted" his way past left back Eric Caldow and pin-pointed a pass that Smith hammered into the net.

So once again a gamble by Spurs' manager Billy Nicholson had paid off.

In a last-minute move to put back the punch and fire in his suddenly goal-shy attack, Nicholson dropped Les Allen and brought in Smith to lead the line.

And using Smith as their "prop", the other Spurs forwards inter-changed with bewildering speed and skill.

Rangers came more into the game after that shock Greaves goal, but Spurs stayed cool and confident in the electric atmosphere.

Then a wave of booing swept across Ibrox after a foul by left half Dave Mackay on Henderson gave Rangers a free kick on the edge of the area.

Two frantic Rangers appeals for penalties

Nicholson gamble pays off as Smith gives Rangers the Cup KO

TWO-GOAL COMEBACK BY BOBBY

By KEN JONES: Rangers 2, Spurs 3 (aggregate 4-8)

IT took ace goal-grabber Jimmy Greaves just eight minutes to wrap up this European Cup Winners Cup-tie for Spurs last night.

Spurs, leading 5—2 after the first leg at White Hart-lane, went flat out from the start for a vital early goal to put the result beyond all doubt.

And Greaves broke the heart of every Rangers fan in the 80,000 crowd that packed Glasgow's Ibrox Park when he whipped Spurs into an impregnable four-goal aggregate lead.

Centre forward Bobby Smith, making his first team come-back in this tension-packed game started the move in mid-field.

He switched the ball to Greaves, and the little inside left out-paced three Rangers defenders to hammer home a brilliant right-foot goal

Drama

Spurs held on to their lead until half-time, but two minutes after the break inside left Ralph Brand pulled a goal back for Rangers.

Outside right Billy Henderson snaked over a cross and Brand rammed the ball into the net with a

WHAM . . . a Jimmy Greaves special on its way past Rangers' goalkeeper Billy Ritchie for Spurs goal No. 1.

were turned down in three minutes before Spurs switched back to another surging spell of sweet Soccer.

A flash of temperament by Rangers ace left half Jim Baxter got him "booked" after a foul on Greaves.

And immediately Greaves should have put Spurs two up in the twenty-seventh minute.

Only three yards from goal, Greaves allowed goalkeeper Billy Ritchie to smother a shot that looked a certainty.

Every Spurs player was back in defence as Rangers forced two corners before goalkeeper Bill Brown made a point-blank save from left winger Davie Wilson.

And Spurs had a fortunate let-off a minute before half-time when a swinging Wilson cross dipped and slipped just wide of the far post with Brown beaten.

Then came the five minutes of furious action after half-time when Spurs lost and then regained their four-goal lead.

But after seventy-four minutes Rangers cut that back when Wilson made the score 2-2.

Just before this goal, Spurs' centre half Maurice Norman had his name taken after his second heavy tackle within a minute.

Four minutes from time Smith set the seal on a great comeback by scoring Spurs' third goal.

It gave Spurs the tie on an 8-4 aggregate and put them into the third round against the Czech side Slovan Bratislava.

Jimmy Greaves putting Spurs 1-0 ahead at Ibrox

LAST-MINUTE WINNER. Bobby Smith scoring his second and Spurs' third in Glasgow

HAPPY SCOTS. Dave Mackay and John White look happy having beaten Glasgow Rangers at home and away.

Sporting News

BRATISLAVA MUD A TRAP ONLY FOR SPURS

HEROIC BROWN HOLDS SLOVAN TO TWO-GOAL LEAD

From Our Association Football Correspondent

RUGBY'S RACKETS EFFORT FOILED

ETON PUT TROUBLES BEHIND THEM

ST. THOMAS'S IN FINAL AGAIN

LONDON HOSPITAL XV OVERPOWERED

Brown, the Tottenham Hotspur goalkeeper, making one of his many fine saves in the match against Slovan at Bratislava. Other Tottenham players are Baker (right foreground), Norman (behind Baker), and Henry (left of Brown).

THE TIMES, Wednesday, March 6, 1963

SLOVAN . . . 2 TOTTENHAM HOTSPUR . . . 0

FROM OUR ASSOCIATION FOOTBALL CORRESPONDENT, BRATISLAVA, MARCH 5

BRATISLAVA MUD A TRAP ONLY FOR SPURS

Heroic Brown holds Slovan to two-goal lead

Once again it is the same dismal story to be told of English football abroad – another defeat. Nine days hence Tottenham Hotspur go into the second leg of their European Cup Winners' Cup tie against Slovan at White Hart Lane, facing an overdraft of two goals. A place in the semi-final is now much in doubt.

Yet they have one consolation, perhaps. It could be far blacker, and at this moment at least they have been offered a glimmer of hope. Indeed, Slovan gratuitously let them off the hook to some extent in the National Stadium here this afternoon, for the difference in speed, craft, and imagination of Slovan might have given them a clearer margin, perhaps in the region of four goals.

So Spurs escaped the drubbing they deserved on a heavy, muddy pitch thawed by spring-like sunshine that many would have expected to suit them. They were in fact, outthought and out-manoeuvred and beaten in their strange tactics of employing Saul, ordinarily a centre forward, at outside right, with instructions to turn his attentions to defence if the tide became unfriendly.

In the event, only for some 15 minutes before half-time, when Slovan were already one up and growing in authority, did we see him fall back purposely to cover the middle, where Hrdlicka, a deep-lying centre foward, linked with his left half Kral to form the fountain head of Slovan's attacking plan. This, no doubt, was based on the stratagem of the Czechoslovakia national side, the World Cup finalists in Chile, who use Masopust and Kvasnak as the hub of their wheel.

Those of us who expected Spurs to employ an all-out defensive policy, as in Prague and Lisbon last year, foresaw Hopkins, a defender, being chosen as a full-time reinforcement of the rear areas. We must now eat our words, yet the germ of the idea was there, for the choice of Saul was designed to cover two contingencies.

As it was, things went wrong nearly all the way round. But for the brave and agile goalkeeping of Brown, at present wearing a plaster across his nose as a badge of honour, the tireless chasing and covering of Marchi and Mackay and some steady screening by Norman the tie would probably already be far out of Tottenham's reach. Yet in a sense they are still alive, hoping for a reversal of events next week with the roar of North London to stir them to life, as happened last season after the defeats at Gornik, Prague and Lisbon in the European Cup.

Next time Spurs must do something to counter the deep-lying centre forward ploy in mid-field. Next time it may be more difficult, since Molnar, the Slovan international, should be fit to play at centre foward, with Hrdlicka forming the link at left half. Next time, too, Tottenham must hope for some response from White, Greaves, Jones and the bustling Smith. All these were now lost almost without trace in the mud, seldom supporting each other, seldom making angles for one another, a lonely line of individuals.

The extinction of White as any sort of connecting link and the usual creator of attacks was perhaps the most serious of all. Without his touches Greaves and the rest fell the easiest of preys to the solid covering of Popluhar and of his full backs and wing halves, none of whom, of course, was loath to use the body check when required. Jones, in particular, was shackled by Urban and blindly tried to break his bonds. All he did was to run constantly into a brick wall. It was pathetic.

Often enough in the past Spurs have been filled with a sort of invisible champagne. But now, within a quarter of an hour, any bubbles they had evaporated and by half-time their potion was flat. How often one finds this when visiting Europe. Still, to repeat it, they may have been let off the hook. That clearly was the feeling of everyone of the 40,000 crowd, grey and silent as it was before the kick-off but chanting their demand later on for the added goals that Slovan deserved.

Yet, as things often go, the two goals they did score, one in each half, might well have been prevented. The first, after half an hour, was well enough executed certainly. Hrdlicka, in his deep-central role, found Kral on his left; Kral put his pass inside Baker and there was Cvetler moving fast to cut in and beat Brown. But in top class football the pass inside the back should be prevented just as Urban and Jankovic cut out any similar attempt by their opponents.

Slovan's second strike arrived after 10 minutes of the second half, which, incidentally, began with a vain protest by Spurs over the apparent substitution of the ball. Now it was two positive errors that led to the goal – a feeble back-heel by White and a disastrous square pass by Baker across his own penalty area. In a couple of passes Mraz and Mravcik punished the crime as Mravcik shot home.

That, virtually, was the end of Tottenham. The soggy pitch became blacker, deeper and more cloying, but it seemed to trap only Tottenham. Slovan, often with the man over, worked their moves cleverly under the direction of Hrdlicka, with Cvetler the master of Baker in speed and footwork. Now it was Brown who rose to the heights. Once, certainly, Mravcik missed a sitter from six yards, but it was a superb diving save by Brown to Cvetler's shot and then an immediate, instinctive reaction to a header by Mraz, all within a few seconds, that again kept Slovan out.

Twice more Brown dived dangerously to keep Tottenham going, and, at the end, but for inches Spurs might have got one back when Marchi lobbed just wide of the far post after one of White's few coherent passes of the day.

DAILY EXPRESS, Friday, March 15, 1963

SPURS . . . 6 SLOVAN . . . 0

SMASH-HIT SPURS AGAIN

Mackay sets off six-goal romp

By CLIVE TOYE

Spurs swept Slovan, the Pride of Czechoslovakia, out of the European Cup Winners' Cup last night.

They did it in nine minutes of surging Soccer that had the blue-shirted men from Bratislava breathless.

They pulled back one goal of the 2-0 lead Slovan gained in the first leg of this quarter-final last week, levelled, burst in front and then went on to slaughter.

All in those nine hectic minutes. And, as the roars rose over brilliantly lit White Hart Lane, Slovan became more and more bemused by the power of the team they shamed so simply in Bratislava nine days before.

It had to be the demon of Tottenham, left half Dave Mackay, who pulled out the stopper on the fantastic pressure Spurs built up from the early seconds. Czech goalkeeper Villem Schroif saved from Jimmy Greaves and then writhed in agony when Bobby Smith charged him in the first minute.

Schroif got up again as soon as Dutch referee Leo Horn whistled for a free kick. But the pattern of the game had been set.

Spurs were out to score or burst their lungs in the attempt. Slovan were to give their blue-clad bodies no rest trying to stop the tide of Tottenham.

And on the tingling tick of the 31st minute a throw-in from Tony Marchi was pushed back to Mackay by John White.

Mackay brought the ball down with his proud chest and sent it scudding into the far corner of the net.

That goal – especially for the screaming fans swaying on the terraces – made up for the moments of anguish when Schroif had saved from Smith then Jones then Smith again.

It made up for that terrifying moment when Slovan broke out of their blockade and Anton Moravcik hit the upright.

But seven more minutes of ferocious action swept the crowd into a frenzy of Hallelujahs before Spurs were level and leaping their joy.

Greaves in mid-field pushed an awkward pass to Jones and shadowed into an open space as Jones slid a return pass.

Greaves wraithed round a lunging Slovan boot and lured Schroif towards him before calmly directing the ball where he had always intended it to go.

Spurs did not even let the leaping hearts of their fans settle down to a subdued thudding before cracking the Slovan curtain of fighting humanity again.

Frank Saul swept a Jones pass high into the middle and burly Bobby Smith headed the ball right out of Schroif's hands into the net.

Could Slovan stop this raging tide of Tottenham? They could not.

The strain on their faces showed they had no hope even when Bill Brown was forced to save superbly from Moravcik.

Right back Mel Hopkins joined the Tottenham attack, roaring up to hit the crossbar and the all-black garb of Schroif, named the Black Panther of Bratislava, turned tawny with the mud as he saved attack after attack.

Twenty minutes into the second half, Schroif came out again to punch a centre from Smith away from the searching head of Jones. And Spurs were two goals ahead.

Schroif fell limp from his effort and Greaves, 25 yards out, almost studiously chipped the ball over his head and inches under the bar.

Slovan were by then staggering from the muscle-tugging effort of keeping Spurs in check.

And two goals in a minute made their fate almost as bad as that of the Polish miners, Gornik, who came to Tottenham 18 months ago with a two-goal lead and went home with an eight-goal thrashing.

In the 75th minute Jones went up to head a centre from Marchi and this time got there before Schroif. His header bulged the net as Schroif lay there abject and dismayed.

Sixty seconds later Schroif's World Cup companion, giant centre half Jan Popluhar, let himself be robbed by frail John White and White ran on unhampered to push the ball past hapless Schroif.

ANTON BULLA (Slovan manager):

"I envy Spurs their supporters. We have never played before such a crowd. It affected our players. Spurs deserved to win but not by six. They were so much better than us in tackling and heading. Completely unrecognisable from the Spurs we beat in Bratislava."

BILL NICHOLSON (Spurs manager):

"This was a victory for power. Slovan are a good football side, but our wing halves tonight powered up the field like they used to do last season and not very often this year. They won us the match."

Two-goal Jimmy Greaves waltzes through the Slovan defence

DAILY HERALD, Thursday, April 25, 1963

OFK . . . 1 SPURS . . . 2

GREAVES SENT OFF!

But Spurs are a goal up

PETER LORENZO

REPORTS THE SHOCK NEWS FROM YUGOSLAVIA

Jimmy Greaves sent off for the first time in his career . . . the crushed Belgrade team whistled off by their own angry fans . . . tiny Terry Dyson ramming in a brilliant opportunist winning goal for 10-man Spurs 20 minutes from time.

This was the tremendous second half drama in this European Cup Winners' Cup semi-final at the crowded Red Army Stadium.

It was in the 55th minute that Greaves became the first Tottenham player to be sent off for nearly 40 years. But from my lofty Press-box perch I didn't see anything that merited such drastic action.

I was following the play. This incident happened some 20 yards away.

In the dressing room afterwards, Hungarian referee Lajo Aranjosi told me: "I sent off Greaves for taking a kick at No. 5 (centre half Krivokuca) when he hadn't got the ball.

"I told Greaves that this wasn't gentlemanly. In fact, Tottenham were a more gentlemanly side when they were down to 10 men.

"This was not a rough game, but Spurs were physically strong."

Angry Spurs manager Bill Nicholson clearly saw things differently. "I am making my own report to the Cup committee," he said. "And the chairman of that committee, Mr Sandor Barcs, was here to see for himself."

At first, Greaves refused to leave the field. He walked away into a crowd of Tottenham players and not until the referee had strode over to Spurs' captain, Tony Marchi, was the 22-year old Cockney persuaded to leave the field.

Then to whistling jeers and howls of derision, Greaves, a lonely, lost figure, made the longest, saddest walk of his Soccer life.

But it speaks for the courage and tenacity of these revengeful Spurs, that even reduced to 10 men, they were still able to control, dictate to and finally conquer these baffled, out-classed Belgrade men.

At the end of their magnificent 90 minutes, all the cheers and applause from the 60,000 crowd were for Spurs.

In their wake came the boos, whistles and jeers as the embarrassed Belgrade team slunk off.

With the return leg at White Hart Lane next Wednesday, Spurs are almost certainly through to the final.

Belgrade were not in the same class. Even with an extra man, they hadn't the guile or method to hold Spurs, every man a furious worker from first whistle to last.

White shot Spurs into the lead after 26 minutes with a superb left foot volley from 20 yards.

The goal ended 90 seconds of Soccer uproar that started when Bobby Smith was bundled over.

Spurs prepared for their usual free kick routine. Next instant the Belgrade right half was seen writhing on the pitch.

Immediately a swarm of Belgrade players surrounded Bobby Smith, pushing and jostling him before the referee raced over.

Still the Belgrade men raved. One almost yanked the arm off the referee, demanding that Spurs' leader be sent off.

But after a brief check with a linesman, the referee returned, censured nobody and pointed for the free kick to be taken.

Marchi promptly flicked the ball forward to Bobby Smith, who tapped it on for White to tear in and volley home.

So much for any suggestion of a defensive performance from Tottenham.

Belgrade's equaliser came nine minutes from the interval – a penalty cracked home by inside right, Popov.

Again, this seemed a harsh decision. The ball hit Mackay's foot and ricocheted on to his hand.

Maurice Norman, playing despite a painful toe, had two stitches inserted over an eye after the game.

GREAVES SENT OFF!

But Spurs are a goal up

BELGRADE, Wednesday: OFK 1, Spurs 2

JIMMY GREAVES sent off for the first time in his career . . the crushed Belgrade team whistled off by their own angry fans . . tiny Terry Dyson ramming in a brilliant opportunist winning goal for 10-man Spurs 20 minutes from time.

This was the tremendous second-half drama in this European Cup-winners' Cup semi-final at the crowded Red Army Stadium.

It was in the 55th minute that Greaves became the first Tottenham player to be sent off for nearly 40 years. *But from my lofty Press-box perch I didn't see anything that merited such drastic action.*

I was following the play. This incident happened some 20 yards away.

More gentlemanly

In the dressing-room afterwards, Hungarian referee Lajos Aranjosi told me: "I sent off Greaves for taking a kick at No. 5 (centre-half Krivokuca) when he hadn't got the ball.

"I told Greaves that this wasn't gentlemanly. In fact, Tottenham were a more gentlemanly side when they were down to 10 men.

"This was not a rough game, but Spurs were physically strong."

Angry Spurs manager Bill Nicholson clearly saw things differently. "I am making my own report to the Cup committee," he said. "And the chairman of that committee, Mr. Sandor Barcs, was here to see for himself."

At first, Greaves refused to leave the . . .

. . and in the other big European game . .

MILAN HIT DUNDEE FOR FIVE

By DOUGLAS RITCHIE

Milan 5, Dundee 1

THAT'S it, Dundee! It's odds-on now that the Scottish champions WON'T be playing in the European Cup Final at Wembley next month.

Their attempt to become the first British club to reach the final crashed in Milan last night.

About 90,000 fans saw Milan go ahead after two min- . . .

BILLY McCULLOUGH . . booked by referee

GEOFF STRONG . . hit vital goal

Real—£10,000 flops

By STEVE RICHARDS

Stoke 2, Real Madrid 2

THE Real Madrid £10,000 Soccer circus must be near its end judging by their . . .

The old pals act

STRONG ROCKS EVERTON HOPE

IT was a great night for Spurs back at home, too. And they've their old Highbury pals to thank for it. Arsenal should be given the freedom of White Hart Lane.

By ALF BALLARD

Everton 1, Arsenal 1

By grabbing a point they put Spurs back in the championship chase with a chance.

The wonder is that any goals were scored. Both sides drew concrete curtains across their goals with jet-speed and threw everything upon a quick breakaway.

Artists like Roy Vernon and George Eastham, both at their best, somehow always found themselves up against a solid wall of defenders when their footwork should have ensured that they were clear.

Priceless

Everton set off as though they would book these priceless championship points right away and went ahead in the eighth minute when Vernon hit in a low shot.

Arsenal were booed for their body-checking tactics.

Outside-left Alan Skirton annoyed the crowd with a tackle which laid out the Everton goalkeeper Gordon West, but he and Eastham formed a dangerous left wing.

The equaliser came in the 30th minute when Geoff Strong, with an amazing flying overhead kick, hooked a Johnny McLeod centre past West.

The second-half was almost . . .

. . . attack against an Everton defence which looked as though it might be tiring.

The Highbury men almost snatched the extra point and would have done so if Strong and Baker had been able to shake off the last ditch defence of centre-half Brian Labone.

● Everton manager Harry Catterick said later that 20-year-old goalkeeper West, who badly damaged his left shoulder in the first half, was unlikely to play again this season.

IS BACK

"Boy! And I thought t' ball of the century was Windsor Castle."

● CHARLES BRAY on the West Indies—Page 12

THOMPSON CASHES IN

Chelsea 0, Wolves 1

A GOAL from winger David Thompson knocked Chelsea out of the fourth round of the F A Youth Cup.

It came after a boob between England Junior World Cup stars John Cowen and Ron Harris in the 15th minute. And it must have been a strange experience for 'keeper Cohen, who did not have a goal scored against him in the youth international or in any of his earlier rounds of this season's Cup competition.

In the second half Thompson rocked the bar with a dipping drive.

POOL PROMOTERS ASSOCIATION CERTIFIED DIVIDENDS For 20th April 1963

SOCCER THIS WEEK 541 DIVIDENDS SHARED BY 2 WINNERS FROM BRIXTON & GLAMORGAN

JIMMY GREAVES

DAILY EXPRESS, Thursday, May 2, 1963

SPURS . . . 3 OFK BELGRADE . . . 1

BLANCHFLOWER'S TRIUMPH

Danny stays cool and steers Spurs to the final

By DESMOND HACKETT

A quiet, unflappable football professor called Danny Blanchflower steered Spurs through a sea of stormy Soccer into the final of the European Cup Winners' Cup last night.

The 5-2 aggregate makes Spurs the first English team to reach a European Cup tournament final. But if the score makes it seem like an armchair ride into the decider against Atletico Madrid in Rotterdam on May 15, it was in fact a harassing and adventurous journey.

Spurs were too easily rattled by the well-drilled moves of OFK. There were moments of agonising ill-luck for the Yugoslavs with shots inches wide, and some cheer-compelling saves from Bill Brown.

Compared with the cool command of Blanchflower, the swashbuckling Dave Mackay, filling in for banished Jimmy Greaves, may have lacked the quality of a truly great artist.

But it was Mackay who smashed up the Yugoslav attacks when they were at their most threatening peak. And it was Mackay who was mightily around to score and make goals when the Spurs outlook was matching the bleak darkness of the night.

The Tottenham defence, superbly led by goalkeeper Bill Brown, were never able to ease against the battling of men of Yugoslavia.

Ron Henry was heroic. Peter Baker celebrated his re-promotion to the team with all his old confidence and calm, unruffled Maurice Norman was patient and persistent.

It was the forwards who patiently tried to take revenge for the body-blocking by the Yugoslavs.

Bobby Smith managed finally to settle down to one of his best and most effective games of the season.

Late in the game, Cliff Jones had to be hauled away from a brawl by the admirable Blanchflower, and Danish referee Sorensen three times rebuked Terry Dyson for over-zealous attention to the opposition.

But it was never a rough or ugly game. The fouls would have passed unremarked in an ordinary English League match.

And this was no ordinary game. It was a wildly exciting, grippingly tensed last stand before a highly rewarding European Cup final.

Mackay got the first goal in 29 minutes from a superb pass from Blanchflower. But six minutes later, to a dramatic hush, Tottenham's defence paused and permitted Skoblar to score.

As the players jittered and the fans muttered there appeared once again the dignified, clear-thinking Blanchflower.

He passed the ball to John White, who smoothed it into the penalty area, and Mackay intelligently chested it down for Dyson to stab it in.

This goal came two minutes before half-time, but Spurs had to survive four minutes of terrifying onslaught after the interval before Smith headed number three.

SPURS IN THE FINAL. Bobby Smith (lying on the ground) has just scored the third goal with a diving header which means Spurs are the first English side to reach a European final

MACKAY STARTS THE SCORING. Inside left Dave Mackay beats Vidinic in the twenty-third minute to put Spurs one ahead in the second leg of the European Cup Winners Cup semi-final at White Hart Lane

DAILY TELEGRAPH, Thursday, May 16, 1963

TOTTENHAM HOTSPUR . . . 5 ATLETICO MADRID . . . 1

ROTTERDAM, WEDNESDAY

DYSON'S DEVOTION PUTS SPURS BACK ON TOP

Spanish defence torn to shreds in first British triumph

From DONALD SAUNDERS

Britain's football prestige, down in the depths for a decade, soared skywards here tonight as Danny Blanchflower and his men trotted round the Feyenoord Stadium, holding aloft the European Cup Winners' Trophy.

Spurs had wrested this glittering Cup from Atletico Madrid, the holders, with a superb display of skilful, fighting football that should make all those Europeans who saw it regard the British henceforth.

Yet Spurs became the first British club to win a major European tournament without the assistance of Mackay, for so long the backbone of their defence, and the inspiration of their attack. The Scottish left half failed a fitness test this morning, and was replaced by Marchi.

When first we heard this news, few of us expected to see Spurs cheered to victory a few hours later. But perhaps it was this apparent blow to their chances that really goaded Tottenham back into full stride. At all events, they rose to the occasion like true champions.

Last autumn 25 teams from 24 countries entered this competition. Tonight Spurs proved themselves indisputably the best of the lot.

During the nervous opening stages they kept their heads and by half-time had moved methodically, calmly, into a two-goal lead. Then, having conceded a penalty two minutes after the interval, they were obliged to call on all their fighting spirit before they could sweep arrogantly to victory over utterly demoralised opponents.

This was, above all, a great triumph of team work. Yet, whenever I look back on the match, one name will immediately spring to mind. For this was Terry Dyson's game.

The little Yorkshireman has never served Tottenham better than he did tonight. He not only scored two goals and provided the passes for two more, but by his example of tireless devotion to duty he inspired the other forwards, who had been out of touch for several weeks, to click back into top gear.

Indeed, there were times tonight when this Spurs attack reached the heights they had scaled en route to the double two years ago.

Consequently, Madrid's defence, considered one of the strongest in Europe, was torn to shreds, with Dyson and Jones, who tortured poor Rodriguez for the greater part of 90 minutes, the chief executioners.

The Spurs defence also played their part nobly. Marchi fitted so neatly into the scheme

10 Daily Telegraph and Morning Post, Thursday, May 16, 1963

European Cup-Winners' Cup

DYSON'S DEVOTION PUTS SPURS BACK ON TOP

Spanish defence torn to shreds in first British triumph

From DONALD SAUNDERS

ROTTERDAM, Wednesday.

Tottenham H. .... 5 Atletico Madrid 1

BRITAIN'S football prestige, down in the depths for a decade, soared skywards here to-night as Danny Blanchflower and his men trotted round the Feyenoord Stadium, holding aloft the European Cup-winners' Trophy.

Spurs had wrested this glittering cup from Atletico Madrid, the holders, with a superb display of skilful, fighting football that should make all those Europeans who saw it regard the British game with rather more respect henceforth.

CUP IN REACH

Sudden change

GREAT TRIUMPH

Greaves dashes in following his shot and the goalkeeper dives too late. Spurs are in the lead and on the way to another triumph.

Scottish Cup

RANGERS LAND THE DOUBLE

Celtic beaten in replay

From DENIS LOWE

GLASGOW, Wednesday.

Rangers ... 3 Celtic ... 0

HAMPDEN PARK was again the scene of a glorious Rangers triumph to-night when they beat Celtic, deadly rivals over the years, in the Scottish Cup Final replay before a huge crowd of more than 120,000.

Salisbury Racing

PICCADILLY AND KOH-I-NOOR LOOK ASCOT HOPES

From MARLBOROUGH

SALISBURY, Wednesday.

WE saw a couple of high class two-year-olds here to-day—either of whom may well be up to Royal Ascot standard. Mr. C. W. Engelhard's Piccadilly beat the Newbury winner Runnymede very easily in the Salisbury Stakes and although Lord Carnarvon's Koh-i-Noor probably had less to beat, he could do no more than win the Westminster Stakes by eight lengths.

Soccer

'STREAMLINED LEAGUE' PLAN

Jimmy Greaves puts Spurs one up against Atletico Madrid in Rotterdam

Atletico Madrid goalkeeper Madinabeytia is beaten by John White for Spurs' second goal

Spurs team on a lap of honour with the Cup

Terry Dyson scores Spurs' third goal from an acute angle

US? WE'RE ANGELS. Following press criticism that Spurs had changed into a team of hard men against Gornik in Poland, the Spurs angels were born. Bobby Smith is seen here giving one of them a lift – or is he flying?

of things that we soon forgot Mackay was not there. Adelardo and Collar, both members of the same World Cup team, were rarely allowed a look in, and the dangerous Chuzo was blotted out by Norman.

On an important occasion like this an early goal is of tremendous value and the one Spurs snatched after 16 minutes certainly helped them take control of their opponents and of themselves.

The move began with a pass by Marchi to Smith, who sent Jones racing past Rodriguez along the right touchline. Then, over came a well-judged centre which Greaves calmly drove home.

Seventeen minutes later Spurs moved further ahead. This time the Spanish goalkeeper failed to cut off a high centre from Greaves and, as the ball bounced away to the left, Dyson smartly pounced on it and chipped it into the middle again. Smith pushed it back to White, who promptly sent it into the roof of the net.

LOOKING BACK WITH TERRY DYSON

Terry Dyson's entry in the record books, for the Tottenham victory in the European Cup Winners' Cup final, states merely that he scored two of the five goals.

But on that exciting night in May 1963 it may have been a piece of defensive work from the winger Dyson that turned the final against Atletico Madrid Tottenham's way.

For after Greaves and White had put Tottenham into the lead in the famous Feyenoord Stadium, Madrid, playing in those days very much in the shadows of the remarkable Real, pulled a goal back.

Dyson recalls: "We suddenly went two goals up but then the penalty by Collar changed the whole face of the match. From being in a clear lead we were battling to survive.

"For 10 minutes Atletico threw everything they had at us and we were fortunate to hang on. Then in another attack the ball broke free to their full back Rivilla."

It was at that moment that Dyson made his most important intervention of the evening. He said: "Dave Mackay was not playing in the game because of an injury but when the full back broke through I wondered what Mackay would do.

"I remembered that he got so many of his injuries by lunging on just throwing himself at people. So I decided to try the same. I launched myself in just as the player shot.

"The ball hit me on the knees and it really did hurt but it was worth it. In that moment I think that the match changed. If the ball had gone in and made it 2-2 who knows what might have happened?"

Within minutes of that Mackay-type tackle, Dyson was the Spurs hero at the other end. "I remember John White putting the ball inside the full back and I kept thinking how close he was to me.

"I rushed the cross a little bit and was disappointed. I thought that it was much too close for the goalkeeper."

In ideal conditions the cross was too close to Madinabeytia but in the pressure of a European final the Spanish goalkeeper flapped at the ball turning it into the net.

Dyson said: "My great memory was of the goalkeeper crying when the ball went into the net. From that second there was no doubt that we were going to win the game."

The goal floored Atletico and Dyson crossed soon afterwards for Greaves to score his second and Tottenham's fourth.

SPURS LIFT THE CUP. Danny Blanchflower holds the European Cup Winners' Cup aloft after Spurs have beaten Atletico Madrid 5-1

IN SAFE HANDS. Bill Nicholson proudly places the Cup Winners' Cup amongst the club's other trophies in the boardroom at White Hart Lane, the first British manager to get his hands on a European trophy.

So Spurs walked off for their half-time cup of tea with the Cup apparently comfortably within reach. Two minutes after the restart the whole picture changed.

Madrid, switching to a more open game, moved up-field and a centre by Collar left Spurs in such a tangle that the unmarked Adelardo was able to bang the ball goalwards. Henry desperately fisted the ball away and Collar quietly converted the penalty.

For 15 minutes Spurs lost their grip and we began to see what a good team the Spaniards might have been, had they been given the opportunity earlier to settle down.

But eventually Spurs broke away and Dyson scored a goal that clinched victory. The little winger picked up the ball out on the left and curled it towards the goalmouth. At the last moment, the wind seemed to catch the ball and it floated over the goalkeeper's head and under the bar.

That was all Spurs needed to regain complete control. They swept their wilting opponents contemptuously aside with an arrogant display of slick, Continental-style Soccer.

Greaves quickly grabbed another goal from a centre by Dyson, then Dyson himself ran 25 yards through the middle, looked up, and hammered the ball into the net.

As the final whistle went Mackay raced from the trainers' bench to embrace Smith. Then, after receiving the trophy, for which they had fought so hard since last autumn, Spurs jogged round the pitch to the deafening cheers of 4,000 faithful supporters.

But perhaps their greatest reward was still to come. As they changed they heard that Leo Horn, one of the world's most experienced referees, considered them the best British team he had ever watched.

"You could send this side anywhere in the world and be proud of them," he said. It is a long, long time since an experienced observer paid this sort of tribute to a British team.

Then Dyson wrapped up the match with a spectacular goal.

Manager Bill Nicholson who was proud to be the first British manager to lead a club side to European success said: "The great recollection of that night was young Terry's shot."

Dyson said: "I played a one-two with Marchi and no-one came to me. I kept going towards goal and when I looked up I could not even see the keeper so I just shot and in it went."

For Tottenham it was the fitting memorial to the double side. They felt that the 3-1 Cup final success against Burnley the season before had not done them justice.

There was a need to leave a greater mark in the history books and this was it. No-one could take from them the fact that they had become the first British side to win a European competition.

Dyson said: "I have never experienced anything like that. It was a totally different occasion. We had won the double and then won the Cup final the following season.

"But it was strange it seemed as though the Cup final success was an anti-climax. We knew that we were a good side but we had not produced it in the final. This however was different. It was probably our best team performance."

In the village hotel outside Rotterdam the team celebrated in style as well. "We went into the nightclub there and let our hair down with the supporters.

"We knew most of them anyway. They were the same people who travelled the country with us during the season and they were the same ones who had gone into Europe with us. That was the way that it should have been."

Dyson was delighted to see that even Bill Nicholson joined the celebrations that night. "It was about the only time that Bill came out with the team. I don't think that I ever saw him looking so pleased."

It is not surprising that Bill looked so proud. Dyson recalled his last words before the team went out that night. He said: "Bill took myself and Cliff Jones to one side and said: "This will be your night. Take on the full backs as often as you can."

He was not wrong.

As holders of the European Cup Winners' Cup, Spurs were automatically given entry to the same competition for the 1963/64 season.

THE HOMECOMING. Danny Blanchflower with the Cup as the team make their way towards the civic reception

DAILY HERALD, Wednesday, December 4, 1963

SPURS . . . 2 MANCHESTER UNITED . . . 0

DUNNE'S BOOB BOOSTS SPURS

Dyson snaps the goal that rocks United's hopes

By PETER LORENZO

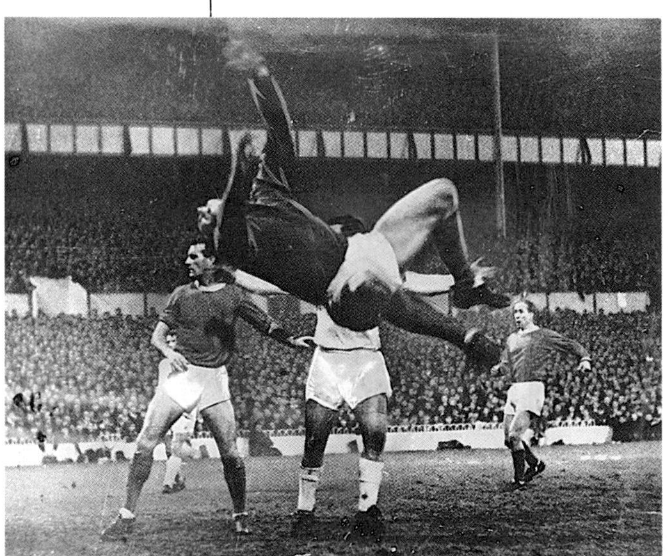

Dave Mackay (out of picture) beats goalkeeper David Gaskett to put Spurs one ahead in the first leg

Three minutes from time an amazing blunder by Manchester United right back Tony Dunne teed up Spurs' second goal in this tremendous European Cup Winners' Cup duel.

It might so easily signal Spurs' survival when they trek to Old Trafford for the second leg of their first round clash next Tuesday.

No danger threatened. No score seemed possible as Dunne gathered a long cross from John White.

Calmly he swept the ball under control, then turned to hit it softly towards goalkeeper Dave Gaskell.

But Dunne hadn't noticed the darting figure of little left winger Terry Dyson speeding up on his blind side.

In a flash Dyson zipped between the two United defenders and cracked the ball in so hard that it rebounded back on to the field before anybody had realised what had happened.

It was a masterly opportunist effort by Dyson. But he would be the first to admit that he should never have been offered the chance.

So Spurs go north with a two-goal lead, instead of the one they just about earned.

And that goal could make all the difference, for the big problem hovering over United is the doubt of Denis Law's availability.

At Leeds today the FA disciplinary committee will adjudicate on the incident when Law was sent off at Villa Park two weeks ago.

Law has gone on record as saying he must accept the blame and suspension will, of course, mean his absence from the return game.

It restores the balance slightly. And I do mean slightly, in Spurs' favour.

Until Dunne faltered, United had thrown up a superb defensive barricade. Skilfully, confidently and aggressively they had contained Spurs' attack.

They allowed Spurs to do most of the pressing. They even allowed them unrestricted mid-field control – until they reached the United penalty area.

The red wall seemed impenetrable. Even when Spurs did pierce their way through, there stood the stubborn, flying figure of Gaskell to foil their best efforts.

Spurs piled on the pressure. The tension mounted. The crowd roared. But still United's tactics and defence stood solid – until the 67th minute.

Then dynamic Dave Mackay, moving like a human rocket, powered his way through to score a brilliant goal. It had to be brilliant to penetrate this superb defence.

Cliff Jones started the move with a cunning back heel to the feet of onrushing Mackay. From a difficult angle Mackay took aim – and smashed in a thunderbolt shot.

The delighted Scot did a double somersault in celebration as the crowd roared their approval of a magnificent effort.

United clearly had one major intent for this match – not to concede goals, rather than try to score any themselves.

Often they had eight or nine men crowding their goal area. Inevitably, they were in attack

14 DAILY HERALD Wednesday December 4 1963

Dyson snaps the goal that rocks United's hopes

DUNNE'S BOOB BOOSTS SPURS

By PETER LORENZO: Spurs 2, Manchester Utd. 0

THREE minutes from time an amazing blunder by Manchester United right-back Tony Dunne teed up Spurs' second goal in this tremendous European Cup-winners' Cup duel.

It might so easily signal Spurs' survival when they trek to Old Trafford for the second leg of their first round clash next Tuesday.

No danger threatened. No score seemed possible as Dunne gathered a long cross from John White.

Calmly he swept the ball under control, then turned to hit it softly towards goalkeeper Dave Gaskell.

But Dunne hadn't noticed the darting figure of little left-winger Terry Dyson speeding up on his blind side.

... flash Dyson zipped between United defenders and ... ball in so hard that it ... on to the field before ... realised what had ...

IAN TODD puts the Cup focus on the team that thinks big

CHELMSFORD

HERE'S WHAT THEY HAD TO SAY

'I wanted to get lost'

TONY DUNNE, on that goal he gave away: — I wanted to find a big hole and get lost. I was to blame . . I should have cleared the ball. The boys had flogged their guts out and deserved something better than this. It may have looked as though I was trying to pass back to Dave Gaskell. I wasn't . . the ball prodded against my leg and just rolled forward.

☆

BILL NICHOLSON, Spurs manager: "I'm not satisfied but goals will take a lot of ... United at O...

● Dave Gaskell sprawls on the ground. Jimmy Greaves' shot thunders into the net . . but the referee has whistled for offside.

Greaves (No. 10) again . . and no luck. 'Keeper Dave Gaskell gets to the ball as the Spurs goal-grabber ...

SHOOT

£5

IS Jimmy Greaves the greatest goal-getter of all time? Is he more explosive near goal than Dixie Dean, Joe Payne or any other giants of the past?

Greaves has smashed 199 League goals in record time. Is it that defences are weaker than they used to be? Or Greaves really great?

● No doubt about Sonny Liston being the ... heavyweight around ... day. How would he have gone against former greats like Joe L... Jack Dempsey, Ro... Marciano, Gene Tu... and Jack Johnson?

● Is Mill House ... greatest steeplechas... racing history? B... than Golden Miller...

SHOOT your ...

only in breakways.

Yet they were always dangerous. When he wasn't back helping his defence, Law operated almost as a one-man forward line.

Three first-time shots from the Scottish international had Spurs' goalkeeper Bill Brown stretching desperately to tip the ball over the bar.

One goal was all that should have separated two fine sides. But now United face the decisive second leg with towering doubts instead of stirring confidence.

DAILY HERALD, Wednesday, December 4, 1963

Here's What They Had To Say

'I wanted to get lost'

BILL NICHOLSON (Spurs manager):

"I'm not satisfied but three goals will take a lot of getting by United at Old Trafford. There was no middle in our team, and little cohesion."

MATT BUSBY (Manchester United manager):

"What a tragedy – but still we must accept it as one of those things. I was delighted with the composure of the side under pressure."

REFEREE HUGH PHILLIPS (regarding Dyson's disallowed goal):

"I whistled before Dyson was in possession. He was offside and there was no question of my consulting the linesman as I was only two yards away."

PAT CRERAND (Manchester United's right half):

"It wasn't slack marking that caused the first goal. Bobby Smith was offside, and we were waiting for the whistle. This was just our lucky night."

MANCHESTER EVENING NEWS, Wednesday, December 11, 1963

This Was An Inside Job!

Touchline tactics spell defeat for so gallant Spurs
Charlton switch turns on heat

By DAVID MEEK

We have waited long and patiently for Bobby Charlton to explode into scoring action. Despite his reputation as a shooting star, five goals from two dozen games was his total this season before the European Cup Winners' Cup clash with Spurs at Old Trafford.

But along with a welcome return among the goals for David Herd, Charlton k.o'd the Cup holders in this competition with a storming display that put the Reds into the quarter-finals.

It was after a touchline tactical switch to his old job of inside forward that Charlton really found his scoring feet.

Manager Matt Busby moved from his place in the stand to the trainers' bench and the order went out for David Sadler to slip out to the wing so that the England man could come into the middle.

Then we saw Charlton, who had been sweeping past players like a gunboat leaving tankers wallowing in its wake, begin to trouble Bill Brown, the Spurs 'keeper.

Charlton and Herd accepted the mantle of the missing Denis Law, and though their shooting was way out in every sense early on they settled down confidently.

Would United have won if Dave Mackay had not broken his leg as early as the eighth minute?

Impossible to answer for sure of course – except that United had already scored the early goal we wanted from them, and I do not see how even a full team could have played better than Spurs' Super Ten.

The Londoners were tremendous with a great game from Terry Dyson, smallest man on the field but surely the one with the biggest heart.

Once again Maurice Setters blotted out Jimmy Greaves, despite nearly a quarter of an hour off the field, and then a brave display for the rest of the game with a gaping gash in his forehead, pulled together by six stitches.

With Bill Foulkes equally masterful against Bobby Smith, the Tottenham threat was blunted.

Pat Crerand made mistakes, but his type of game with adventurous passing that tries to create openings, always will slip up at times. But I thought he was the key to United's constant pressure and forceful forward play.

Spurs played so well and were so unlucky to lose Mackay that a replay would probably have been a fairer result. Much of their football was more poised and mature than some of United's enthusiastic surges.

But United have also had their share of misfortune in the course of the two legs of this tie with Tony Dunne's unluckily conceded goal at White Hart Lane and then being robbed of the services of Denis Law.

So all credit to the Reds, who destroyed the idea that they are a one-man team who would be lost without Law.

Touchline tactics spell defeat for so gallant Spurs

THIS WAS AN INSIDE JOB!

CHARLTON

Charlton switch turns on heat

By DAVID MEEK

WE have waited long and patiently for Bobby Charlton to explode into scoring action. Despite his reputation as a shooting star five goals from two dozen games was his total this season before the European Cup Winners' Cup clash with Spurs at Old Trafford.

But along with a welcome return among the goals for David Herd, Charlton k.o.'d the Cup holders in this competition with a storming display that put the Reds into the quarter finals.

It was after a touchline tactical switch to his old job of inside forward that Charlton really found his scoring feet.

Manager Matt Busby moved from his place in the stand to the trainers' bench and the order went out for David Sadler to slip out to the wing so that the England man could come into the middle.

Then we saw Charlton, who had been sweeping past players like a gunboat leaving tankers wallowing in its wake, begin to trouble Bill Brown, the Spurs' 'keeper.

Charlton and Herd accepted the mantle of the missing Denis Law, and though their shooting was way out in every sense early on they settled down confidently.

SPURS' SUPER TEN

Would United have won if Dave Mackay had not broken his leg as early as the eighth minute?

Impossible to answer for sure of course—except that United had already scored the early goal we wanted from them, and I do not see how even a full team could have played better than Spurs' Super Ten.

The Londoners were tremendous with a great game from Terry Dyson, smallest man on the field but surely the one with the biggest heart.

Once again Maurice Setters blotted out Jimmy Greaves, despite nearly quarter of an hour off the field, and then a brave display for the rest of the game with a gaping gash in his forehead, pulled together by six stitches.

With Bill Foulkes equally masterful again against Bobby Smith, the Tottenham threat blunted.

David Herd (half hidden) clips the ball out of the reach of the outstretched Spurs 'keeper Bill Brown for United's second goal.

Six Notts men aim to prove us wrong

BY KEEP NET

ANGLERS from Lancashire and Nottingham clash this week-end in two matches on the River Trent, and the only referee needed will be a set of accurately balanced scales to weigh the fish caught by either side.

National attention will be focused on the six-a-side challenge between Ken Booth's team of Lancashire matchmen and six of the finest Trentmen Nottingham can muster.

It will be fished on the Nottingham Piscatorials' private length of the Trent near Fiskerton on Sunday.

This challenge from the Midlands is the result of an opinion expressed by Ken that the best reel to use when match-fishing the River Trent is a fixed spool . . . a remark that set the city anglers by the ears.

The honours go to Spurs — Dyson was great

By Noel Cantwell

Manchester United skipper and Eire international, who writes every week in the "Manchester Evening News and Chronicle."

DON FRAME'S Postbag is held over until to-morrow.

FIVE FOR DANTE

MANCHESTER EVENING NEWS, Wednesday, December 11, 1963

The Honours Go To Spurs – Dyson Was Great

By NOEL CANTWELL

MANCHESTER UNITED SKIPPER AND EIRE INTERNATIONAL, WHO WRITES EVERY WEEK IN THE "MANCHESTER EVENING NEWS"

So Manchester United go into the quarter-finals of the European Cup Winners Cup.

There was all the drama – possibly more – of the great European Cup win over Bilbao in 1957.

But the honours go to Spurs.

I said this in my short official speech at the after-the-match banquet in the early hours of this morning, and after sleeping on it this is still my summing up.

No team has ever played better with 10 men.

But at the same time it is no use talking about what might have happened if that wonderful wing half, Dave Mackay, had not broken his leg in a tackle with me in the seventh minute.

For in the short time the teams were at full strength I thought WE played better. But THEY played better when they were down to 10 . . . it is one of those strange twists that a handicapped team can often surpass the form shown at full strength.

I will admit that delighted though I am to have won, truly I would have liked the game to have gone to a replay. Yes, there is sentiment in sport, and it does affect you on these occasions.

Maybe our manager, Matt Busby, felt the same way, for with six minutes to go and the scores level on aggregate, he was shouting "hold it".

Outstanding of the 10 fighting Spurs was the smallest of them all – wee winger Terry Dyson, who stands only 5ft 3in. He dropped back to an extra centre half position where he displayed a heart as big as a lion. He looked like a pocket Dave Mackay – and you cannot hand out bigger praise than that.

What did happen in the accident to Mackay? Everybody is asking that and I will save myself a lot of answering if I do it here.

He smashed the ball as I went to block it. He ran into me and went right over the top of my tackle. He thinks he broke the leg as he fell and everyone knew it was a break the minute he landed.

This is the first time I have been involved in a serious injury and I felt terrible. And I still do.

The first thing I did when we got to the banquet, which was held at the hotel in which Spurs were staying, was to go and see Dave. He said: "It could have happened to either of us." It gave me a little consolation but no-one would wish such a tragic accident on anyone.

He took it philosophically, adding that a tough player like himself must expect something serious in his soccer life.

All I can add is that everyone at Old Trafford will not be completely happy until the day is announced that Dave will return to the game.

If Dyson was Spurs' star, then Bobby Charlton was certainly ours. It was his finest hour and the best game I have seen him play. I think the secret was his added responsibility in the absence of Denis Law. Bobby took over so much of the scheming and shooting role of Law – plus his own, too – that he just had to come inside in the last quarter which finally swung the game our way.

And now my sincere thanks to every Manchester United fan among the crowd of 48,639 – and they all sounded Red Devil supporters. If there were any Spurs fans at the game their voices were drowned out.

In last week's article I said we were not out despite being two goals down after the first leg and the fans played a tremendous part by cheering us on.

How well you did your bit. You were tremendous and I cannot tell you how much this meant to the team.

Players will often say they do not hear the crowd's remarks. Perhaps not, but you know when they are really rooting for you.

When we were attacking and I had a moment of respite, I kept thinking: "These fans mean us to win." And you did. I HAVE NEVER HEARD ANYTHING LIKE IT SINCE I CAME TO OLD TRAFFORD.

Our centre half Bill Foulkes, the only player who appeared in the Bilbao match, said the enthusiasm of the fans topped even that game.

Our tremendous pressure, backed by the Old Trafford roar, eventually wore down the gallant Spurs.

But we can never take the honour away from them . . .

20—EVENING STANDARD, WEDNESDAY, DECEMBER 11, 1963

Spurs greatest hour!

NOW FOR NEW BLOOD —MAY BE A LONDONER

By BERNARD JOY

THE SAD TRAIL HOME

DAVE MACKAY leaves Manchester Central Station for London and home today. In the background is Spurs' trainer, Cecil Poynton.

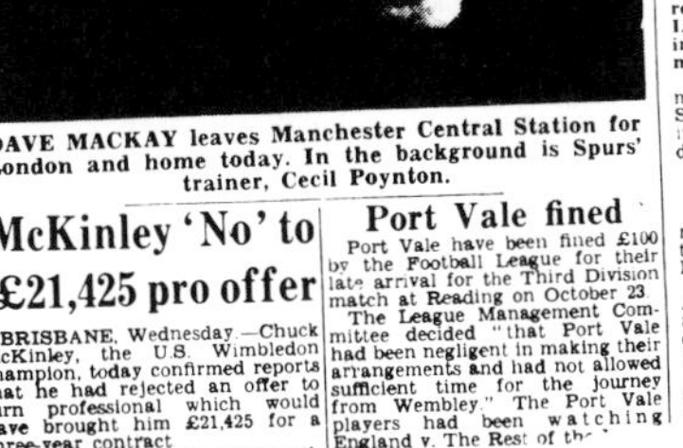

McKinley 'No' to £21,425 pro offer

BRISBANE, Wednesday.—Chuck McKinley, the U.S. Wimbledon champion, today confirmed reports that he had rejected an offer to turn professional which would have brought him £21,425 for a three-year contract.

The offer was made last month by the Professional Tennis Players' Association, [illegible] Frank Sedgman.

Port Vale fined

Port Vale have been fined £100 by the Football League for their late arrival for the Third Division match at Reading on October 23.

The League Management Committee decided "that Port Vale had been negligent in making their arrangements and had not allowed sufficient time for the journey from Wembley." The Port Vale players had been watching England v. The Rest of th[illegible]

TOMORROW'S CARD AT WINDSOR

SPORTRAIT

EVENING STANDARD, Wednesday, December 11, 1963

SPURS GREATEST HOUR!

Now for new blood – maybe a Londoner

By BERNARD JOY

Spurs' finest hour since they took the van in British football three and a half years ago was followed today by the reckoning after their defeat on a 4-3 aggregate in the European Cup Winners' Cup by Manchester United. And seen in the raw light of a December day the cost is heavy.

For an hour after Dave Mackay fractured his left leg until Matt Busby switched Bobby Charlton into the middle where he hit two vital goals as Spurs' stamina began to run out, Tottenham gave the most glorious rearguard action I have seen.

It was not as dour in defence as Arsenal in the 1952 Cup final against Newcastle because Spurs insisted on attacking whenever possible. THEY HAVE NEVER GIVEN A BETTER EXAMPLE OF THE MAJESTIC POISE AND ASSURED SKILL WHICH MAKE THEM THE FINEST BRITISH TEAM OF THE GENERATION.

United centre half Bill Foulkes, who has played in the record number – for an Englishman – of 20 European ties, says: "It was the toughest tie United ever had. We had to go flat out for the whole 90 minutes – and against 10 men for most of the time!"

Mackay, who returned today with his teammates, cannot play before the end of March and will not be his boisterous self for the rest of the season.

Danny Blanchflower has had a recurrence of a knee injury and is considering retirement at the end of the season.

These two wing halves were the motor of the team in their climb to the top in Europe.

Of less moment, perhaps, is the fact that left back Ron Henry will have an X-ray to a badly bruised left instep.

To maintain urgency in the players and interest among the spectators, Spurs must stay in Europe and that means winning either the League or the Cup. That in turn means obtaining reinforcements.

Even before being knocked out by United, I believe Spurs had decided to go into the transfer market as soon as the tie was over.

So I am prepared for manager Billy Nicholson to make a secret dash to sign a player.

If it is north of the border it could be Billy McNeill, of Celtic, who can play in most defensive positions, or St. Mirren winger Jimmy Robertson.

BUT NICHOLSON MAY CONCENTRATE ON A BIG DEAL WITH A LONDON CLUB.

Mackay is, of course, irreplaceable. He refused to have an anaesthetic when the leg was set and held court in his hotel room until the early hours to a stream of callers, including Noel Cantwell, whose tackle caused the break, Terry Dyson who told him, with tears in his eyes, "You have lost your place at left half to me now," and Denis Law.

Mackay told me, "The specialist says it is a clean break and has set well. I broke bones in the right foot three times when with Hearts and so I am used to making a comeback."

Mackay's bedside reading is a James Bond thriller, Thunderball. An apt title for the 007 of Soccer.

That amazing little man, Dyson, rose to the occasion as he always does, while Peter Baker celebrated his 32nd birthday by holding Charlton, when he was outside left, and also being an extra forward.

As Everton are out of the European Cup, United are left to carry the Football League banner in the top European competitions. Their strongest rivals in the last eight are MTK Budapest, who play Chelsea in a friendly tonight, Glasgow Celtic, Slovan, whom Spurs defeated on a 6-2 aggregate last season, and Hamburg.

None are as powerful as Spurs and in future rounds United will have former Chelsea inside right Graham Moore and Law.

They will win the trophy if Charlton recaptures, as he did last night, the crusading form which took United to the 1958 final after the Munich crash.

DAILY EXPRESS, Wednesday, December 11, 1963

MAN. UNITED . . . 4 SPURS . . . 1

EUROPEAN CUP WINNERS CUP' – SECOND ROUND. SECOND LEG. UNITED WIN 4-3 ON AGGREGATE

DAVE MACKAY BREAKS LEG

BY DESMOND HACKETT

Spurs are out of the European Cup Winners' Cup. But, by the glowing glory of football, they were never down in the greatest man-to-man duel I have seen.

Sixty seconds at dynamite-charged Old Trafford last night were enough to switch this Cup tie of Cup ties.

It came after six minutes. It brought a goal to Manchester United and a crash that sent Dave Mackay, the iron man of Spurs, off to hospital with a broken left leg.

Spurs, who had come here with a challenging two-goal lead from the first leg, found themselves on the panic line of a one-goal margin.

Mackay and his merry men had been pounding away with all the threat of a conquering confident team. Sadly, two of United's boy reserves changed the course of it all.

Twenty-year old Phil Chisnall aimed a through pass so close to goal that goalkeeper Bill Brown was compelled to come out.

But Brown was beaten by 17-year old David Sadler, the Kentish lad who had been pitched in to replace banned £116,000 Denis Law.

Sadler crossed the ball with the calm of a veteran and David Herd, unchallenged, scored a goal to send 48,000 fans erupting.

In the next minute Mackay was going through to hurl his dangerous power into a Spurs raid when he clashed with United captain Noel Cantwell.

There was a hush as a sickening crack sounded above the cheers.

Mackay, defiant to the last, was sitting up leaning on one elbow as he was carried off the field for the first time in his fighting football life.

Mackay departed but oh, how he left his fighting spirit stamped on the remaining Magnificent Ten!

This tense duel became almost hysterical when early in the second half we had two goals in two minutes.

In the 53rd minute the ball was bounding

20

DAILY EXPRESS WEDNESDAY DECEMBER 11 1963

Tottenham tragedy

MOMENT OF DRAMA. SPURS' SUPER SCOT IS CARRIED OFF AND 48,000 OLD TRAFFORD FANS ARE HUSHED

DAVE MACKAY BREAKS LEG

By DESMOND HACKETT

Man. United 4 Spurs 1

European Cup Winners' Cup — Second Round. Second Leg. United win 4—3 on aggregate.

SPURS are out of the European Cup Winners' Cup. But, by the glowing glory of football, they were never down in the greatest man-to-man duel I have seen.

Sixty seconds at dynamite-charged Old Trafford last night were enough to switch this Cup tie of Cup ties.

It came after six minutes. It brought a goal to Manchester United and a crash that sent Dave Mackay, the iron man of Spurs, off to hospital with a broken left leg.

Two-goal lead

Spurs, who had come here with a challenging two-goal lead from the first leg, found themselves on the panic line of a one-goal margin.

Mackay and his merry men had been pounding away with all the threat of a conquering confident team. Sadly, two of United's boy reserves changed the course of it all.

Twenty-year-old Phil Chisnall aimed a through pass so close to goal that goalkeeper Bill Brown was compelled to come out.

But Brown was beaten by 17-year-old David Sadler, the Kentish lad who had been pitched in to replace banned £116,000 Denis Law.

Sadler crossed the ball with the calm of a veteran and David Herd, unchallenged, scored a goal to send 48,000 fans erupting.

In the next minute Mackay was going through to hurl his dangerous power into a Spurs raid when he clashed with United captain Noel Cantwell.

There was a hush as a sickening crack sounded above the cheers.

Defiant

Mackay, defiant to the last, was sitting up leaning on one elbow as he was carried off the field for the first time in his fighting football life.

Mackay departed but oh, how he left his fighting spirit stamped on the remaining Magnificent Ten!

This tense duel became almost hysterical when early in the second half we had two goals in two minutes.

In the 53rd minute the ball was bounding almost out of control among a surge of players outside the Spurs goal and Herd scored.

Within seconds there was an admiration-compelling burst by Spurs with John White centring for Greaves to head home superbly.

Manchester United were reduced to 10 men just on the hour mark when Maurice Setters collided in mid-air with White.

Setters went off with a sponge over his forehead, but came back after 11 minutes. Later Setters had six stitches put in a cut over his right eye.

Again the tumult bayed to a frightening roar as Charlton, a crimson ghost, beat the entire Spurs' defence.

Hammered

Charlton drew goalkeeper Brown out to meet him, but then earned only a mighty groan as he shot high over an empty goal.

Then at 78mins. Charlton the villain became Charlton the hero when he hammered the ball in off the far post to tie the overall score for the second time in this heart-bursting match.

Two "unbearable" minutes from time came the greatest goal of this game.

Herd, going at full speed, back-heeled to Crerand, who put the ball forward and Charlton racing forward incredibly turned the ball into goal to send the crowd into a crazy victory roar.

This was a night when men played with all their power, without the tarnish of a vicious tackle or petty abuse of the rules.

quotes

'We are back at the top' —Busby

MATT BUSBY (Manchester United manager): "This is a wonderful tonic for Manchester United. This has put us right back at the top of football. Bobby came along at the right time and did the job for us wonderfully well.

"We are terribly sorry about Dave Mackay. It was a tragedy for Spurs and they played splendid football even without him. In fact it was a great tragedy that both clubs couldn't have met at full strength in what has been a great European Cup Winners tie."

DAVE MACKAY (Spurs wing half): "It was just one of those things. Two of us went for the ball. I got there first and the thing just happened. I knew my leg was broken, I heard it break."

EDDIE BAILY (Spurs assistant manager): "We just can't say how long this injury will keep Dave out of the game. It could be months, it depends on how quickly the leg heals.

"He is a strong man and he has been very brave about it."

. . . but they're 9–1 for F.A. Cup

Spurs, who meet Chelsea in the third round of the F.A. Cup, are clear favourites at 9–1 following last night's Victoria Club call-over made before the Cup game at Manchester United.

The prices :—

Looking for a tycoon? Then try Highbury

THERE are only 120 millionaires in Britain.

But two of them were sitting together at Highbury last night enjoying their common interest—Soccer.

John Moores, pools millionaire chairman of Everton, was watching his team being beaten 6—0 by Arsenal. Harold Needler, gravel-pit millionaire chairman of Hull City, was studying form because his club play Everton in the F.A. Cup third round on January 4.

Needler has given Hull shares worth £400,000 in his desire to make his Third Division club equal to those he was watching last night.

Moores has backed his club in terms almost as extravagant to make sure Everton never slip from the top to where, for example, Hull are now.

HERE'S an item for the it's-never-happened-before records: Toilet rolls were hurled among the Varsity match crowd at Twickenham yesterday.

Officials were so incensed they broadcast a warning at half-time: "Will the crowd kindly refrain from this stupid habit of throwing paper!"

I have a horrible feeling they will not!

BILLY GRAY, Millwall's new manager, makes his first signing today. His new boy is Chris Clarke, 16-year-old ex-Chelsea amateur left winger.

BRIAN HUGGETT, Romford's little Ryder Cup golfer, smashed the West Essex course record by five strokes with a 61 at Chingford yesterday.

He scooped £3-a-head off seven opponents. Next objective: To scoop the big prizes on the Far East circuit this winter.

LEYTON ORIENT travel to Grimsby in Rolls-Royces for their Boxing Day match.

Orient directors are putting on the style for their East End team and loaning their cars so that the players can spend Christmas Day at home.

ENGLAND are the world's biggest underdogs for an international match tonight. They face Scotland at Murrayfield at curling—and a local bookmaker rates England 100—1 shots.

—PATRICK ROBINSON

DOG WINNERS / SUMMARY

CUP WINNERS' CUP Second Rd., Second Leg

MAN UTD (1) 4 TOTTNHM (0) 1

F.A. CUP Second Rd. Replay

DIVISION 1

Dave Mackay, on crutches and with his left leg in plaster, leaves hospital with John Smith (left) and Eddie Baily

Highbury goal-men bring some joy to London

BAKER LAUNCHES ARSENAL BLITZ

Joe Baker heads the first of Arsenal's six

By CLIVE TOYE: Arsenal 6 Everton 0

ARSENAL swamped champions Everton last night with football that makes them serious challengers for the next League title.

Two goals apiece from Joe Baker and George Eastham, and one each from Geoff Strong and George Armstrong made it a great night for the forwards, who flitted past so many clumsy Everton tackles.

There were only three shots at Jim Furnell from the talent-packed Everton attack, which testifies to the firm strength of Arsenal's remoulded defence.

It was solid and safe and if Ian Ure was not the star defender then he was only shaded by new boy John Snedden.

Everton can hardly offer their weakened team as a defence. Their reserves cost them a small fortune. But they performed as if they had never heard of the First Division, let alone played in it.

If Arsenal had not eased up in the second half, they would have passed the 10-goal mark.

The rush for goal started in five minutes when Baker finished off an Eastham-McLeod-Strong move.

Strong jabbed in the second in the 12th minute, and Baker made it three six minutes later.

PENALTIES

Eastham scored the first of his two penalties in the 29th minute at the start of Everton left-back Mick Meagan's private nightmare. Meagan had handled a header from Armstrong.

Three minutes after half-time Meagan punched over a shot from Baker, and Eastham again scored from the spot.

With a minute to go Armstrong cheated down a pass from Strong and scored.

England go down again

TBILISI (Georgia), Tuesday.—England's amateur boxers crashed 9—0 to the Soviet Union here tonight—their second defeat by the Russians in four days.

W. Brom ten are told 'You can't go'

By ALAN WILLIAMS

WEST BROMWICH ALBION directors came out firmly in support of manager Jimmy Hagan last night.

They turned down all 10 transfer requests by the club's senior players, who claim they cannot get on with the manager.

Club secretary Alan Everiss announced after a 60-minute meeting had considered the £270,000 bombshell:—

"The board have fully discussed the transfer requests of the various players and these will not be acceded to. The players will be notified accordingly."

Club captain Don Howe, who is acting as the players' spokesman, said they would wait and see how they were notified of the decision.

"We shall almost certainly call a meeting of players as soon as we can get together," he said.

Manager Hagan took part in a practice match with reserves and third team players yesterday morning. He still refused to comment.

Gibson's genius crushes Oxford

By PAT MARSHALL

Cambridge 19 Oxford 11

CALL this Mike Gibson's match! And what a match for the Cambridge outside half to call his own.

This 82nd Varsity clash produced a tremendous second half and threw up heroes as fast as an erupting volcano throws up lava.

Sapping

Swinging

Baldwin defies junior Spurs

Charlton 0 Spurs 1

F.A. Youth Cup, Second Rd.

TONY BALDWIN, 19-year-old Charlton apprentice professional goalkeeper, defied an experienced Spurs side with a gallant display at The Valley last night.

But the goal after five minutes by Keith Weller was sufficient to give Spurs victory.

Knowles topples West Ham

THE GAMBOLS . . . . by Barry Appleby

almost out of control among a surge of players outside the Spurs goal and Herd scored.

Within seconds there was an admiration-compelling burst by Spurs with John White centring for Greaves to head home superbly.

Manchester United were reduced to 10 men just on the hour mark when Maurice Setters collided in mid-air with White.

Setters went off with a sponge over his forehead, but came back after 11 minutes. Later Setters had six stitches put in a cut over his right eye.

Again the tumult bayed to a frightening roar as Charlton, a crimson ghost, beat the entire Spurs defence.

Charlton drew goalkeeper Brown out to meet him, but then earned only a mighty groan as he shot high over an empty goal.

Then at 78 mins. Charlton the villain became Charlton the hero when he hammered the ball in off the far post to tie the overall score for the second time in this heart-bursting match.

Two "unbearable" minutes from time came the greatest goal of this game.

Herd, going at full speed, back-heeled to Crerand, who put the ball forward and Charlton racing forward incredibly turned the ball into goal to send the crowd into a crazy victory roar.

This was a night when men played with all their power, without the tarnish of a vicious tackle or petty abuse of the rules.

"We are back at the top" – Busby

MATT BUSBY (Manchester United manager):

> "This is a wonderful tonic for Manchester United. This has put us right back at the top of football. Bobby came along at the right time and did the job for us wonderfully well.
>
> "We are terribly sorry about Dave Mackay. It was a tragedy for Spurs and they played splendid football even without him. In fact it was a great tragedy that both clubs couldn't have met at full strength in what has been a great European Cup Winners' tie."

DAVE MACKAY (Spurs wing half):

> "It was just one of those things. Two of us went for the ball. I got there first and the thing just happened. I knew my leg was broken. I heard it break."

David Herd scores for Manchester United

DOWN BUT NOT OUT. Dave Mackay smiles away the pain in his hospital bed the day after he broke his leg. From left: Jimmy Greaves, Dave Mackay, Terry Dyson, Denis Law, Bill Brown

JONES GOES CLOSE. Noel Cantwell (No. 3) about to clear off the line from Cliff Jones at Old Trafford

2

DAILY MIRROR, Wednesday, July 22, 1964

SPURS STAR KILLED BY LIGHTNING

International John White dies on golf course

by MIRROR REPORTERS

Soccer international John White, 26, star of the Spurs and Scotland forward lines, was killed by lightning yesterday in a storm which flailed a wide area of Southern England.

A flash struck him as he sheltered from the rain under an old oak tree at Crews Hill golf club, Enfield. He had been playing alone – and two groundsmen found him lying dead.

White, who was regarded as one of the finest inside forwards of recent years, was sometimes called "The Ghost" because of his will-o'-the-wisp play.

He played for Scotland twenty-two times and it is reckoned that it will cost Spurs an £80,000 transfer fee to get a replacement of his calibre.

Mr C. F. Cox, a Tottenham director, said last night: "White's death is a tragic loss to Tottenham and football in general. He was a vital link in our successful run in recent years."

Soon after White was found dead, his 24-year old wife Sandra arrived at the golf course with their six-month old son Robert. She intended to pick up her husband in the family car – but was met by police officers at the entrance to the club.

They broke the news to her, and fifteen minutes later she was driven away in tears.

Mrs White, who has a two-year old daughter, Amanda, married John in June, 1961.

Club steward Albert Burr, 55, said last night that White decided to have a round of golf while his wife went shopping.

Sudden death came to John White – "a true man of Soccer," writes Ken Jones on Page 22 – on the first fairway. A one-minute cloudburst sent him scurrying for cover under a tree at the side of the course.

As he sat beneath the tree, with his golf bags by his side, lightning struck. It is thought that he died instantly.

The club's professional, Leonard Mitchell, 42, said: "I was playing about 150 yards from where he was found. I could smell burning in the air, and there was a tingling in my fingers."

Daily Mirror

Wednesday, July 22, 1964 No. 18,844

International John White dies on golf course

SPURS STAR KILLED BY LIGHTNING

By MIRROR REPORTERS

SOCCER international John White, 26, star of the Spurs and Scotland forward lines, was killed by lightning yesterday in a storm which flailed a wide area of Southern England.

A flash struck him as he sheltered from the rain under an old oak tree at Crews Hill golf club, Enfield. He had been playing alone—and two groundsmen found him lying dead.

White, who was regarded as one of the finest inside forwards of recent years, was sometimes called "The Ghost" because of his will-o'-the-wisp play.

He played for Scotland twenty-two times and it is reckoned that it will cost Spurs an £80,000 transfer fee to get a replacement of his calibre.

Mr. C. F. Cox, a Tottenham director, said last night: "White's death is a tragic loss to Tottenham and football in general. He was a vital link in our successful run in recent years."

Weeping

Soon after White was found dead, his 24-year-old wife Sandra arrived at the golf course with their six-month-old son Robert. She intended to pick up her husband in the family car—but was met by police officers at the entrance to the club.

They broke the news to her and fifteen minutes later she was driven away in tears.

Mrs White, who has a two-year-old daughter, Amanda, married John in June, 1961.

Club steward Albert Burr, 55, said last night that White decided to have a round of golf while his wife went shopping.

Sudden death came to John White—"a true man of Soccer," writes Ken Jones on Page 22—on the first fairway. A one-minute cloudburst sent him scurrying for cover under a tree at the side of the course.

As he sat beneath the tree, with his golf bags by his side, lightning struck. It is thought that he died instantly.

The club's professional, Leonard Mitchell, 42, said: "I was playing about 150 yards from where he was found. I could smell burning in the air and there was a tingling in my fingers."

John White and his wife Sandra with their daughter Amanda and baby Robert—in one of his father's international caps.

Great storm holds up trains

The savage summer storm held up rush-hour trains in London . . .

Floodwater built up in a tunnel just outside King's Cross station and halted all trains, an Eastern Region spokesman said last night.

The centre two tracks of the station were flooded, and within fifteen minutes all outgoing tracks were swamped.

... at Alexandra Park was abandoned because of the downpour.

The last of the three Royal Garden Parties given by the Queen and the Duke of Edinburgh in the past week ended in a thunderstorm and torrential rain last night.

Dashed

The Queen and the Duke carried on with presentations in the royal tea tent. Then women in light summer frocks and drooping straw hats dashed under umbrellas through the peak-hour traffic to reach ...

Round the South coast ... were battered by high ... and rough seas . . .

A record-breaking ... was made off the coast.

IT'S DANCING CILLA

... rehearsing for "The Night of 100 Stars," the big charity show which ...

Bloom

...hief in ...ood ...ws' ...ddle

By ROBERT HEAD

THE LATE, GREAT JOHN WHITE. The whole of British football was stunned with the news on 21 July 1964 that the Spurs inside forward John White had been killed by lightning whilst sheltering from the rain at Crews Hill Golf Club. Spurs were never quite able to recover from this blow.

He was a true man of Soccer

KEN JONES writing about his pal . . JOHN WHITE

IT couldn't be true. It mustn't be. But it was. "Whitey" was dead.

Somehow the stunning news, telephoned to me at my home late yesterday, wouldn't sink in. Lightning doesn't strike down your friends. Not people you know.

It's something that happens to other people in other places. Impersonal and soon-forgotten tragedies.

But John White's death is neither impersonal nor will it soon be forgotten. The tragedy of it will not be isolated in his home or in the suburb of sorrow that will be Tottenham today.

Because John White belonged to more than just one club and one country. He was not just of Spurs and Scotland, but of Soccer.

In an age when artistry is at a premium he remained faithful to the traditional skill and elegance of Scottish football.

When he came to Spurs from Falkirk in 1959 he was virtually an unknown, despite a place in his national side.

Bargain

He was bought for a bargain £20,000 on the back of rave reports by his international teammates Dave Mackay and Bill Brown.

And it was soon apparent why.

His cultured control of the ball, perfection in passing and an uncanny ability to drift clear of the men detailed to mark him soon made him one of the great inside forwards of our time.

Faith

By 1961, the year of Spurs' Cup and League triumphs, he had established himself as a world-clas...

...many things. For the hours we spent talking with his room-mate Cliff Jones. For the jokes we had together on European Cup trips.

For the "cert" he and Denis Law told me to back before the Scotland-England game at Hampden Park last April. A "cert" that was beaten. And it was the only horse that John had backed all year.

For his ever ready smile. For his concern and sympathy when I was sick. For his willingness to listen to advice. For his football and his faith in that football, even when the boot was coming in high and hard.

His death is a bitter blow. To his family, to his club, to his country and to his friends.

There will be an empty peg in the dressing room when Spurs players report back for training today. It will take a great player to fill it.

CAROLE GETS U.S. TRIP: 'FABULOUS!'

CAROLE ROSSER (Devon) is to partner Virginia Wade (Kent) in the American tennis doubles championships in Boston next month.

"It's unbelievable—fabulous," said Carole, who ... yesterday by ... they had

I'm heartbroken, says Tottenham skipper

A few of the many tributes paid to John White last night . . .

TONY MARCHI, Spurs' skipper: "It's tragic. John was a great player and a fabulous character. If John had an off-day, the Spurs team had an off-day. That's how valuable he was to us. I'm heartbroken."

BILL BROWN, Spurs' Scottish international goalkeeper: "... was my bu... years ...

... played with Falkirk and I was with Rangers . . . And we have been room-mates on many Scottish tours. I don't know of a better positional footballer."

BOBBY ROBSON, Fulham and England wing half: "Of all the inside forwards I've played against, he rated as one of the very best. You could never get near him. I often muttered to myself when marking him: 'Why can't you stand still for a moment.'"

... President of

DAILY MIRROR, Wednesday, July 22, 1964

He Was A True Man Of Soccer

It will take a great player to fill the gap at Spurs

By KEN JONES

It couldn't be true. It mustn't be. But it was. "Whitey" was dead.

Somehow the stunning news, telephoned to me at my home late yesterday, wouldn't sink in. Lightning doesn't strike down your friends. Not people you know.

It's something that happens to other people in other places. Impersonal and soon-forgotten tragedies.

But John White's death is neither impersonal nor will it soon be forgotten. The tragedy of it will not be isolated in his home or in the suburb of sorrow that will be Tottenham today.

Because John White belonged to more than just one club and one country. He was not just of Spurs and Scotland, but of Soccer.

In an age when artistry is at a premium he remained faithful to the traditional skill and elegance of Scottish football.

When he came to Spurs from Falkirk in 1959 he was virtually an unknown, despite a place in his national side.

He was bought for a bargain £20,000 on the back of rave reports by his international team-mates Dave Mackay and Bill Brown.

And it was soon apparent why.

His cultured control of the ball, perfection in passing and an uncanny ability to drift clear of the men detailed to mark him soon made him one of the great inside forwards of our time.

By 1961, the year of Spurs' Cup and League triumphs, he had established himself as a world-class performer in a side of world-class stature.

I shall remember him for many things. For the hours we spent talking with his room-mate Cliff Jones. For the jokes we had together on European Cup trips.

For the "cert" he and Denis Law told me to back before the Scotland-England game at Hampden Park last April. A "cert" that was beaten. And it was the only horse that John had backed all year.

For his ever-ready smile. For his concern and sympathy when I was sick. For his willingness to listen to advice. For his football and his faith in that football, even when the boot was coming in high and hard.

His death is a bitter blow. To his family, to his club, to his country and to his friends.

There will be an empty peg in the dressing room when Spurs' players report back for training today. It will take a great player to fill it.

"I'm heartbroken," says Tottenham skipper. A few of the many tributes paid to John White last night . . .

TONY MARCHI, Spurs' skipper: "It's tragic. John was a great player and a fabulous character. If John had an off-day, the Spurs team had an off-day. That's how valuable he was to us. I'm heartbroken."

BILL BROWN, Spurs' Scottish international goalkeeper: "John was my buddy for the last five years at Tottenham. He was one of the greatest inside forwards of his type and time. He had a dry humour, and was great company."

ALEC SCOTT, Everton's Scottish international forward: "I knew John when he played with Falkirk and I was with Rangers . . . And we have been room-mates on many Scottish tours. I don't know of a better positional footballer."

BOBBY ROBSON, Fulham and England wing half: "Of all the inside forwards I've played against, he rated as one of the very best. You could never get near him. I often muttered to myself when marking him: 'Why can't you stand still for a moment.'"

TOM REID, President of the Scottish FA: "He will be missed as much as a man as he was a player. I have known John since he came into the Scotland team in 1959 and he always gave grand and loyal service."

Jimmy Greaves and Alan Gilzean in action against Liverpool. Spurs bought the elegant Scot in December 1964 from Dundee. He proved to be one of Bill Nicholson's finest signings.

1966. Mike England (centre) seen signing for Spurs from Blackburn Rovers in a £95,000 deal – a record fee at the time for a centre half; Spurs had faced stiff competition from Manchester United – Spurs' chairman Fred Wale (right) and manager Bill Nicholson seem pleased with their capture.

"SPURS ARE ON THEIR WAY TO WEMBLEY", 1967. Cup finalists Tottenham Hotspur, pictured at EMI Studios, St John's Wood, where they have since returned on a few occasions, recording their Cup final song, "Glory, Glory Hallelujah" on an LP which included two solos, "Bye bye blackbird" from Terry Venables and "Stolen" from Jimmy Greaves. Dave Mackay, Jimmy Robertson and Alan Gilzean sang "I belong to Glasgow". Alan Mullery, Frank Saul, Cyril Knowles and Eddie Clayton rendered "Maybe it's because I'm a Londoner" and Pat Jennings, Joe Kinnear and Mike England performed "When Irish eyes are smiling". Other songs included "Hello Dolly" and "The bells are ringing". From left: Dave Mackay, Mike England, Jimmy Greaves, Cyril Knowles, Pat Jennings, Terry Venables, Joe Kinnear and Jimmy Robertson.
PS. The producer pointed out that the beer was for lubrication rather than inebriation.

LOOKING BACK WITH DANNY BLANCHFLOWER

The party was over all too soon. The double team lost its way after 1964 and the special side disintegrated.

Captain Danny Blanchflower pin-pointed the reasons. He said: "When I finished in 1964 I was lucky. I had won all the medals there were.

"The majority of the team thought that it was just starting. They had tasted success and wanted more, but it was not to be.

"This was a very special team and a special time. There was only one way the team could go in those days though and that was down."

Blanchflower knew that the Tottenham set up was going to collapse in the season before their exit from the Cup Winners' Cup.

"It was brought home to me when I was 37. It was the season before I retired. I had a knee injury. I went to a doctor who took over from the usual Tottenham specialist.

"The doctor that normally looked after us had gone to Argentina on a three month holiday and was not available. The stand in told me: 'You have done your cartilage.'"

Blanchflower went into hospital and had the operation. He woke up and was met by the doctor. He told him: 'The cartilage operation has been done.

'The problem Mr Blanchflower is that there is nothing wrong with the cartilage. It appears to have been a ligament injury.'

When the regular returned Blanchflower said: 'How do you know the difference between a cartilage and a ligament injury?' He replied: 'Experience'.

"That was the problem with the Spurs team. When it started to crumble the experience on the field was missing. I was the most experienced player and there was no one to replace me.

"It happens to most great sides unless you have that special blend of youth and experience. Liverpool are one of the few teams that have managed to achieve it.

"As soon as their most experienced players are getting older the younger ones in the team have developed. Therefore they just find some young men to bring on.

"It is a kind of stepping stone process. They were a rare breed. The Tottenham double side though was a rare product indeed.

"They were very special days. Most players thought that they would go on for ever. That was never my philosophy because I said that if we had special days every day they would stop being special.

"As soon as the team started to lose, it became a shock for some of the players as well. It hurt them. To me losing or winning did not matter.

"As a youngster in Northern Ireland I would play a match in the morning for a team that would lose 6-0 and then in the afternoon for a side that would win 7-0.

"That is the sort of thing that the experienced players learn very quickly. If you cannot do that then you are in trouble.

"It was a shame but the party came to an end . . . like they all do."

1967: YOU CAN'T KEEP A GOOD MAN DOWN. Dave Mackay lifts the FA Cup as captain of Spurs after having suffered two broken legs. Seen here chaired by Alan Gilzean and Pat Jennings.

SUNDAY EXPRESS, May 21, 1967

TOTTENHAM . . . 2 CHELSEA . . . 1

GLORY, GLORY SPURS

Chelsea fall for the old Wembley one-two

by ALAN HOBY

Playing smooth and sophisticated football at their own pace in the classic manner . . . three, four, and sometimes even five players pushing the ball around to one another and backing each other up as if their minds were mirrors reflecting each other's thoughts, Spurs won their fifth Cup final of the century and their third in seven years.

Their heroes were centre forward Alan Gilzean, who won almost total supremacy in the air from Chelsea centre half Marvin Hinton, right half Alan Mullery, who rose to giant stature both in defence and attack, and right winger Jimmy Robertson, who coolly crashed in that first crucial goal one minute before half-time.

This psychological blow right to Chelsea's solar plexus happened after they had held elegant Spurs through that tight-marking and tactics-ridden opening period.

Yet the danger signals for Chelsea were at red almost from the opening whistle.

Twice Robertson had fired great drives at the West Londoners' goal.

The first, in the 13th minute, was struck with such force that the goal-roar was rising in every Tottenham throat when that prince of goalkeepers, Peter Bonetti, executed a fantastic trapeze dive to his left to fingertip the ball away.

It was a sizzling Robertson volley and this was the decisive difference between the two sides. Spurs played with flair and killer finish.

Chelsea were also-rans whenever they got near the Tottenham box.

A little later the jetting Robertson hooked another splendid shot, taken from a difficult angle, just high and wide of the Chelsea goal.

Then, just as referee Ken Dagnall was looking at his watch, John Boyle, Chelsea's chunky defensive winger, stupidly fouled Terry Venables out on the left just over the half-way line.

From Dave Mackay's free kick the mobile Mullery, playing his finest game, picked up the ball and ran irresistibly on Chelsea's packed goal.

Once again Tommy Docherty's blue-vested men waited to soak up this Spurs attack like a sponge before counter-punching in their own hard-running style.

But Mullery kept on coming and suddenly unleashed a thundering shot which struck poor Ron Harris' shin to rebound, as if directed by Lady Luck herself, straight to the unmarked Robertson standing on the edge of the penalty area.

Robertson, transferred from St Mirren in March 1964 for £23,000, thumped an unbeatable drive on the half volley past the helpless Bonetti.

Robertson proved that he is a 100 per cent competitor when, on the great football occasion of the year, he took his chance with brilliant aplomb.

Until then despite the complete lack of penetration shown by their two strikers – Bobby Tambling, who could do little right, and Tommy Baldwin, who looked even more unhappy – Chelsea had still managed to contain a superior all-round football team with efficiency and composure.

But it was that first all-important goal which, as I forecast, really swung this all-London Cockney final.

Up to then there had been a lack of enthusiasm among the crowd. Perhaps the football was too tactical, too copybook.

But as Spurs' skipper Dave Mackay, that indestructible, 32-year old Scottish warrior who had shrugged off two broken legs to take his third Cup-winners' medal, rushed up to

Chelsea fall for the old Wembley one-two

ONE! It's seconds from half-time as a shot from Jimmy Robertson (right) hits the back of the Chelsea net for Spurs' first goal

TWO! Sixty-seven minutes gone . . . Frank Saul (left) screws the ball around Chelsea skipper Ron Harris. Moments later it had beaten Peter Bonetti to put Spurs two up. And Spurs were set for another Wembley triumph.

GLORY, GLORY SPURS

TOTTENHAM (1) .... 2 CHELSEA (0) 1
Robertson (45 min.), Saul (67 min.) Tambling (86 min.)
(at Wembley—100,000. Receipts: £109,649—record)

ALAN HOBY REPORTS

PLAYING SMOOTH and sophisticated football at their own pace in the classic manner . . . three, four, and sometimes even five players pushing the ball around to one another and backing each other up as if their minds were mirrors reflecting each other's thoughts, Spurs won their fifth Cup Final of the century and their third in seven years.

Their heroes were centre forward Alan Gilzean, who won almost total supremacy in the air from Chelsea centre half Marvin Hinton, right half Alan Mullery, who rose to giant stature both in defence and attack, and right winger Jimmy Robertson, who coolly crashed in that first crucial goal one minute before half-time.

the mobile Mullery, playing his finest game, picked up the ball and ran irresistibly on Chelsea's packed goal.

Once again Tommy Docherty's blue-vested men waited to soak up this Spurs attack like a sponge before counter-punching in their own hard-running style.

But Mullery kept on coming and suddenly unleashed a thundering shot which struck poor Ron Harris's shin to rebound, as if directed by Lady Luck herself, straight to the unmarked Robertson standing on the edge of the penalty area.

Robertson, transferred from St. Mirren in March 1964 for £23,000, thumped an unbeatable drive on the half volley past the helpless Bonetti.

CUP FINAL SPECIAL PAGE

SWUNG

Spurs' skipper Dave Mackay—with the Cup—is chaired in triumph by his team-mates

PICTURES BY LARRY ELLIS

The captains' own stories

DAVE MACKAY

RON HARRIS

I AM STAYING, SAYS THE DOC

STIRRING

QUOTES as told to JAMES CONNOLLY

congratulate the overjoyed Robertson Spurs' supporters were bawling and cheering.

Yes, the sun had gone in for Chelsea.

Indeed, in the second half, Spurs settled down and their football flowed rhythmically and elegantly across the turf like ripples across a pond. Their defence, at times, mastered Chelsea's biteless forwards with almost cocky contempt.

We had seen, it is true, some brilliant things from right half John Hollins.

We had watched without surprise Ron Harris' captain's steely part in shackling and tackling Jimmy Greaves until the little goal-poacher was forced wide on the wings – despite one free kick which grazed the bar.

We had even seen some quite pretty footwork from Chelsea's £100,000 Tony Hateley, who is more renowned for his heading, but the Chelsea build up was far too sluggish and this was the other biting difference between the two teams.

Far from being "Bonnie Prince Charlie" Cooke's obsessive dribbling slowed the tempo.

And always ready to strike, like a coiled snake at the central heart of the battle, was the great Gilzean, spraying the ball around with those flick-tongue headers which time and again had the Chelsea defence worried.

Also in this final of alternating sun and violent cloudbursts, Spurs were able to kill and push the ball around a vital split-second faster than Chelsea.

There were, of course, sudden Chelsea breakways. In the 43rd minute Cooke brilliantly dribbled past Mackay as if the Spurs skipper had prison chains on his legs.

Cooke beat the sprawling Mackay again before firing a terrific cross drive which forced Tottenham's acrobatic Irish goalkeeper Pat Jennings to a magnificent save.

In the second half too, after Greaves had at last escaped his jailer Ron Harris to let loose a left foot swerver which Bonetti punched away, Cooke unpredictably flashed on the scene again.

He brilliantly flighted a ball with the outside of his foot, but Jennings plucked it out of the air as if it were a tennis ball.

Then, with Spurs in elegant ascendency, Chelsea crashed again.

Mackay flung a characteristic throw-in deep into the Chelsea defence. Robertson touched the ball on and there was Frank Saul, who had to sit on the touchlines when Spurs won their last two finals in 1961 and '62.

A goal did not look "on" but dramatically Saul swivelled and hit a surprise shot which slid into the corner of the net.

Chelsea looked dead. Their shoulders sagged. Their spirits dropped and with Venables, hands fluttering endlessly and directing the game like a traffic cop, it seemed virtually over.

But, as so often happens in football, Chelsea were not as finished as they looked.

With five minutes to go Chelsea, so predictable with their high balls to Hateley's head, leaped back with a move which was fittingly inspired by the courageous Hateley.

What heart this six-footer from Aston Villa has! How often has he been accused of playing like a man with chapped feet!

But just to prove how wrong all criticism of Chelsea – and of his own uncertain control – can be, Hateley suddenly exploded into dynamic action.

Dribbling cleverly, Hateley pushed a sweet pass to indomitable Ron Harris. Chelsea's left half swung the ball out to Boyle out on the left.

Boyle crossed another beauty which goalkeeper Jennings, rushing from his goal like a frightened householder when the building is on fire, punched wildly out.

Unfortunately for Jennings – and Spurs – the ball hit Tambling on the head and skidded into goal.

It was a stirring Chelsea rally, but it came too late and soon Spurs' Mike England re-established his authority on the tight Tottenham defence which has now taken them to 24 games without defeat.

Then, as referee Ken Dagnall blew up, Mullery threw himself on the turf and thumped it with delight.

Spurs had won, and the cheers of their passionately involved supporters rang out on all sides.

Every Tottenham heart was singing as manager Bill Nicholson quietly stood on the touchline and shook hands with every one of his players.

No doubt he had a particular warm word for Mackay, the match-winning Robertson, little Kinnear, and the deadly Gilzean.

As the gale blustered Mackay led his team on the traditional lap of honour.

Meanwhile, sporting Chelsea lined up in the centre-field and waved a last sad farewell to the crowd.

There was no disgrace in losing to a team of such grace and talent as Tottenham Hotspur.

SUNDAY EXPRESS, May 21, 1967

THE CAPTAIN'S OWN STORIES

DAVE MACKAY

Every sportsman has his supreme moment. I had mine yesterday when the Duke of Kent presented me with the FA Cup.

Of course, I'd been to Wembley twice before with Spurs and collected a winners' medal, but here was I, the boy who had played his first organised Soccer game in plimsolls, having led a fine Tottenham side to victory over gallant Chelsea, collecting the greatest prize English Soccer has to offer.

They say I'm a tough guy, but my eyes began to cloud over and the multitude of blues and whites worn by the fans just mingled together as I moved up the steps to the royal box to collect the trophy.

Yes, a memorable moment, and one I will never forget.

I felt we gained a worthy victory. It made me proud that it was gained under my leadership.

Whatever success I have had as a captain in recent years is in no small part due to playing under the man who led Tottenham to their great League and Cup double success in 1960/61, Danny Blanchflower.

Danny and I may be as different as chalk and cheese when it comes to temperament, but I'm a far better skipper for having played under his wing.

Even I must admit that I had long lingering doubts about ever feeling the sun and rain on my back on this great day after twice breaking my left leg.

In all humility, I can honestly say that this well-earned success has not really surprised me.

In fact, I said before our third round replay win over fighting Millwall that this relatively young and skilful team was capable of winning something big.

Tottenham can be a far greater team, and should give a good account of themselves in Europe next season. I am firmly convinced the side can develop even further.

I may be the veteran of the team, but that lush Wembley turf never gave me the slightest worry, although a couple of my much younger colleagues evidently felt it pulling at their leg muscles.

I thought the whole side played well – especially the youngsters. We made one mistake, and it led to Chelsea's goal – but I never really had any doubts about victory.

Chelsea manager Tommy Docherty helped make my great day. He said we were a fine, young side. As a 32-year old, I hasten to agree.

RON HARRIS

We lost, but I am proud of the way we went down, and especially of the fighting finish our boys made.

I thought we were unlucky to be a goal down by half-time. That goal came at just the wrong time for us when we seemed to be containing Spurs.

The ball came off my shin to Jimmy Robertson. He took it well. Disappointing? Of course it is. But the big thing is that we got through to Wembley and I think we're young enough to do it again.

The turning point in theory came with Spurs' second goal.

But I think the turning point came just before Spurs scored their first goal. Pat Jennings made a fantastic save from Charlie Cooke. A save that swung the game. We could easily have been one up.

But despite the disappointment I think we produced a good tactical game. It wasn't as tough as some people thought it would be. But you can't take it away from Spurs. They were a good side, and took their chances well.

TIMES, Thursday, September 21, 1967

HADJUK SPLIT . . . 0 TOTTENHAM HOTSPUR . . . 2

SPLIT, YUGOSLAVIA, SEPT. 20

TOTTENHAM OFF TO FINE START

From GEOFFREY GREEN

Having suspected they might be flung to the wolves, Tottenham Hotspur achieved rather more than they expected here today by taking a two goal lead in the first leg of their European Cup Winners' Cup tie.

Spurs won as aeroplanes swooped overhead, dropping leaflets, rockets exploded, sirens screamed and every rooftop and every tree overlooking the ground blossomed with young, agile figures. Here might have been Christmas trees decorated with coloured baubles. But the gifts of the day belonged to the visitors.

To beat Hadjuk, the local heroes, was a solid performance indeed, a talented side backed by a 30,000 crowd unabashedly partisan, with humidity, heat and a hard ground all in their support. These Slavs are always awkward to face in their own backyard and Hadjuk for one are known along this Dalmatian coast as the "masters of the sea".

But now they have had the wind spilled from their sails and since by the rules of this particular competition goals scored away from home are worth twice their face value, the second leg at White Hart Lane a week hence should wear a formal air.

Thus Spurs, unchanged from last Saturday, have redeemed themselves for the moment in the eyes of their followers after two recent unnerving defeats on their travels at home. And let it be said at once they now beat a cunning foe of clever technicians largely by their own practical knowledge. For two-thirds of the hot afternoon – the temperature was up in the seventies – Hadjuk swarmed forward in wave after wave of attack.

But Spurs remained composed and compact to build a fortress inside their penalty area. And having snatched a vital lead inside the opening four minutes they held their seams together. Bit by bit they wore the opposition down and finally became the masters over the last 20 minutes. The steam ran out of the Slavs and Spurs underlined their whole effort with their second killing goal only three minutes from the end. Robertson, from Saul's break and Greaves' unexpected low pass from the left, knocked in the first quick nail; Greaves himself, with one of his old time efforts – a 40-yard run past three tackles, with Mullery's through pass at his toe, and a perfectly placed left foot shot to the top corner – closed the coffin. Tottenham, with inscrutable discernment and taste, did what they came hoping they might.

There are weary limbs this evening to show that they have been in a hard but sporting match. All that spoilt it was the incessant whistle of the Bulgarian referee who had eyes only for the Slavs, an official who must have learnt the rules from a book unknown to the original lawmakers.

Still Tottenham kept their heads calmly, turning away from every frustration in a match played out to an incessant screech of whistles in the crowd and to a non-stop rocket barrage that would have silenced even a Brazilian gathering. More than once, in fact, Greaves and Gilzean – often caught offside – stopped in their tracks thinking the referee was playing his usual serenade only to find too late that it was some joker up on the open terraces.

If the attack won its plaudits for making those two important bricks from a minimum of straw, it was the defence generally who took the major honours. England was a colossus in the air; Beal stuck to the insidious clever Vardic like a leech; and Mullery was always at hand to cover and to pick up the loose ball to start a counter attack. Twice or so Beal and England cleared off their line at a critical period midway through the first half. And to this stern rearguard the wingers – especially Saul – added their support.

Tottenham, in fact, gave every ounce today as they enticed Hadjuk into their defensive net. Up to the edges of the penalty area the Slavs were subtle purveyors, pressed on by the talented Holcer, Hlevnjak, and Vardic.

Vardic, however, for once overdid his own cleverness and dribbled himself into ever-decreasing circles. Before the kick off he swore that in defeat he would remove his dark beard. He now has an appointment with his barber as the price of his own over-elaboration. The longer he held the ball the better Spurs liked it.

Tottenham Hotspur packing their goal at Split to preserve their two goals lead. Playing in dark shirts, they are (from left): Knowles, Beal, Kinnear, England, Mullery and Robertson.

TOTTENHAM OFF TO FINE START

HORSE TRIALS

Selectors watch for

DAILY TELEGRAPH, Thursday, September 28, 1967

TOTTENHAM . . . 4 HADJUK SPLIT . . . 3

SPURS WIN 6-3 ON AGGREGATE

SPURS THROUGH 6-3 DESPITE SHOCKS IN LAST 10 MINUTES

Lights – and Hadjuk – fail

By BYRON BUTLER

Spurs last night completed the meal they began on the Adriatic coast last week. They enjoyed themselves, with all the trimmings, against Hadjuk, even though indigestion caught up with them.

Hadjuk scored three times in the final 10 minutes, two in 60 seconds, the third a penalty with the last kick of the match, but this late flourish was nothing more than an interesting postscript.

Spurs won the first leg of this European Cup Winners' Cup first round tie by 2-0 in Split eight days ago, and were three up at half-time last night. Hadjuk then needed six themselves to survive: a tall order.

But the 38,623 spectators will probably remember the three goals Hadjuk did manage after they have forgotten the four that Spurs scored. The Yugoslavs have lived a little and the crowd, champions of the underdog, were happy for them.

This second leg merely confirmed, however, what the first had proved: Hadjuk were no match for the FA Cup holders. Spurs are out of sorts at the moment but they still looked fitter, seemed braver and were certainly cleverer and better co-ordinated.

Hadjuk's forwards were quite unable to take any of the weight off their defenders. They often appeared to lose the ball before they got it and England, Mullery and company held the game in a massive grip.

Not that the Spurs crowd was always confident their team would win. They had doubts for fully the first three minutes of the game when Hadjuk, with Vardic, a bearded little sprite, flickering about meaningfully, promised all manner of good things.

But the threat proved a thing of no substance and, until the last 10 minutes Vukcevic, Hadjuk's black-clad goalkeeper, a tall, elastic man, must have felt Spurs' forwards bore him some personal grudge. He did well despite everything.

Robertson (22nd minute), Gilzean (24th), Venables (40th) and Robertson again (84th) scored Spurs' goals and Greaves went near, so near, on half a dozen occasions. Jones, though, was the man I would like to have seen score.

He took the place of Saul to give Spurs more power in the air, and looked prepared to take any chance to get a goal. Once he flung himself at a centre so hard that he hit the back of the net bounced off and then, somehow, managed to get his foot caught in the netting. A fair try.

Hadjuk had only themselves to blame for the first goal. Ristic tried to dribble his way out of trouble. Gilzean challenged, Robertson got the ball and, from the right corner of the penalty area, scored with a shot to the top left corner. Gilzean got his with a header from a cross by Knowles and a flick by Greaves gave Venables the third.

The Yugoslavs came more into the game in the second half with Spurs, understandably if not wisely, not now firing on all cylinders. Eleven of the lights on each of White Hart Lane's four pylons went out and the crowd, grateful for the unexpected on an apparently unremarkable night, greeted the failure with a kingsize roar.

But then, suddenly, in the 81st minute, Hadjuk scored twice. First Vardic netted, after being allowed room on the right, and then Musovic snatched successfully at the rebound after Hlevnjak had hit the bar. Robertson squeezed in this second, Spurs' fourth, three minutes later, but the game had one more surprise left.

Knowles handled, the referee, J F Campos (Portugal) unhesitatingly awarded a penalty and Hlevnjak scored easily. It was interesting, no more. The match might have been in danger for Spurs, just, but never the tie.

Beal s fair head clears danger for Tottenham at White Hart Lane last night. Fellow detenders, Knowles (LEFT) and Jennings, are ready to clamp down on any action from bearded Jugoslav forward, Vardic.

Cup Winners' Cup

SPURS THROUGH 6-3 DESPITE SHOCKS IN LAST 10 MINUTES

LIGHTS–AND HAJDUK–FAIL

By BRYON BUTLER

Tottenham .... **4** **Hajduk (Split)** **3**

DAILY MAIL, Thursday, November 30, 1967

OLYMPIQUE LYONNAIS . . . 1 SPURS . . . 0

RIOT: MULLERY ORDERED OFF

BRIAN JAMES

Spurs, among the least muscular or mean-tempered of English sides, found themselves involved in a riot here tonight.

It was a scene that once threatened to repeat the disgrace of Montevideo.

Play in this European Cup Winners' Cup match with Olympique Lyonnais was held up for eight appalling minutes in the first half as the teams fought with fist and foot.

Uproar came when Alan Mullery was kicked full in the face by French forward Andre Guy. Fans poured on to the pitch to support their team in an overall attack on Spurs.

Mullery was lying unconscious throughout, a victim if ever I saw one. He got groggily to his feet to be sent off with Guy as Czech referee Krnavek's gesture to good order.

At half-time Spurs' manager Bill Nicholson was struck as he tried to prevent Guy attacking Gilzean.

Only the later sense of the Tottenham players, gradually regaining their self-control and overcoming their sense of outrage, enabled the game to be completed. The French merely used more discretion in their use of violence until the end.

Nicholson said later: "Some of their tackling was a disgrace, they were body-checking from the start. I can only assume Mullery was sent off for retaliating in that scuffle."

Spurs lost the first leg of this first round tie to a Di Nallo goal in the 75th minute, but clearly have the overwhelming skill to reverse the result with ease in two weeks' time.

What must hurt them more deeply, and must take longer to erase, is the loss of their world-wide reputation for trouble-free football.

Who was to blame? Study the sequence of events:

In the first 15 minutes every Spurs defender plus forwards Jones and Venables was penalised for tackles, aimed at the ball but with an opposing player standing in between. None was delivered with more than ordinary firmness.

Such tackling is allowed in England. The world, as represented here by Czech referee Krnavek, does not. And though the French had been permitted to obstruct and body-check the effect of this tackling on Lyon was frightening.

Spurs players were tumbling. Robertson was kicked to the ground with the ball 20 yards away. Then, after keeper Chaveau was hurt punching a centre, both Greaves and Gilzen were punched in the face. Neither answered with more than a steady stare.

But in the 33rd minute came that awful interlude. Mullery tackled Guy and both fell. As they struggled to rise the Frenchman kicked Mullery full in the face with sole of his boot.

Spurs men sprinted to Mullery's rescue and were met by the French team streaming from every part of the pitch, aiming blows and kicks. Schwinn ran 15 yards to lunge with his boot chin-high at Greaves, who had the sense to duck.

The French team were followed by dozens from the 10,000 crowd, who vaulted a thin picket fence to take part.

A long scene of pushing and protesting, of recurrent flashes of violence followed before the pitch was cleared, and Mullery, with blood trickling down his face, and Guy trudged to the touchline.

If you blame Spurs on this evidence you are blaming them only for the way they have been taught, the way they are permitted at home. The charge must be made at the national game rather than these 11 representatives.

Half-time provided the chance for the teams to reassess their attitude. Spurs played throughout the entire second half determined to keep possession both of the ball and of their tempers.

They managed it despite more appalling provocation. Robertson was bowled over five times in quick succession, bouncing up each time to play on with admirable restraint.

Throughout, Spurs were the quicker, cleverer side and three times desperate French defenders kicked clear after Chaveau was beaten.

The French were merely workmanlike. So, tonight, even the result was utterly unjust.

BRIAN JAMES reporting on a European night of violence

RIOT: Mullery ordered off

Olympique Lyons 1
Spurs 0
Lyons, Wednesday

SPURS, among the least muscular or mean-tempered of English sides, found themselves involved in a riot here tonight.

'This Lyon side played more like Rugby League

Jimmy Robertson | Terry Venables | Alan Mullery | Cliff Jones | Alan Gilzean

THE FIVE SPURS CROCKS INJURED IN THE BATTLE OF LYONS

Disgraceful, rages Nicholson

flew back to London today suffering

of Lyons

of the

EVENING NEWS, Thursday, November 30, 1967

Disgraceful, Rages Nicholson

"This Lyon side played more like Rugby League than Football League"

From JOHN OAKLEY

LYON

Spurs flew back to London today suffering heavy casualties after the Battle of Lyon with Jimmy Robertson by far the worst of the wounded.

The Londoners were not only surprisingly beaten 1-0 by Olympique Lyonnais in their European Cup Winners' Cup first round, first leg, but five players were injured.

In addition, Alan Mullery, rather harshly sent off in the first half, is automatically ruled out of the second leg at White Hart Lane on December 13 and also faces a possible suspension when his case comes up before the FA disciplinary committee.

Robertson, pulled, kicked, tripped and hacked in turn by Olympique left back Bernard Lhomme, had to have 10 stitches for a deep cut in his left shin after the match.

He will not be able to play in the home game with Newcastle on Saturday and could be inactive for two or three weeks. Robertson thinks differently. "Mark my words," he said, "I shall play in the return match if I have to stand on one leg."

Terry Venables (swollen knee), Alan Gilzean (bruised side), and Cliff Jones (gashed right leg) should be fit by Saturday with Venables the most doubtful of the trio.

Mullery, kicked in the face by Andre Guy in the incident that led to both players being sent off, chipped a tooth and cut the inside of his mouth, but is looking forward to a "return to the peace and quiet of English Soccer."

Poor Mullery! It seemed cruelly unjust that he should go off but the Czech referee, Josef Krnavek, said, "Mullery was fouled. As he went down he kicked at Guy and then the French player stuck a boot in his face. I had to send them both off to stop a riot."

Krnavek might have been right. As Mullery and Guy tangled and other players went in with boots and fists in a general scuffle, the excitable crowd swarmed on to the pitch.

Said the referee: "I told Olympique officials that they had three minutes to clear the pitch otherwise I would have called the match off."

But the referee was responsible for the match getting completely out of hand. French manager Louis Hon said: "He lost control altogether at times," and Bill Nicholson, whom I have never seen so angry, made veiled hints about the official's eyesight.

"I think the match was a disgrace," stormed Nicholson, "and this Lyon side played more like Rugby League than Football League. They pulled and shoved all through the game, yet the referee let them get away with it.

"Guy should have been sent off on his own. Mullery was, perhaps, not entirely blameless but he was heavily provoked."

Nicholson had good cause to criticise Guy, for the Olympique forward carried on the war at half-time in the tunnel leading to the dressing rooms.

Guy went to attack Gilzean and Nicholson was struck in the eye by the Frenchman's elbow as he intervened.

Nicholson, having simmered down, made light of the matter but he was bitterly disappointed at losing the game. "We had enough chances to have won easily," he said, "and I am upset to think we lost to such a bad team as this.

"Jimmy Greaves had a wonderful chance early on, Cliff Jones had a shot stopped on the line and Alan Gilzean might have scored when he had only the goalkeeper to beat. But that's football. Sometimes things go all wrong."

Nicholson agreed that the main trouble with these European games is the differing ideas of what is fair play.

Olympique did not like Spurs' strong but generally fair tackling and the Londoners could not tolerate the body-checking and shirt-pulling of the Frenchmen.

But as they limped home today the Tottenham party have two consoling points.

First, they should win the return leg at White Hart Lane very easily to qualify for the next stage as the French team have only one really good player, skipper Fleury Di Nallo.

Secondly, Roger Hoy, their only recognised centre half now that Mike England is recovering from a cartilage operation, came through the game without trouble.

Hoy bruised his left foot a month ago and jarred it again in training yesterday. There might have been after-effects but as Hoy said today, "I never felt a thing during the match."

SPURS TO BLAME SAY FRENCH

Spurs were largely to blame for last night's brawl, the French sports daily L'Equipe said today.

Though football at this competitive level was not "a game reserved for young ladies," it was difficult to swallow "the repeated anti-sporting gestures of players like Mackay or Mullery," continued the newspaper.

But the newspaper also quoted Andre Guy, whose fight with Mullery led to both players being sent off, as saying: "I admit a little blame on my side.

"But Mullery deliberately struck me on the thigh. Then I replied with a kick."

DAILY MAIL, Thursday, December 14, 1967

SPURS . . . 4 LYON . . . 3

AGGREGATE 4-4: LYON WIN ON AWAY GOALS

DIABOLICAL!

Nicholson admits: defence errors threw my Spurs out of Europe

By BRIAN JAMES

PAGE 12

Diabolical! Nichols defe

The goal Nicholson described as 'the finish': Jennings is too late as Bonassa charges in the French winner

Reading hit five before relaxing

Reading .... 6 **Aldershot** 2

READING blasted Fourth Division Aldershot out of the FA Cup in a most unneighbourly style, scoring five crisp first-half goals and a sixth late in the game.

Their prize is a plum second-round home draw against the Athenian League amateurs Dagenham.

Eased

Aldershot's defence split at the seams as Reading linkmen Allen and Foster schemed intelligently.

Silvester started the Reading goal riot from a Sainty pass after only three minutes. They then survived a snap Aldershot reply before Harris added a second from a Foster-Bacuzzi move.

Allen completely deceived Aldershot keeper Godfrey with a 30yd. free kick for the third and three minutes later Collins added a fourth with the Aldershot defence in a hopeless tangle.

Allen added the fifth after robbing full-back Waller, but Reading eased up after the interval.

Silvester then netted an easy sixth from another Sainty through pass after 69 minutes.

Plucky Aldershot, who substituted Rafferty for Walden at half-time, kept peeging away and were rewarded for their persistence with two late goals from Priscott and Howarth after careless defensive errors.

Seconds from time Dixon robbed them of a third with a penalty save from Walker.

Lamble substituted for the injured Bacuzzi in the second half.

Reading.—Dixon, Bacuzzi, Dean, Meldrum, Chapman, Foster, Allen, Collins, Sainty, Silvester, Harris. Sub: Lamble.

Aldershot.—Godfrey, Walker, Renwick, Dawes, Madden, McAnearney, Priscott, Walden, Howarth, Kearns, Gowans. Sub: Rafferty.

Keeper taken off

Dennis Loney, Nemean League goalkeeper, had ten stitches in his knee last night after being taken off in a representative Soccer match against the Southern Olympian League at Molesey. His side lost 3—1.

All Blacks' 'finest tour game yet' is reported in Page 11 by

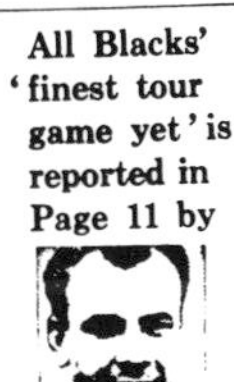

TERRY

Chelmsford fight back for replay

By ALEX BANNISTER: Oxford U......3 Chelmsford......3

After extra time. Score at 90mins.: 3—3.

SOUTHERN LEAGUE Chelmsford, twice trailing by two

The Bigges
in Pools Hi
THIS WEEK
HARTLEPOOL

Spurs went out of the European Cup Winners' Cup last night, beating the Lyon team they had come to loathe, but leaving the last laugh with the "losers".

For away goals in this competition count double in the event of an aggregate tie. And Spurs' defence opened like a wound to give Olympique Lyonnais three in the second half, each a little masterpiece of clumsiness.

Manager Bill Nicholson was in doubt about the needlessness of defeat. His scathing comment:

RETROSPECTIVE VIEW BY ALAN MULLERY

Alan Mullery has still got the 'chip' in one of his front teeth to remind him of the attack by Andre Guy, hard man of Olympique Lyonnais, the French Cup holders.

It was one of the most ferocious matches Mullery ever played in. In his illustrious career with Spurs and England, he went on to suffer the dubious distinction of becoming the first player sent off in an England shirt.

"In fact," recalls Mullery, "I was sent off twice within a year for England.

"The first time was in Florence and that was a personal disgrace, as it was the first sending off for an England player. Then, the next year, 1969, I was sent off in a friendly against Guadalajara, but that was a joke. Colin Harvey got kicked in a place it hurts most. Mayhem broke out and I got involved in dragging a player off Colin and got sent off for my troubles."

But nothing compares with the night of European madness against Olympique Lyonnais and a fighting Frenchman Andre Guy.

"The funny thing was, he was such a good player," recalls Mullery, who went on to a management career with Brighton, Charlton, Crystal Palace and QPR after his playing days with Spurs.

"But he was an absolute animal. I went into the tackle and he turned round and kicked me full in the mouth.

"There's a lot of people in the game who have said that I had a big mouth, so when an Adidas boot came my way it was odds-on my mouth would catch it!

"I retaliated. I punched him. And both of us got sent off. It was what you'd expect playing on foreign soil."

But it didn't end there. Far from it. As the players marched off at half-time a fight broke out in the tunnel.

Mullery takes up the story: "He went off first, dashed around the corner and hid. He then pounced and laid into me.

"Bill Nicholson had to pull us apart. Our manager slung me into our dressing room but four yards away there was virtually a free-for-all with a ten-a-side punch-up as that fellow Guy stood outside

our dressing room door shouting abuse.

"I've never experienced anything like it, and Bill Nick was so furious he said we will tear this team apart in the second leg back at White Hart Lane. It's the only time I can recall Bill saying something like that.

"Unfortunately I was banned from the game and we went out on the away goal rule. Certainly, the intimidation in the first leg in Lyon cost us the tie.

"We were one of the few sides in those days regularly in Europe and we had a big reputation. They were a physical team and they decided to 'tank in'.

"But we had a few people in our team who could look after themselves, even though we were not an over-physical team."

Interestingly Mullery talks about the style of play Spurs adopted at the time in Europe.

"I can't remember going away from home to defend. We always felt we were good enough to win home or away and we always played the same way . . . 4-2-4.

"It meant a tremendous amount of work for the two mid-field players, myself and Terry Venables.

"His three years at Tottenham were not his happiest," Mullery recalls of Venables.

"He didn't really have a good time. He found it difficult to adapt after arriving from Chelsea where he was the king pin in Tommy Docherty's young side.

"I remember talking to Ron Greenwood recently who told me that he had tried to sign Venables for West Ham, but he chose Tottenham instead.

"The crowd got on his back and he eventually went to QPR where he was very successful. But at least at Tottenham he was in the FA Cup winning side of 1967."

"This was diabolical, we just made a series of mistakes from beginning to end. The last goal was the finish. I felt Jennings should have got back for it. Even then there were two blokes standing by the far post doing nothing.

"This match should have been a formality. The biggest disappointment was losing over there when the forwards missed their chances. They took them here, but the defence let them down."

Tottenham chairman Fred Wale added his condemnation: "I am most disappointed, we just threw it away."

Only the mathematicians among the 41,000 crowd realised immediately the enormity of Tottenham errors.

Throughout a see-sawing second half the away goals rule made it certain there could be no extra time. Once Lyon had scored a single goal Spurs had to win this home leg by two clear goals to qualify.

They were 2-0 up at half-time only for the French to cut the margin to 2-1 in the 54th minute. Each time Tottenham restored their winning lead, Lyon cut it back again to a winning aggregate draw.

At the end thousands still stood uncomprehending as the Frenchmen jubilantly congratulated each other. It was left to the knowing to explain how a "victory" had become in fact the blackest of defeats.

Apologists for Tottenham will tell you this defence was destroyed before the start, with England in hospital, Mullery suspended and three deputies – Beal, Clayton and Johnson – all injured.

All this is true. But it is true also that even those who were left could and should have held that lead.

The French, who had cowered around their goal lashing in frenzy at all who drew near through the first half, came out gingerly into attack at the start of the second. They had no choice.

Then they could hardly believe their luck. They found they had only to strike directly at Spurs with swift dribbles to provoke the most appalling errors.

Mackay threw himself about like a Dervish, going into slide tackles heedless of risk. But one man's cunning and courage was not enough.

Too many of the youngsters around him were found wanting in composure and judgement at this moment of trial.

And when Spurs summoned up all they had left in a final challenge for victory, too many forwards had given everything already.

Especially Robertson, the brave winger of the first leg who survived brute tackle after brute tackle in this first half, before finally being overwhelmed.

Especially Bond, the youngster who came in to play mid-field and make it his own domain with intelligence and impudent skill before losing his stamina.

Venables and Jones worked themselves to exhaustion . . . but there was too little remaining strength around them for the effort to be enough.

I suspect that Lyon, good as they were allowed to look in the second half, were the worst team Tottenham have faced during their years in Europe. I know this was the worst game Tottenham have produced.

Spurs' first goal in the 20th minute was a chain reaction. It began when Bond shot brilliantly from 20 yards to force a corner.

This was scrambled out but returned by Venables and Gilzean to the unmarked Greaves, who scored with a tremendous drive.

I thought he was clearly offside and so did several French defenders who had to be beaten away by the referee's flailing arms.

Just before half-time the agile Chauveau was beaten again, this time from the penalty spot by Greaves, after Bond was tripped. Three goals came in six minutes in the second half.

In the 54th minute Bouassa shot from 20 yards on the left to hit a post and Di Nallo was first to the rebound to score.

In the next minute Robertson broke away to centre from the line and, as Gilzean fell, Jones dived with fantastic courage among the flying feet to head Spurs' third. Now they led 3-2.

Five minutes later Rambert, again cutting in down the left, beat Jennings with the shot and Knowles could only help the ball across the line. That put the French 5-3 up on aggregate. It was confusing but undeniably exciting.

In the 70th minute Spurs regained the overall lead. Robertson centred and Gilzean found space and time to chest it down and drive past Chauveau.

With ten minutes left the Frenchmen took the final, ridiculously easy goal. Pin crossed from the right and, with Jennings rooted to his line, Bouassa slumped forward to his knees to charge the ball into the net at the far post.

NEWS OF THE WORLD, Sunday, February 28, 1971

TOTTENHAM . . . 2 ASTON VILLA . . . 0

SPURS BACK ON THE GLORY TRAIL

Chivers – you're a cracker

By FRANK BUTLER

It was Hallelujah for Spurs when they smashed the Third Division jinx of the Football League Cup with two late goals from Martin Chivers at Wembley.

But it was glory! glory! for plucky Aston Villa, never two goals inferior to their lucky conquerors.

Spurs' class was supposed to have told. But not even Cockney pride could argue that, after the first 20 minutes when Alan Gilzean strolled nonchalantly along the wing threatening all sorts of mischief to Villa, the London club kept on top.

A stranger among the 100,000 crowd who paid a record £132,000 might have been excused for asking who were the First Division side. After that first 20 minutes Spurs played like a side with a hangover.

Gilzean faded as a menace. And where was Martin Peters? Spurs had so much advantage at mid-field and in goal-power that they should have settled down and rubbed the noses of their Birmingham challengers into the Wembley turf.

But it never happened. Not even skipper Mullery of England fame stood out. Like Peters, he became obscure in a game that lacked an outstanding star and threatened to go on for ever without a goal, unless somebody made a mistake.

Full credit to Villa, for while Spurs made little impression, the Birmingham boys went into battle and dominated the match for more than half the first half and most of the second.

It took Chivers to pull Spurs out of their rut. This was in the 79th minute, when we looked set for yet another League Cup final with extra time.

Spurs broke away. Gilzean put the ball through to Neighbour. The winger shot and, though Dunn got down to it with one hand, he couldn't stop the ball rolling on into an empty space.

The rest was easy for Chivers, who never lets a defence off the hook with a chance like that.

It was so tough on Villa, who had fought all the way and never deserved to be a goal down at any stage.

A now cock-a-hoop Spurs hammered home another goal three minutes later when Chivers again scored. This was a great goal.

Chivers had reason to feel proud because he fought off the Villa defence and under real pressure turned and hit the ball with his left foot into the back of the net.

Dunn, Tiler, Turnbull and Bradley just looked on completely dejected at this final blow.

Villa would, I think, have caused another Wembley upset if they could have scored. And they were certainly unlucky 14 minutes after half-time.

Collins – who seemed to be pushed – crashed into his own goalkeeper and while he and Jennings were on the ground, Lochhead sent the ball trickling towards the goal.

It would certainly have crossed the line but for Steve Perryman chasing after it and hooking it over the touchline.

Some thought the whistle had gone, but referee Jim Finney only awarded a throw-in after Collins and Jennings had recovered.

So, but for Perryman, it would have meant a Villa goal and then, I believe, they would have won.

There had been so few scoring opportunities from both sides, and it was always on the cards that the team to score first would win the Cup.

And Villa had come close to scoring within a minute of the second half starting. Lochhead pushed the ball between Knowles' feet to Hamilton.

The inside left ran forward and let go with a drive which grazed the top of the bar as it went over. It was not to be Villa's day.

SPURS Back on the glory trail

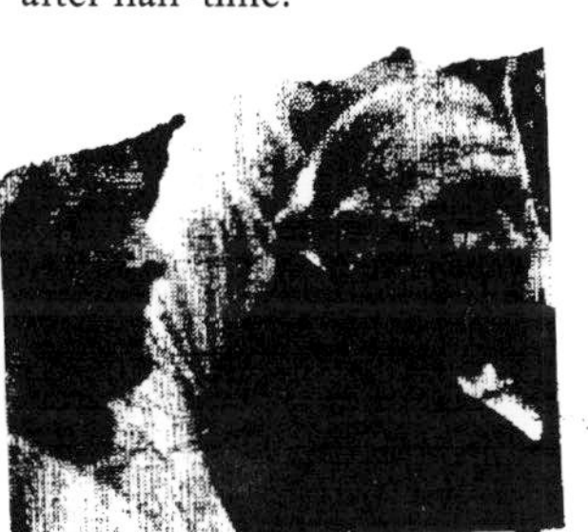

IT'S WEMBLEY and it's all over . . . triumphant Spurs manager Bill Nicholson and skipper Alan Mullery hold up the League Cup

VICTORY starts here . . . Martin Chivers slams Spurs ahead

Chivers—you're a cracker

By FRANK BUTLER

Tottenham (0) 2	A. Villa (0) 0
Chivers (79 min, 82)	
Attendance 100,000	Receipts £132,000

IT WAS Hallelujah for Spurs when they smashed the Third Division jinx of the Football League Cup with two late goals from Martin Chivers at Wembley.

But it was glory! glory! for plucky Aston Villa, never two goals inferior to their lucky conquerors.

Spurs' class was supposed to have told. But not even Cockney pride could argue that, after the first 20 minutes when Alan Gilzean strolled nonchalantly along the wing threatening all sorts of mischief to Villa, the London club kept on top.

Excuse

A stranger among the 100,000 crowd who paid a record £132,000 might have been excused for asking who were the First Division side. After that first 20 minutes Spurs played like a side with a hangover.

Gilzean faded as a menace. And where was Martin Peters? Spurs had so much advantage at mid-field and in goal-power that they should have settled down and rubbed the noses of their Birmingham challengers

came obscure in a game that lacked an outstanding star and threatened to go on forever without a goal, unless somebody made a mistake.

Full credit to Villa, for while Spurs made little impression, the Birmingham boys went into battle and dominated the match for more than half the first half and most of the second.

It took Chivers to pull Spurs out of their rut. This was in the 79th minute, when we looked set for yet another League Cup final with extra time.

Spurs broke away. Gilzean put the ball through to Neighbour. The winger shot and, though Dunn got down to it with one hand, he couldn't stop the ball rolling on into an empty space.

The rest was easy for Chivers, who never lets a defence off the hook with a chance like that.

Tough

Steve Perryman chasing after it and hooking it over the touchline.

Some thought the whistle had gone, but referee Jim Finney only awarded a throw-in after Collins and Jennings had recovered.

So, but for Perryman, it would have meant a Villa goal and then, I believe, they would have won.

There had been so few scoring opportunities from both sides and it was always on the cards that the team to score first would win the Cup.

Danger

And Villa had come close to scoring within a minute of the second half starting. Lochhead pushed the ball between Knowles' feet to Hamilton.

The inside-left ran forward and let go with a drive which grazed the top of the bar as it went

VICTORY is certain . . . Chivers rubs it in with his second
WEMBLEY PICTURES BY BRIAN TH

NOW FOR EUROP

Chivers was the most consistent Spurs forward. Apart from his goals, he always looked the danger man in a forward line that was disappointing.

Collins had a tough struggle against Lochhead and I've seen much better performances from Mullery. And the Spurs defence at times shook badly.

Praise for Villa must be collective. I liked Anderson and Rioch. Lochhead kept working without getting a goal. And the defence held up well until the last 11 minutes.

NOW FOR EUROPE HOW THEY SAW IT

By REG DRURY

Skipper Alan Mullery takes Spurs back into Europe after a three-year absence.

But last night he praised brave Villa.

"They certainly made it very difficult for us," he said. "Until we scored that first goal you could say that Villa's tactical plan had worked perfectly. It was only when we got in front that our class really told."

Mullery was particularly pleased with the win. "It will cheer up my two-year old daughter Samantha who has to go into hospital tomorrow for a minor operation," he said.

"I hope I will be able to take the Cup to show her."

Two-goal hero Martin Chivers talked about his luck in getting the first goal – and his pride in getting the second.

"I could hardly miss the first one after their goalkeeper John Dunn had pushed out Jimmy Neighbour's shot," said Chivers. "But the second – I thought I did well with that one.

"Originally I intended to hit it with my right foot, but it bounced awkwardly so I had to swivel and whack it with my left.

"Villa did well. But we might have got on top earlier if we had gone at them and not been so apprehensive of them getting a breakaway goal."

Chivers had only one Wembley disappointment.

"When I went up to get my award, I was hoping to spot my mother in the crowd," he told me.

"But I just couldn't see her – it was harder than trying to get through the Villa defence."

The game was a hard luck story for Villa – who fully deserved the lion's share of the cheers which they got at the final whistle.

Manager Vic Crowe said afterwards: "I am proud of the boys. If we had scored first, I don't think Spurs would have recovered.

"I was so pleased at half-time that I did not vary our tactics other than to tell Fred Turnbull to mark Chivers a lot tighter. He was so obviously their danger man."

"It could all have been so different if Steve Perryman had not cleared that shot from Andy Lochhead when it was rolling into an empty goal. But that's life."

Spurs' boss Bill Nicholson summed up; "I thought it was a great game – in that last twelve minutes! If I had a drink handy I would get everyone to propose a toast to Martin Chivers."

With domestic victory in the League Cup, Tottenham once more gained entry to the European arena.

WEMBLEY 1971. Martin Chivers (No. 9) is seen turning away after having scored the first of his two goals in the League Cup final in which Spurs beat Aston Villa 2-0. Spurs were back in Europe again for the first time in four years

DAILY MAIL, Wednesday, September 15, 1971

KEFLAVIK . . . 1 SPURS . . . 6

GREAT GILZEAN BREAKS ICE

Hat-trick for spearhead of Spurs' strolling win

By BRIAN SCOVELL

IN REYKJAVIK

Spurs gained their easiest-ever victory in Europe when they crushed feeble opposition in the first round of the UEFA Cup here tonight.

The play of the Keflavik amateurs, who had to pay for their own meal before the game, was embarrassingly naive. They made mistake after mistake and Tottenham could well have scored 20.

Their first goal took only seven minutes. Martin Chivers sent in a thunderous right foot shot which 20-year old goalkeeper Olafsson could only beat out. Alan Gilzean, running across the goal area, calmly turned the ball back into the net.

The 10,000 crowd in this pretty little stadium nestling under the mountains were silent except for the 200 Spurs supporters.

Steve Perryman, Chivers, Gilzean and Peters all fired over the bar after being given free shots and the second goal did not come until the 25th minute.

Gilzean chipped the ball across goal for Alan Mullery to head back and Ralph Coates, standing unmarked at the far post, calmly headed in. It was Coates' first goal for Spurs in ten matches and he did an enthusiastic little shuffle to celebrate.

In the 26th minute Keflavik had their first shot at goal but it went well wide. Four minutes later international centre forward Johannsson hit a shot on the turn from 25 yards which Pat Jennings had to dive to save. The crowd erupted.

Back at the other end Phil Knowles made a fine run on the left but his shot was blocked. Alan Mullery hit in the third goal in the 31st minute from a low Gilzean cross which bounced off a defender.

It was the most one-sided contest they've had in these parts since the British Navy took on the Icelandic fishing protection vessels in the 'Cod War' a year or two back.

Just before half-time Knowles struck the crossbar from a free kick and ten minutes after the interval Chivers again rattled Olafsson's bar. Spurs slowed down on the spring turf and obviously didn't want to be too cruel.

Mullery scored a fourth in the 59th minute when his 30-yard shot went in off the goalkeeper.

Coates was helped off the field in the 62nd minute after injuring his left knee in the penalty area. Jimmy Pearce took his place.

A minute later Gilzean scored the best goal of the contest, if you can call it that, with a glancing header from a 25-yard Chivers throw.

Mullery, his work done, went off in the 74th minute and was replaced by Scot Graeme Souness. The light was so poor at this stage it was difficult to pick up the ball.

That must have been the feeling of Jennings in the 76th minute when he dived to block a shot from Johannsson only to see blonde right winger Juliusson left clear to bang in the rebound to make it 1-5.

Spurs' series of misses continued. Chivers struck the bar for the third time.

Gilzean headed a sixth in the 86th minute to complete his hat-trick.

Great Gilzean breaks ice

JON'S SPORTING TYPES

Keflavik ....1 Spurs 6

SPURS gained their easiest-ever victory in Europe when they crushed feeble opposition in the first round of the UEFA Cup here tonight.

The play of the Keflavik amateurs, who had to pay for their own meal before the game, was embarrassingly naive. They made mistake after mistake and Tottenham could well have scored 20.

Their first goal took only seven minutes. Martin Chivers sent in a thunderous right-foot shot which 20-year-old goalkeeper Olafsson could only beat out. Alan Gilzean, running across the goal area, calmly turned the ball back into the net.

BRIAN SCOVELL in Reykjavik

an enthusiastic little shuffle to celebrate.

In the 26th minute Keflavik had their first shot goal but it went well wide. Four minutes later int national centre forward Johannsson hit a shot on t turn from 25 yds which Pat Jennings had to dive t save. The crowd erupted.

Back at the other end Phil Knowles made a fine run on the left but his shot was blocked.

DAILY EXPRESS, Wednesday, September 29, 1971

TOTTENHAM . . . 9 KEFLAVIK . . . 0

UEFA CUP – FIRST ROUND: SECOND LEG: TOTTENHAM WIN 15-1 ON AGGREGATE

15. SPURS ONE SHORT OF RECORD

By STEVE CURRY

Tottenham turned their White Hart Lane stadium into a mock-up of a Roman amphitheatre last night as they continued the slaughter of the innocent amateurs from Iceland.

Keflavik were saved the ultimate embarrassment of a double-figure second leg only because the Spurs forwards squandered a succession of chances.

There was embarrassment enough in any case, in the aggregate total of 15, just one short of the British record in Europe set by Leeds United.

It was too much to ask a team of play-for-pleasure youngsters from Soccer's backwoods to match the power and prowess of a team worth well over a million pounds.

But if the game has made Spurs' fans more aware of the jewel they have in big Martin Chivers, then it will have served a useful purpose.

The England striker, who still does not get the credit from the fans that his ability justifies, scored three goals . . . all of them well taken on a night when goals were there for the taking. They came in this order:

CHIVERS (8 mins) forced the ball over from six yards when Alan Mullery headed down Alan Gilzean's cross.

CHIVERS (19) put in a dramatic 30-yard pile-driver from Steve Perryman's pass.

PERRYMAN (24) scored in the corner when the ball was deflected out to him on the edge of the area.

RALPH COATES (44) climaxed a run from the half way line with a shot which Keflavik goalkeeper Olafsson misjudged.

CHIVERS (58) headed in at the far post when Mullery chipped over a short corner from Coates.

CYRIL KNOWLES (65) scored with an oblique shot from the edge of the area.

GILZEAN (77) scored from within the six-yard box when Jimmy Pearce headed down a left wing cross.

GILZEAN (78) scored with the kind of headed flick at which he is a master from a Knowles cross.

PHIL HOLDER (86) substitute for Peters, got his reward for an industrious second half display.

ICELAND HAILS ENGLISH SOCCER

Bill Nicholson, Tottenham manager said after last night's win: "Obviously this was a very lopsided game.

"However, I think it is a good thing for football in general to have sides like this playing in European football. It is all part of the game's goodwill.

"And Keflavik played with great sportsmanship."

KEFLAVIK chairman Hafsteinn Gudmundsson: "We are terribly disappointed, because we thought we could have kept the score down.

"But it is a wonderful experience to play against English clubs. They are the best in Europe."

LAST NIGHT: TOTTENHAM GO MARCHING ON . .

15

OF RE

CHIVERS

ICELAND HAILS

TOTTENHAM turned their White Hart Lane stadium into a mock-up of a Roman ampitheatre last night as they continued the slaughter of the innocent ... from Iceland.

By STEVE CURRY

Tottenham 9 Keflavik 0

E.U.F.A. Cup — first round: second leg: Tottenham win 15—1 on aggregate

when goals were there for the taking. They came in this order:—

CHIVERS' HAT-TRICK. Martin Chivers scoring his third goal on a night which saw Spurs reach their record by scoring 15 times in one European tie

DAILY TELEGRAPH, Thursday, October 21, 1971

NANTES . . . 0 TOTTENHAM . . . 0

CHIVERS BOOKED AS SPURS FUMBLE AWAY TO DRAW

By DAVID MILLER

Tottenham's near-million pound team gave one of their worst-ever displays against Nantes in this UEFA Cup match last night, yet they achieved a draw – such is football. The French, clever but brittle, were individually faster and sharper.

Yet they wasted their early chances and tired over the last half-hour when Spurs might have snatched a goal they never deserved.

Against four strikers who controlled the ball superbly and repeatedly interchanged at great speed, Spurs' rearguard were in trouble from the start. Seldom will Tottenham survive such a roasting without punishment.

Facing a front line of four, Spurs had no proper cover at the back, with Beal having to pick up and mark one of the opposition.

In attack, Spurs never got going. The inaccuracy of Mullery, Peters, Chivers and Gilzean was sometimes hard to believe as they fluffed move after move.

Tottenham's only effective ploy was the high ball in search of the head of Chivers or Gilzean. Neighbour dribbled too often and too far, and he missed his club's best chance 10 minutes from time as Peters' header fell at his feet seven yards out.

Nantes set off with a firework display, and after only seven minutes Courtin, put through by Blanchet, shot first time and was as surprised as the rest of us to see the ball stick as if magnetised in Jennings' hands high above his head.

Moments later, Jennings, completely beaten, was thankful to see the ball go wide as Courtin shot across the face of the goal, from a free kick by Marcos.

Bertrand-Demanes, the French goalkeeper, did well to hold the powerful drive by Mullery, and around the half-hour, Peters and Chivers put shots over the bar, both from glancing headers by Gilzean.

This was one of Spurs' few concise spells. It was backs-to-the-wall again at the start of the second half and repeatedly it was Beal to the rescue. Morgan came on for Gilzean with a quarter of an hour to go, and three minutes from time Peters nearly scrambled a goal from a cross by Knowles.

On an evening Spurs will want to forget Chivers found himself booked – his third caution in 12 months.

Chivers booked as Spurs fumble away to draw

By DAVID MILLER

Nantes .... **0 Tottenham Hotspur ... 0**

TOTTENHAM'S near million-pound team gave one

NANTES. French international goalkeeper Bertrand-Demanes clears from Jimmy Neighbour (left) and Martin Peters.

Mike England gets up high to clear a Nantes attack

TIMES, Wednesday, November 3, 1971

TOTTENHAM . . . 1 NANTES . . . 0

TOTTENHAM'S MISSES DENY THEM WIN BY A MILE

By GEOFFREY GREEN

Tottenham Hotspur, who won the European Cup Winners' Cup in 1963 and reached the semi-final of the European Cup the year before that, last night edged themselves fussily into the last 16 of the new UEFA Cup. They did so with a narrow victory – which should, in fact, have been by a mile – against Nantes at White Hart Lane.

Tottenham will have to find something deeper within themselves if they are to keep up the English record of the past four years when the trophy has come to these shores through Leeds, Newcastle, Arsenal and then Leeds again. In the field are sides like AC Milan and Juventus, of Italy, Real Madrid, Ferencvaros of Hungary, even Wolverhampton Wanderers. All these, on their day, might take a deal of beating.

Last night Spurs should have had everything quietly wrapped up by half-time. Before the quarter-hour they had taken the lead through Peters, their captain for the night in the absence of Mullery. Taking a pass from Pratt, he shot home under the bar from the edge of the penalty area to round off one of the few flowing moves of the night, begun deep in the Tottenham half by Beal and carried on by Knowles, Neighbour and Perryman. That suggested a healthy beginning. But that was the only time the penny was to drop.

Yet how Nantes escaped before the interval, when Chivers once missed from Gilzean's square header almost on the French goal-line, was beyond belief; and there were near misses too from Gilzean and a couple of near things from Chivers and Gilzean again as they worked through a packed defence. Once also Chivers, using his weight and height, burst through a crowd of Frenchmen and stung Bertrand-Demanes, under the French crossbar, with a powerful left foot rocket.

Indeed up till then it was one-way traffic and Jennings – a lonely figure at the other end – might well have laid himself a table and helped himself cross-legged, to a bottle of aperitif so little did the action come his way. Yet, curiously, it was only within seconds of the kick off, with Tottenham apparently half asleep, that Blanchet was put through the Tottenham defence for the only really dangerous situation achieved by the French all night. The winger's shot went just wide of Jennings' far post but, apart from that, there was nothing truly to worry Beal at the side of England and company.

There was little real body or drive in the game. It was light-weight and stilted, especially the French game. Certainly there were many clever triangular movements between Blanchet, Rampillon and Marcos, an Argentinian international centre forward, and a bit of pace suggested by Maas.

Spurs, by the interval, should have been three or at least four up. In the second half the game somehow became insulated from reality. Waves of impatience rose from the crowd as both teams began anxiously to stammer and stutter as the standard of the affair rapidly began to depreciate. Both sides were now in a brittle equipoise with Peters trying to use the long ball and get Chivers to burst through the middle.

The Polish referee seemed to lose track of things. Anxiety and frustration arose and the whistle was heard loud and often as though a gendarme was controlling the traffic in the centre of Paris during the rush hour.

With half an hour left Marcos was cautioned and then when Rampillon was writhing on the ground the French trainer was ordered off the field. The situation was all confusion. The French brought on Eo while Rampillon was recovering on the touchline; then Rampillon decided to return to the fray making 12 Frenchmen on the field. Laughter mingled with irritation; things had reached the point of the clowns at a circus.

Near the end Barot was also cautioned and in the last few minutes Morgan was substituted for Gilzean. If only Barot had had a 'd' in his name that at least might have cheered up things.

Tottenham's misses deny them win by a mile

By Geoffrey Green
Football Correspondent

Tottenham 1 FC Nantes 0

Tottenham Hotspur, who won the European Cup Winners Cup in 1963 and reached the semi-final of the European Cup the year before that, last night edged themselves fussily into the last 16 of the new UEFA Cup. They did so with a narrow victory—which should, in fact, have been by a mile—against Nantes at White Hart Lane.

Tottenham will have to find something deeper within themselves if they are to keep up the English record of the past four years when the trophy has come to these shores through Leeds, Newcastle, Arsenal and then Leeds again. In the field are sides like AC Milan and Juventus, of Italy, Real Madrid, Ferencvaros, of Hungary, even Wolverhampton Wanderers. All these, on their day, might take a deal of beating.

Last night Spurs should have had everything quietly wrapped up by half-time. Before the quarter-hour they had taken the lead through Peters, their captain for the night in the absence of Mullery. Taking a pass from Pratt, he shot home under the bar from the edge of the penalty area to round off one of the few flowing moves of the night, begun deep in the Tottenham half by Beal and carried on by Knowles, Neighbour and Perryman. That suggested a healthy beginning. But that was the only time the penny was to drop.

Nantes escaped before [...] line, was beyond belief; and there were near misses too from Gilzean and a couple of near things from Chivers and Gilzean again as they worked through a packed defence. Once also Chivers, using his weight and height, burst through a crowd of Frenchmen and stung Demanes, under the French crossbar, with a powerful left-foot rocket.

Indeed up till then it was one-way traffic and Jennings—a lonely figure at the other end—might well have laid himself a table and helped himself cross-legged, to a bottle of aperitif so little did the action come his way. Yet, curiously, it was only within seconds of the kick-off, with Tottenham apparently half asleep, that Blanchet was put through the Tottenham defence for the only really dangerous situation achieved by the French all night. The winger's shot went just wide of Jennings's far post but, apart from that, there was nothing truly to worry Beal at the side of England and company.

There was little real body or drive in the game. It was light-weight and stilted, especially the French game. Certainly there were many clever triangular movements between Blanchet, Rampillon and Marcos, an Argentinian international centre forward, and a bit of pace suggested by Maas.

Spurs, by the interval, should have been three or at least four up. In the second half the game somehow became insulated from reality. Waves of impatience rose from the crowd as both teams began anxiously to stammer and stutter as the standard of the affair rapidly to depreciate. Both sides [...]

The Nantes goalkeeper punches clear from the head of Gilzean.

ball and get Chivers to burst through the middle.

The Polish referee seemed to lose track of things. Anxiety and frustration arose and the whistle was heard loud and often as though a gendarme were controlling the traffic in the centre of Paris during the rush hour.

With half an hour left Marcos was cautioned and then when Rampillon was writhing on the ground the French trainer was ordered off the field. The situation was all confusion. The French brought on Eo while Rampillon [...] the touchline; then Rampillon decided to return to the fray making 12 Frenchmen on the field. Laughter mingled with irritation; things had reached the point of the clowns at a circus.

Near the end Barot was also cautioned and in the last few minutes Morgan was substituted for Gilzean. If only Barot had had a d in his name that at least might have cheered up things.

TOTTENHAM HOTSPUR: P. Jennings; R. Evans, C. Knowles, J. Pratt, M. England, P. Beal, J. Neighbour, S. Perryman, M. Chivers, M. Peters, A. Gilzean (sub, R. Morgan).

FC NANTES: J.-P. Bertrand-Demanes; P. Barot, G. de Michele, J.-C. Osman, B. Gardon, M. Pech, B. Blanchet, H. Michel, A. Marcos, G. Rampillon (sub, G. Eo), E. Maas.

Referee: S. Eksztajn (Warsaw).

SPURS' WINNER. Bertrand-Demanes is beaten as Peters scores from the edge of the penalty area

DAILY MIRROR, Thursday, December 9, 1971

SPURS . . . 3 RAPID BUCHAREST . . . 0

TWO FOR CHIVERS

Comedy keeper 'Radu' adds to the fun

By KEN JONES

When Spurs defend their goal in snow-swept Bucharest next Wednesday, they may have cause to regret the chances they squandered at White Hart Lane last night.

A goal up in twenty seconds, they always seemed within reach of an unassailable lead in this UEFA Cup third round first leg tie. But a mixture of poor finishing, bad luck and the pantomime antics of goalkeeper Raducanu leaves them with some apprehension.

Raducanu, a towering giant of 6ft 5in, fumbled his way through a match which at one time he looked as though he was about to quit.

His troubles began in Spurs' first attack when he stood motionless beneath his cross-bar as a long throw from Martin Chivers bounced invitingly in front of Martin Peters.

The Rumanians might have been deceived by Alan Gilzean's unsuccessful attempt to flick the ball on.

But, certainly, Raducanu was immobile for almost the only time in the game as Peters thrust his head forward to score a remarkable goal.

Encouraged by this early success Spurs struck some of their most certain form and the volume of their attacks suggested that they might emulate one of the overwhelming victories achieved in European competitions by former Spurs teams.

But although there was an avenue of space along the Rumanian left into which Spurs could push players, Raducanu kept his goal intact for a further thirty-six minutes.

Then Spurs scored the goal which angered him to the point where it looked as though he would walk out of the contest.

A Rumanian defender fell in pain as Neighbour pushed a pass forward to Chivers, and Chivers, using his impressive strength, held off two tackles before scoring, close in.

As the ball hit the net, Raducanu rose in protest, arguing that Neighbour had been guilty of a foul.

The Rumanians, with their manager on the pitch, continued to protest and when the game restarted Raducanu stood waving angrily.

Almost immediately he allowed a back-pass from one of his defenders to sit invitingly in front of his goal. But as Gilzean sprinted forward, the giant Rumanian moved to the ball, signalling that he was indeed going to continue.

With two goals to comfort them, Spurs moved eagerly after others, but they were occasionally reminded of the quality of Rapid's own forwards.

Nasturescu was always a threatening raider, and he almost made a goal for Neagu. The cross was perfect, but Neagu's header was angled too high. A Rapid attack early in the second half also had Spurs in confusion.

Chivers' towering throw-ins and the centres which Spurs poured in from both flanks tested the Rumanians in the air, but it was not until the 62nd minute that Spurs scored again.

By then, they had replaced £170,000 Ralph Coates with Jimmy Pearce who was deployed along the right, but it was from the left that Spurs' goal came.

Gilzean glanced the ball down and Chivers shot his second goal of the night.

The Rumanians now strung together some neat attacks, but were foiled by the splendid covering of Phil Beal.

A three-goal lead might be enough to see Spurs through next week but Rapid have a habit of scoring at home against good teams, and the test is far from over.

MIRROR, Thursday, Decem...

LONDON'S BIG CUP NIGHT

TWO FOR CHIVERS

By KEN JONES: Spurs 3, Rapid Bucharest 0

WHEN Spurs defend their goal in snow-swept Bucharest next Wednesday, they may have cause to regret the chances they squandered at White Hart Lane last night.

A goal up in twenty seconds, they always seemed within reach of an unassailable lead in this EUFA Cup third round first leg tie. But a mixture of poor finishing, bad luck and the pantomime antics of goalkeeper Raducanu leaves them with some apprehension.

Raducanu, a towering giant of 6ft. 5in., fumbled his way through a match which at one time he looked as though he was about to quit.

His troubles began in Spurs' first attack when he stood motionless beneath his crossbar as a long throw from Martin Chivers bounced invitingly in front of Martin Peters.

Deceived

The Rumanians might have been deceived by Alan Gilzean's unsuccessful attempt to flick the ball on.

But, certainly, Raducanu was immobile for almost the only time in

Comedy keeper 'Radu' adds to the fun

the Rumanian left into which Spurs could push players, Raducanu kept his goal intact for a further thirty-six minutes.

Then Spurs scored the goal which angered him to the point where it looked as though he would walk out of the contest.

A Rumanian defender fell in pain as Neighbour pushed a pass forward to Chivers, and Chivers, using his impressive strength, held off two tackles before scoring, close in.

Raducanu sprawls—beaten by Martin Chivers (right) for Spurs' third and his own second in last night's White Hart Lane clash.

goal. But as Gilzean sprinted forward the giant Rumanian moved to the ball, signalling that

was angled too high. A Rapid attack early in the second-half also had Spurs in confusion.

Chivers' towering throw-

Peters on target again against Rapid Bucharest

Martin Peters wheels away having put Spurs ahead against Rapid Bucharest

TIMES, Thursday, December 16, 1971

RAPID BUCHAREST . . . 0 TOTTENHAM HOTSPUR . . . 2

THREE ESCAPES THEN TOTTENHAM WEAR DOWN RUMANIANS

Bucharest, December 15

From GEOFFREY GREEN

Tottenham Hotspur, victorious, bloody but unbowed, limped painfully out of the 23rd August Stadium here today and into the quarter-finals of the UEFA Cup with a valuable win. So now they have behind them trips to Iceland, France, and Rumania with five victories and one draw on the way.

They next await the draw for the last eight of the competition which is to be made on January 12 as they join Wolverhampton Wanderers, the two Italians, Juventus and AC Milan with UT Arad (Rumania) Ferencvaros (Hungary) Sarajevo (Yugoslavia) and Lierse (Belgium) making up the company.

Spurs are through, yet they were so nearly bundled out of it in the first half today when they had three desperate escapes in the fifth, 28th and 40th minutes. On those occasions Codreanu only missed by a whisker as he dived to head a cross at the far post. Next it was a valiant save by Collins on his goal-line from Ene with Jennings lost in a melee. Then finally Perryman put a diabolical back-pass clean into the path of Ene who had only Jennings to beat. But somehow Jennings with a gallant dive at his feet and a completing save by Evans rescued the situation.

So at half-time with the scoreline blank Tottenham were half way there with their three-goal lead from White Hart Lane last week still solvent in the bank.

In the end, having survived the opening barrage Tottenham took control against a fading opponent to round off a coldly efficient performance at the back where a first-class demolition job was done by Collins, in place of the injured England, Pratt, Beal and the energetic Coates, who played a vital part in Tottenham's 4-4-2 formation which his speed every now and then changed into a fluid 4-3-3 when Tottenham counter-attacked from depth. All this while the Rumanians threw everything at them except the giant floodlights of this 80,000 stadium and they turned on a fullscale offensive from the start in 4-2-4 formation. Having taken the weight up to the interval Tottenham's long counter-attacks slowly began to eat into the foe and it was then that the goals came. The first arrived a quarter of an hour after the interval, a header by Pratt saw the powerful Chivers break through in full stride. His shot hit Raducanu, the goalkeeper but there was Pearce to shoot in the rebound in spite of a despairing effort to save on the line by Codrea. Number two came six minutes from the finish when Chivers once more took a through pass from Peters and with flowing footwork and powerful shoulders scored a great individual goal, working his way in on a wide arc down the left, along the byline, to shoot home magnificently from an acute angle.

If the first half had been coldly strategic the flesh and blood came after the interval. The fun and games – if that is the right expression – began with Tottenham's opening goal which virtually put the Rumanians out of court. In protesting that Chivers was offside Lupescu and Raducanu, the captain (throwing the ball at the Italian referee in fiery anger) both had their names taken. That set a spark to the proceedings. Within another minute, Knowles, of Tottenham, was also booked. Then, to add fuel to the fire, Pearce and Pop tangled in an ugly way and both were sent off the field.

Those 12 minutes that Pearce had spent on the field had given him a short life but a gay one. In that spell he had a goal disallowed for offside; scored the vital first goal and then found himself dismissed from the battle – not a bad performance for a substitute who had come on for Gilzean shortly after the start of the second half.

There were other substitutes too as the fur flew; Naylor for Perryman, who was winged in the first half with a damaged shoulder; Angelescu for Dumitru, then another Rumanian substitute, Nasturescu for Ene. That completed both sides' quota of substitutions but it was those moments after Tottenham's first goal that really injected the bitterness into the Rumanians, of whom Mr Billy Nicholson, the Tottenham manager, later said: "We have never played against a dirtier side," and certainly I have never seen a more unruly period in the fire of European competition.

Just to add to the drama of that second half, Codreanu hooked up Coates as he broke down the right – an obvious penalty. But there was Peters to miss from the spot as he clipped his shot outside Raducanu's right-hand post. So all this emerged – all this fire, anger and bile – on a cold day which brought a distinct nip in the air. So much so that one lost one's toes and one's fingers as the temperature plunged down. To add to it all there was a crowd no more than 10,000 strong. Among them were 100 Tottenham supporters; they at least must have enjoyed what was a tactical triumph.

12

SPORT

Football

Three escapes the
Tottenham wear
down Rumanians

From Geoffrey Green
Football Correspondent
Bucharest, December 15

Rapide Bucharest 0
Tottenham Hotspur 2

Tottenham Hotspur, victorious, bloody but unbowed, limped painfully out of the 23rd August Stadium here today and into the quarter finals of the UEFA Cup with a valuable win. So now they have behind them trips to Iceland, France, and Rumania with five victories and one draw on the way.

They next await the draw for the last eight of the competition which is to be made on January 12 as they join Wolverhampton Wanderers, the two Italians, Juventus and A C Milan with U T Arad (Rumania) Ferencvaros (Hungary) Sarajevo (Yugoslavia) and Lierse (Belgium) making up the company.

Spurs are through, yet they were so nearly bundled out of it in the first half today when they had three desperate escapes in the fifth, 28th and 40th minutes. On those occasions Codreanu only missed by a whisker as he dived to head a cross at the far post. Next it was a valiant save by Collins on his goalline from Ene with Jennings lost in a melee. Then finally

TIMES, Wednesday, March 8, 1972

UT ARAD . . . 0 TOTTENHAM . . . 2

TOTTENHAM FORCE ARAD TO STRUGGLE ALONG POINTLESS AVENUES

Arad, Rumania, March

From BRIAN JAMES

ARAD WELCOME SPURS. From left: Roger Morgan, John Pratt, Steve Perryman, Ray Evans, Pat Jennings, Martin Peters

With the unnerving confidence of sappers sprinting through their own minefield, Tottenham Hotspur endured the totally predictable assaults of totally unknown opponents to take a fine victory in the UEFA Cup quarter-final here today.

In the end it was easily enough accomplished. UT Arad, the best team in Rumania, were shown to be neither sophisticated enough nor possessed of sufficient stamina to deter a Tottenham team growing fast to the state of resolution and discipline that wins not only matches in Europe, but also competitions.

The oddities of the pitch and ball, the unfamiliarity of the rival players, the complexity of strange sights, sounds, even smells, all these were either ignored or overcome by Tottenham. By the end we wondered why there should ever have been doubts.

But all that is looking back. In the beginning, Tottenham had to hold Arad's busy and persistent raids while they made their instant assessment of their task and then settled to the style which made this newly acquired knowledge work.

Work was the operative word. Only two men, Chivers and Gilzean, were left up front to battle for the ball which hung tantalizingly in the wind as though striking an invisible barrier about the half way line. The rest dug in in two ranks mid-field and forced Arad to struggle along pointless avenues until their patience gave out and they were left with Jennings and his goal as long-range targets for optimistic shooting.

They were all good at this spoiling and harassing task, and no-one was better than Morgan, perhaps the player to whom it should have come hardest. A winger, who has endured more than his share of bad luck for two years, his display in Rumania showed that his troubles have left no scar on either his

Martin Chivers in determined mood

Football

Tottenham force Arad to struggle along pointless avenues

From Brian James
Arad, Rumania, March 7

UT Arad 0, Tottenham 2

With the unnerving confidence of sappers sprinting through their own minefield, Tottenham Hotspur endured the totally predictable assaults of totally unknown opponents to take a fine victory in the UEFA Cup quarter-final here today.

In the end it was easily enough accomplished. UT Arad, the best team in Rumania, were shown to be neither sophisticated enough nor possessed of sufficient stamina to deter a Tottenham team growing fast to the state of resolution and only ... ing an invisible barrier about the halfway line. The rest dug in in two ranks midfield and forced Arad to struggle along pointless avenues until their patience gave out and they were left with Jennings and his goal as long-range targets for optimistic shooting.

They were all good at this spoiling and harassing task, and no one was better than Morgan, perhaps the player to whom it should have come hardest. A winger, who has endured more than his share of bad luck for two years, his display in Rumania showed that his troubles have left no scar on either his courage or his skill.

It was Morgan, also, who scored ... first goal. Sprinting ... not he shot well as ... in the twelfth ... bad blow for ... de was the ... ovoscki,

Morgan scores Tottenham's first goal in Arad yesterday.

...the crossbar, w...

For ever under the eye of the British Press. Second left, Peter Blackman (Evening Standard), third left, Norman Giller (Daily Express), fourth left, Brian James (The Times), fifth left, John Oakley (Evening News), far right, Brian Scovell (Daily Mail)

MORGAN ON THE MARCH. Roger Morgan puts Spurs ahead in Rumania

courage or his skill.

It was Morgan, also, who scored Tottenham's first goal. Sprinting to the critical spot he shot well as Peters centred neatly in the twelfth minute. This was a bad blow for Arad, for whom Flavio Domide was the keenest plotter and Brosovoscki, who struck a post with one shot, the biggest threat.

If Tottenham knew little of Arad, then Arad knew nothing of Tottenham. We saw this before half-time when Tottenham scored again with a set-piece goal quite famous in football, which yet caught Arad quite unprepared. Morgan's short corner, Gilzean's back-header at the near post and England's stabbing volley at the far post were the goal's well-rehearsed components.

There were strange doings at half-time when Tottenham had to replace in their attack the clever Gilzean who was still dazed from an earlier collision, and chose centre half Collins for the job. And then Arad replaced their uniform. For the second half they came out with unnumbered red tunics worn over their cream shirts.

But it was too late now to confuse Tottenham, their grip on the game was absolute and they even found occasion to show a little more of their essential football without allowing their delight in elegance to undermine the need for safety. A shot from Biro, which struck the crossbar, was always there to remind them.

When it was done Tottenham could reflect that the real problem of this match may lie still in the future, for Chivers and Knowles both had their names taken and, having been also cautioned in earlier European games, may be penalized in this Cup's later rounds. It must be said that in a match that was never more than hearty the booking of these two, and that of Biro, reflected more the referee's strange anxieties rather than the players'.

Some Arad householders had climbed into their lofts and removed the slates of their roofs to provide extra grandstands around the ground. As today they labour to make their homes once again weather-proof they will be sharing the feelings of the 19,000 who had paid to see – at no moment were the losers permitted to look anything but.

DAILY EXPRESS, Wednesday, March 22, 1972

TOTTENHAM . . . 1 UT ARAD . . . 1

GILLY GOAL LIFTS SAD SPURS

By NORMAN GILLER

Alan Gilzean, as graceful as a Nureyev on grass, last night lifted Tottenham into the UEFA Cup semi-finals.

It was just the pick-up Tottenham needed after the despair of their FA Cup quarter-final defeat by Leeds on Saturday.

But their performance looks better on paper than it did on the pitch for this was no glory-glory-night for Spurs.

They almost allowed Arad, a stilted, sterile side, to become the first team ever to win a European tie at Tottenham.

Spurs went through to the semi-finals with jeers from their frustrated fans echoing in their ears after they had made a mess of a dozen scoring chances.

It seemed as if the pounding they got from Leeds had left them demoralised.

Arad were nowhere near the Leeds class. They were bankrupt of ideas and trespassed deep into Tottenham territory only three times in a weak bid to shake off their two-goal hangover from the first leg in Rumania.

Yet Arad incredibly stole into the lead with their only menacing move of the second half when World Cup international Flavio Domide swept a low shot into the net in the 63rd minute.

It was Gilzean who fittingly restored sanity to the scoreline with a neatly headed goal nine minutes from the end.

Gilzean, perhaps in his final season with a Tottenham team he has served so well, had stitched the few magnificent moments into this not very memorable match.

This gazelle of a player shaved a post with a shot, struck the bar with a header and went close with six other gliding headers.

Gilzean played as a central striker in place of the banned Martin Chivers, and Terry Naylor efficiently deputised for injured Philip Beal at the back of the defence.

Arad goalkeeper Miroslav Vidac had a magic night and even the Tottenham players had to applaud some of his stunning saves.

The outstanding save was when he turned a Ralph Coates, goal-bound shot off target. Coates, playing wide out on the right, had earlier powered a header against the bar.

It could so easily have been a seven-goal romp for Spurs. But the important thing is that they are through to the semi-finals of a competition in which Wolves are still taking a more than passing interest. Wolves face Juventus at Molineux tonight and should join Tottenham in the semi-final draw on Friday.

Spurs' manager Bill Nicholson insisted afterwards that Chivers' absence had made no difference to their performance. He said: "Alan Gilzean did a great job. He deserved a hat-trick.

"I was very pleased with Terry Naylor. He's a determined player who made the others work – he reads the game well."

Gilzean said: "The longer it went on, the better they got. It was just one of those nights. I was beginning to wonder if one would ever go in."

Arad skipper Petescu said: "It is tremendous that we should be able to hold Spurs. We are so out of condition. We haven't played in the Rumanian League for more than a month."

Martin Peters heads for goal against Arad

EURO-NIGHT AT TOTTENHAM

GILLY GOAL LIFTS SAD SPURS

Alan Mullery (left) exchanges pennants with AC Milan captain, Gianni Rivera

DAILY MAIL, Thursday, April 6, 1972

TOTTENHAM . . . 2 AC MILAN . . . 1

HATCHETS OUT FOR SPURS

By JEFF POWELL

Spurs – shamefully brutalised by the hatchetmen of Milan – somehow kept enough of their limbs and their football together to sustain some hope of reaching the UEFA Cup final.

It was no accident that one of their bravest players, young Steve Perryman, volleyed the two fine goals which give Tottenham a slender lead to defend in Italy in a fortnight.

This was a night when only a hero would have gone looking for goals in the face of the cynical chopping with which Milan sullied the good name of football.

Milan, who had Sogliano sent off in the 61st minute, were delighted with the result for their away goal counts double.

Milan were a downright disgrace and their coach Nerro Roçco stands accused as an accomplice to the Soccer crimes his team committed.

So, too, does Spanish referee Iglesias. He was so out of touch that he awarded 38 free kicks against Tottenham, 22 against Milan.

Never has an international defender been so inaptly nicknamed as Baby Face Rosato, who tried so hard to eliminate Martin Chivers but hurt his own back in the process.

Never before has a man with Benetti's violent tendencies been credited in a match programme with such an unlikely hobby as keeping pet canaries.

Benetti personified the split personality of his team. He burst on to Terry Naylor's 25th-minute half-clearance to strike an opening goal full of skill and power.

No-one after seeing that, and some of the other talents, will argue that these are great players, even though they were misguided last night.

It was to Tottenham's credit that they raised their game after the sickening blow of Benetti's goal.

The way they battled was also a tribute to the returning Alan Mullery who gave Spurs renewed drive and direction.

It was much to do with Mullery's urging that Spurs forced surprising cracks in one of the world's greatest defences.

Alan Gilzean and Martin Peters combined to lay the ball into Perryman's path for the first of his 20-yard goals in the 33rd minute.

Immediately before the interval, Gilzean was booked for arguing and Milan's great German, Schnellinger, for time-wasting. Both trivialities amid last night's mayhem.

Sixteen minutes after the break, Sogliano was sent off for his last part in an hour-long running feud with Mullery.

Milan were left to survive half an hour with ten men and they got through four minutes.

Then they fumbled an attempt to clear Mullery's corner and Perryman buried his second goal low to the right of Cudicini.

Milan sent on Zazzaro for Golin and Tottenham substituted Neighbour for Coates in the last stages of the battle.

. . . and for the League championship drama, turn to Page 31.

Hatchets out for Spurs

Tottenham .... 2 AC Milan .... 1 : By JEFF POWELL

Cudicini's fingers are just inches away but Perryman's second goal is a winner.

Steve Perryman is mobbed having given Spurs the lead

PERRYMAN'S DOUBLE FOR SPURS. AC Milan goalkeeper Cudicini dives full length but is beaten by a rocket from Steve Perryman. Karl Heinz Schnellinger, the West German international, looks on

RESTROSPECTIVE VIEW BY STEVE PERRYMAN

Steve Perryman has never been renowned for his goal-scoring achievements, even though he has managed at least one goal per season since his debut in 1969. Two goals in one game therefore, especially against one of Europe's top sides, in a UEFA Cup semi-final was a feat that remains one of his most treasured memories. His goals came to Spurs' rescue after they went behind in the first leg tie at White Hart Lane, and with away goals so valuable, the Spurs team and their fans feared the worst.

Then, up stepped Perryman. He recalls: "Milan had a fabulous team with players like Gianni Rivera and Romeo Benetti. Being one goal down at home, bearing in mind we had to go to the San Siro to face a hostile crowd, was far from ideal. We were fully aware that the Italians would relish a defensive job of holding onto their lead, particularly an away goal.

"I'm not exactly noted for my goals. Certainly, not for scoring from outside the box, but that was the only way through their well-drilled defence.

"I scored my first from the edge of the box and the second from 25 yards!

"The Italians feared the aerial ability of Alan Gilzean, and marked 'Gilly' very tightly. They were shocked by my goals. It was just my night, perhaps my best in Europe – certainly for scoring!"

6
9

Mike England, surrounded by five Milan defenders, heads for goal

DAILY MIRROR, Thursday, April 20, 1972

AC MILAN . . . 1 TOTTENHAM . . . 1

TOTTENHAM WIN 3-2 ON AGGREGATE

SPURS IN UEFA CUP FINAL – AGAINST WOLVES

MILAN, WEDNESDAY

From HARRY MILLER

Tottenham survived a tense and tremendous finish here at the San Siro stadium tonight to march magnificently forward to the final of the UEFA Cup.

An early goal by skipper Alan Mullery had seemed to push Milan to the point of surrender.

But Rivera scored from the penalty spot in the 68th minute, and Tottenham were stretched to the limit of their strength and character to hold on.

Tottenham can look back on this European night with pride. And Mullery's cup of contentment must indeed be overflowing.

Two weeks ago he was wandering in the Second Division wilderness with Fulham.

SPURS AHEAD. Mullery (partly hidden, extreme right) beats Cudicini from just outside the penalty area

Tottenham recalled him to their colours for that trouble-torn first leg 2-1 win over Milan.

Sir Alf Ramsey recalled him to the England squad yesterday and tonight he showed all his old command of the mid-field to help inspire Tottenham to a two leg final with Wolves on May 3 and 17.

Tottenham could not have wished for a better boost than the one Mullery gave them after just seven minutes.

Cyril Knowles, excellent at left back, started the move with a fine overlapping run and cross from the left. Martin Chivers had a shot blocked and the ball broke for Steve Perryman to set up a 20-yard Mullery shot that curved into the top corner of the net.

Tottenham had moments of error and anxiety – once when Mike England headed against his own bar and was happy to see Knowles clear the ball for a corner.

But Tottenham's particular strength was in mid-field, where Mullery, Perryman and Peters dominated.

Ralph Coates, who played with intelligence and enthusiasm, made one fine 60-yard burst from mid-field that ended when he was hauled down on the edge of the penalty area.

Belgian referee Loraux kept the game moving smoothly with his firm control. And he was quick to stamp on the only explosive situation. That came when Phil Beal clashed

SPURS IN EUFA FINAL—A W

Alan Mullery's shot flies into the net *Picture: MONTE FRESCO.*

TOTTENHAM survived a tense and tremendous finish here at the San Siro stadium tonight to march magnificently forward to the final of the EUFA Cup.

An early goal by skipper Alan Mullery had seemed to push Milan to the point of surrender.

But Rivera scored from the penalty spot in the 68th minute, and Tottenham were stretched to the limit of their strength and character to hold on.

Tottenham can look back on this European night with pride. And Mullery's cup of contentment must indeed be overflowing.

Two weeks ago he was wandering in the Second

From HARRY MILLER, Milan, Wednesd
AC Milan 1, Tottenham 1
(Tottenham win 3-2 on aggregate)

Division wilderness with Fulham.

Tottenham recalled him to their colours for that trouble-torn first leg 2—1 win over Milan.

Sir Alf Ramsey recalled him to the England squad yesterday and tonight he showed all his old command of the midfield to help inspire Tottenham to a two-leg final with Wolves, on May 3 and 17.

Tottenham could not have wished for a better boost than the one Mullery gave them after just seven minutes.

Anxiety

Cyril Knowles, excellent at left back, started the move with a fine overlapping run and cross from the left. Martin Chivers had a shot blocked and the ball broke for Steve Perryman to set up a twenty-yard Mullery shot that curved into the top corner of the net.

Tottenham had moments of error and anxiety — once when Mike England headed against his own bar and was happy to see Knowles clear the ball for a corner.

But Tottenham's particular strength was in midfield, where Mullery, Perryman and Peters dominated.

Burst

Ralph Coates, who played with intelligence and enthusiasm, made one fine sixty-yard burst from midfield that ended when he was hauled down on the edge of the penalty area.

Belgian referee Loraux kept the game moving smoothly with his firm control. And he was ... to stamp on the ... situation

of the brush with referee showing the low card of caution

But in the sixty-eig minute Tottenham s... denly found themselve with a furious fight ... their hands.

Knowles missed a

DEANS' PENALTY MISS DASHES CELTIC HOPES

Celtic 0 Inter-Milan 0
(after extra time. Celtic lose 5—4 on penalties)

By CHRIS HARRIGAN

CELTIC'S hopes of reaching the European Cup Final for the third time ended last night because of the magnificent Inter defence—and the nerves of one of their young stars.

The Italians, held to a goal-less draw in Milan in the first leg of this semi-final, played brilliantly to keep out Celtic through ninety minutes and then extra time.

As the 75,000 capacity crowd held its breath, World Cup referee Rudi Glockner indicated that this match would be decided on penalties.

Inter's captain Sandro Mazzola slotted the first past Celtic's Evan Williams.

Then up stepped Dixie Deans, Celtic's reserve striker, who had come on in the second half for his first taste of European action.

Deans blasted the ball over the bar. He, and the Celtic players and the crowd, knew it was all over.

Artists like Inter do not make mistakes in these situations.

Facchetti, Frustalupi, Pellizzaro and Brazilian star Jair all scored from their spot-kicks to make sure of victory.

Celtic's other four penalties were all put in, but the Scots should never have allowed the game to get to this stage.

In the final Inter will meet the holders Ajax of Holland, who beat Benfica of Portugal 1—0 on aggregate.

Rangers make it for third time

By TED CORBETT: Rangers 2, Bayern Munich 0

RANGERS won through to their third Cup-Winners' Cup final since 1961 with two goals at Ibrox last night for a 3—1 aggregate against Bayern Munich.

On May 24 they will meet either Moscow Dynamo or East Berlin Dynamo, who complete their semi-final tonight.

The Germans offered little challenge once

PENALTY-SAVER PARKES DOES IT AGAIN!

By PETER INGALL

Wolves 2, Ferencvaros 1

WOLVES reached the final of the EUFA Cup at Molineux last night thanks to another penalty save by goalkeeper Phil Parkes.

Parkes made it possible for Wolves to win this semi-final on a 4—3 aggregate with a repeat of the penalty save he made in the 2—2 draw in Budapest two weeks ago.

Steve Daley, making his debut in the competition, gave Wolves a great start with a 25-second goal. Frank Munro headed the second just before half-time.

MURDER SQUAD

LIFT OFF. Cyril Knowles prepares to take off from Milan, destination London and the UEFA Cup final

with Benetti and the Italian came out of the brush with the referee showing the yellow card of caution.

But in the 68th minute Tottenham suddenly found themselves with a furious fight on their hands.

Knowles missed a tackle on Bignon and the Italian raced forward into the penalty area where he was brought down by Beal. Rivera blasted the ball in from the spot.

Tottenham called off John Pratt, sent on substitute Terry Naylor and held on.

The bonfires now burning on the huge terraces seemed like a funeral pyre for Milan's hopes. They might also be tribute to a memorable Tottenham performance.

BOOKED! BUT HE'S NOT EVEN PLAYING

SPURS flew home today following their EUFA Cup semi-final triumph over AC Milan still uncertain whether Belgian referee Pierre Loraux will go through with the biggest howler of the season.

For Loraux, who for the most part had an excellent game, insists he booked Steve Perryman and Milan's Giorgio Biasiolo in the 61st minute.

In fact he cautioned Phil Beal and Romeo Benetti after a scuffle in the Spurs penalty

back, but he didn't wave any card at me. If he did I didn't know anything about it."

Beal was also critical of the referee for awarding a penalty after he had stopped Milan centre-forward Bigon breaking clear after a rare mistake by Cyril Knowles.

"I took the ball cleanly off Bigon's feet and then he did this perfect swallow dive over my legs," said Beal.

"I don't think the referee was going to give a penalty. He changed his mind because of the screaming fans."

Rivera convert-

EVENING NEWS, Thursday, April 20, 1972

BOOKED! BUT HE'S NOT EVEN PLAYING

Refereeing fiasco in Milan as smooth Spurs swing into the UEFA Cup final

By JOHN OAKLEY

Spurs flew home today following their UEFA Cup semi-final triumph over AC Milan still uncertain whether Belgian referee Pierre Loraux will go through with the biggest howler of the season.

For Loraux, who for the most part had an excellent game, insists he booked Steve Perryman and Milan's Giorgio Biasiolo in the 61st minute.

In fact he cautioned Phil Beal and Romeo Benetti after a scuffle in the Spurs penalty area. But he got his numbers the wrong way round.

Afterwards Loraux said: "I cautioned the No. 8 of Spurs and the No. 6 of Milan. I have not made a mistake."

Loraux could not be shaken even when it was pointed out that Beal has fair hair and Perryman is dark and that Biasiolo was not even on the field at the time, having been substituted six minutes earlier.

To add to the confusion Beal did not know the referee had booked any Spurs player – and neither did manager Bill Nicholson.

Now Spurs will wait to hear from UEFA before deciding whether to protest. But Perryman was certainly not involved.

"When the referee was showing his yellow card, I was 30 yards away," he said.

Beal added: "There is no doubt the ref booked Benetti for sticking his knee in my back, but he didn't wave any card at me. If he did I didn't know anything about it."

Beal was also critical of the referee for awarding a penalty after he had stopped Milan centre forward Bigon breaking clear after a rare mistake by Cyril Knowles.

"I took the ball cleanly off Bigon's feet and then he did this perfect swallow dive over my legs," said Beal.

"I didn't think the referee was going to give a penalty. He changed his mind because of the screaming fans."

Rivera converted the penalty, in the 68th minute, cancelling a seventh-minute goal from Alan Mullery.

But Spurs, who won the first leg 2-1 at White Hart Lane had little difficulty in holding on to win 3-2 on aggregate.

Mullery, who was playing for Fulham at Orient in a Second Division relegation battle only 17 days ago, was thrilled by his goal.

He said: "It was the most valuable of my career. What we wanted most of all was a quick goal to shake them and I was thrilled when I was the one who got it.

"Perryman set it up with a perfect pass and by the time the ball reached me I had decided to have a go.

"I cracked it as hard as I could and in it went.

"I was sure then that we would win. For it meant Milan had to get three goals to beat us and that never looked on.

"Even after their penalty I wasn't really worried because we were playing so well and holding them without much trouble."

Ralph Coates, in a European final in his first season with Spurs, was more cautious.

"I didn't really think we would lose, but when they got that penalty I did become a bit anxious.

"But it is wonderful to be in a European final. Coming to Spurs is the best thing that has happened to me in Soccer. I wanted to get away from Burnley and into the big time. Now it's all beginning to happen."

Martin Peters, who strained his groin, was the only Spurs casualty, although Alan Gilzean, kept out of the match by similar trouble, is also doubtful for the League game at Southampton on Saturday.

Nicholson said afterwards: "I wanted to play Gilly but when he told me he didn't think he would last more than 20 minutes I reluctantly decided to leave him out."

Nicholson said today: "Of course I am delighted we are in the final against Wolves, but I am not making any forecasts.

"Wolves are a good side. But we have an advantage. The final is over two legs, on May 3 and 17, and we play the first match at Molineux, just the way we like it."

DAILY MAIL, Thursday, May 4, 1972

WOLVES . . . 1 SPURS . . . 2

GIVE US THAT CUP – CHIVERS

By JEFF POWELL

Martin Chivers, without whose goals Tottenham would be no nearer an honour than the lower reaches of the First Division, produced two more monumental efforts last night to put one Spurs hand firmly on the UEFA Cup.

Chivers, the sleeping England giant of Saturday's rout by West Germany, not only reduced Wolves to outsiders in Europe's first all-English final but also reaffirmed his right to lead the England bid for Nations Cup revenge.

First, with the sort of crushing header he produces too seldom for a big man, Chivers lifted Spurs ahead. And then three minutes from time with one of the best of even his 43 goals this season, Chivers restored that first leg advantage which Spurs had lost to a Wolves sucker-punch approved by one of the most controversial referees in football history.

Said Spurs' manager Bill Nicholson: "Martin took his goals really well and they came at just the right moments – the first when Wolves were pressing us hard and the second when we were hanging on for a draw."

Tottenham, who have never lost a Cup final and who are unbeaten in Europe this season, are not now in danger of losing either record. Wolves go to White Hart Lane on May 17 facing a towering task.

Yet neither club could shift the mood of anti-climax from Molineux last night. There were spasms of Wolves pressure, moments of genuine excitement, some nail-biting escapes. Yet there was no escaping the ordinary feeling of a League game.

Although Shaw was booked for a kick at Coates early on, it was 20 minutes before the first thrill lit a damp Midlands evening.

Then Jennings ran out of his penalty area to effect a clearance which Hegan drove back so quickly from the halfway line that the Spurs goalkeeper only just regained his goal-line in time to touch the ball over.

Kinnear's booking for a tackle from behind on Wagstaffe was the only remaining remarkable moment of the first half.

Twelve minutes into the second Wolves were punished for Taylor's rash tackle on Gilzean. England took the long free kick and Chivers ran majestically to head the ball deep into the net.

Russian official Tofik Bakhramov sanctioned a sharp piece of Wolves gamesmanship in the 71st minute.

The Spurs defence were still challenging a free kick decision on the edge of their penalty area as Richards rolled the ball quickly for McCalliog to equalise in off Jennings.

Spurs remained under pressure and Coates was pulled off, in favour of substitute Pratt, until Chivers won the match. He gathered Mullery's pass and turned inside to hit a thunderous 25-yard right foot drive.

Martin Chivers heads Spurs in front

Daily Mail, Thursday, May 4, 1972

quits the international scene—Page 31

e us that
—Chivers

By JEFF POWELL

bals Tottenham would r reaches of the First tal efforts last night to Cup.

ing England giant of Saturermany, not only reduced n Europe's first all-English ned his right to lead the ns Cup revenge.

ort of crushing header he r a big man. Chivers lifted three minutes from time with s 43 goals this season. Chivers advantage which Spurs had lost to a Wolves sucker-punch approved by one of the most controversial referees in football history.

Said Spurs manager Bill Nicholson: 'Martin took his goals really well and they came at just the right moments the first when Wolves were pressing us hard and the second when we were hanging on for a draw.'

Towering

Tottenham, who have never lost a Cup Final and who are unbeaten in Europe this season, are not now in danger of losing either record. Wolves go to White Hart Lane on May 17 facing a towering task.

Yet neither club could shift the mood of anti-climax from Molineux last night. There were spasms of Wolves pressure, moments of genuine excitement, some nailbiting escapes. Yet there was no escaping the ordinary feeling of a League game.

Although Shaw was booked for a kick at Coates early on, it was 20 minutes before the first thrill lit a damp Midlands evening.

Then Jennings ran out of his penalty area to effect a clearance which Hegan drove back so quickly from the halfway line that the Spurs goalkeeper only just regained his goal line in time ...

● Spurs show they can defend as well as attack and Mike England and Cyril Knowles cut out this danger from John Richards.

QUICK CROSSWORD

EXPERT'S TIME RATING: 5-10 min.—Outstanding. 10-20 min.—First class. 20-30 min.—Very good.

ACROSS

Fans salute Brighton

By JOHN PARSONS

Brighton ....1 Rochdale 1

Brian Bromley and Ken Beamish combined to give John Templeman a chance

Chivers arises from lethargy to put Tottenham in front

By Geoffrey Green
Football Correspondent

Wolverhampton Wanderers 1
Tottenham Hotspur 2

Tottenham Hotspur last night got their noses in front of Wolverhampton Wanderers at Molineux in the first leg of the UEFA Cup final. If they keep their heads for the return match at White Hart Lane on May 17 then they should add this new trophy to their Cup Winners' Cup triumph of 1963, though one will scarcely expect it to be in the same expansive vein.

There was a curious irony here, for though these two sides this winter had scored 52 goals in this competition at home and abroad, night scarcely offered anything was adventurous. Indeed for an hour the n

sodic, fragmentary and often disconnected until the last hour when the goals tumbled. The first came some 12 minutes after the interval when Chivers rose to head home a long free-kick by England as the Wolves defence hesitated. But with 18 minutes left, Wolverhampton were back in it when McCalliog slipped home a quickly taken free-kick by Richards which caught Tottenham unawares as they were preparing their wall on the edge of the penalty area.

Then, three minutes from the end, came the winner. Mullery, out on the left, robbed McAlle, found Chivers and there was the hefty centre forward to bang home his thunderbolt from a full 20 yards to mark up his 43rd goal of the season.

TIMES, Thursday, May 4, 1972

Chivers From Lethargy To Put Tottenham In Front

By GEOFFREY GREEN

Tottenham Hotspur last night got their noses in front of Wolverhampton Wanderers at Molineux in the first leg of the UEFA Cup final. If they keep their heads for the return match at White Hart Lane on May 17 then they should add this new trophy to their Cup Winners' Cup triumph of 1963, though one will scarcely expect it to be in the same expansive vein.

There was a curious irony here, for though these two sides this winter had scored 52 goals in this competition at home and abroad, last night scarcely offered anything that was adventurous. Indeed, for nearly an hour the night was bankrupt and it seemed that we were heading for a stalemate. By the end, however, two goals emerged from set positions of free kicks – one to each team – and in the dying moments Chivers suddenly arose from a lethargy to thunder home one of his special shots to take the night into Tottenham's keeping.

The concrete truth was that the game lacked magnetism. Wolves, in the end, were victims of their own realism, which proved a poor guide, as they swung the ball about in long passing. Tottenham's strength lay in their collective effort, but in many ways the best performance of all came from the Russian team of officials led by the referee, Bakhramov, always to be remembered as the linesman who gave that important goal to Hurst and England in the World Cup final of 1966.

The match as a whole was episodic, fragmentary and often disconnected until the last hour when the goals tumbled. The first came some 12 minutes after the interval when Chivers rose to head home a long free kick by England as the Wolves defence hesitated. But with 18 minutes left, Wolverhampton were back in it when McCalliog slipped home a quickly taken free kick by Richards which caught Tottenham unawares as they were preparing their wall on the edge of the penalty area.

Then, three minutes from the end, came the winner. Mullery, out on the left, robbed McAlle, found Chivers and there was the hefty centre forward to bang home his thunderbolt from a full 20 yards to mark up his 43rd goal of the season.

There was the odd near miss and full-length save, of course, but the other only real highlight came some 20 minutes after the start when Jennings, running far outside his penalty area to kick a clearance, had to hare back at full speed to tip over the crossbar an instant return shot from Hegan aimed from the half-way line. It reminded one of Pele's effort in the World Cup in Guadalajara two years ago.

Basically, both teams seemed to find football difficult on a soft surface following a night and day of drizzle. There were moments when the 39,000 crowd roared Wolverhampton on, but the great, brilliant light and the sight and the feeling of those days at Molineux in the 1950s, when a kind of collective euphoria gripped the Midlands, was missing.

Chivers, the bombardier, though doing little else, in the end set himself in a place apart by his two valuable goals. But the spirit and drive belonged to Hegan, of Wolves, and Mullery, of Tottenham, in mid-field. Peters' voice again seemed muted.

No one truly presided over, much less ruled, the battle. Spurs eventually emerged from two dark patches of danger in the twilight, having settled for a 4-4-2 tactical switch over the last quarter of an hour when Pratt was substituted for the energetic Coates. Though turning to defence, at the last they won. There it rests for a fortnight.

After the game Mullery, who has 38 international caps, said he had written to Sir Alf Ramsey, the England team manager, asking not to be considered for future international matches.

Mullery wrote the letter before the England party for the second leg in the European championship quarter-final against West Germany was announced. He said he wanted to spend more time with his family and less time travelling.

THE UEFA CUP COMES TO TOTTENHAM

IT'S ALL YOURS, MULLERY

By NORMAN GILLER : Spurs 1 Wolves 1

(Spurs win 3-2 on aggregate)

ALAN MULLERY'S astonishing season ended last night with him displaying the E.U.F.A. Cup in a one-man victory parade around White Hart Lane.

...and fans a

DAILY EXPRESS, Thursday, May 18, 1972

SPURS . . . 1 WOLVES . . . 1

SPURS WIN 3-2 ON AGGREGATE

IT'S ALL YOURS, MULLERY

By NORMAN GILLER

Alan Mullery's astonishing season ended last night with him displaying the UEFA Cup in a one-man victory parade around White Hart Lane.

The rest of the triumphant Tottenham players left him to it and retreated to the safety of the dressing room as he became engulfed in a swarm of supporters.

Tottenham's fans will claim that Mullery's name should be engraved on the trophy following his spectacular goal that clinched the Cup for Spurs in this first ever all-English European final.

He threw himself full-length to head in a Martin Peters free kick in the 29th minute . . . but was about the only person in the capacity-crammed ground who could not describe the goal. Mullery knocked himself out as he landed face-first in the goalmouth and was helped off for treatment. He returned in time to play a reluctant part in the Wolves equaliser in the 41st minute.

The ball bounced off him as it was played into the packed penalty area and ran into the path of David Wagstaffe, who scored from 25 yards with a spiteful left foot shot that made something of a circular tour before swinging into the net high off the left post.

Wolves, carrying a 2-1 hangover from the first leg at Molineux, needed a second goal to force extra-time and had Tottenham stretched near to breaking point in a frantic, final 20 minutes.

Club captain Mike Bailey came on as substitute for his first top-flight action for four months and gave Wolves new momentum for their late revival movement.

But superb saves by goalkeeper Pat Jennings, an offside decision against Derek Dougan and disciplined defensive play took the whip out of the Wolves whirlwind.

There was a sign of staleness in the Tottenham team even in triumph. They were playing their 68th competitive match of the season and the marathon run had drained them of energy and initiative.

Only captain Mullery, clutching the UEFA Cup between his arms like a baby, had the stamina for the traditional lap of honour. He had at least 4,000 Spurs fans as companions on the disorganised journey around the perimeter of the pitch.

It was just six weeks ago that Mullery returned to Tottenham after his controversial loan transfer to Fulham.

He voluntarily ended his England career two weeks ago and then capped his see-saw season with last night's remarkable goal . . . the goal that he knows nothing about.

Modest manager Bill Nicholson refused to come out and acknowledge the cheering, chanting fans after a victory that gives him the honour of having won more major trophies than any other manager in the Football League.

Since he took charge at White Hart Lane in 1958, Spurs have played in three FA Cup finals, one League Cup final, one European Cup Winners' Cup final and this season's UEFA Cup final. They have now won the lot.

The only top title now eluding him is the European Cup. And his Spurs players – now hoping for the reward of improved contracts for next season – have promised to complete the full house for him.

LOOKING BACK WITH MARTIN CHIVERS

The West Midlands is not usually the place to find a European final. But in 1972 Molineux played the unlikely host to the first leg of the UEFA Cup final.

To Martin Chivers and the rest of the Tottenham team it proved to be a bit of an anti-climax. Chivers explained: "The previous round had been at Milan.

"The firecrackers were so low they seemed to be about to touch you. That was real European atmosphere. Playing Wolves did not seem to be a European final at all."

But Chivers was the last to complain about a trip to Wolves. He had an outstanding goal-scoring record against the Midlands side and scored twice again in the final.

"I think that if they had been against a European side it would have been more memorable. They would have been shown to the nation regularly. It just took the edge off the matches that it was an all English clash.

"I am sure that was the way Wolves looked at it as well. They had beaten Ferencvaros in the semi-final and would have enjoyed a trip to West Germany or somewhere as much as us."

But the victory that Chivers' goals produced was as vital as any in Tottenham's European history. Alan Mullery completed the win at White Hart Lane in the second leg.

Chivers looks back on those days with great feeling. "It was the in-between time

Alan Mullery scores Spurs' goal in the UEFA Cup final second leg

I think. The great era of football when you were guaranteed big gates for big matches was coming to an end.

"I don't think that the players have ever had it so good. It was and still is a marvellous profession but I still think that was a great time."

Chivers has no doubts that in a period not renowned for its great teams Spurs were as good as any team in the country.

He said: "Between 1971 and 1974 we had a squad that could not be matched. We lacked the consistency to win the League but we were outstanding in the Cups.

"We used to pick each other to pieces at the time but we now look back and think what a good side it was.

"I remember the dressing room teasing that Mike England used to get but he was a great centre half. Looking at his performances he was about as good as anything there has been.

"Players around you made you outstanding. To play with people like Alan Gilzean was an honour. I knew where the goal was but other people created the chances.

"By that Feyenoord Cup final in 1974 we knew the side was coming to a watershed. It was a sad time once Bill Nicholson went. We were close knit and once it started to break up it was over quickly.

"They were days that we would never forget, the full houses, the outstanding matches in Europe . . . the glory days."

'rd Joy sees Tottenham make history
ıail-biting night of suspense

Glory, glory! Spurs are Cup Kings

Extra time

Subdued

EVENING STANDARD, Thursday, May 18, 1972

LONDON'S TOP DOGS – AND IT'S GREAT

The MARTIN PETERS COLUMN

We have had our passports stamped in Iceland, Rumania, France and Italy on the way to the UEFA Cup final and it has been a long, hard slog starting way back in September. But it was all worth while just to see Alan Mullery holding up the trophy.

That was a very proud and happy moment for all of us connected with the club – players, management, staff, and, above all, the supporters.

So Tottenham Hotspur will be the first name to be engraved on the new trophy and we go into the competition again next season as the holders.

We will be London's only representatives in Europe too, as neither Arsenal nor Chelsea managed to get in this time. I must say it feels good to be top dogs in London again after last year when we were very much in Arsenal's shadow.

The European Cup may have a bit more glamour about it but I don't think anyone would dispute that the UEFA Cup is just as hard to win.

Before the season began our manager, Bill Nicholson, warned us that this competition would be the toughest of them all. After the first round we thought he must have been joking as we beat Keflavik, the amateurs from Iceland, 15-1 on aggregate.

In fact, out of the 64 teams, there were only a few duffers. Teams like Leeds, Juventus, AC Milan and Ferencvaros went into the hat. So I think we have every reason to feel tremendously proud that we have come out on top.

Wolves fought well but they had left themselves with just a bit too much to do after losing the first leg 2-1 on their own ground.

If they had scored first it could have been very interesting but fortunately we opened the scoring and it was nice to have a hand in the goal myself.

I curled a free kick from near the left touchline and Alan Mullery flung himself forward to head a spectacular goal. I'm especially delighted with our victory for Alan's sake. Barely a month ago he was on loan at Fulham and must have had grave doubts about his future.

But what a tremendous comeback he has made and he has scored vital goals against Milan in the semi-final and against Wolves last night.

To cap it all, Alan finished up with a little unintentional solo performance. He was left stranded on the pitch on his own with the cup. The rest of the lads couldn't get near him because of the crush and Alan was left to do a lap of honour on his own – with an escort of about 5,000 young fans.

While most of the players will be putting their feet up Martin Chivers and I will be reporting to the Hendon Hall Hotel later today to join the England squad for the home internationals.

I have shaken off the cold that was bothering me in Germany last week and am hoping very much to be in the side against Wales on Saturday and so win my 54th cap.

Most of us have been feeling the effects of this very strenuous season but I must say I don't feel half as weary now as a few days ago. But then, they do say that it's only losers who feel tired, don't they?

Martin Peters was talking to Alexander Clyde.

EVENING STANDARD, Thursday, May 18, 1972

GLORY, GLORY! SPURS ARE CUP KINGS

Tottenham make history on a nail-biting night of suspense

By BERNARD JOY

Although Spurs' manager Bill Nicholson confesses, "We have had too much football, some of the players are knackered," Spurs will embark on the same ambitious programme next season of trying to win four competitions – the UEFA Cup as well as the three domestic tournaments.

The 1-1 draw at White Hart Lane with Wolves which made them the first holders of

CHAMPAGNE IN THE DRESSING ROOM. From the left: Joe Kinnear, Cyril Knowles, Ralph Coates, Martin Peters, Philip Beal, Martin Chivers

the UEFA Cup – the successor to the Fairs Cup – was their 26th Cup match of the season, making 68 competitive matches in all.

Nicholson says: "The side that wins the UEFA Cup very often goes on to take the League Championship as Leeds and Arsenal did. The side in the European Cup very rarely retain the League title.

"Any club that is in the European Cup and feels confident about the strength of the side – as they should be as champions – ought to withdraw from the FA Cup. The tough European matches come after Christmas when they are entangled in the FA Cup programme.

"It is different in our case. We have yet to prove our ability and both the players and club want to be in every competition, both from the income point of view, and insurance for securing entry into Europe again.

"We have been involved in a helluva lot of football, more than ever before by this club.

"Every match has been important because we did well in the League and wanted to maintain a high position. We had a fair run in the FA Cup, reached the semi-final of the League Cup and had 12 games in Europe.

"It has been a tremendous drain on the players and some have looked knackered. Martin Chivers for example.

"You can play too much football for the general well-being of the club. Games tumble over each other so that you have no chance to catch up with yourself, and there is no opportunity to get on the training ground to work on your problems.

"You accept this and when you win something all is worth while. The important thing is that we are in Europe again next season and that brings a special atmosphere to the club."

Spurs have a remarkable record. They have won all eight finals in which they have taken part (six under Nicholson's managership) and are the first British club to win two different European trophies.

The nail-biting suspense in which the second half was played last night lifted the game to one of the most exciting in Spurs' colourful history.

And it all started from a change of tactics at half-time. In the first half Spurs went at Wolves, as they had planned, in order to put pressure on the weakest department, the back four.

The dressing room at the interval was subdued and tense as Wolves had just equalised with a great goal by David Wagstaffe, after Alan Mullery had put Spurs in front.

It was decided to play safe, keep a tight defence and be less aggressive. The ball was kicked instead of passed, the initiative handed over to Wolves' dangerous forwards and Spurs had their worst 45 minutes in the competition.

Yet the result was gripping entertainment which had fans on the edge of their seats with suspense.

Len Shipman declared: "I am very proud to be president of the Football League with two teams like that in it. It was a magnificent match, a credit to English football."

The final was won at Molineux, where Spurs established a 2-1 lead, and the game at White Hart Lane turned on a magnificent save by Pat Jennings from John Richards.

Jennings dismisses it: "It looked better than it actually was. Although Richards was only three or four yards out he hit the ball with the inside of his right foot and there was only one way it could go."

Nicholson had no doubt where credit was due, saying to Jennings: "You won us the Cup."

With 15 minutes to go Derek Dougan had a goal rightly disallowed for offside and Wolves' manager Bill McGarry says, "As long as I live I won't be able to puzzle out why he was in an offside position.

"It was from a corner and Richards headed the ball back to him at a post. It's a situation that is on 99 times out of 100 with at least one person on the goal-line with the keeper. But everyone had moved out."

After the match the Spurs players pushed Mullery out for a one-man lap of honour with the Cup.

He says: "It was terrible. I was lynched, dragged, pushed, everything, and the Cup weighed a ton.

"That came on top of my goal when I dived behind Martin Chivers to head and got a big fist in an ear. My ankle got a nasty bang in the first half as well.

"But what a great finish to the season, which at one time was so depressing with my pelvic strain."

Clubs retain their home gates in the UEFA Cup and Spurs' income will be almost £150,000 of which the final leg realised nearly £48,000 – a record. But expenses are high, amounting to about £50,000.

Despite a poor domestic season, Spurs carried the English banner into Europe as defenders of the UEFA Cup.

RETROSPECTIVE VIEW BY STEVE PERRYMAN

"Bill Nicholson walked into the dressing room at 6.30pm to announce that Martin Peters had failed a fitness test and that I would be captain for the night and vice-captain of the club."

Steve Perryman, at the age of 21, was "shocked". He had become the youngest player to skipper Spurs in the history of the club, when he led the team in Europe against Lyn Oslo.

He served the club for 11 years as skipper when he eventually got the job on a permanent basis – not from Nicholson, who had groomed him carefully for leadership – but from Nicholson's successor Terry Neill, when Peters left the club.

Perryman made a fine start as Peters' understudy. Spurs won 6-3 in Norway.

"There were many experienced international players in that dressing room when Bill Nick walked in an hour before kick off. I'm sure Bill, in his wisdom, was looking to the future.

"I can remember wondering if there would be any resentment, but I am not sure whether I recall it or read it somewhere, that the players showed their delight by cheering.

"Certainly, I didn't know what captaincy was all about in those days, but it was a nice introduction, almost a carefully thought out baptism.

"Martin Peters was injured in our League game with West Ham, but he was soon back and the following season played 35 games, including captaining the team in the UEFA Cup final against Feyenoord.

"Bill Nick started the next season but didn't stay for very long. I don't think Terry Neill realised that I was club vice-captain when he appointed me skipper in succession to Martin."

Perryman's recollection of his first game as captain against Lyn Oslo was his surprise that the Norwegians managed to score against them!

Spurs had a happy knack of adjusting to a variety of Continental styles.

No matter how poor the club's League form, they seemed to come to life in Europe.

Perryman eventually played in more European campaigns than any other Tottenham player.

There is no-one more qualified to describe the special meaning of European football to Spurs.

"Foreign coaches would come to watch us play in a League game just before our European ties and we'd play badly and probably lose.

"They would go away thinking they've got nothing to beat. They would be shocked to think that our team could possibly have won the UEFA Cup.

"But European nights always brought the best out in our team. Somehow we produced something special.

"There was only one night I didn't think we deserved to go through. That was against Nantes, when Bill Nick had a furious row with Martin Chivers.

"We had an expertise of playing away. We'd go on our travels talking about concentrating on defence, getting behind the ball, and making sure we're safe . . . and score ourselves inside 10 minutes!

"Away goals are so vital. And scoring in Eastern bloc countries early on considerably eased the pressure.

"Sometimes, it seemed strange playing the away leg in the afternoons.

"It was also difficult to get used to some of the places, particularly behind the Iron Curtain. It made us appreciative of our own country and facilities.

"We'd always take our own food, even our own chef! Steak and cornflakes always went with us, plus, of course, tomato sauce."

Perryman praised the organisation of Nicholson and his assistant Eddie Baily on these trips.

"Eddie would come back with photos of the players we'd be up against.

"He'd always give a glowing report of the opposition, no doubt to keep us on our toes.

"Once, he returned from watching Tbilisi in Georgia, southern Russia and was adamant that we would not beat them.

"He went into raptures about their skills, their movement off the ball, everything he would like to see from his own team.

"Looking back, I'm convinced he was using a bit of kidology. Well, it worked. It motivated us.

"But Eddie was right in one respect: they were an outstanding team.

"We rose to the challenge and got through, in two excellent matches with the Russians."

Spurs' youngest captain, Steve Perryman, had his sports shop in Greenford; in the background is his father Ron.

Alan Gilzean on the mark.

DAILY MAIL, Thursday, September 14, 1972

LYN OSLO . . . 3 TOTTENHAM . . . 6

THE JOKERS!

Spurs circus stars settle for six goals

by JEFF POWELL

It was cabaret time in old Oslo last night. The Tottenham circus came to town to score six goals . . . but to let in half as many to keep the good people of Norway rolling in the aisles.

Spurs' defenders, trying to join their forwards in turning this into a UEFA Cup night of a thousand skills, were for a time almost a party to a bigger sensation than if the Christians had sorted out the lions in Rome.

Fantasia had nothing on the Nordic laugh-in. Little wonder Spurs' manager Bill Nicholson and assistant Eddie Baily were stunned by the way their team chose to begin the defence of the trophy.

For the sake of the game in Norway, perhaps it is just as well that Spurs showed the lighter side of England's Soccer character. A gate of fewer than 11,000 suggested that the public here had grown tired of seeing their gallant amateurs cut to pieces.

And not until the last ten minutes, when Martin Chivers at last broke his duck with two goals in two minutes, did the scoreline taken on the shape of a promised massacre.

Tottenham were a goal down in eight minutes as Pat Jennings was left unprotected and beaten by a chip from Austnes.

They replied through Martin Peters within 20 seconds and John Pratt put them ahead from 25 yards in the 24th minute. Before half-time, we were to be treated to the phenomenon of three goals in a minute – the 38th to be precise.

Alan Gilzean scored the first two of them after crosses by Ray Evans . . . But Christophersen put Lyn within two-goal touching distance at half-time.

Christophersen scored again in the 58th minute.

Through all this the giant England centre forward Martin Chivers had fumbled in vain for his goal-scoring touch. The famine ended in the 82nd minute with a header from a cross by Evans . . . then he struck again with a header from a Pearce centre.

Martin Peters equalises in Oslo.

The jokers!

Spurs circus stars settle for six goals

Lyn Oslo.........3 Tottenham.........6

From JEFF POWELL in OSLO

IT WAS cabaret time in old Oslo last night. The Tottenham circus came to town to score six goals . but to let in half as many to keep the good ... aisles.

their forwards in
ght of a thousand
to a bigger sensa-
out the lions in

n. Little
ssistant

THE goal-rush is on! Spurs skipper Martin Peters sweeps the ball past Lyn goalkeeper Sven Bjorn Olsen to open the account. Martin Chivers, following up behind Peters, approves. Olsen was beaten another five times.

SPURS' STARTING LINE-UP. Spurs began their defence of the UEFA Cup with the above line-up. Front row from the left: Perryman, Pearce, Pratt, England, Knowles, Naylor. Back row from the left: Gilzean, Jennings, Evans, Peters, Chivers.

DAILY MIRROR, 28 September, 1972

SPURS . . . 6 LYN (OSLO) . . . 0

AGG. 12-3

CHIVERS HITS HAT-TRICK

Now he waits for Sir Alf's verdict

By HARRY MILLER

Martin Chivers scores the first goal of his hat-trick against Lyn Oslo.

CHIVERS HITS HAT-TRICK

Now he waits for Sir Alf's verdict

By HARRY MILLER: Spurs 6, Lyn (Oslo) 0 Agg. 12-3

MARTIN CHIVERS, the man who waits more anxiously than most for the England squad Alf Ramsey names today, shot a European hat-trick last night.

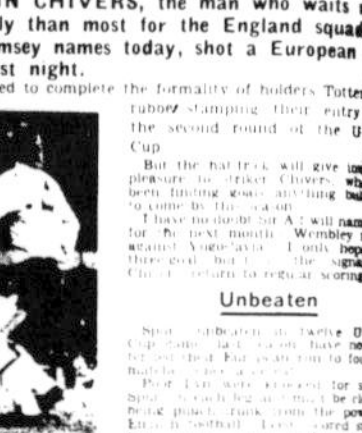

Unbeaten

Ralph Coates (No 11) thrilled at his goal—Spurs' sixth

casual side foot flick and it's a second goal for Spurs—and Martin Chivers—against Lyn (Oslo) in the UEFA Cup last night.

Oxford surge halted by sad Clarke's slip

WIGG RESCUES WATFORD'S HOME RECORD

Wrexham hit back—then Sutton strikes

REVIE'S GREAT GOAL SHOW FIZZLES OUT

Martin Chivers, the man who waits more anxiously than most for the England squad Sir Alf Ramsey names today, shot a European hat-trick last night.

It helped to complete the formality of holders Tottenham rubber-stamping their entry into the second round of the UEFA Cup.

But the hat-trick will give immense pleasure to striker Chivers, who has been finding goals anything but easy to come by this season.

I have no doubt Sir Alf will name him for the next month's Wembley match against Yugoslavia. I only hope this three-goal burst is the signal for Chivers' return to regular scoring.

Spurs, unbeaten in 12 UEFA Cup games last season, have now extended their European run to 14 matches since a defeat.

Poor Lyn were knocked for six by Spurs in each leg and must be close to being punch-drunk from the power of English football.

Chivers, who scored the last two goals in the 6-3 first leg win in Oslo, grabbed the first two last night.

The Norwegian amateurs held out for 20 minutes before Alan Gilzean, suspiciously offside, fastened on to a long clearance from Pat Jennings and banged a shot against Lyn 'keeper Sven Olsen. Chivers was there to drive in the rebound.

Thirteen minutes later John Pratt crossed accurately to the near post and Chivers, right-footed, flicked in the second goal.

With 53 minutes gone, the enterprising Gilzean headed down a cross from the right, and Ralph Coates sent a fierce left foot shot past Olsen.

Five minutes later, Jimmy Pearce put his name on the scorers' list with a superb right foot volley and Chivers shot his third in the 71st minute.

Tottenham had called off Pratt and Phil Beal and sent on substitutes Terry Naylor and Phil Holder by the time Coates completed the demolition job in the 83rd minute.

Cyril Knowles made the goal with a fine pass and Coates raced 20 yards to lash the ball wide of the luckless Olsen.

GUARDIAN, Thursday, October 26, 1972

TOTTENHAM H . . . 4 PIRAEUS . . . 0

SPURS SETTLE FOR FOUR

By DAVID LACEY

For once Tottenham punched their weight last night, with the result that their second round UEFA Cup tie against Olympiakos Piraeus looks by no means as difficult now as it did at the start of the week.

Spurs, the UEFA Cup holders will take a 4-0 lead to Athens for the second leg in a fortnight's time. They answered the muscular, not unskilled but often crude, challenge of the Greeks with football of renewed pace and rediscovered finishing power. In the past Tottenham have often pussyfooted with a packed defence; last night, with Coates, Evans, Perryman, and Knowles driving them forward, Chivers playing with much of his old confident power and Pearce always alert, they scarcely gave Olympiakos pause for breath.

The only fear about the next match from Tottenham's point of view is that it may explode into an ugly situation if the control is not firmer than it was last night. Alfred Delcourt, the Belgian referee, would have needed the visual qualities of an Argus to spot some of the shirt-pulling that was going on as the Greeks tried desperately to stop Tottenham from running away with the game; at the same time he appeared stricken with the limitations of a Cyclops as Gilzean was hacked at from behind by Glezos when he challenged the goalkeeper and barged bluntly off the ball by Sinetopoulos as he started to go up for a centre.

The guilt was not all Greek. Perryman hip-checked Gloustos sharply in the opening minutes, and Knowles made a dangerous open-studded challenge to the same player as both went up for the ball a little while later.

Neither did Delcourt distinguish himself over the penalty awarded to Tottenham on the house after Knowles, running long and clear into the penalty area was brought down by Glezos. Kelessidis, agile enough in the Olympiakos goal, was not so quick that he could reach Peters' kick without moving before it was taken and after he had saved the shot, the referee ordered it to be taken again. Once more Peters ran up, again the goalkeeper moved and again he saved, pushing the ball behind. But now the referee merely signalled a corner kick. Spurs seemed more perplexed than angry, as well they might, for by that time they were four goals up.

The first goal came in the twelfth minute, Chivers withstanding Siokos's challenge as he met Evans' centre and laying the ball off low for Pearce to score the first of his two goals. After 25 minutes Chivers himself added the second, rising in his old manner to meet Coates' cross and four minutes after half-time he laid on a third for Coates after Gilzean had intercepted a slack pass out of defence by his tormentor, Sinetopoulos. Pearce scored the fourth with a physically explosive shot a minute before the penalty incident.

For the last half-hour the Greek side played some clever football, Gloutsos and Delikaris moving the ball forward quickly and perceptively in mid-field, with Jennings being brought increasingly into action. It was all to no avail, but it did emphasise the value of Tottenham's lead. Tottenham made two substitutions late in the game, bringing on Naylor for Beal and Neighbour for Gilzean. Olympiakos replaced Vierra with Argiroudis at half-time and later Triantafilos with Losanta.

Martin Peters has a header cleared off the line

Spurs fear Greeks less even without gifts

By DAVID LACEY : Tottenham Hotspur 4, Olympiakos Piraeus 0

For once Tottenham punched their weight last night, with the result that their second round U E F A Cup tie against Olympiakos Piraeus looks by no means as difficult now as it did at the start of the week.

Spurs, holders of the cup, will take a 4-0 lead to Athens for the second leg in a fortnight. They answered the muscular, not unskilled but often crude challenge of the Greeks at White Hart Lane with football of renewed pace and rediscovered finishing power. In the past Tottenham have often pussyfooted with a packed defence. Last night with Coates, Evans, Perryman and K...

... and Knowles made a dangerous open-studed challenge to the same player as both went up for the ball, a little while later.

Neither did M. Delcourt distinguish himself over the penalty awarded to Tottenham on the hour after Knowles, running long and clear into the penalty area, was brought down by Glezos. Kelessidis, agile enough in the Olympiakos goal, was not so quick that he could reach Peters's kick without moving before it was taken and, after he had saved the shot, the referee ordered it to be taken again. Once more Peters ran up, once again the goal-keeper moved ...

... action. It was all to no avail b... it did emphasise the value ... Tottenham's lead.

Tottenham made two su... stitutions late in the game brin... ing on Naylor for Beal a... Neighbour for Gilzean. Oly... piakos replaced Vierra wi... Argiroudis at half-time and late... Triantafilos with Losanta.

Tottenham Hotspur. — Jennings, Evans, Knowles, Pearce, England, Bea..., Gilzean, Perryman, Chivers, Pete..., Coates.

Olympiakos. — Kelessidis; Gyatzi..., Angoulis, Siogos, Glezos, Sinetopoulo..., Papadimitriou, Gloutsos, Vierra, Bell..., aris, Triantasiolos.

Referee.—A. Delcourt (Belgium).

DAILY EXPRESS, Thursday, November 9, 1972

OLYMPIAKOS . . . 1 SPURS . . . 0

TIRED TOTTENHAM SOLDIER ON

From NORMAN GILLER

Tottenham shrugged and smiled in defeat here this afternoon like millionaires who have lost a little pocket money in a poker game.

They still held the winning hand at the finish, thanks to their overwhelming 4-0 victory against Olympiakos in the first leg of the UEFA Cup tie in London.

Spurs now go through to the last 16, but must considerably improve on this performance if they are to retain the trophy won with such style last season.

Manager Bill Nicholson said after the game: "We came here determined not to lose the lead we had built up in London. While we are never happy to lose, we are satisfied to be through to the next round."

This was Tottenham's sixth match in 14 days – and they played like tired men. They will remember the beautiful setting for the game rather than their contribution to it.

The historical harbour of Piraeus was just a goal kick away, but there was nothing pretty or spectacular about the football.

Tottenham concentrated on containing the Greeks and protecting their first leg lead. They were always cool and composed in the pressure-cooker atmosphere, but their attacking movements stuttered rather than flowed.

Mike Dillon and Terry Naylor were drafted into the defence after skipper Martin Peters had pulled out at the last minute with a stomach upset. Both Dillon and Naylor did well and it was not their fault that Spurs were trailing 1-0 at half-time.

Ray Evans had twice cleared off the line and it looked as if Tottenham were going to survive the first half without conceding a goal. Then goalkeeper Pat Jennings threw a goal into the lap of the Greeks.

Jennings, astonished even himself when he failed to gather a harmless-looking shot from Lossanta. He pushed the ball into the path of Argiroudis who had the simple job of jabbing the ball into the net.

It was the last kick of the first half and suddenly Spurs had to live on their nerves. But, with deputy captain Steve Perryman driving them on from his mid-field command post, Tottenham held together in a tense second half when the anxiety spilled over on to the touchline bench.

Nicholson and coach Eddie Baily were pelted with rubbish by the fanatical fans as they shouted orders to their players. Police moved in to protect them.

Martin Chivers produced two old-style moments of magic, once having the ball taken off his toes after a 40-yard run and then powering in a spectacular overhead shot that was turned off target.

Perryman and Alan Gilzean combined to give Chivers a clear sight of goal and his left foot shot thudded against a post.

But mainly it was a back-pedalling performance from Tottenham.

West German referee Hans Weiland handled the game firmly and fairly, but I thought he was harsh to book John Pratt for a tame first half tackle.

Tired Tottenham soldier on

From NORMAN GILLER
Olympiakos 1 Spurs 0

TOTTENHAM shrugged and smiled in defeat here this afternoon like millionaires who have lost a little pocket money in a poker game.

Mike England hobbling in what proved to be an ill-tempered match

TIMES, Thursday, November 30, 1972

TOTTENHAM . . . 2 RED STAR, BELGRADE . . . 0

SPURS GO FROM PROMISE TO FULFILMENT

By GEOFFREY GREEN

Martin Peters (right) exchanges pennants with the world-famous Yugoslav international Dragan Dzajic, captain of Red Star Belgrade

Tottenham Hotspur put a small blight upon Yugoslavia's Republic Day last night by their 2-0 win over Red Star at White Hart Lane. But there could still be a lot for them to do in Belgrade in the return match on December 13 if they are to retain their hold on this UEFA Cup. This tie is only at the half-way stage for a place in the quarter final round and a great deal can happen yet.

But Spurs need scarcely be warned. If this was only Red Star's second defeat in all the season they can be red hot at home as they have proved more than once and time may have shortened ahead for Tottenham. But looking at this Red Star side one can only appraise and approve. They are a group of talented technicians, possessing a fine ball control. All they truly lacked last night was a finishing punch inside the penalty area, where Lazarevic proved the main culprit.

If fame and merit are not necessarily compatible their football was certainly ordered, patterned and harmonious. It was Spurs who found an immediacy in a match which bore the dominating theme of attack in spite of Red Star's 5-2-3 formation. Not that this line-up was defensive in a physical way that British football knows. It was based on touch play with possession football at the heart of it.

But it was Tottenham, in the end, who moved from promise to achievement. We shall see in a fortnight's time whether fulfilment is to follow. You have got to play your own game in a world like this and play it properly or go to the wall. At least Spurs were true to themselves as they scored a goal midway through each half. The first breakthrough came at the twenty-sixth minute when Chivers, using his shoulders powerfully, put a low left foot shot inside the far post to complete a move between himself, Gilzean and Peters, who made the last diagonal pass while still on the ground.

No. 2 came 20 minutes after the interval when Peters again made the incision. Taking a long pass, as Knowles drove powerfully up the left flank, he centred from the left byline and there was the faithful Gilzean, always nosing around searching for the half-opening, who hit the roof of Petrovic's net with a swift shot. Around these two central points came a number of misses – four of them could be marked against Red Star and Lazarevic, Jankovic, Karasi and finally Novkovic, chipping over Jennings' bar from an open position to put his head in his hands, all threw away their openings.

12 THE TIMES THUR

SPORT

Football

Spurs go from promise to fulfilment

By Geoffrey Green
Football Correspondent

Tottenham 2 Red Star, Belgrade 0

Tottenham Hotspur put a small blight upon Yugoslavia's Republic Day last night by their 2—0 win over Red Star at White Hart Lane. But there could still be a lot for them to do in Belgrade in the return match on December 13 if they are to retain their hold on this UEFA Cup. This tie is only at the halfway stage for a place in the quarter final round and a great deal can happen yet.

But Spurs need scarcely be warned. If this was only Red Star's second defeat in all the season they can be red hot at home as they have proved more than once and time may have shortened ahead for Tottenham. But looking at this Red Star side one can only appraise and approve. They are a group of talented technicians, possessing a fine ball control. All they truly lacked last night was a finishing punch inside the penalty area, where Lazarevic proved the main culprit.

If fame and merit are not necessarily compatible their football was certainly ordered, patterned and harmonious. It was Spurs who found an immediacy in a match which bore the dominating theme of attack in spite of Red Star's 5-2-3 formation. Not that this line-up was defensive in a physical way that British football knows. It was based on touch play with possession football at the heart of it.

But it was Tottenham, in the end,

Gilzean seizes a half chance to strike a shot against a Red Star post.

self, Gilzean and Peters, who made the last diagonal pass while still on the ground.

No 2 came 20 minutes after the interval when Peters again made the incision. Taking a long pass, as Knowles drove powerfully up the left flank, he centred from the left by-line and there was the faithful Gilzean, always nosing around

who might have made it 3—0—blasted wildly over the bar from an open position. In the second half, too, there was a great save by Petrovic from Chivers as the centre forward—coming back to England form it seemed—powered his way through from the halfway line; at the other end in the dying minutes there was Jennings to keep out a

Tottenham's heroes were clearly Evans and Knowles well supported by Perryman and Peters in midfield with Chivers the power point up front.

The expected Red Star danger, Dzajic, who had torn England apart at Wembley last month, was continually seeking an outlet. But Evans remained a shadow to him

Alan Gilzean (right) foiled by Petrovic, the Red Star goalkeeper but:

Gilly scores the all-important second goal for Spurs

For Tottenham Pearce followed suit at the half hour shooting wildly from the right and later Gilzean – who might have made it 3-0 – blasted wildly over the bar from an open position. In the second half, too, there was a great save by Petrovic from Chivers as the centre forward – coming back to England form it seemed – powered his way through from the half-way line; at the other end in the dying minutes there was Jennings to keep out a cunning cross lob from Dzajic under the far angle. If that had gone in it would have meant a valuable away goal for the Slavs.

It was a fine match, hard, competitive but clean in spite of the fact that the names of Karasi and Knowles went into the French referee's book. Otherwise the official had little to do except keep his eyes sharp on a damp night where rain hung like a curtain for most of the second half as it swirled across the pitch.

Tottenham's heroes were clearly Evans and Knowles well supported by Perryman and Peters in mid-field with Chivers the power point up front.

The expected Red Star danger, Dzajic, who had torn England apart at Wembley last month, was continually seeking an outlet. But Evans remained a shadow to him sometimes behind but for most of the time containing him beautifully. This must have had a positive effect on the outcome. Krivokuca at right back, but playing right across the field, was unpredictable and impromptu.

DAILY EXPRESS, Thursday, December 14, 1972

RED STAR . . . 1 TOTTENHAM . . . 0

TOTTENHAM WIN 2-1 ON AGGREGATE

SPURS ECLIPSE RED STAR

Nick gambles – and Kinnear makes it pay

From NORMAN GILLER

BELGRADE, WEDNESDAY

Tottenham kept their grip on the UEFA Cup here today with one of the greatest defensive displays I have seen from a British team in Europe.

They lost today's battle 1-0 but the war was won by the two goals Tottenham collected in the first leg in London two weeks ago.

It took tremendous discipline and determination for them to survive to the quarter-finals against a team flowing with talent.

Manager Bill Nicholson was the mastermind behind the triumph.

He gambled by playing three full backs in the back line with Joe Kinnear given the sweeper role alongside commanding Mike England.

Transfer-seeking Kinnear did not know until 30 minutes before the kick off that he was playing. It was the first time he had performed in this central position and he did it with great skill and style.

He was always on hand to give support to any defender under pressure and showed sharp anticipation and tackling power in helping Ray Evans keep world star Dragan Dzajic under control.

Fans are lighting bonfires all around this giant concrete Red Star stadium but the flames are like a funeral pyre for their team.

Spurs came here without star striker Alan Gilzean and with Martin Chivers gamely playing despite an attack of 'flu.

But all the Tottenham players gave 100 per cent and then a little more to assert their authority over a team containing six full Yugoslav internationals.

It was a match to remember for Ralph Coates who sprinted marathon distances to help ease the pressure when Red Star were pressing for a second goal in the second half.

And John Pratt played like two men in midfield for Tottenham. He made a 40-yard run in the 34th minute which ended with him getting the ball in the net, a fist in the face and a booking.

Goalkeeper Petrovic came out to try and save at his feet but got kicked in the head as Pratt forced his way past and ran the ball into the net.

Italian referee Mario Gonela blew up for a foul on Petrovic and Pratt was punched and pummelled as he was surrounded by Red Star players.

Signor Gonela separated them like a boxing referee and booked Pratt and Red Star defender Dojcinovski.

Red Star showed more individual skill and finesse than can ever be seen in an English League match.

All their players were masters of ball control but they indulged in too much unnecessary dribbling which gave the Tottenham defenders time to regroup.

Red Star managed to create only one clear scoring chance in the first half. Centre forward Lazarevic fired a shot past Pat Jennings in the 28th minute but somehow the goalkeeper managed to reach back to turn the ball off target.

There was pandemonium when Lazarevic threatened to break Tottenham's command with a 48th-minute goal. He scored with a diving header after Evans had been dispossessed by the gifted Dzajic.

The 70,000 Yugoslav fans, silent through out most of the first half, stood waving banners and letting off fireworks for 10 full minutes as Red Star powered forward in search of an equaliser.

But the stadium was soon as quiet as a cemetery as Spurs buried this comeback with cool, controlled defensive work.

DISALLOWED. John Pratt has the ball in the net but the referee blew up for a foul on the goalkeeper

Lazarevic (centre) scores the only goal with a diving header in front of a 70,000 crowd but Spurs won the tie 2-1 on aggregate

Martin Peters has a shot blocked by the Setubal defence

DAILY MIRROR, Thursday, March 8, 1973

SPURS . . . 1 VITORIA SETUBAL . . . 0

SPURS 'SUB' HERO AGAIN

By HARRY MILLER

Ray Evans, the tall defender who talked of a transfer when he was omitted from Tottenham's League Cup final side, left the substitute's bench to become the hero of White Hart Lane last night.

Sent on in the seventy-sixth minute of this UEFA Cup quarter-final, he scored the only goal four minutes later.

It was like Saturday's final all over again – and Evans' goal may yet prove as valuable as the winner that Wembley substitute Ralph Coates scored against Norwich.

But Tottenham will go to Portugal for the return later this month knowing that they still have much to do before a semi-final place can be claimed.

Tottenham had seemed to be heading for the dubious distinction of failing for the first time to score in the home leg of a European tie.

When Alan Gilzean went off fourteen minutes from the finish, Jimmy Neighbour appeared the obvious choice to send on.

Instead, full back Evans – so unhappy at finding there was no room for him at Wembley – was pushed into the frenzied action.

He promptly showed the sort of determination that makes it easy to see why manager Bill Nicholson wants him to star with Spurs.

A long throw-in by Martin Chivers was nodded on by Martin Peters and then Evans stormed forward to head in off a post.

Up to then, Tottenham had hurled themselves at a Setubal defensive wall that looked more impregnable the longer the game went on.

Keeper Joaquim Torres was in constant and brave action as Tottenham sent a series of centres into a crowded goalmouth.

Chivers drove a fierce shot narrowly over the bar and Peters had another blocked just short of the line.

The aerial threat of big striker Jose Torres was limited by the pressure Setubal had to soak up. But he promises to cause all sorts of problems in the second leg.

Carrico was shown the yellow card as a caution for dissent after fouling Coates in one of the rare displays of temper by this disciplined Setubal side.

Setubal may well have cause to regret a bad last-minute miss by Conceicao.

He shot wide with only keeper Pat Jennings to beat.

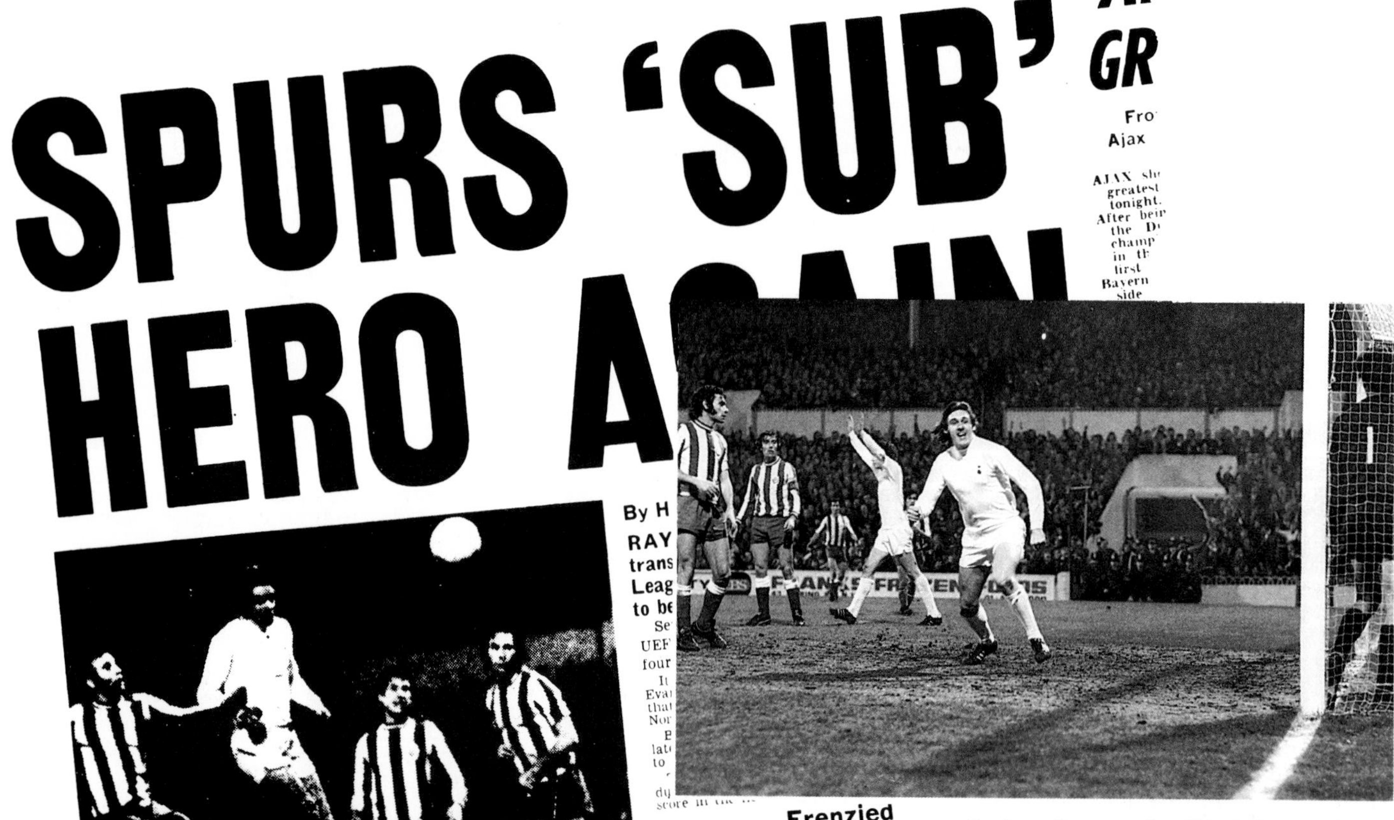
SPURS 'SUB' HERO A
Frenzied

Ray Evans (foreground) and Martin Peters with hands aloft celebrate Spurs' winning goal at White Hart Lane

DAILY MAIL, Thursday, March 22, 1973

VITORIA SETUBAL . . . 2 TOTTENHAM . . . 1

AGGREGATE 2-2. SPURS WIN ON AWAY GOALS

SPURS SNATCH IT

Chivers power-strike sinks Portuguese

By JEFF POWELL

One crushing blow from the right foot of Martin Chivers was just enough to spirit Tottenham above all the aggravation of this Portuguese night into the semi-finals of the UEFA Cup.

The England centre forward smote a 35-yard free kick high into the Vitoria Setubal net after 69 minutes to decide an apparently lost quarter-final for Spurs on the technicality of that one away goal.

Spurs, frustrated by a 15-minute delay at the start, looked in deep trouble after surrendering their slender quarter-final advantage after only 20 minutes.

The one goal they brought with them in defence of their European trophy was lost by the posse of Spurs defenders who hesitated over a freakish bounce of the feather-light ball.

England and Beal were at the heart of the confusion, between them failing to clear Joao's free kick.

There was a doubt about the justice of the German referee's decision against Gilzean's tackle, but there was no questioning the quality of the finishing shot.

Campora strode forward to swerve his drive past Jennings from 16 yards.

After their score, the vein of artistry running through the Portuguese team came richly to the surface. And Spurs, who knew they were facing one of the sternest examinations in their recent European history, were in all sorts of trouble.

One fast-hit shot by skipper Martin Peters was an isolated Tottenham threat in the first half.

The Portuguese were encouraged by a near-miss header from Joao and close range shots in quick succession from Turres and the Brazilian Duda which were blocked in front of a gaping Spurs goal.

Mike England, the one defender capable of dealing with Torres, was left limping by a late tackle from the giant centre forward. Spurs breathed more easily as England ran off the painful effects of that knock.

As Tottenham tackled and ran their way back into the match, Peters was booked for a foul on Rabelo, and Perryman was at the heart of a flare-up after Octavio had been floored.

Setubal climbed ahead in the 65th minute. Cardoso tempted Jennings into no man's land with a free kick, Duda headed down and Torres finished the business with his left foot.

But the phenomenal surge of Chivers' power secured Tottenham the priceless away goal four minutes later.

That awesome effort was greeted by a monumental silence.

Spurs snatch it

N'S SPORTING TYPES

'...stay in this ...ing, dear, got an... ...r important White ...aper to read'

TE WIRE

...from Doncaster: ...ARMAINE (3.0, RUGBY SPECIAL

Hector is the hero

BY JEFF FARMER

Derby ....2 Spartak Trnava ...0

Derby win on aggregate 2-1

DERBY moved into the European Cup semi-finals last night with a victory which owed more to their strength and determination than the skills which made them First Division champions.

Two goals from Kevin Hector—the first nudged over the line by his right knee, the second thumped home while all around him were arguing about a penalty claim—took Derby past the defiant challenge of a Spartak side who currently dominate Czech football.

Hector's priceless goals, which made Derby only the fifth English club to survive this far in the battle for Europe's crown, came in a 13-minute spell either side of the interval.

The first, which cannoned in off Hector as John McGovern's cross flew into the goalmouth, was the vital breakthrough after Derby had spent 39 minutes of uphill struggle against a splendidly organized defence.

Those of us who had rated the return leg a formality for Derby after watching Spartak perform so unimpressively during the one-goal win in Czechoslovakia soon

MARTIN CHIVERS . . . his goal puts Spurs into semi-finals .

MULLER GOALS NOT ENOUGH

WORLD CUP star Gerd Muller scored two first-half goals to give Bayern a 2—1 revenge win over Ajax Amsterdam in Munich.

But it was not enough to stop holders Ajax moving into the semi-finals of the European Cup. They had crushed the West German side 4—0 in the first leg two weeks ago.

Chivers power-strike sinks Portuguese

ONE crushing blow from the right foot of Martin Chivers was just enough to spirit Tottenham above all the aggravation of this Portuguese night into the semi-finals of the UEFA Cup.

The England centre-forward smote a 35-yard free-kick high into the Vitoria Setubal net after 69 minutes to decide an apparently lost quarter-final for Spurs on the technicality of that one away goal.

Vitoria Setubal ...... 2 Tottenham 1

(Aggregate 2—2. Spurs win on away goal)

BY JEFF POWELL

Spurs, frustrated by a 15-minute delay at the start, looked in deep trouble after surrendering their slender quarter-final advantage after only 20 minutes.

The one goal they brought with them in defence of their European trophy was lost by the posse of Spurs defenders who hesitated over a freakish bounce of the feather-light ball.

England and Beal were at the heart of the confusion, between them failing to clear Joao's free-kick.

There was a doubt about the justice of the German referee's decision against Gilzean's tackle, but there was no questioning the quality of the

to swerve his drive past Jennings from 16 yards.

After their score, the vein of artistry running through the Portuguese team came richly to the surface. And Spurs, who knew they were facing one of the sternest examinations in their recent European history, were in all sorts of trouble.

One fast-hit shot by skipper Martin Peters was an isolated Tottenham threat in the first half.

The Portuguese were en-

succession from T... and the Brazilian ... which were blocked ... front of a gaping S... goal.

Mike England, the ... defender capable of ...ing with Torres, was limping by a late ta... from the giant cen... forward. Spurs breat... more easily as Engl... ran off the painful effe... of that knock.

As Tottenham tack... and ran their way ba... into the match Peters wa...

DAILY MAIL, Wednesday, April 11, 1973

LIVERPOOL . . . 1 SPURS . . . 0

LINDSAY FREAK CHECK SPURS

By JEFF POWELL

The trainload of Londoners who cavorted away from Anfield last night would do well to remember that Spurs are no longer an irresistable force at White Hart Lane.

Liverpool strove frenziedly for the insurance of a second goal to take with them into the second leg of this semi-final in a fortnight.

But one freakish rebound off the shins of Alec Lindsay may yet prove enough to end Spurs' ownership of the UEFA Cup and send Liverpool into their second European final.

In a courageous performance by Spurs there is special praise for another, if less extravagant, performance by Pat Jennings.

There are honourable mentions in this dispatch for the desperate heroics of men like Mike England and John Pratt, who as Liverpool fragmented their defence resorted to putting their bodies painfully in the way of many thunderous shots.

There was some chagrin in the judgement by Liverpool manager Bill Shankly, who said: "We never stopped. We should have had a lot of goals.

Chivers bursts through only to be foiled by Ray Clemence

RETROSPECTIVE VIEW BY RAY CLEMENCE

Few players are better qualified than Ray Clemence to appreciate the true significance of nights of European glory.

"The highlight of my career," says Clemence, "was the night Liverpool won the European Cup in 1977."

Clemence can trace back Liverpool's domination of Europe to the time of a night of European misery for Spurs.

Clemence was in goal for Liverpool when Spurs were knocked out of the UEFA Cup at the semi-final stage in 1973.

Spurs, as UEFA Cup holders, lost on the away goal rule, ending a marathon run in Europe that had begun with a 6-1 win in Keflavik two years previously.

Suddenly Liverpool began to emerge as the real European force in English Soccer.

"I remember little about that UEFA Cup semi-final," admits Clemence, "apart from the fact that Steve Heighway had a habit of scoring at Tottenham in those days, and he did it again. That proved the vital away goal that took us through."

Clemence reflects on the significance of the victory. "Spurs had won the trophy the previous season and had a bigger reputation in Europe than ourselves."

Borussia Moenchengladbach beat FC Twente 5-1 on aggregate in the semi-finals to move on to face Liverpool at Anfield on 23 May, 1973 in front of 41,169 and were humbled 3-0 with Kevin Keegan scoring two.

Despite a 2-0 defeat 13 days later at Moenchengladbach with Heynckes scoring twice, Liverpool took the trophy.

But as champions, Liverpool entered the European Cup the next season going out to Red Star Belgrade in the second round, while Spurs went on to yet another UEFA Cup final finally losing to Feyenoord.

Finally, in Rome on May 25 before a 57,000 gate, Liverpool beat Borussia Moenchengladbach 3-1 to win Europe's greatest prize to begin an incredible domination of English clubs in the European Cup.

Liverpool retained the title of kings of Europe the following May, winning at Wembley against FC Bruges.

Nottingham Forest then won it in successive seasons beating Malmo and SV Hamburg, with Liverpool beating Real Madrid in 1981 and Aston Villa overcoming Bayern Munich in '82.

Villa fell to eventual finalists Juventus,

Daily Mail, Wednes...

Lindsay freak checks Spurs

Liverpool .... 1 Spurs .... 0 **By JEFF POWELL**

THE trainload of Londoners who cavorted away from Anfield last night would do well to remember that Spurs are no longer an irresistible force at White Hart Lane.

Liverpool strove frenziedly for the insurance of a second goal to take with them into the second leg of this semi-final in a fortnight.

But one freakish rebound off the shins of Alec Lindsay may yet prove enough to end Spurs' ownership of the UEFA Cup and send Liverpool into their second European final.

In a courageous performance by Spurs there is special praise for another, if less extravagant, performance by Pat Jennings.

ugh bargain buy ...2 m Europe test

From JEFF FARMER in Turin

"I thought the referee was good, but we should have had a penalty when Keegan was tripped."

That late and justified penalty claim for England's foul on Keegan was the last of the major incidents of a frantic night which happened too fast for the Swedish official.

Jennings, the Irish goalkeeper whose phenomenal performance in a League game on this ground ten days ago established him as a favourite to succeed Gordon Banks as Footballer-of-the-Year, made three more outstanding saves to justify the Kop's appreciation of his talent.

All came after the almighty 27th-minute scramble in which he was beaten. Jennings had blocked Smith's free kick and one of a cluster of Spurs defenders saw his attempted clearance ricochet off Liverpool full back Lindsay and deep into the corner of the net.

Spurs not only refused to lie down under pressure from Liverpool and the weight of the Anfield roar but also created fleeting chances of their own.

Chivers volleyed wide as he swept on to a marvellous pass from Peters. Coates fired over from an even better chance fashioned by Chivers and Gilzean.

The two forwards who missed those chances were taken off five minutes from time as manager Bill Nicholson sent on substitutes Evans and Pearce to relieve his beleaguered troops.

After watching his reshaped team survive the last perilous moments without further disaster Nicholson said, "I had hoped for a goal because away goals are so important in these competitions.

"But it is always hard at Liverpool and I suppose that in the circumstances I have to be happy with this result."

---

and in '84, Liverpool regained their crown on penalties against AS Roma, taking the title for the first time without Clemence in goal.

Bruce Grobbelaar had taken over from Clemence, who joined Spurs in a £300,000 deal in the summer of 1981.

Clemence says: "The 1977 year was vintage for Liverpool. We were going for the treble, and if any team was going to win everything in sight, it was us.

"We won the League, and then four days after losing the Cup final, we went to Rome for the European Cup. We proved that the treble is impossible.

"At that time we beat a very good side in Moechengladbach, but in the early '70s Bayern Munich, with Beckenbauer and Gerd Muller, were one of the best teams I ever faced in Europe.

"We were also shocked by the superb skills of Dinamo Tblisi, who knocked us out in the early rounds."

Clemence joined Spurs for "a new challenge" and found himself with new glories . . . UEFA Cup, FA Cup-winning medals and runners-up in the Milk Cup to add to his fabulous collection from Anfield.

"The last thing on my mind when we played Spurs in that semi-final was that one day I'd be joining them.

"I'd only been at Liverpool about six years, and only the past three in the first team.

"I enjoyed a great time at Anfield, but I've also had my memorable moments at Tottenham."

How do European nights at Anfield compare with White Hart Lane?

"When both clubs reached their heights the atmosphere was on a par. Night matches are always special, and European games that bit more special. In fact, there is nothing really to compare.

"In more recent years, it's been more special at Tottenham . . . because they've not had so many.

"At Liverpool, with almost 20 years in Europe, the fans have become more choosy and sometimes the terraces have been a little barren.

"Of course, we're all missing the European game now. The chance to pit your individual skill against the Continentals has always been the high point of a season for a player.

"It's fascinating to see the different styles and it provides a useful insight for international football."

DAILY MIRROR, Thursday, April 26, 1973

SPURS . . . 2 LIVERPOOL . . . 1

AGGREGATE 2-2 LIVERPOOL THROUGH ON AWAY GOALS

STEVE STUNNER KO'S SPURS

His goal worth double to cancel Peters' two UEFA Cup semi-final

By HARRY MILLER

Martin Peters (centre) nets Spurs' second goal

Two goals by Martin Peters and victory from a marvellous match were not enough last night to send Tottenham forward to a second successive UEFA Cup final.

Like so many fine sides before them, they became victims of the rule that says away goals count double.

So the one that Steve Heighway sandwiched between Peters' double blast puts Liverpool in sight of a fabulous double.

League champions in all but name, the Merseysiders now have the chance to win their first European trophy tackling West Germans Borussia Moenchengladbach in the two legged final next month.

They were cheered on the pitch for this semi-final second leg by a sporting 46,919 crowd and cheered off after going to the centre circle to salute the fans.

Pat Jennings dives in vain as Steve Heighway scores the away goal which knocked the holders out of the UEFA Cup

STD code 01—353 0246

STEVE STUNNER KO's SPURS

High and handsome—Heighway's winner.

UEFA Cup semi-final

By HARRY MILLER

Spurs 2, Liverpool 1

His goal worth double to cancel Peters' two

TWO goals by Martin Peters and victory from a marvellous match were not enough last night to send Tottenham forward to a second successive U E F A Cup Final.

Like so many fine sides before them, they became victims of the rule that says away goals count double.

Gruelling

Tottenham won the League Cup-tie in a replay and Liverpool will regard this triumph as ample revenge.

High and inspiring—that's Peters' first goal

A long Chivers throw to the near post was headed across goal by Alan Gilzean and in zoomed Peters to hook the ball wide of Ray Clemence.

As they kept going forward with a frenzied wave of attacks, Mike England was caught upfield unable to cut out an Emlyn Hughes clearance.

Kevin Keegan raced on to the ball and his low cross into the goal-mouth was carefully side-footed in by Heighway.

Joe Kinnear limped out of the action in the 70th minute to be replaced by Ray Evans and Tottenham came alive again with Peters' second goal one minute later.

A Gilzean header and a Pratt shot were blocked following a Cyril Knowles cross before Peters crashed the ball into the roof of the net.

FOUR MEN HANGED

Three Africans and coloured man convicted of separate murders hanged in Pretoria, South Africa

WHAT A WEEK—SHANKLY

BILL SHANKLY, Liverpool boss, said: "It's been a tremendous week for us. The players are getting their reward for the season's work over more than sixty matches.

"Now the big thing for us is to get home and play before our fans on Saturday. I'm confident we can complete the Championship - U E F A Cup double."

Martin Peters said: "It's disappointing to lose on an away goal, but we won that way in the last round against Setubal. Liverpool are a great side and if we had to lose the cup to any team, I'm glad it's them."

Somehow their gesture symbolised the four tremendous Cup games these clubs have played this gruelling season.

Tottenham won the League Cup tie in a replay and Liverpool will regard this triumph as ample revenge.

But Tottenham should emerge from defeat with heads held high.

They went into the match seeking an early goal to wipe out the 1-0 lead Liverpool brought from Anfield.

The leveller for which they fought so hard came in the 48th minute. A long Chivers throw to the near post was headed across goal by Alan Gilzean and in zoomed Peters to hook the ball wide of Ray Clemence.

As they kept going forward with a frenzied wave of attacks, Mike England was caught up-field unable to cut out an Emlyn Hughes clearance.

Kevin Keegan raced onto the ball and his low cross into the goalmouth was carefully side-footed in by Heighway.

Joe Kinnear limped out of the action in the 70th minute to be replaced by Ray Evans and Tottenham came alive again with Peters' second goal one minute later.

A Gilzean header and a Pratt shot were blocked following a Cyril Knowles cross before Peters crashed the ball into the roof of the net.

Ray Clemence has the ball firmly in his grasp whilst under pressure from Gilzean and Peters

SUNDAY TIMES, March 4, 1973

TOTTENHAM HOTSPUR . . . 1 NORWICH CITY . . . 0

JUST ANOTHER TROPHY TO SPURS

Thank heaven for Coates, who saved us from a replay

By BRIAN GLANVILLE

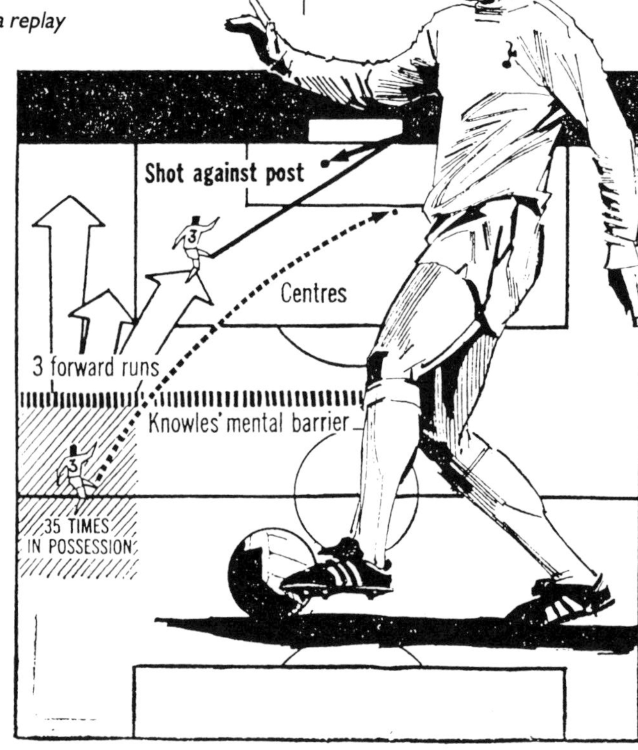

If you are one for true romance, schoolboy heroics and stones that the builder rejected, perhaps you will indulge and excuse this awful League Cup final for the sake of Ralph Coates. Coates it was who was so bitter at not being chosen originally to play; Coates it was who came, bald and bustling, off the substitutes' bench in the first half, and Coates it was who scored the solitary goal. Thank heaven for Coates, who saved us from having to go through the whole tedious business again.

On the face of it, the Football League's decision to allow no extra time seemed irresponsible in the extreme, a piece of gratuitous selfishness at a time when there is already far too much football. In retrospect, perhaps they had some premonition that this match would be so abysmally mediocre that it was hard enough to bear the 90 minutes, let alone an additional half-hour.

For this Tottenham, the team with far the higher potential, must take the greater share of the blame. Nor can they offer the excuse that they were disrupted by the injury to Pratt, mid-way through the first half, which caused them to bring on their eventual hero, Coates. Even by that point, their mid-field had been palpably found wanting, though certainly it got no better thereafter.

Peters' contributions, though something polished, were as rare as they so often are. He is not a general, a player who can take steady control of a game, but rather one who can occasionally turn it on a sudden inspiration. It must be admitted and remembered that it was his header which in turn was headed off the line by Forbes in the first half, his header, again, which paved the way for Coates to score.

Perryman, for the moment, lacks the depth to be an orchestrator; to supply the chances which Chivers and Gilzean looked tantalisingly capable of taking. There was the mystery, too, of why Knowles was so reluctant to overlap against such cautious opposition.

THE WINNING LINE-UP: Martin Peters lifts the League Cup for 1973 and Spurs are back in Europe. Back row from the left: Pratt (who was injured and substituted after 25 minutes), Knowles, Jennings, Peters, England, Perryman, manager Bill Nicholson, coach Eddie Baily, Chivers, Gilzean. Front row from the left: Coates (who came on as substitute and scored the only goal), Kinnear, Pearce, Beal

Just another trophy to Spurs

Brian Glanville thanks heaven for Coates, who saved us from a replay

Tottenham Hotspur 1   Norwich City 0

IF YOU ARE one for true romance, schoolboy heroics and stones that the builder rejected, perhaps you will indulge and excuse this awful League Cup Final for the sake of Ralph Coates. Coates it was who was so bitter at not being chosen originally to play; Coates it was who came, bald and bustling, off the substitutes' bench in the first half, and Coates it was who scored the solitary goal. Thank heaven for Coates, who saved us from having to go through the whole tedious business again.

On the face of it, the Football League's decision to allow no extra time seemed irresponsible in the extreme, a piece of gratuitous selfishness at a time when there is already far too much football. In retrospect, perhaps they had some premonition that this match would be so abysmally mediocre that it was hard enough to bear the 90 minutes, let alone an additional half hour.

For this Tottenham, the team with far the higher potential, must take the greater share of the blame. Nor can they offer the excuse that they were disrupted by the injury to Pratt, midway through the first half, which caused them to bring on their eventual hero, Coates. Even by that point, their midfield had been palpably found wanting, though certainly it got no better thereafter.

Peters' contributions, though something polished, were as rare as they so often are. He is not a general, a player who can take steady control of a game, but rather one who can occasionally turn it on a sudden inspiration. It must be admitted and remembered that it was his header which in turn was headed off the line by Forbes in the first half, his header, again, which paved the way for Coates to score.

Perryman, for the moment, lacks the depth to be an orchestrator; to supply the chances which Chivers and Gilzean looked tantalisingly capable of taking. There was the mystery, too, of why Knowles was so reluctant to overlap against such cautious opposition.

As one has remarked before, the present Norwich side, however successful, has none of the endearing characteristics of some of its postwar predecessors, those teams which had such exciting FA Cup runs in the early and late 1950s. They have a very proper, even an exaggerated, awareness of their own technical shortcomings, and cut their coat most narrowly according to their cloth.

They are, in fact inclined, as they were yesterday, to be a functional and unenterprising bore, a team dourly committed to the most parsimonious of 4-4-2 formations. This is a great pity because they have, in Anderson, one of their four midfield men, a natural winger who can, if given the chance, roast a fullback with the best of them.

There is another talented player in the midfield phalanx in the blond Paddon, but he, again, simply doesn't get sufficient opportunity to go forward and make it count; all the less on this huge expanse of Wembley. Blair and Cross, the two front runners, are precisely that: runners, chasers without subtlety who hope endlessly for the best.

It says much for the drab quality of their team's play that it was well into the second half before the Norwich fans raised their vigorous, traditional chorus of: "On the ball the City. Never mind the danger!"

It was after 24 minutes that Pratt, who had collapsed and had treatment a little earlier, clutching his groin, hobbled off the field and gave way to Coates. Three minutes later, the boredom was at last relieved by the prospect of a goal; though it required the complicity of some very poor goalkeeping to bring it about. Chivers took one of his mighty soaring throws in from the right, Keelan dashed out and merely flapped at it. Peters headed over him into the goalmouth, but Forbes, jumping on the line with other defenders, resourcefully headed away.

After 35 minutes Keelan, who had by now settled down to catch the ball authoritatively, more than redeemed his lapse. Once again, a long throw from the right by Chivers made the chance. Gilzean, that inextinguishable wizard, turned cunningly on the ball at the near post to leave Stringer helpless, then shot. Keelan took it with splendid solidity.

By now, Tottenham were at last beginning to deploy their superior skills and imagination. Norwich were still quick and forceful in the breakaway, but just before the interval their defence was caught ominously square. Knowles and Pearce sent Chivers through a gap on the left, Butler racing to the rescue with a brave tackle. Gilzean then touched Pearce's left-wing corner neatly back to England, whose powerful first-time shot flew just over the top.

We had to wait until the 27th minute of the second half before there was the ghost of another goal; and prophetically, it was Coates who made the running. He had a fine long burst down the right wing, past Butler, was brought down, but squeezed the ball to Peters. The inside left crossed, the ball skimmed Forbes's head, and Pearce met it to graze the outside of the left hand post.

Ninety seconds more, and we at last had the solace of a goal. Inevitably, it was a throw by Chivers which began it, this time from out on the left. Peters, at the near post, nodded it across goal, Gilzean helped it on its way, England swung at it and missed, and the Norwich defenders were caught off balance as Coates drove home a smashing cross shot.

In the 88th minute, there was almost another Tottenham goal, as Norwich belatedly flung themselves into attack, and left gaps in the process. Away came Tottenham down the left, Knowles at long last went through on the overlap, received from Pearce, and shot low across a remarkably tardy Keelan. The ball went under his dive, hit the base of the far post, and rebounded. So Tottenham, that endless devourer of trophies, have regained the League Cup after lending it for a year to Stoke City.

Weather: bleak. **Ground:** firm.
Goals: Coates (73min).
Tottenham Hotspur (4-3-3): Jennings; Kinnear, England, Beal, Knowles; Pratt (sub. Coates, 24min), Perryman, Peters; Gilzean, Chivers, Pearce.
Norwich City (4-4-2): Keelan; Payne, Stringer, Forbes, Butler; Briggs, Livermore, Paddon, Anderson; Blair (sub. Howard, 79min), Cross.
Referee: D. Smith (Gloucestershire).

Quiet one, Cyril. Quiet one, son

by Brian James

THERE WERE just a few half-embarrassed choruses yesterday of "Nice one, Cyril," the pop song devoted to the exploits of Cyril Knowles. For Knowles himself was strikingly out of tune. The wide inviting spaces of Wembley, and the lack of ... Norwich, had seemed to ...

zean and Peters, was the sum of Spurs' advantage from the 35 passes he prodded, or lobbed forward.

Only twice in the match did he allow himself forward to a point within 15 yards of the corner flag—usually his favourite haunt ...

As one has remarked before, the present Norwich side, however successful, has none of the endearing characteristics of some of its postwar predecessors, those teams which had such exciting FA Cup runs in the early and late 1950s. They have a very proper, even an exaggerated, awareness of their own technical shortcomings, and cut their coat most narrowly according to their cloth.

They are, in fact inclined, as they were yesterday, to be a functional and unenterprising bore, a team dourly committed to the most parsimonious of 4-4-2 formations. This is a great pity because they have, in Anderson, one of their four mid-field men, a natural winger who can, if given the chance, roast a full back with the best of them.

There is another talented player in the mid-field phalanx in the blond Paddon, but he, again, simply doesn't get sufficient opportunity to go forward and make it count; all the less on this huge expanse of Wembley. Blair and Cross, the two front runners, are precisely that: runners, chasers without subtlety who hope endlessly for the best.

It says much for the drab quality of their team's play that it was well into the second half before the Norwich fans raised their vigorous, traditional chorus of: "On the ball the City. Never mind the danger!"

It was after 24 minutes that Pratt, who had collapsed and had treatment a little earlier, hobbled off the field clutching his groin, and gave way to Coates. Three minutes later, the boredom was at last relieved by the prospect of a goal; though it required the complicity of some very poor goalkeeping to bring it about. Chivers took one of his mighty soaring throws in from the right, Keelan dashed out and merely flapped at it. Peters headed over him into the goalmouth, but Forbes, jumping on the line with other defenders, resourcefully headed away.

After 35 minutes Keelan, who had by now settled down to catch the ball authoritatively, more than redeemed his lapse. Once again, a long throw from the right by Chivers made the chance. Gilzean, that inextinguishable wizard, turned cunningly on the ball at the near post to leave Stringer helpless, then shot. Keelan took it with splendid solidity.

By now, Tottenham were at last beginning to deploy their superior skills and imagination. Norwich were still quick and forceful in the breakway, but just before the interval their defence was caught ominously square. Knowles and Pearce sent Chivers through a gap on the left, Butler racing to the rescue with a brave tackle. Gilzean then touched Pearce's left wing corner neatly back to England, whose powerful first-time shot flew just over the top.

We had to wait until the 27th minute of the second half before there was the ghost of another goal; and prophetically, it was Coates who made the running. He had a fine long burst down the right wing, past Butler, was brought down, but squeezed the ball to Peters. The inside left crossed, the ball skimmed Forbes' head, and Pearce met it to graze the outside of the left hand post.

Ninety seconds more, and we at last had the solace of a goal. Inevitably, it was a throw by Chivers which began it, this time from out on the left; Peters, at the near post, nodded it across goal, Gilzean helped it on its way, England swung at it and missed, and the Norwich defenders were caught off balance as Coates drove home a smashing cross-shot.

In the 88th minute, there was almost another Tottenham goal, as Norwich belatedly flung themselves into attack, and left gaps in the process. Away came Tottenham down the left, Knowles at long last went through on the overlap, received from Pearce, and shot low across a remarkably tardy Keelan. The ball went under his dive, hit the base of the far post, and rebounded. So Tottenham, that endless devourer of trophies, have regained the League Cup after lending it for a year to Stoke City.

And so Spurs, knocked out of Europe by an English team, proved their indomitable spirit and, having won the League Cup, moved back into Europe.

DAILY EXPRESS, Thursday, September 20, 1973

GRASSHOPPERS . . . 1 TOTTENHAM . . . 5

THANKS, JENNINGS

By NORMAN GILLER

ZURICH, WEDNESDAY

Daft as it sounds, Tottenham owe this 5-1 UEFA Cup first round first leg victory to goalkeeper Pat Jennings.

Grasshoppers, an imaginative team of part-time professionals, might easily have emerged as 6-5 winners but for the genius of Jennings.

The Tottenham defenders should have a whip round and hand their win bonuses to a player the Swiss fans are tonight describing as "even better than Gordon Banks."

Jennings made a dozen superb saves as the Tottenham defence was continually driven to disorder during a rush-hour of attacks by the fast, skilful Grasshoppers forwards.

It was a traumatic experience for centre half Mike England who was having his first major match since a cartilage operation eight weeks ago.

England got something more than the match action he was seeking in his bid to regain full fitness before joining the Wales World Cup campaign against Poland next week.

It was not until veteran Alan Gilzean was summoned from the substitutes' bench in the 62nd minute that Tottenham at last took command of a match of many moods and movements.

Martin Chivers had given Spurs a smart start, heading in a Cyril Knowles free kick in the fifth minute.

Jennings was left as exposed as a man facing a firing squad for the next 25 minutes. He smothered shots from all angles and it was right against the run of play when Ray Evans hammered a shot low into the Grasshoppers net after neat combination between John Pratt and Ralph Coates in the 31st minute.

The gallant Grasshoppers finally found a way past Jennings from the penalty spot in the 43rd minute, Adolf Noventa scoring after Jimmy Neighbour had handled.

Stocky Phil Holder substituted for Coates (sprained ankle) in the second half and brought much-needed urgency to a defence that was in danger of a complete breakdown.

Jennings was taking Grasshoppers on again single-handed and made four more flying saves before the cultured Gilzean came on for Neighbour.

A mighty Jennings clearance opened the way for Chivers to make it 3-1 in the 76th minute.

Then Gilzean glided on to the scoring scene with superbly-taken goals in the 80th and 85th minutes with the Grasshoppers defence looking even more distressed than Tottenham's.

Tottenham's forwards must have felt they were seeing double at times. Identical twins Hans Niggl and Thomas Niggl were partners at the back of a Grasshoppers defence that was continuously in trouble because of being too adventurous.

Spurs' manager Bill Nicholson admitted later: "It could have been a much different story but for Pat Jennings. He played a blinder. Grasshoppers were brilliant at times and could have been 3-1 up at one stage."

Ralph Coates bursts through to shoot at goal

Pat Jennings to the rescue—saving from Ove Grahn

Thanks, Jennings

ZURICH, Wednesday: — Daft as it sounds, Tottenham owe this 5 — 1 U.E.F.A. Cup first round first leg victory to goalkeeper Pat Jennings.

Grasshoppers, an imaginative team of part-time professionals, might easily have emerged as 6-5 winners but for the genius of Jennings.

The Tottenham defenders should have a whip ...

By Norman Giller: Grasshoppers 1 Tottenham 5

... ence for centre-half Mike England, who was having his first major match since a cartilage operation eight weeks ago.

England got something more than the match action he was seeking in his bid to regain full fitness before joining the Wales World Cup campaign against Poland next week.

In command

... for the next 25 minutes. He smothered shots from all angles and it was right against the run of play when RAY EVANS hammered a shot low into the Grasshoppers' net after neat combination between John Pratt and Ralph Coates in the 31st minute.

The gallant Grasshoppers finally found a way past Jennings from the penalty spot in the 43rd minute, ADOLF NOVENTA scoring after Jimmy Neighbour had ...

A mighty Jennings clearance opened the way for CHIVERS to make it 3-1 in the 76th minute.

Then GILZEAN glided on to the scoring scene with superbly taken goals in the 80th and 85th minutes with the Grasshoppers defence looking even more distressed than Tottenham's.

Tottenham's forwards must have felt they were seeing double at times. Identical twins Hans Niggl and Thomas Niggl were partners at the back of a Grasshoppers ... nce that was continually ...

DAILY TELEGRAPH, Thursday, October 4, 1973

TOTTENHAM HOTSPUR . . . 4 GRASSHOPPERS ZURICH . . . 1

TOTTENHAM WIN 9-2 ON AGGREGATE

SPURS KEEP EUROPEAN RECORD BUT ARE FLATTERED

By ROBERT OXBY

Scoring their last three goals in the last 16 minutes, Tottenham gained another flattering result in their UEFA Cup first round tie at White Hart Lane last night. The Grasshoppers defence cracked again after they had led from the 24th minute.

Until Lador turned a low cross from Evans into his own goal in the 74th minute, the gallant Swiss, with four reserves, had seemed likely to become the first team to win a European leg at White Hart Lane.

As in Zurich two weeks ago, however, their part-timers tired in the last quarter, and Evans was able to achieve a remarkable "hat-trick" of assists. The first three goals came from his crosses, and one from Knowles, his full back partner, brought the fourth.

Earlier, Becker and Elsener showed all the striking skill and footwork which forced Pat Jennings, the Spurs goalkeeper, into such stupendous form in the first leg. Last night, however, despite Elsener's 24-minute goal, they felt the paucity of opportunities from their reserve mid-field men.

Grasshoppers, who had to leave out their injured mid-field players Noventa, Grahn and Olhauser, brought in Capro and Lador for their senior debuts. But they took the game to Spurs, and only a save on the line by Daines prevented a goal by Becker in the fifth minute.

Spurs responded with intense mid-field pressure, but their attacks lacked penetration. Grasshoppers' goal followed a superb dribble by young Becker, who beat three men before interchanging with Elsener.

The Swiss defenders, who capsized so badly in the second half in Zurich, soon showed how their covering had improved as Spurs at last hit them with strong attacks in the second half. The Niggl twins were constantly prominent at the back.

Deck made a fine falling save from Coates, who also had a shot blocked, and from an astute running header by Gilzean, Peters produced an acrobatic bicycle kick and the ball sped inches wide of the goal. On the hour Chivers was just wide with a shot on the turn.

But Grasshoppers remained dangerous with their ability to break away from deeper positions, and Meyer, who had joined Becker and Elsener up front, shot wildly over when he had only Daines to beat.

The Swiss defence cracked at last in the 74th minute when Evans centred low and hard from the right. Challenged by Knowles, the unfortunate Lador could only steer the ball past his own goalkeeper.

Six minutes later, Deck could only beat out a fierce shot from Evans to the oncoming Peters, who put Spurs ahead. England scored the third in the 86th minute, and Peters' header in the 89th minute made it a flattering 4-1.

Alan Gilzean outjumps a Grasshop pers defender to get in his header.

Spurs keep European record but are flattered

FOOTBALL RESULTS

EUROPEAN CUP
1st Rd, 2nd Leg

CELTIC ...(2) 3 TPS Turku (0) 0
Deans —18,000
Johnstone 2
(Celtic win 9-1 on agg.)
DINAMO CRUSADERS (0) 0
BUCH'ST (4) 11
Georgescu 4
Nunweiler 4 —10,000
Dumitrache
Dinu

By ROBERT OXBY

Tottenham Hotspur ... 4 Grasshoppers (Zurich) ... 1
(Tottenham win 9-2 on aggregate)

SCORING their last three goals in the last 16 minutes, Tottenham gained another flattering result in their UEFA Cup first-round tie at White Hart Lane last night. The Grasshoppers' defence cracked again after they had led from the 24th

Overweight Best

DAILY EXPRESS, Thursday, October 25, 1973

ABERDEEN . . . 1 SPURS . . . 1

PENALTY BLOW CAN END SPURS EUROPE BID

By STEVE CURRY

Trevor Whyma

most promis... was led off with his righ... arm in a sling.

Penalty blow can end Spurs Europe bid

By Steve Curry: Aberdeen 1 Spurs 1

TOTTENHAM HOTSPUR last night conceded a penalty two minutes from time at Aberdeen—a goal that diminished their chances of a future in Europe.

A rare goal from Ralp...

Tottenham Hotspur last night conceded a penalty two minutes from time at Aberdeen – a goal that diminished their chances of a future in Europe.

A rare goal from Ralph Coates in the 15th minute had looked to be enough to ensure Spurs' passage into the third round of the UEFA Cup.

But as the Scots pressed for an equaliser, Spurs' full back Ray Evans nudged substitute Berty Miller two yards inside the area and Jim Hermiston drove the penalty kick beyond Spurs' deputy 'keeper Barry Daines.

Spurs began without three internationals – Pat Jennings, Cyril Knowles and Martin Chivers. And during the course of the game lost another two internationals – Joe Kinnear and Coates – through injury.

There were times during this lively game when Spurs' authority seemed beyond challenge.

They took the lead in the 15th minute. Alan Gilzean headed into a ruck of players, McGrath released the ball for Ralph Coates to drive the ball into the net.

But Spurs' defensive strength was upset in the 34th minute when Kinnear was carried off.

In the second half Spurs' general lack of confidence this season became apparent. Mike England had to make a lunging clearance when Joe Smith broke through in the 49th minute. Ray Evans had to clear off the line from a Willie Young header to a left wing corner two minutes later.

Ralph Coates seen giving Spurs the lead against Aberdeen in Scotland.

DAILY MIRROR, Thursday, November 8, 1973

SPURS . . . 4 ABERDEEN . . . 1

AGG. 5-2

PADDY THE SUPER SUB

McGrath hits great double to clinch win for Spurs

By NIGEL CLARKE

Paddy McGrath scored his first goals for Tottenham to clinch this second round UEFA Cup tie at White Hart Lane last night.

The eighteen-year old Irish striker struck twice in nine minutes after coming on as a seventy-first minute substitute for Jimmy Neighbour.

His first goal in the eightieth minute came when Aberdeen, 2-1 down and 3-2 behind on aggregate, were causing Spurs all kinds of problems.

Martin Chivers crossed, Martin Peters headed the ball down, Cyril Knowles flicked it on and McGrath turned it joyously into the net.

McGrath struck again a minute from time. He danced past David Robb with clever footwork and then drove a shot beneath goalkeeper Bobby Clark.

Spurs, with Chivers back after injury, had taken the lead after fourteen minutes.

Ray Evans' low cross was back-heeled by Peters, the ball hit Willie Miller and Peters reacted instantly to half-volley past Clark from fifteen yards.

But Spurs showed none of the sophistication that has been a feature of their European campaigns.

They allowed Aberdeen to upset them with quick breaks and twice before half-time the Scots came so close to a goal.

After sixteen minutes Spurs survived a penalty score when Evans clearly tripped Drew Jarvie.

Referee Kurt Tschenscher pointed to the spot but Spurs protested passionately, with Chivers racing fifty yards back from the half way line to join in.

They persuaded the West German official to consult a linesman who had been flagging. And after the brief consultation Aberdeen were waved aside, presumably because Jarvie was offside.

Then on the half-hour goalkeeper Pat Jennings had to save bravely at Jarvie's feet, and a brilliant move set up a chance for Alex Willoughby that the winger curled only inches wide.

Spurs came back to score again in the thirty-seventh minute. Chivers headed down Mike England's cross and as Eddie Thomson failed to clear, Neighbour side-footed the ball home.

Chivers was then involved in a barging match with Thomson that needed teammates to separate them. Both were booked.

Aberdeen got the goal they deserved nine minutes after half-time to throw the match wide open again.

Willoughby, who had missed another fine chance, brilliantly crossed on the half volley and Jarvie closed in to score off the far post.

Another goal then would have put Aberdeen ahead on aggregate because of the away goals ruling.

Chris McGrath (white shirt) beats Aberdeen goalkeeper Bobby Clark to score Spurs' third goal.

Thursday,
Telephone: (STD code 01)—

team—out of the UEFA Cup 6—1 on

full report to

PADDY THE SUPER SUB

By NIGEL CLARKE

Spurs 4, Aberdeen 1 (agg. 5-2)

PADDY McGRATH scored his first goals for Tottenham to clinch this second round UEFA Cup-tie at White Hart Lane last night.

The eighteen-year-old Irish striker struck twice in nine minutes after coming on as a seventy-first minute substitute for Jimmy Neighbour.

UPR

Cha

DAILY MIRROR, Thursday, November 29, 1973

TBILISI . . . 1 TOTTENHAM . . . 1

COATES' CANNON

Spurs battle on

From HARRY MILLER

IN RUSSIA

Ralph Coates and Pat Jennings showed the Soviet Union yesterday what heroes of Soccer are all about as Tottenham achieved a magnificent UEFA Cup result.

On a rubble-heap of a pitch deep in the heart of Georgia, Coates scored the goal that should give Tottenham the impetus to go through to the quarter-finals of this competition.

"It was the best goal I've ever scored," he said. "It was particularly pleasing because it was with my left foot and I've been practising my shooting all week."

Coates' goal came in the twenty-fifth minute of a match that was a credit to the now rather tarnished ideals of European football. And it was at that important point that Jennings took over.

He repelled a stream of Tbilisi attacks with some splendid saves until Kakhi Asatiani beat him seventeen minutes from the end.

The glum looks of these normally happy Georgian fans told its own story as they filed from the ground. With away goals counting double they knew that Tottenham had done enough.

Coates did more than score a goal of goldmine value. He had the sort of game that was almost a public message to manager Bill Nicholson.

"Sell me if you dare," might have been echoing round the mountains that surround all four sides of the picturesque Locomotive Stadium.

There has been mounting speculation in the past fortnight that Nicholson might use Coates as bait for Sunderland's transfer-listed Dennis Tueart.

Coates demonstrated all that was best about Tottenham's performance yesterday. Twice in his own penalty area he made successful tackles to kill off Tbilisi.

Terry Naylor was brought in to reinforce the mid-field at the expense of Alan Gilzean and, with Martin Chivers striking from deep

COATES' CANNON

Spurs battle on

and, with Martin Chivers striking from deep positions there was often only superb skipper Martin Peters left up front.

It was a triumph for Tottenham after the disappointing 3—1 crash to Wolves last Saturday.

John Pratt, disgracefully heckled by Tottenham's supporters and pulled off in that match, had a fine game 2,500 miles from home. So did Naylor and Steve Perryman.

Chivers so nearly scored with a glancing header before Coates struck after twenty-five minutes. Chivers neatly laid-off a Mike England pass and Coates found the net with a ferocious twenty-yard drive.

Rapturous

The Russians lost a lot of their legendary discipline for a while after that. But they should have scored just before half-time when David Kipiani broke clear and shot wide with only Jennings to beat.

It was different in the second-half as the Russians finally got shots on target.

Jennings saved brilliantly from Murtaz Khurtsilava, captain of the Russian national side, and from Manutvar [illegible] twice. They were saves that brought gasps of admiration from the capacity 42,000 crowd.

The Russians saved their faces, if not the tie, in the 73rd minute as Asatiani equalised. He took a low cross and burst past a cluster of defenders to drive a shot wide of Jennings.

RALPH COATES — "Sell me if you dare" message to Nicholson.

EARLE SIGNED IN £100,000 DEAL

By JACK STEGGLES

FULHAM striker Steve Earle signed for Leicester last night in a £100,000 deal that now depends only on the formality of a medical exam today.

Leicester manager Jimmy Bloomfield plans to field Earle against Tottenham at Filbert Street on Saturday.

West Ham yesterday let Dudley Tyler return to his former club, Hereford, for £10,000.

Grimsby full-back Dave Worthington moved to Southend for £6,000.

Millwall's Eire international Eamonn Dunphy is expected to join Charlton for £20,000 today.

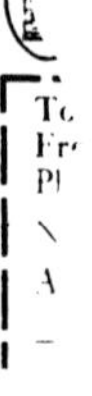

positions, there was often only superb skipper Martin Peters left up front.

It was a triumph for Tottenham after the disappointing 3-1 crash to Wolves last Saturday.

John Pratt, disgracefully heckled by Tottenham's supporters and pulled off in that match, had a fine game 2,500 miles from home. So did Naylor and Steve Perryman.

Chivers so nearly scored with a glancing header before Coates struck after twenty-five minutes. Chivers neatly laid off a Mike England pass and Coates found the net with a ferocious twenty-yard drive.

The Russians lost a lot of their legendary discipline for a while after that. But they should have scored just before half-time when David Kipiani broke clear and shot wide with only Jennings to beat.

It was different in the second half as the Russians finally got shots on target.

Jennings saved brilliantly from Murtax Khurtsilava, captain of the Russian national side, and from Manutyar Machaidze twice. They were saves that brought gasps of admiration from the capacity 42,000 crowd.

The Russians saved their faces, if not the tie, in the seventy-third minute as Asatiani equalised. He took a low cross and burst past a cluster of defenders to drive a shot wide of Jennings.

The players cross swords at the official banquet

The players in training on the morning of the game

Martin Peters (No.10) heads home Spurs' third

GUARDIAN, Thursday, December 13, 1973

TOTTENHAM H . . . 5 DINAMO TBILISI . . . 1

LIKE OLD TIMES FOR TOTTENHAM

By FRANK KEATING

Old memories were summoned up in a glorious evening at White Hart Lane last night when Tottenham Hotspur found inspiration in the clean, fair, open talents of Dinamo Tbilisi, from Georgia, and beat them at their own attacking game by 5-1.

The Russians looked good on the break but, with an away goal to catch up, were increasingly hesitant. They seemed to be funking the issue. And as they did so Tottenham's palpitating hearts seemed to beat more contentedly. And just past the half-hour they took the lead.

Immediately after Khurtizlavia's free kick from 20 yards had grazed Jennings' crossbar, the non-stop Coates broke clear from the goal kick: for once he flighted in a scooped sort of centre instead of side-footing to the overlapping Evans as usual. The centre curled goalwards, Chivers embarked on a dummy run to the near post, and the ball sailed over his head to the unmarked McGrath who headed into the net – one-nil – and the Russians needed to show their mettle now.

Sure enough they did: first Asatiani, then the menacing Machaidze set up assaults on Jennings. And on the stroke of half-time Khurtizlava's wicked drive from 20 yards slapped against the post with Jennings stranded and Kipiani put the rebound into the side netting. Tottenham went in reasonably happy but they were by no means home yet.

After three close calls at the other end, Tottenham had increased their lead in the 52nd minute. Yet another determined run down the line by Coates ended with an accurate centre which Chivers met perfectly to head home. Four minutes later Ebralidze turned in a low cross from the right, but after 62 minutes Tottenham scored again.

England headed a corner by Pratt back into the packed goalmouth and Peters glanced it home with his head. The Soviet side could not master the Tottenham centres, as men ran on to them at the near post or waited for them by the far woodwork. Yet another centre by Peters from the left, after 76 minutes, was headed home by Chivers before the goalkeeper could reach the ball. Four minutes later Peters met a centre by Pratt with his head to complete Dinamo's humiliation.

Like old times for Tottenham

By FRANK KEATING : Tottenham H 5, Dinamo Tbilisi 1

Old memories were summoned up in a glorious evening at White Hart Lane last night when Tottenham Hotspur found inspiration in the clean, fair, open talents of Dinamo Tbilisi, from Georgia, and beat them at their own attacking game by 5-1.

drive from 20 yards slapped against the post with Jennings stranded and Kipiani put the rebound into the side netting. Tottenham went in reasonably happy but they were by no means home yet.

After three close calls at the [illegible] end, Tottenh[illegible]

2
10

TIMES, Thursday, March 7, 1974

COLOGNE . . . 1 TOTTENHAM . . . 2

TOTTENHAM LIVE UP TO THEIR MOTTO

From GEOFFREY GREEN

COLOGNE, MARCH 6

Tottenham Hotspur kept up their unbeaten record in the UEFA Cup here this evening to give themselves a fine platform for a semi-final place in the competition when the second leg is played at White Hart Lane in a fortnight's time. It was a magnificent performance of shadow boxing; of a rearguard action; and of breakaways that turned the match against the odds and the ceaseless pressure of the Germans, Tottenham's way.

Tottenham inflicted on Cologne only their second defeat at home in 31 Continental competition matches over the last few years. That in itself is a major feather in their caps. At times in the second half the Tottenham goal became almost a shooting gallery as the Germans pounded from left, right and centre, but could find no way of breaking down this magnificent barrier.

So Tottenham, after a complicated and protracted journey, return home with a deep sense of heroic quest, their pockets crackling with the notes of money and music. The match was probably won on the drawing board of Room 108 in the Bad Godesberg Hotel on the banks of the Rhine – the room where the Führer did much of his planning. Let us hope that Bill Nicholson's planning will have a happier ending.

For Tottenham it was a closely-shared experience, yet the future is not necessarily over for these Germans, for Cologne are a highly-talented and skilful side with internationals in their ranks of the quality of Overath, Cullmann (both of whom, no doubt, we shall see in the World Cup this summer), Weber, who played in the World Cup final at Wembley in 1966, Flöhe and Löhr. This

Chris McGrath beats Cologne goalkeeper Weiz to give Spurs the lead after 18 minutes

Jennings, the Tottenham goalkeeper, makes a fine save during last night's match.

Tottenham live up to their motto

From Geoffrey Gr

Germans, for Cologne are a highly-talented and

hour left, in one of their sudden

match stood out in stark relief, with the Germans holding, running and passing off the top of their heads; in contrast, Tottenham were absorbing like a sponge everything thrown at them in defence and counter-punching dangerously as McGrath showed his ability to beat a man on the wing outside and inside, and the big Chivers throwing his weight about in the middle in dangerous thrusts.

It was Chivers who opened the way for Tottenham's first goal after 18 minutes. Taking a pass from Peters, he torpedoed his way down the left, shot across the goal, and there was McGrath, reading the play, to shoot home at the far post. Ten minutes after the interval Cologne at last got a reward for all their attacking when Müller (not the great Müller) took a chipped pass from Simmet, kept off England's challenge, and slid home the equaliser. After that the fury of the German attacks mounted, but somehow Tottenham held on bravely with England, Beal and Evans the particular heroes in front of the alert Jennings.

Under constant attack Tottenham's spirit burned while Cologne denied their rights, touched the outskirts of their skill. Tottenham lived up to their Boy Scout motto, "Be Prepared". They were just that and with a quarter of an hour left, in one of their sudden breakouts from their rampart, they sneaked the winner. Evans passed to Naylor, overlapping on the right flank; Naylor got to the byline, pulled back his centre and Peters came in on the blind side to head the winner.

These two goals, snatched away from home, could mean everything at White Hart Lane. As for the rest of a fine, exciting match, I can hardly note all the near things and other misses. Chivers, for instance, might have scored twice for Tottenham, before the Germans had got going; Müller did likewise at the other end, as did Löhr and even their left back Hein, in the second half. Once, too, Evans saved a sizzling shot from Overath on the Tottenham goal-line with Jennings beaten! But that was all on the stage. I return to Room 108, where Mr Nicholson planned his campaign.

He did it by reverting to a 4-4-2 formation, bringing in Dillon with a figure 11 on his shirt, yet drafted into defence as a further reinforcement. The ringmaster, however, was Overath, with his educated left foot. Yet when it was all over, for all his brilliant prompting, he left the field looking as alone as a sole survivor of a shipwreck adrift on a raft in an empty ocean. Tottenham will be seeing more of him on March 20.

DAILY MAIL, Thursday, March 21, 1974

TOTTENHAM . . . 3 COLOGNE . . . 0

SPURS GO IT ALONE

Cologne crumble as Chivers strikes

By PETER MOSS

Tottenham are left alone to carry the England flag into Europe. These pale players of League football are men inspired when they turn to the UEFA Cup.

For six years English teams have won this competition under its present title and its previous name – the Fairs Cup. It will take an outstanding team to end that run this year.

Not that Spurs had to be magic for long last night. They killed this tie as a contest in the first 14 minutes. The two goals they scored by then gave them a 4-1 overall lead against a team sprinkled with West German internationals.

After that, it was bloodless progress towards their third consecutive semi-final in this competition. In that early spell, Martin Chivers, so often the dullest of a team of bores in League matches, scored one goal and majestically made the other.

Cologne defenders helped by playing statues. They stood admiringly as Spurs' left back Terry Naylor overlapped in the tenth minute.

When he centred, Chivers flicked the ball to a defender who obligingly returned it. The big man then had only to turn and knock the ball in.

Four minutes later Chivers jumped beyond the far post to re-direct Chris McGrath's centre towards Ralph Coates. As the ball came towards him, Coates was able to pick his spot then head the ball wide of the static goalkeeper.

The rest was a matter of record. The third goal – in the 48th minute – was the one patented by Martin Peters. Again, it was begun by Naylor and once more Chivers steered the ball on with his head. This time Peters appeared like a ghost after a 20-yard run to snap up the ball and place it in the net.

Television changed their minds about showing this match which was a pity. A capsuled version of it would have been a delight.

For the 40,968 who attended there were too many spells when the only thing to wonder at was Cologne's incompetence.

Many had come to chant the old "Glory, Glory Hallelujahs" but the occasional sparse chorus hung heavily on the air.

Martin Peters turns away in triumph having beaten Cologne goalkeeper Harald Schumacher

classic
See Pages 43, 44, 45.

Spurs go it alon

Cologne crumble as Chivers strikes

TOTTENHAM 3 COLOGNE 0: By PETER MOSS

UEFA CUP: Spurs win 5–1 on aggregate

TOTTENHAM are left alone to carry the England flag into Europe. These pale players of League football are men inspired when they turn to the UEFA Cup.

For six years English teams have won this competition under its present title and its previous name—the Fairs Cup. It will take an outstanding team to end that run this year.

Not that Spurs had to be magic for long last night. They killed this tie as a contest in the first 14 minutes. The two goals they scored by then gave them a 4–1 overall lead against a team sprinkled with West German internationals.

After that, it was bloodless progress towards their third consecutive semi-final in this competition. In that early spell Martin Chivers, so often the dullest of a team of bores in League matches, scored one goal and majestically made the other.

Cologne defenders helped by playing statues. They stood admiringly as Spurs left-back Terry Naylor overlapped in the tenth minute.

When he centred Chivers flicked the ball to a defender who obligingly returned it. The big man then had only to turn and knock the ball in.

Four minutes later Chivers jumped beyond the far post to redirect Chris McGrath's centre towards Ralph Coates. As the ball came towards him Coates was able to pick his spot then head the ball wide of the static goalkeeper.

The rest was a matter of record. The third goal in the 48th minute was the one patented by Martin Peters. Again it was begun by Naylor and once more Chivers steered the ball on with his head. This time Peters appeared like a ghost after a 20-yard run to snap up the ball and place it in the net.

IPSWICH OUT
LS OFF

RALPH COATES dives in to head Spurs' second goal

Bowles magic destroys Scots

Football League 5
Scottish League 0
By JEFF POWELL

STAN BOWLES who ... create four goals and scored an outrageous ... stole the ... last night as a ...

Martin Chivers scores again for Spurs.

Coates watches his diving header find the net

PLAYERS

DAILY MAIL, Thursday, April 11, 1974

LOCOMOTIV . . 1 TOTTENHAM . . . 2

IN LEIPZIG

BRILLIANT SPURS LAND A GREAT GAMBLE

From JEFF POWELL

IN LEIPZIG

Spurs screwed up all their courage here yesterday to put one foot firmly into yet another major European final.

Two goals inside half an hour were a glorious vindication of manager Bill Nicholson's decision to gamble Tottenham's UEFA Cup lives on attack.

Nicholson had reasoned that the best chance of taking goals from the notoriously defensive East Germans was to surprise them on their own pitch.

He was brilliantly right. But Tottenham have a lead of one goal and the extra insurance of two away goals should surely guarantee their progress through the second leg of this semi-final in London in a fortnight.

Nicholson scored caution by selecting winger Jimmy Neighbour in place of injured striker Chris McGrath. And Spurs were not to be deterrred from their optimism . . . not by 75,000 banner-waving, klaxon-blowing fans, or the suffocating heat.

Martin Peters and Ralph Coates scored the early goals which launched Spurs towards another remarkable achievement in distant Europe. It is extraordinary the way Spurs rise to the UEFA Cup challenge.

Tottenham might have had even more goals in their opening burst. They they defended heroically to limit Locomotiv's enraged second half comeback to one goal.

Wales' centre half Mike England stood firm through the frenzied closing stages despite having had treatment for a gash sustained on his forehead late in the first half.

Tottenham's attacking gamble made for an exhilarating match rich in chances at both ends. And Peters had shot against the outstretched leg of German goalkeeper Friese in between menacing shots by Lowe and Macoul before he opened the scoring in the 15th minute.

England drove the ball forward from the half way line, and Neighbour chested it down but too far away from him.

But Peters cut commandingly across the path of his own winger to half-volley a mighty left foot shot high into the corner of the net.

Ten minutes later Neighbour's through-ball launched Evans into a run and battle to reach the byline and hammer over a cross which Martin Chivers swung and missed but which Coates was able to drive in off the crossbar.

Spurs were then denied a third goal in the most freakish circumstances. Chivers met a cross from Evans with a firm header which hit the post and then rebounded into play off the unknowing head of goalkeeper Friese.

Chivers put his hands to his head and fell back onto the turf in amazement.

Locomotiv were transformed in the second half when Spurs were required to take increasing punishment.

The Germans pulled a goal back in the 58th minute, World Cup striker Lowe meeting Geisler's free kick with a decisive header at the near post.

Coates, who had carried his injured ankle through his vital contribution to the Tottenham performance, limped off in favour of substitute Phil Holder for a last 15 minutes which saw Matoul hit a post, Lowe hit the legs of Pat Jennings. But Tottenham survived.

Ralph Coates scores Spurs' second goal in Leipzig. Chivers and Peters show their delight.

EUROPE SEMI-FINAL NIGHT

Brilliant Spurs land a great gamble

FROM JEFF POWELL IN LEIPZIG

LOKOMOTIVE 1
TOTTENHAM 2

SPURS screwed up all their courage here yesterday to put one foot firmly into yet another major European final.

Two goals inside half an hour were a glorious vindication of manager Bill Nicholson's decision to gamble Tottenham's UEFA Cup lives on attack.

Nicholson had reasoned that the best chance of taking goals from the notoriously defensive East Germans was to surprise them on their own pitch.

He was brilliantly right. But Tottenham have a lead of one goal and the extra insurance of two away goals should surely guarantee their progress through the second leg of this semi-final in London in a fortnight.

Optimistic

Nicholson scored caution by selecting winger Jimmy Neighbour in place of injured striker Chris McGrath. And Spurs were not to be deterred from their optimism . . . not by 75,000 banner waving, klaxon-blowing fans, or the suffocating heat.

Martin Peters and Ralph Coates scored the early goals which launched Spurs towards another remarkable achievement in distant Europe. It is extraordinary the way Spurs rise to the UEFA Cup challenge.

Tottenham might have had even more goals in their opening burst. Then they defended heroically to limit Lokomotive's enraged second-half come back to one goal.

Exhilarating

Wales centre-half Mike England stood firm through the frenzied closing stages despite having had treatment for a gash sustained on his forehead late in the first half.

Tottenham's attacking gamble made for an exhilarating match rich in chances at both ends. And Peters had shot against the outstretched leg of German goalkeeper Friese in between menacing shots by Lowe and Macoul before he opened the scoring in the 15th minute.

England drove the ball forward from the halfway line, and Neighbour chested it down but too far away from him.

But Peters, cut commandingly across the path of his own winger to half-volley a mighty left-foot shot high into the corner of the net.

Ten minutes later Neighbour's through ball launched Evans into a run and battle to reach the byeline and hammer over a cross which Martin Chivers swung at and missed but which Coates was able to drive in off the crossbar.

Spurs were then denied a third goal in the most freakish circumstances. Chivers met a cross from Evans with a firm header which hit the post and then rebounded into play off the unknowing head of goalkeeper Friese.

Amazed

Chivers put his hands to his head and fell back on to the turf in amazement.

● RALPH COATES . . . scored the second for happy Spurs.

Finalists put extra time case

CUP finalists Liverpool and Newcastle told the FA yesterday that they want extra time, if necessary, at Wembley on May 4.

And if a replay is needed they want it to be staged at Hillsborough and not at Wembley, where it is scheduled for the following Wednesday.

Newcastle were surprised 2-1 by Burnley at St James's Park last night.

Tommy Craig dislocated his left elbow which could make him doubhtful for the final.

Magnificent Morley

Newbridge 9
Bristol 25

Gloucester 10
Newport 16

By MERVYN THOMAS

ALAN MORLEY, former England wing-threequarter and a British Lions standby for South Africa, shone for Bristol.

He added two brilliant tries to an opening penalty by lock Steve Gorvett.

Newbridge, beaten 32—0 at Bristol over Christmas, had a spirited, fast rucking pack but could not match their opponents' handling.

Gorvett converted Morley's 28th try of the season and Trevor Hoskins replied with a penalty that left Newbridge trailing 13—3 at half-time.

Bristol added 12 points in three minutes through tries by right-wing Robbie Carter and centre Peter Williams, both converted by Gorvett.

Jeff Jones scored a Newbridge try, goaled by Hoskins.

GLOUCESTER fullback Peter Butler took his points total to 487 by scoring all his side's successes.

He opened with a penalty but lively Newport hit back with an opportunist try through Clive Jenkins, Richie Pugh goaling.

A David Ford try increased Newport's lead and, although Butler kicked his second penalty, the Welsh side scored a further try through Paul Watts, with Pugh converting.

Butler scored a late try for Gloucester but his goal attempt hit an upright.

Three . . . and . . . booked

TWO Atletico Madrid players were sent off within a minute of each other in Celtic's stormy European Cup semi-final first leg in Glasgow.

And that was after . . . had earlier been booked . . . of them Spaniards.

LATE WIRE. Best from Haydock: VOSTIZZA (3.15, . . .)

QUICK CROSSWORD

DAILY MIRROR, Thursday, April 25, 1974

SPURS . . . 2 LOCOMOTIV LEIPZIG . . . 0

SPURS WIN 4-1 ON AGGREGATE

SPURS IN FINAL!

Chris and Chiv give Germans a double blow

By HARRY MILLER

Tottenham last night walked away from a season of domestic mediocrity and towards a glorious European finale.

Goals from Chris McGrath and Martin Chivers at White Hart Lane enabled them to clear the hurdle at which Wolves and Ipswich fell, and reach the UEFA Cup final for the second time in three years.

If Tottenham did it with a performance that made the old "Glory, glory" anthem the most muted of sounds around North London, the facts still speak for themselves.

This win, built on the firm foundations of a 2-1 first leg semi-final success in Leipzig, means that Tottenham have qualified for a two leg summit clash against Feyenoord on May 22 and 29 without losing one of their ten games on the way.

To that fact must be added the impressive statistic of 29 goals scored, and only seven conceded. The East Germans are left to reflect that with better finishing in both legs they might have knocked Tottenham off a road they now know better than any other side in Europe.

Tottenham, in the first half, were sometimes forced to resort to tackling that was uncharacteristically crude. But Phil Beal and Mike England steadied them up at the back.

And as Locomotiv began to leave large gaps through their anxious rushes forward to bridge the 2-1 deficit, Beal nearly surprised them with a low 35-yard drive that keeper Friese nearly lost as he finished on his backside.

It was the sort of night when Chivers suffered anguish and enjoyed admiration in equal parts. He had a penalty appeal turned down when Grobner appeared to handle his shot early on.

He later rounded Grobner, and with a clear opening lashed the ball high over the bar. And he got in at the far post for a fine header from McGrath's cross, but Sekora cleared off the line.

Yet East German World Cup star, Wolfram Lowe, missed a chance just before half-time that surely changed the whole course of the evening's proceedings.

A badly-placed Joe Kinnear clearance was headed down to him by Lisiewicz. He raced forward, made the mistake of trying to take the ball round Pat Jennings, and lost it.

The tide really began to turn Tottenham's way early in the second half. An England right foot shot seemed certain to find the net, until Martin Peters somehow got in the way and diverted the ball over the bar.

Then in the 55th minute came the goal that delighted the 41,280 Tottenham fans and marked the beginning of the end for Locomotiv. The busy Ralph Coates went wide on the right, crossed – and McGrath was there at the far side of the six-yard box to beat Friese with a dipping header.

It was the fifth goal in five UEFA games for the talented teenager from Belfast.

Locomotiv, even as the end drew near, refused to accept that Tottenham were about to achieve what Wolves and Ipswich could not. Jennings, who has saved Tottenham so often in recent months, needed to be at his most agile and alert to divert a firm header from Matoul.

Finally, four minutes from the finish, Chivers set the seal on Tottenham's march to the final. Steve Perryman set him up with a fine run and pass, and Chivers bore in from the left to score with a low left foot shot.

SPURS IN FINAL!

Chris and Chiv ... a double blow

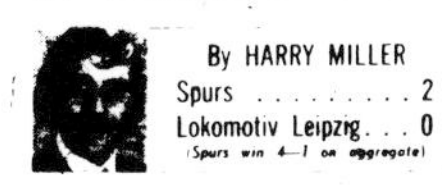

By HARRY MILLER
Spurs 2
Lokomotiv Leipzig. . . 0

Feyenoord watch out . . . Martin Chivers hits the second goal as Spurs sail into the final of the U E F A Cup.

Yeo record sends fans home happy

•England is axed by Wales

RESULTS, SCORERS

DAILY MIRROR LEISURE GUIDE

Martin Chivers scores Spurs' second goal.

DAILY MIRROR, Wednesday, May 22, 1974

SPURS . . . 2 FEYENOORD . . . 2

SPURS ON THE BRINK!

Dutchmen hit them with a late goal

By HARRY MILLER

Mike England celebrates after putting Spurs ahead in the UEFA Cup final.

Tottenham are on the brink of being pushed from the top of the European mountain they have climbed so sucessfully this season.

A carbon copy of the grit and courage which has characterised their UEFA Cup crusade was not enough in a thrilling first leg of the final at White Hart Lane last night.

Tottenham twice led, were twice pulled back and now go to Rotterdam for the second leg next week knowing that only a performance pulled from their triumphant past will be good enough.

Feyenoord, once the masters of European club football and now the new champions of Holland, really are something special.

They made the teams Tottenham have beaten in the previous rounds these past nine months look positively pedestrian.

Eight of their players are Dutch internationals. Some of them will be in the World Cup next month. Let other competing countries be warned.

In the sorrow that crowded in over North London there was no-one more dejected than Mike England.

The big centre half who has suffered pain from injuries in silence as Spurs progressed from one round to the next, scored his side's first goal and was very involved in the second.

But these Dutchmen – and one outstanding Dane, Jorgen Kristensen – always gave the impression that anything Tottenham did they could do better.

And with away goals counting double in the event of a tie, they will surely regard their performance last night as good enough.

For as well as men like England, Steve Perryman and Martin Chivers played, Spurs cannot have been left with anything but an inferiority feeling. I hope however I am wrong.

Tottenham started like a whirlwind. Feyenoord were pushed back to the extent that it was twenty minutes before Pat Jennings touched the ball – and that was to collect a pass back from Phil Beal.

DAILY MIRROR Wednesday May 2

SPURS ON THE BRINK!

Dutchmen hit them with a late goal

TOTTENHAM are on the brink of being pushed from the top of the European mountain they have climbed so successfully this season.

A carbon copy of the grit and courage which has characterised their ... leg of the final

GOAL! Mike England celebrates after heading Spurs in front. Picture HARRY P.

Top: England scoring Tottenham's first goal. Bottom: Van Hanegem scoring Feyenoord's first

Feyenoord earn a priceless draw

By Geoffrey Green
Football Correspondent

Tottenham Hotspur 2 Feyenoord 2

After six years on these shores the Uefa Cup looks to be on its way to the Netherlands. Tottenham must go across the Channel next Wednesday for the second leg of this final, having failed to beat the Dutch champions at White Hart Lane last night. To hold on to the trophy for England, Spurs must win in the stadium where 11 years ago they became the first British club to win a Continental trophy—the European Cup Winners' Cup—either that or force a draw with any score from 3—3 upwards.

Feyenoord came to London yesterday to achieve their draw. They

from a sharp angle. That is how football should be played.

It was a lively second half but after the interval Tottenham showed their poor league form in this competition for the first time. They simply could find little inspiration against the technically efficient Dutchmen who played a possession game when it was necessary. Tottenham were hard working and straightforward, but nothing more and paled beside the subtle touches of the Dutchmen. De Jong, van Hanegem and Jansen were always posing the more difficult questions in midfield as they worked the ball up to the long-legged and dangerous Schoenmaker at centre forward.

Little Kristensen, also on the left wing, was as tricky as a waggonful of monkeys, and only the lively Coates could live with them

ally trickling into the net by of England's head and the foo Feyenoord's central defe Israel.

It was an action-packed at the change of ends. De and Evans both scraped the side of the posts with fla shots from 20 yards. There dazzling save by Jennings a came out to thwart de Jong. In the battle Kristensen, as as van Hanegem, was "bool van Hanegem for dissent Kristensen for refusing to yards back from the fre which brought Tottenham's ing goal.

So ended a night which in slanting rain in front of spirited 46,000 crowd mad lively by the klaxons and ony of noise from the Dutch

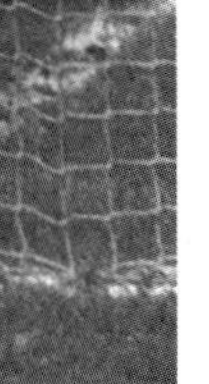

The threatened goal came in the thirty-ninth minute. Kristensen twice obstructed Ray Evans as he went to take a free kick out on the right, earning him a booking.

At the third attempt Evans got the ball across and England charged in to score with a forcing downwards header.

Tottenham's joy lasted just four minutes. Then Wim van Hanegem equalised with a free kick from the edge of the penalty area which he bent round Tottenham's defensive wall with his left foot.

Van Hanegem had earlier been cautioned for dissent and will miss the second leg, having been booked in a previous UEFA Cup match.

Tottenham picked up the tempo in the second half and regained the lead in the sixty-second minute again following a free kick.

Once more Evans took it. This time he chipped the ball forward, keeper Eddy Treytel missed it, England was involved in the scramble and Dutch defender Joop van Daele got the final touch before the ball crossed the line.

Beal limped off with an ankle injury nine minutes from the end to be replaced by Mike Dillon. Three minutes later Feyenoord equalised for the second time.

Tottenham were split open as the superb Kristensen sent Theo de Jong through to score with a low shot.

But Tottenham manager Bill Nicholson was quick to warn: "This tie is not over yet.

"Feyenoord are a really fine side. But they would be foolish to take anything for granted. We shall fight all the way for victory in Rotterdam next Wednesday."

DAILY MIRROR, Thursday, May 30, 1974

FEYENOORD . . 2 SPURS . . . 0

HOLIGANS SHAME SPURS

Nick's braves fail in a final wrecked by fans

From HARRY MILLER

IN ROTTERDAM

England's monopoly of the UEFA Cup was broken here last night as Tottenham lost a final that will be remembered for all the wrong reasons.

The huge gaps on the terraces behind one goal at the finish bear testimony to the carnage caused by Tottenham's rioting supporters.

This infamous evening – a permanent blot on the name of one of Britain's greatest clubs – will not easily be forgotten. And the reckoning, when UEFA launch what must be a massive inquiry into the behaviour of a hooligan minority among the fans, is still to come. Feyenoord, who staged this final, are in dire danger of a heavy fine for the happenings off the pitch as much as Bill Nicholson's Tottenham.

Ralph Coates and Martin Peters look on as the ball is kept out by the Feyenoord keeper.

Mirror Sport

Thursday, May 30, 1974
Telephone: (STD code 01)—353 0246

HOOLIGANS SHAME SPURS

Nick's braves fail in a final wrecked by fans

From HARRY MILLER in Rotterdam

Feyenoord 2 Spurs 0 (Feyenoord win 4-2 on agg)

ENGLAND'S monopoly of the U E F A Cup was broken here last night as Tottenham lost a final tha...

GERMANY —YOU LUCKY BEGGARS!

The real tragedy is that the fighting on the terraces over-shadowed the excellent football played by both sides.

Tottenham lost a battle that had turned against them even before a ball was kicked in this second leg.

Their failure to achieve more than a 2-2 draw at White Hart Lane last week proved their undoing as Feyenoord won on their own soil with a goal in each half.

So a run in which English clubs had won the trophy for the previous six seasons, was ended. But it was a gallant failure.

Tottenham were a team patched up and under pressure from personal worries.

Phil Beal played with his injured left ankle heavily strapped. Ray Evans was feeling a bruised instep. And Ralph Coates had the worry of his five-year old daughter in hospital with a ruptured appendix.

Feyenoord went ahead three minutes from half-time. Peter Ressel made the telling pass and Wim Rijsbergen scored with a shot through the massed ranks of defenders strung across Tottenham's goal.

The second goal came seven minutes from the end when substitute Jan Boskamp crossed and Ressel drove firmly into the net.

arrested, 200 hurt as Tottenham lose in Holland

IOTING FANS
HAME BRITAIN

Baton wielding Dutch police battle it out with the mobs on the terraces last night

Now Ulster goes back to direct rule

Turn to Page 2.

Steve Perryman goes close.

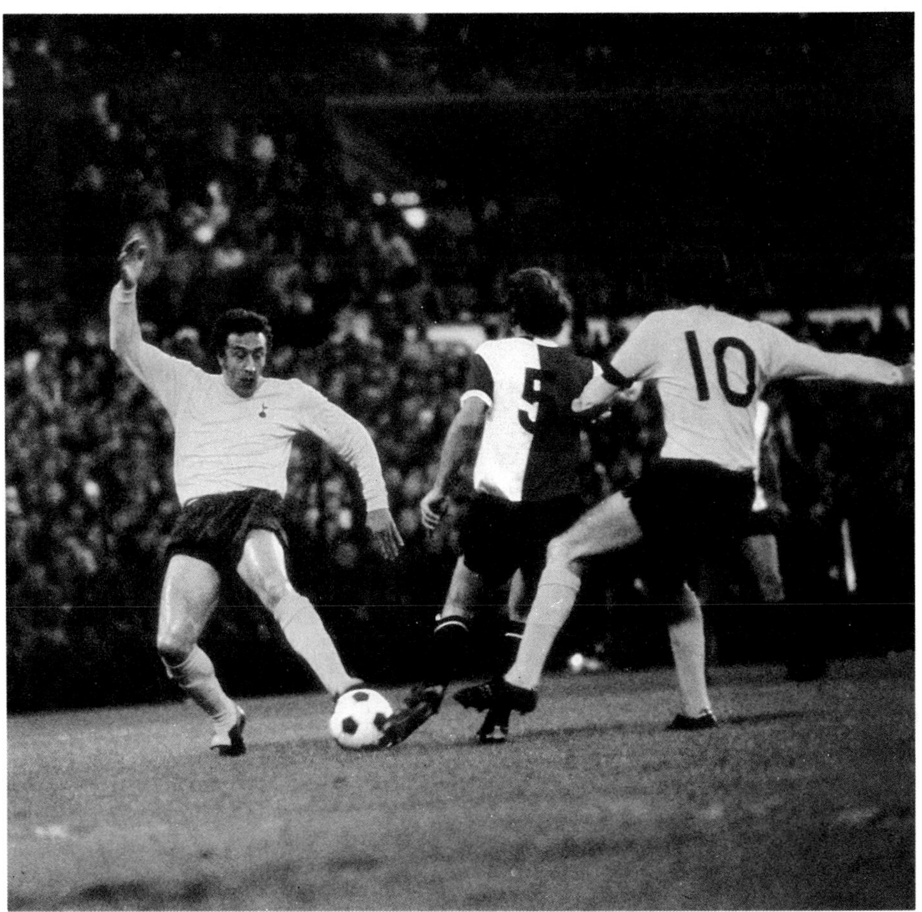

Martin Chivers and Martin Peters pressurise a Feyenoord defender.

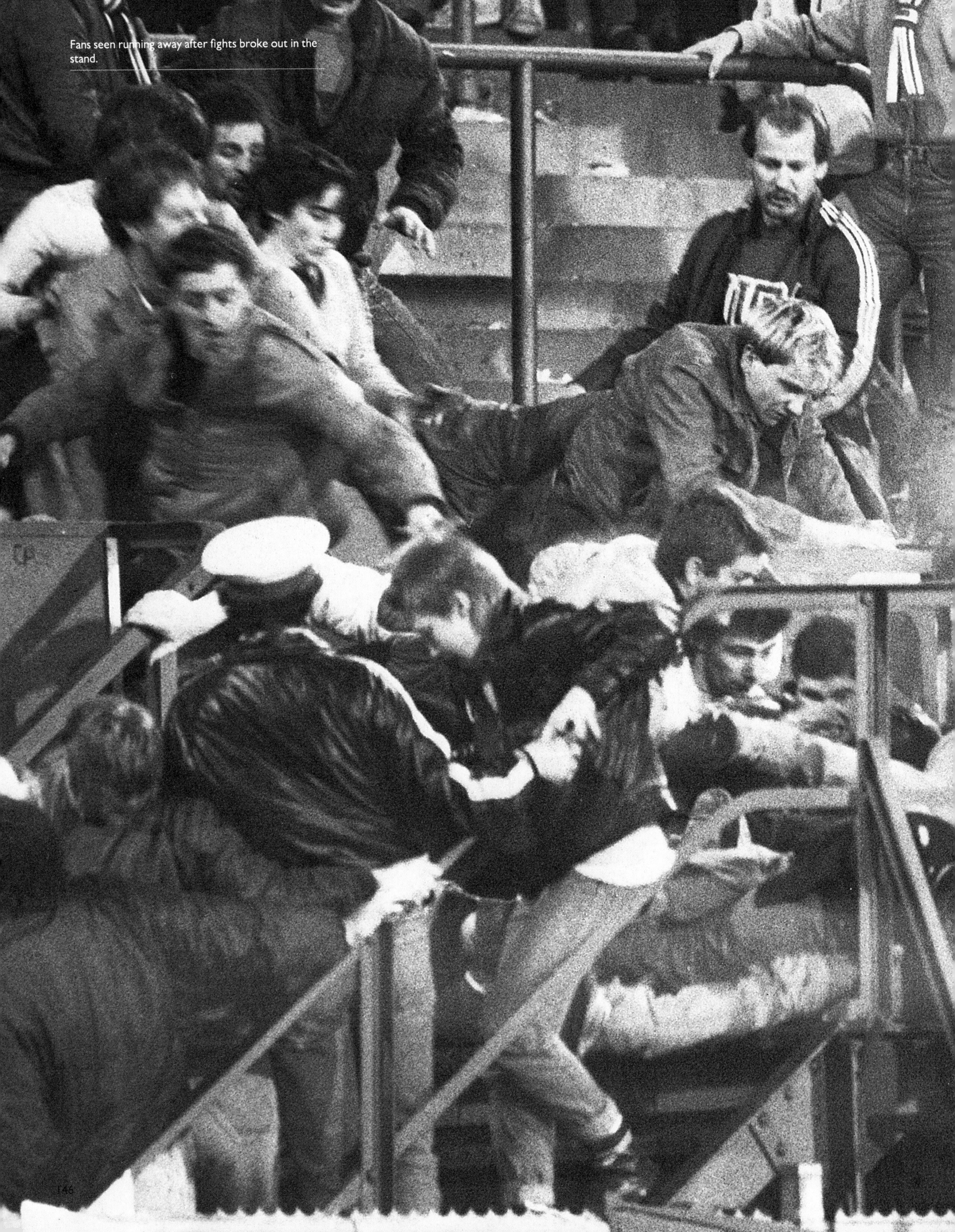

Fans seen running away after fights broke out in the stand.

DAILY MAIL, Thursday, May 30, 1974

SPURS FACE A BAN IN EUROPE

The Front Page riot match . . . this could be the outcome

From BRAIN SCOVELL

IN ROTTERDAM

Spurs face severe disciplinary action by UEFA because of the behaviour of their fans as they lost in the final of the UEFA Cup at Rotterdam last night.

In 14 years' reporting football in Europe, I have never seen scenes like these. Hundreds of Dutch fans were bombarded by bottles, banners and broken chairs.

An embarrassed Spurs chairman Sidney Wale apologised to Feyenoord officials afterwards. "The whole thing makes me sick," he said. "It was a disgrace.

"It is certain we'll be in trouble with UEFA. But I'm sure it was only a minority of fans involved."

Spurs had played well in the first half, creating far more chances than the Dutch champions. Skipper Martin Peters twice put headers just wide.

The goal that ended the match came when Pat Jennings dropped a cross, and Rijsbergen headed the ball into the net.

When Spurs came out for the start of the second half, they were booed, and there were cries of "British go home."

Skipper Peters tried to make a placatory gesture, but was screamed down.

Italian referee Concetto Lo Bello booked Steve Perryman and Ray Evans for dissent and inflamed the crowd by giving an indirect free kick near the penalty spot for an obstruction on Martin Chivers.

Players jostled each other, and one feared that the crowd trouble might spread to the pitch.

But the kick was taken a second time and cleared. But near the end Peters was involved in a tackle with a Feyenoord defender, and there was another ugly scene.

In the 83rd minute Feyenoord winger Ressel struck home Feyenoord's second goal.

It had been a gallant performance by Spurs, but the second leg confirmed what we knew from the first – that this side is not good enough to win a major honour.

Manager Bill Nicholson will have to rebuild.

Feyenoord looked much inferior to the side that impressed English critics so much in the first leg. They were surprised at Tottenham's approach.

The Front Page riot match . . . this could be the outcome

Spurs face a ban in Europe

SPURS face severe disciplinary action by UEFA because of the behaviour of their fans as they lost in the final of the UEFA Cup at Rotterdam last night.

In 14 years' reporting football in Europe. I have never seen scenes like these. Hundreds of Dutch fans were bombarded by bottles. banners and broken chairs.

An embarrassed Spurs chairman Sidney Wale apologised to Feyenoord officials afterwards. 'The whole thing makes me sick,' he said. 'It was a disgrace.

Minority

'It is certain we'll be in trouble with UEFA. But I'm sure it was only a minority of fans involved.'

Spurs had played well in the first half. creating far more chances than the Dutch champions. Skiper Martin Peters twice put headers just wide.

The goal that ended the match came when Pat Jennings dropped a cross. and Rijsbergen headed the ball into the net.

When Spurs came out for the start of the second half. they were booed. and there were cries of 'British go home.'

Skipper Peters tried to make a placatory gesture. but was screamed down.

FEYENOORD 2 SPURS 0

From BRIAN SCOVELL
in Rotterdam

Italian referee Concetto Lo Bello booked Steve Perryman and Ray Evans for dissent and inflamed the crowd by giving an indirect free kick near the penalty spot for an obstruction on Martin Chivers.

Players jostled each other. and one feared that the crowd trouble might spread to the pitch.

But the kick was taken a second time and cleared. But near the end Peters was involved in a tackle with a Feyenoord defender. and there was another ugly scene.

Gallant

In the 83rd minute Feyenoord winger Ressel struck home Feyenoord's second goal.

It had been a gallant performance by Spurs. but the second leg confirmed what we knew from the first — that this side is not good enough to win a major honour.

Manager Bill Ni...

RAY EVANS causes bother in the Feynoord defence in a Spurs attack

Thursday, Ma

Sportsn goe wher actic

ENGL reveal their tru spirit in Leipzig draw after Eas with all the lu ahead. JEFF ports in

BU goes one b hagen, beati Baruzzi on his Europe title in a PETER MO Page

BOYC at last shows t in the trial a His unbeaten l land against th rightly worry ALEX BANNIS in Page

LION last, but surely th Britain's big sp

LOOKING BACK WITH BILL NICHOLSON

Bill Nicholson's love of European football was crushed in the sad night in Feyenoord's De Kuip stadium.

A man who had put so much effort into the game was sickened by sights that were to be repeated all too often during the next 10 years.

The warnings of Brussels were posted in Rotterdam and the lessons went unheeded. English football had declined and the standards were to plummet further.

Nicholson saw on that May night football go mad. The Feyenoord stadium was wrecked by hooligans as Tottenham slumped to their UEFA Cup final defeat.

It was a scene that sickened the battle hardened Nicholson. His daughter was in the 55,000 crowd that night. It was a night Nicholson won't forget.

He stood in the police room under the Feyenoord stadium making appeal after appeal for the crowd to behave. Each appeal was ignored.

His team were sitting stunned through half-time in the nearby dressing room.

Nicholson does not like to think back. He said: "We had such a good relationship with the Feyenoord club. The stadium, such a lovely place, was just smashed to pieces.

"It proved to football that there is a certain section who if hell bent on trouble will cause trouble. It is something that has been proved all too regularly since those days.

"I cannot understand why people should do such things. I don't know why they don't respect law and order. In the old days we had a respect for that sort of thing.

"But that night in Rotterdam was so bad. I don't think I have ever seen anything like it. I remember the days of battles during the depression but this was much worse.

"My daughter went over on the boat and coach and they said that the fans were so drunk they had to lock themselves in the cabin. There was so much drinking going on and there was so much trouble.

"We knew nothing of what might happen while we were preparing for the match. It was never an excuse for our defeat but they were not ideal conditions in which to play a match.

"It showed the controls that were needed for fans travelling away and what could happen if things went wrong. You have to be aware of what might happen.

"I still cannot forget the scenes of the seats spinning down the stands. It was fortunate a lot more people did not get hurt."

For Nicholson the 1970s were the end of the great footballing years. He said: "Money took over. It became such an influence, people became frightened of losing.

February 75 – Bill Nicholson receives the OBE

"People therefore started playing more and more mid-field players and it became like piggy back in the centre circle, with everyone on top of each other.

"Inflation hit the clubs trying to build for the future. Staffs were cut and if you lost, you lost your support because they could not afford to watch a losing team.

"Defence became exaggerated and the goals fell away. There were no free attacking matches and the game was spoilt as a spectacle. Couple that with hooliganism and the game has never recovered."

LOOKING BACK WITH JOHN PRATT

Bill Nicholson simply walked into the Spurs dressing room in the bowels of the Feyenoord stadium, screwed up his coat and hurled it in the corner.

John Pratt remembers it well. "He just said: 'They are tearing the place to pieces.' He stormed out and we never saw him again."

It was the night of shame in the De Kuip stadium. Spurs' fans were on the rampage. Pratt said: "The immediate reaction of the players was to worry if their families were all right.

"I had my mother, father, mother-in-law and wife out there for the match. We wondered where they were in the ground and if the trouble was near them.

"When we left the dressing room for the second half we spent most of our time looking around the stands to try and catch a glimpse of our families.

"It was no way to play a football match – not one as important as a European final. We could see the seats coming down the stands. No one could concentrate."

Pratt is convinced that without the intervention of the Tottenham hordes Spurs could have won the match and the UEFA Cup.

"We were only a goal down at half time and we had created some clear cut chances and Chris McGrath had even had a goal disallowed.

"We were confident that we could come back and tie the game up. We just needed a good talking to and some new thoughts and you never know.

"Instead there were a stream of police and stadium officials coming to the dressing room and Bill was dragged away to make his appeal. It was terrible."

Spurs went on to lose the game and the Cup. Next day Pratt recalls. "It was a day off. We were supposed to be with our families and take a stroll through Rotterdam.

"You just couldn't open your mouth. We were ashamed to be English. We just wanted to keep our heads down and get out as quickly as possible. I just wanted to crawl into a hole and die."

It was the start of another great upheaval in Tottenham's history. Bill Nicholson was to leave quickly afterwards and Terry Neill took over.

Out went players like Martin Chivers, Mike England and Martin Peters. Pratt said: "It was such a shock. We all thought that Bill was going to be at Tottenham for ever.

"It was only when Terry Neill came in that we realised that the great era was over and rebuilding was underway. I remember one morning turning up for training and saying to Steve Perryman 'Heck, we are the only ones left'.

"Until then everyone had known Bill and known that they were wanted. I was only ever on a one-year contract in 16 years at White Hart Lane.

"Suddenly we did not know what sort of players the manager was looking for and if we were going to be in a job any longer. It was an unsettling time. There again, periods of change always are."

The appalling events at Feyenoord seemed to bode ill for Spurs in domestic and therefore European terms. In 1977 they were relegated to the Second Division.

Then, with the arrival of Villa and Ardiles, things began looking up. In 1981, four years to the day since their relegation, they won the FA Cup and so became once more a serious contender in the 1981/82 European Cup Winners' Cup.

NEWS OF THE WORLD, Sunday, 15 May, 1977

SPURS . . . 2 LEICESTER . . . 0

THAT'S IT – NOW YOU'RE REALLY ON TRIAL SPURS

By REG DRURY

Spurs' chairman Sydney Wale kept his feet on the ground last night as the relegation trap door opened and dropped his club into the Second Division amidst the most bizarre scenes.

As teenage fans demonstrated their loyalty in an atmosphere normally associated with championship-winning teams, Wale told me:

"We are on trial next season. It's make or break . . . time isn't on our side . . . we must gain promotion. Otherwise we will become just another Second Division side.

"The board are behind manager Keith Burkinshaw. He may have made mistakes – Keith would be the first to admit that – but I believe he can lead us back to the top."

As Wale spoke, thousands of youngsters still swarmed over the pitch, more than half an hour after the final whistle, chanting "We all agree . . . Tottenham Hotspur are magic."

Skipper Steve Perryman appeared in the directors' box to take a bow, as though Spurs had cause for celebration, and the "Glory, Glory Hallelujah" chorus echoed around the ground – as it did when Spurs achieved the double 16 years ago.

"I expected a demo, but not this kind," said the bewildered Spurs chairman. Like Wale, I found the situation totally unreal.

Spurs' slide into the Second Division after 27 years is hardly a cause for celebration – especially as the present team isn't good enough to win promotion at the first attempt.

Star goalkeeper Pat Jennings seems certain to move on to a club more deserving of his talents, and of the remainder only youngster Glenn Hoddle – and the industrious Perryman – have the style which was once a Spurs hallmark.

In the past year, Spurs have spent nearly half a million on new players. But the present side is still no more than ordinary.

This final victory owed as much to Leicester's shortcomings as it did to Spurs' ability. Leicester never even made a game of it after going a goal behind in the third minute when Jimmy Holmes thumped in a right wing cross from Gerry Armstrong.

John Pratt added a second a couple of minutes after the interval when Peter Taylor sent him clear. Pratt rapped his first shot against the post and then netted the rebound.

It could have been more. Ian Moores, who has had an unhappy time since Spurs signed him from Stoke in September, lobbed the ball over the bar from a few yards out.

Leicester 'keeper Mark Wallington made several good saves, the best of them to turn a tremendous Pratt blast past the post.

That's it—now you're really on trial Spurs

SPURS chairman Sydney Wale kept his feet on the ground last night as the relegation trap door opened and dropped his club into the Second Division amidst the most bizarre scenes.

As teenage fans demonstrated their loyalty in an atmosphere normally associated with championship-winning teams, Wale told me:

"We are on trial next season. It's make or break . . . time isn't on our side . . . we must gain promotion. Otherwise we will become just another Second Division side.

"The board are behind manager Keith Burkinshaw. He may have made mistakes—Keith would be the first to admit that—but I believe he can lead us back to the top."

As Wale spoke, th[illegible] youngsters still [illegible]

By REG DRURY
Spurs 2 Leicester 0

in the directors' box to take a bow, as though Spurs had cause for celebration, and the "Glory, Glory, Hallelujah" [illegible] echoed around the ground [illegible] did when Spurs achieved the [illegible] 16 years ago.

"I expected a demo, but not this kind," said the bewildered Spurs chairman. Like Wale, I found the situation totally unreal.

TALENTS

Spurs' slide into the Second Division after 27 years is hardly a cause for celebration—especially as the present team isn't good enough to win promotion at the first attempt

In the past year, Spurs have spent nearly half-a-million on new players. But the present side is still no more than ordinary.

This final victory owed as much to Leicester's shortcomings as it did to Spurs' ability. Leicester never even made a game of it after going a goal behind in the third minute when Jimmy Holmes thumped in a right wing cross from Gerry Armstrong.

John Pratt added a second a couple of minutes after the interval when Peter Taylor sent him clear. Pratt rapped his first shot against the post and then netted the rebound.

I could have been more. Ian Moores, who has had an unhappy time since Spurs signed him from Stoke in September, lobbed the ball over the bar from a few yards out.

Leicester 'keeper Mark Wallington [illegible] good saves, the best of [illegible]

DAILY EXPRESS, Tuesday, July 11, 1978

SPURS SCOOP THE WORLD

Burkinshaw buys Argentine stars

By MALCOLM FOLLEY

Tottenham manager Keith Burkinshaw yesterday signed two of Argentina's all-conquering national side – Osvaldo Ardiles and Ricardo Villa – in a £750,000 deal.

Ardiles masterminded Argentina's World Cup triumph in Buenos Aires last month.

But while the Italians drooled over his skills and the Spaniards awaited developments, Burkinshaw caught a plane to the Argentine capital.

By last night Tottenham's £1,500 investment in his airline ticket had reaped rewards which will make the North London club the focal point of British football.

Ardiles and Villa, both 25 and mid-field players, had signed three-year contracts and begun to organise their travel arrangements to arrive in London on Sunday.

The whole transaction, which breaks shattering new ground in the British game, had taken just 72 hours to complete.

Burkinshaw only arrived in Buenos Aires on Saturday. His first appointment was with Ardiles and after brief negotiations he went ahead and set up the £400,000 transfer with his club Huracon.

Next, he saw Villa, "considered by many," says Burkinshaw, "to be the best player in Argentina," and was given the encouragement to clinch the double-deal with Racing Club.

Burkinshaw's mission was eased by the discovery that the two players and their wives were firm friends.

The Tottenham manager, whose club reclaimed their First Division status last season, conducted negotations through an interpreter.

"Both men are extremely intelligent and want to have English lessons as soon as they arrive," Burkinshaw told me.

"Little Ardiles can read English and already makes himself understood with me."

Burkinshaw does not envisage the players having any difficulty getting work permits. "The Department of Employment told me last week that there wouldn't be any problem," he explained.

Burkinshaw had spent months combing the country for suitable players to make Tottenham great again. All his inquiries drew a blank.

Then he watched Argentina win the World Cup. "My board gave me the go-ahead to try to get Ardiles," he said.

"I knew Harry Haslam (manager of Sheffield United) had done a lot of work on Argentinian players. He has an Argentinian coach, Oscar Arce, and was looking for players in a cheaper bracket.

"He helped me a great deal and arranged for Tony Rattin, the Argentinian captain sent off in the infamous World Cup match with England at Wembley in 1966, to act for me.

"I never expected to get the pair of them. It proves that Tottenham think big and want to be the best club in the country.

"Even by their standards, the signings must be one of the biggest things in the club's history."

Now Burkinshaw hopes to fly home to complete the signing of Fulham defender John Lacy.

Haslam expects to sign two Argentinian players before the weekend, but they will be strictly small fry.

DAILY EXPRESS Tuesday July 11 1978

***

SPURS SCOOP THE WORLD

EXPRESS EXCLUSIVE

Ardiles and Villa sign in £750,000 double deal

By Malcolm Folley

TOTTENHAM manager Keith Burkinshaw yesterday signed two of Argentina's all-conquering national side — Osvaldo Ardiles and Ricardo Villa — in a £750,000 deal.

Ardiles masterminded Argentina's World Cup triumph in Buenos Aires last month.

But while the Italians drooled over his skills and the Spaniards awaited developments, Burkinshaw caught a plane to the Argentine capital.

By last night Tottenham's £1,500 investment in his airline ticket had reaped rewards which will make the North London club the focal point of British football.

Here on Sunday

Ardiles and Villa, both 25 and midfield players, had signed three-year contracts and begun to organise their travel arrangements to arrive in London on Sunday.

The whole transaction, which breaks shattering new ground in the British game, had taken just 72 hours to complete.

Burkinshaw only arrived in Buenos Aires on Saturday. His first appointment was with Ardiles and after brief negotiations he went ahead and set-up the £400,000 transfer with his club Huracan.

Next, he saw Villa, "considered by many," says Burkinshaw, "to be the best player in Argentina," and was given the encouragement to clinch the double-deal with Racing Club.

Burkinshaw's mission was eased by the discovery that the two players and their wives were firm friends.

The Tottenham manager, whose club reclaimed their First Division status last season, conducted negotiations through an interpreter.

Intelligent

"Both men are extremely intelligent and want to have English lessons as soon as they arrive," Burkinshaw told me.

"Little Ardiles can read English and already makes himself understood with me."

Burkinshaw does not envisage the players having any difficulty getting work permits. "The Department of Employment told me last week that there wouldn't be any problem," he explained.

Burkinshaw had spent months combing the country for suitable players to make Tottenham great again. All his inquiries drew a blank.

Then he watched Argentina win the World Cup. "My board gave me the go-ahead to try to get Ardiles," he said.

"I knew Harry Haslam (manager of Sheffield United) had done a lot of work on Argentinian players. He has an Argentinian coach, Oscar Arce, and was looking for players in a cheaper bracket.

"He helped me a great deal and arranged for Tony Rattin, the Argentinian captain sent off in the infamous World [illegible] match with England at Wembley in 1966, to act for me.

"I never expected to get the pair of them. It proves that Tottenham think big and want to be the best club in the country.

"Even by their standards, the signings must be one of the biggest things in the club's history."

Now Burkinshaw hopes to fly home to complete the signing of Fulham defender John Lacy.

Haslam expects to sign two Argentinian players before the weekend, but they will be strictly small fry.

Ardiles ... Argentine ace

Burkinshaw buys Argentine stars

Scotland blacklist Masson, Macari

By John Mann

DON MASSON (Derby County) and Lou Macari (Manchester United) were added to Scotland's World Cup blacklist yesterday.

The S.F.A. sentences come largely as a result of comments made by the players about their stay in Argentina.

Now three of Scotland's [illegible] strong World Cup pool have been banned. Willie Johnston of West Brom was sent home in disgrace from Argentina for taking drugs.

Yesterday's decision came after the Association's selection committee reconvened their inquiry in Glasgow following last Friday's session at which Ally MacLeod's future as manager was assured.

The S.F.A.'s decision was that:—

"Don Masson, having admitted giving false information to the Association's manager and medical officer on a most important issue in Argentina, and having expressed publicly that he would prefer not to play for Scotland, could be accommodated in his desire."

Complaints

On Macari, they said: "The team manager, in selecting players in future, is recommended to bear in mind the vehement complaints against the Association and its arrangements by the player Lou Macari.

"He should give serious consideration to the advisability of subjecting the player again to these arrangements which he professes to find unsatisfactory."

They added that their decision to send Willie Johnston home and ban him for life from playing for Scotland has been added to by FIFA, who have barred the player from all international and club commitments in Europe till June 12, 1979.

Scotland's next match is a Nations Cup-tie with Austria in September.

[illegible] PAGES 29 AND 31

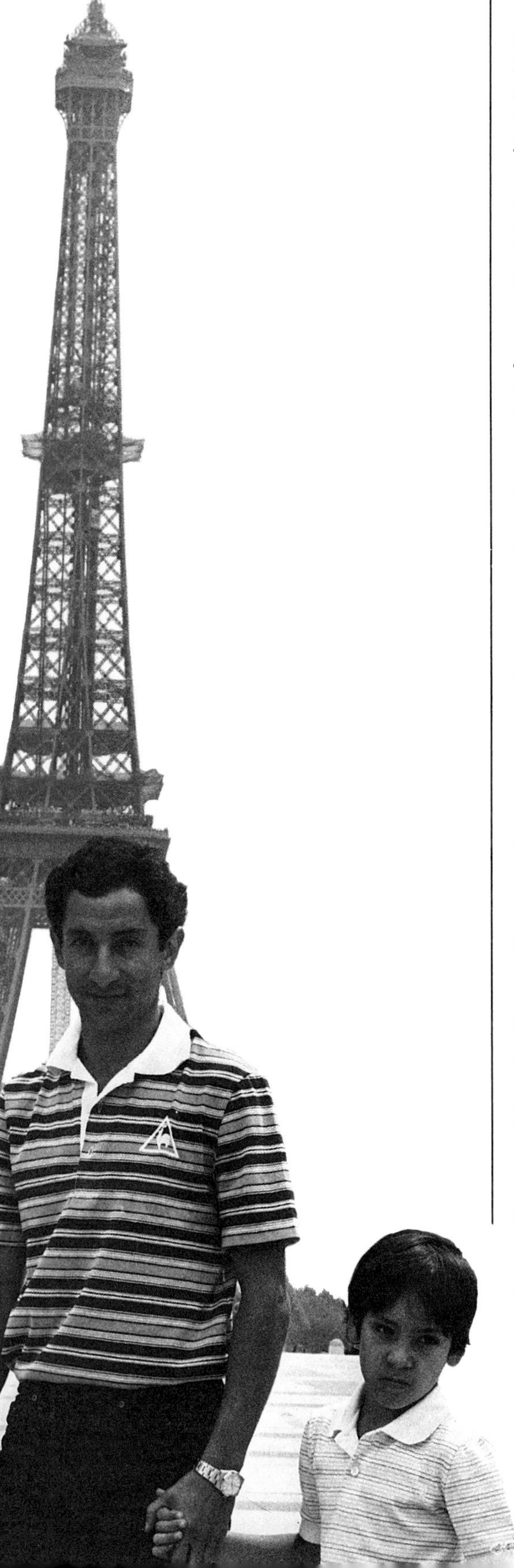

WELCOME OSSIE

Ossie Ardiles came to Tottenham Hotspur in the summer of 1978 fresh from the successes of the Argentina World Cup triumph. European football was a strange stage for the great Ardiles.

"You never seemed to get the space in English football," Ardiles said. "European football was so different. It was a great break from the day to day battles we used to face."

The tiny little Argentine was destined to be the greatest import that the English game was ever to have. His mid-field skills and his ability to help the younger players on gave Tottenham that extra piece of magic.

"It was hard at first though," remembers the man who stunned British football with his £325,000 transfer from Argentina in the summer after the World Cup. "There are a great deal of differences between football in Europe and football in South America.

"In South American football there are only a few teams each year that are going to win anything. There are also great differences in style between the respective countries in South America.

"They don't for example play the same style in Argentina as they do in Brazil perhaps. The main link between all the types of play though is the time that you get on the ball.

"When we came to England there was always someone on you from the start. They never gave the mid-field players the room they needed to play and that is the factor that has led to some disappointing play.

"I don't think that the game ever improved in Britain during the eight years that I played there. The players were becoming less skilful and more about workrates. The best were always ready to go abroad."

Because of the Falklands War between Britain and Argentina Ossie Ardiles was forced into temporary exile in France with the leading club Paris St Germain. It was a six-month break that Ardiles enjoyed.

"The football in France was much less intense than that in England. The clubs did not take the matches so seriously and the fans did not either. The crowds were much smaller and the atmosphere is missing from the games.

"But they do allow their players to express themselves more and that is why they produce players like Platini and the likes."

The six-month exile ended with injury and a dramatic return at the start of 1983 to White Hart Lane. Once again though a series of serious injuries ruined what should have been a golden time for Ardiles.

"In fact I was recovering from the latest in a long line of shin problems when I made my most telling contribution to Tottenham's European campaigns in the 1980s. It came against Anderlecht in that UEFA Cup final of 1984."

Ardiles was called on by manager Keith Burkinshaw with just 10 minutes to go in the gruelling final. The White Hart Lane crowd roared its approval as Ardiles began his warm up.

When he came on he made an immediate impact. A corner fell to him on the edge of the six-yard area and Ardiles lashed the ball against the bar in a mad goalmouth scramble. It seemed that the chance had gone but the ball came back to Graham Roberts via Mick Hazard for the vital equaliser.

"It was a special night but there again all the nights in Europe tended to be a bit special. It was one of the highlights of the season to be involved in those European games.

"They added something to a season. All the players knew that they were playing for a big club if they were playing in Europe. The trips into those sort of competitions made you learn things. We enjoyed ourselves yes but we learnt a lot as well.

"They helped Glenn Hoddle and players like that establish themselves as stars. Look at the advantages that exposure to Europe gave a player like Steve Archibald. Off he went to Barcelona. It is a special thing Europe."

Ossie Ardiles and his son during their six-month stay in France

FA CUP FINAL REPLAY . . . THE SAGA ENDS

It's viva Villa for hot Spurs

RICKY VILLA, who was branded a failure on Saturday, led Spurs to unforgettable FA Cup victory last night.

In a full-blooded contest of skill and passion, his two goals as Spurs took the lead, lost it, and then regained it proved decisive.

It was breathtaking and exhilarating football with City showing courage and commitment, and Spurs at last capturing some of their scintillating skills.

The two famous clubs had promised to make this 100th Final memorable. If they did not reach the height in their first match on Saturday, then certainly they achieved it last night.

And Villa's 78th-minute goal which clinched the Cup for Spurs is likely to be replayed over and over again in years to come, a superb bit of individualism.

That Spurs were going to play with greater commitment and intent was obvious from the very first minute.

Ossie Ardiles held off two muscular challenges to free Garth Crooks down the right and Spurs' coloured striker pulled the ball back to the edge of the box where Ricky Villa hit the ball on the full only to see it strike Steve Archibald.

The challenges were vigorous with Spurs clearly not prepared to allow themselves to be intimidated as ... Saturday.

By STEVE CURRY

Tottenham	 3
Man. City	 2

edge of the penalty area Glenn Hoddle curled the ball superbly round City's wall ...

City flier . . . Kevin Reeves takes off between Rick...

That goal was the sp... ignite ...

Albio...

WEST Bromwich Albi... have slapped a £1 milli... price tag on Pet... Barnes.

Manchester City are ... pared to pay £500,00... the unsettled Engl... winger who cost ... £650,000 two years a...

But Albion boss Ron... son says: "It woul... something extra spe... make us reconsid... decision to turn d... transfer request he ... few weeks ago."

Meanwhile Albi... renew their interest ... transfer-listed stri... Biley. The clubs ag... exchange deal ... Albion's unsettle... David Mills in M... fell through whe... injured.

Good news for ... 35-year-old Kevin ... accepted an ... renewed contra... season.

Hector, retu... Baseball Grou... League Burto...

DAILY EXPRESS, Friday, May 15, 1981

TOTTENHAM . . . 3 MAN. CITY . . . 2

It's Viva Villa For Hot Spurs

By STEVE CURRY

Triumphant. Ardiles lifts the FA Cup that takes Spurs back into Europe

Ricky Villa, who was branded a failure on Saturday, led Spurs to unforgettable FA Cup victory last night.

In a full-blooded contest of skill and passion, his two goals as Spurs took the lead, lost it, and then regained it proved decisive.

It was breathtaking and exhilarating football with City showing courage and commitment, and Spurs at last capturing some of their scintillating skills.

The two famous clubs had promised to make this 100th final memorable. If they did not reach the height in their first match on Saturday, then certainly they achieved it last night.

And Villa's 78th-minute goal which clinched the Cup for Spurs is likely to be replayed over and over again in years to come, a superb bit of individualism.

That Spurs were going to play with greater commitment and intent was obvious from the very first minute.

Ossie Ardiles held off two muscular challenges to free Garth Crooks down the right and Spurs' coloured striker pulled the ball back to the edge of the box where Ricky Villa hit the ball on the full only to see it strike Steve Archibald.

The challenges were vigorous with Spurs clearly not prepared to allow themselves to be intimidated as they were on Saturday.

And the London team had the bonus of opening the score in the seventh minute.

Ardiles, prepared to run with the ball manoeuvred an opening on the edge of the City area and as he drilled the ball at goal it struck Archibald involuntarily on the heel.

He spun to strike the loose ball which Joe Corrigan could only block, Villa collecting it coolly to hammer Spurs into the lead.

The jubilation of the London fans, however, was to last only three minutes, the time it took City to equalise with a quite spectacular goal.

Ray Ranson pumped a free kick into the Spurs penalty area, it was half-cleared and Tommy Hutchison headed sideways for Mackenzie to strike the ball on the volley and leave Milija Aleksic no chance.

From a free kick on the edge of the penalty area Glenn Hoddle curled the ball superbly round City's wall and as Corrigan flung himself to his right, the ball hit the upright and rebounded to safety.

It was proving an absorbing game, City competing just as vigorously as they did on Saturday and Spurs providing the finer touches from the passing of Hoddle, the running of Ardiles and the competitiveness of Villa.

Referee Hackett was having to use all his refereeing experience to keep the excessive enthusiasm in check and in the 40th minute cautioned City's Tommy Caton for scything down Crooks.

But five minutes into the second half City dramatically took the lead.

A long free kick by Caton was headed on to Bennett by Mackenzie, City's striker chested the ball down and as he turned for goal went sprawling under the weight of clumsy challenges from Paul Miller and Hughton.

It was a clear penalty and Kevin Reeves stepped forward to place his kick positively into the right hand corner.

That goal was the spark to ignite some ill-tempered tackling and in the space of the following eight minutes, Hackett had to caution four players: Ransom for a foul on Tony Galvin; Galvin for a foul on Hutchinson; Archibald for dissent; and Gow, fourth player, for a tackle on Ardiles.

The little Argentinian was understandably angered by the foul.

Squeezed between that note taking was a superb left foot shot from Hoddle which Corrigan had to turn spectacularly over.

Suddenly, in the 71st minute, the pendulum swung again and Hoddle at last got some reward for one of the countless cleverly-weighted passes he had been spraying round Wembley for most of the night.

As his pass fell into the heart of City's area, Archibald controlled it but before he could get in his shot, Crookes pounced, to shoot low to Corrigan's right hand, and into the net.

Amazingly, Spurs then took the lead as the match reached a breath-taking climax with a piece of superb individualism from Villa who weaved past four challenges in City's area to score an unforgettable goal.

STANDARD, Thursday, September 17, 1981

AJAX . . . 1 SPURS . . . 3

FALCO GLORY SETS A £1½M HEADACHE

By PETER BLACKMAN

FIRE ONE . . . Spurs lift off in Europe as Ajax keeper, Piet Schrijvers is left helpless goal. Ricky Villa looks on.

Falco glory sets a £1½m headache

TOTTENHAM'S two-goal hero in Amsterdam, Mark Falco, is about to set manager Keith Burkinshaw a £1½-million headache.

The 20-year-old Hackney lad modestly accepted the praise after helping Spurs to a magical 3-1 lead over Ajax in the European Cup-Winners Cup.

But Falco is aware that the expensive strike partnership of Steve Archibald and Garth Crooks could be only two weeks away from being re-united.

Archibald returned after an ankle injury lay-off in Amster-dam last night and cartilage victim Crooks, after watching the first leg tie, told me: "I could be back for the second leg at our ground."

Dream

Burkinshaw hit a few shots on the golf course today, pondering the fact that Falco

PETER BLACKMAN reports

Falco stayed late in bed today at his parents' Hackney home: "First, some sleep . . . then some eggs and bacon from my mum . . . that's my plan today," he said.

"It was my first game in Europe last night, and it's against a really famous team, so it was a real dream come true for me when those goals poured in."

Burkinshaw said: "It was a sup-

And there was genuine appreciation from Crooks, who said: "There was marked maturity about him. He hit both goals superbly, but all my thoughts right now are aimed towards getting back in the side, and if luck is on my side, then I could be facing Ajax in the return."

Appeal

Falco could have had a hat-

ht before Ricky

Spurs should now go into the next round, and this opening victory was achieved with patience and a sharp awareness that the tactics had to be right.

"So often tactics have not proved our strong point," said captain Steve Perryman, who appealed over the loudspeakers in the Olympic Stadium for good behaviour among the group of travelling Spurs fans.

"But we got it right this time, and I hope we don't throw away all the good work here with any recklessness at home."

The fans? Inside the stadium the official group were excellently behaved, and there were only isolated incidents elsewhere in the heavily-policed stadium.

The official UEFA observer from Finland told Spurs chairman, Arthur Richardson, that the security arrangements were in order.

Tottenham's two-goal hero in Amsterdam, Mark Falco, is about to set manager Keith Burkinshaw a £1½-million headache.

The 20-year old Hackney lad modestly accepted the praise after helping Spurs to a magical 3-1 lead over Ajax in the European Cup Winners' Cup.

But Falco is aware that the expensive strike partnership of Steve Archibald and Garth Crooks could be only two weeks away from being re-united.

Archibald returned after an ankle injury lay-off in Amsterdam last night and cartilage-victim Crooks, after watching the first leg tie, told me: "I could be back for the second leg at our ground."

Burkinshaw hit a few shots on the golf course today, pondering the fact that Falco brilliantly grabbed his chance while the big stars have been absent in the past month.

Falco stayed late in bed today at his parents' Hackney home: "First, some sleep . . . then some eggs and bacon from my mum . . . that's my plan today," he said.

"It was my first game in Europe last night, and it's against a really famous team, so it was a real dream come true for me when those goals poured in."

LOOKING BACK WITH KEITH BURKINSHAW

Tottenham's return to Europe in 1981 was a sad reminder of their last disastrous experience – a trip to Holland.

This time it was to Amsterdam not Rotterdam where the dreadful 1974 riot took place. At the helm was a new manager Keith Burkinshaw.

It was a time of celebration. Spurs had brought the South American flair of Ossie Ardiles and Ricky Villa to the world of British football.

Villa's magnificent goal against Manchester City in the FA Cup final replay that May had earned Spurs their ticket to Europe and back to the big time.

Burkinshaw said: "That reappearance in Europe lifted the side into a different bracket. Now we were one of the big teams.

"In England there are only a handful of teams who regularly qualify for the European competitions. To reach Europe as we were about to do for four consecutive seasons made us into a Liverpool class team.

"The team gains more experience and more confidence from that exposure to European tactics and styles. They get the knowledge of how to handle different systems.

"That is something that you cannot learn from the domestic game because you don't come up against that many differing approaches.

"It helps them as young players and rounds them into more mature and commanding players. Europe is the great schooling ground."

"The young fellas started to find their feet and blossom. People like Micky Hazard developed spendidly in European competition.

Burkinshaw said: "It was a superb team effort and young Mark has snaffled his first-team chance with both hands. I'm delighted for him."

And there was genuine appreciation from Crooks, who said: "There was marked maturity about him. He hit both goals superbly, but all my thoughts right now are aimed towards getting back in the side, and if luck is on my side, then I could be facing Ajax in the return."

Falco could have had a hat-trick last night before Ricky Villa added the third goal with a spectacular, swashbuckling, breakaway goal that floored the dazed Dutch team.

Spurs should now go into the next round, and this opening victory was achieved with patience and a sharp awareness that the tactics had to be right.

"So often tactics have not proved our strong point," said captain Steve Perryman, who appealed over the loudspeakers in the Olympic Stadium for good behaviour among the group of travelling Spurs fans.

"But we got it right this time, and I hope we don't throw away all the good work here with any recklessness at home."

The fans? Inside the stadium the official group were excellently behaved, and there were only isolated incidents elsewhere in the heavily-policed stadium.

The official UEFA observer from Finland told Spurs' chairman, Arthur Richardson, that the security arrangements were in order.

Spurs' assistant secretary, Peter Day remained in Amsterdam to offer his help to the police.

RETROSPECTIVE VIEW BY MARK FALCO

Mark Falco joined Spurs straight from school and watched the European games against Split and Lyons in 1967 from the 'Shelf', which was his favourite vantage point on the terraces.

"European nights were always special for the fans and for me. It brings out the patriotism in the Spurs crowd. The atmosphere in other matches just isn't the same no matter what the game."

What a thrill then to be playing his first European game against one of the Continent's greatest clubs, Ajax of Amsterdam.

And, in the true spirit of Roy-of-the-Rovers, young Mark Falco made his presence felt with two of the goals which saw Spurs take a 3-1 advantage from the first leg in Holland.

"Recall those matches against Ajax? That's no trouble," enthused Falco, "I'll never forget them.

"After the glory of winning the FA Cup, we were still on a high when we went into Europe, but we didn't really know what to expect.

"Ray Clemence and Steve Perryman had plenty of experience while Glenn Hoddle had played in Europe for England, but the rest of us couldn't know what was in store until we had tried it for ourselves.

"Although we didn't know what to expect we were keyed up alright. Everyone was eager to impress on their first venture into European football.

"We produced one of that team's best displays in Europe that night. The first half against Feyenoord when we went four goals up, the 2-0 win over Bayern Munich after losing in Germany, and the UEFA Cup final against Anderlecht, I'd select as special performances.

"But we reached heights against Ajax that even surprised us. The fact that I scored two goals as well means so much.

"We took Ajax apart. My first goal came from a corner. The ball was knocked out, and as Ajax pushed forward to catch us offside, Ricky Villa slipped a pass to me and I slipped the ball round the 'keeper.

"My second again came from a corner. I slid the ball in at the far post."

The honest Falco was generous with his praise for Tottenham's third goal scored by the brilliant Ricky Villa. "He ran from the half way line, beating a few players before going round the 'keeper and walking the ball in."

Falco was in the middle of a hot run at the start of the season with nine goals in eleven games, keeping his place for Spurs' return to Europe.

Spurs comfortably won the second leg and a 6-1 aggregate score was a terrific start to a new European adventure.

"The young goalkeeper Tony Parks suddenly came through and thrived in the extra responsibility of the European competition. It all gave them added confidence.

"If the young players are developing then the club benefits too, obviously because they have a growth of talent which tends to help everything improve.

"If you get into Europe you seem to find that your League position improves and that the general professionalism of the clubs develops.

"It helps add interest and impetus to seasons and the City benefits from the exciting prospect of the visit of top continental glamour sides."

Certainly there cannot be many more glamorous sides in Europe than Ajax of Amsterdam. In the early 1970s Ajax were the pioneers of the 'total football' concept.

They formed the backbone of the great Holland team of the 1974 World Cup with stars like Johan Cruyff, Johnny Rep and Johan Neeskens.

Now Burkinshaw was told they were on the verge of a revival. Burkinshaw said: "They had a side that people warned would emerge to be one of the great European powers.

"They had Jesper Olsen, Soren Lerby and many Dutch youngsters in their team. Instead of thrashing us as we feared we went out and gave them a footballing lesson."

It was the start of a brave new era for Spurs.

Glenn Hoddle in action against Ajax

Mark Falco celebrates his goal as Spurs go through 6-1 on aggregate

DAILY STAR, Wednesday, September 30, 1981

SPURS . . . 3 AJAX AMSTERDAM . . . 0

SPURS WIN ON AGGREGATE 6-1

SPURS SPREE

By BOB DRISCOLL

Spurs unleashed 12 thunderous minutes of striking power last night to crush the last Cup Winners' Cup breath out of Ajax of Holland.

Having built a commanding 3-1 lead away, Spurs cruised through much of this second leg.

Then came that incredible burst of scoring action started in the 70th minute by Tony Galvin.

Six minutes later young Mark Falco accepted a simple chance and Ardiles followed up in the 82nd minute with a curling shot.

Having flattened Ajax in Amsterdam, Spurs were content to gently box their ears.

Spurs found themselves able to command the mid-field in much the same way as they had in Amsterdam.

The only problem this time was that their feared finishing power seemed to lack much of its usual venom.

After just two minutes Ricardo Villa dummied over a low centre for Hoddle to move on to a scoring chance.

But the England mid-fielder clipped his shot a foot over the bar.

It looked then as though Spurs were in the mood to demolish the once mighty Dutch club again.

Perhaps the best chance of the first half came in the 28th minute when Villa steadied himself on the goal-line and hit a ground pass to the edge of the box towards Hoddle.

Hoddle met the ball first time keeping his shot low and straight towards the corner of the net.

But as the crowd roared expectantly, goalkeeper Galje dived late to keep the ball out.

There was very little in reply from the Dutchmen.

But Spurs made sure of the tie in the 70th minute when a 40-yard ball from Hoddle gave Falco the chance to lay on a perfect chance for Tony Galvin who scored with a right foot shot.

Six minutes later Falco made it 5-1 on aggregate after good work by Hoddle and Archibald.

And it became a rout in the 82nd minute when Ardiles looped in a header.

SPURS SPREE

by BOB DRISCOLL

Spurs 3, Ajax Amsterdam 0

(Aggregate: 6—1)

SPURS unleashed 12 thunderous minutes of striking power last night to crush the last Cup Winners' Cup breath out of Ajax of Holland.

Having built a commanding 3—1 lead away, Spurs cruised through much of this second leg.

Then came that incredible burst of scoring action started in the 70th minute by Tony Galvin.

Six minutes later young Mark Falco accepted a simple chance and Ardiles followed up in the 82nd minute with curling shot.

Having flattened Ajax in Amsterdam, Spurs were content to gently box their ears.

Spurs found themselves able to command the midfield in much the same way as they had in Amsterdam.

The only problem this time was that their feared finishing power seemed to lack much of its usual venom.

After just two minutes Ricardo Villa dummied over a low centre for Hoddle to move on to a scoring chance.

But the England midfielder clipped his shot a foot over the bar.

It looked then as though Spurs were in the mood to demolish the once mighty Dutch club again.

Roared

Perhaps the best chance of the first half came in the 28th minute when Villa steadied him-

Shaw steps back

GARY SHAW makes a dramatic return for Aston Villa tonight.

Shaw (left) replaces Tony Morley, who has been sensationally dropped, for the European Cup match against Icelandic amateurs Valur.

Manager Ron Saunders said: "Maybe being left out will provide an extra stick on Morley's backside and perhaps he will start performing again."

FULL STORY — Page 26

Danger.. it's Ward

by BRYAN COONEY

Southampton 1, Limerick 1

Aggregate: 4—1

BRAVE little Limerick fought tooth and nail to keep out

Limerick should have done more with the chance.

The Irish side were full of running and had plenty of spirit. In wet conditions which made control difficult, Southampton suffered the frustration of almost

Last night's

CUP WINNERS' CUP

First round, second leg

SPURS 3 AJAX 0

Spurs: Galvin, Falco, Ardiles. H.T. 0—0. Att.: 34,606. Agg.: 6—1.

UEFA CUP

First round, second leg

BEVEREN WAAS 5

Waas: Martens (4), Pfaff. H.T. 0—2. Agg.: 0—8.

SOUTHAMPTON 1 LIMERICK 1

Southampton: Keegan. Limerick: Morris. H.T. 0—0. Att.: 12,841. Agg.: 4—1.

LEAGUE TWO

Ossie Ardiles threads his way through the Ajax defence

DAILY EXPRESS, Thursday, October 22, 1981

DUNDALK . . . 1 SPURS . . . 1

SORRY SPURS GET THE LUCK OF THE IRISH!

By ALAN THOMPSON

Sorry Spurs were out-played, out-fought, out-thought and eventually out-lasted by the part-timers of Dundalk last night.

The scoreline credited them with a draw but the story is one of incredible luck and unbelievable defensive slackness that could have ended in overwhelming defeat in this Cup Winners' Cup second round, first leg.

And even when, after a series of heart-stopping escapes, they managed to go into a second half lead, it was quickly nullified by a man who was told five years ago that he would never play again.

Garth Crooks scored for Spurs in the 63rd minute with a split second of splendid opportunism. He out-ran the Dundalk defence to latch on to a through ball from Glenn Hoddle which he took round goalkeeper Blackmore before slotting into an empty net.

That should have tightened Tottenham up, but incredibly they allowed the Irish to level.

Mick Fairclough, who thought his career had ended five years ago after an injury with Huddersfield, flashed round the immobile Graham Roberts before cutting into the penalty area and firing in a shot which gave Ray Clemence not the slightest chance.

That was the signal for the Dundalk fans to erupt in sheer, unrestrained joy.

And it was nothing less than the Irishmen deserved.

Spurs could easily have been one goal down in three minutes or two in seven minutes. Even three in 25 minutes – all due to defensive uncertainty and misunderstanding.

A bad back-pass by Roberts left Clemence 15 yards out of goal and although Carley managed to reach the ball, the angle was too narrow and the ball trickled tantalisingly across a goalmouth that was as wide open as the Grand Canyon.

Then Hughton got into the act with another pass that was intended for his goalkeeper but was about 10 yards short.

Clemence raced out of goal and out of the penalty area but Roberts managed to clear from Carlyle's boot and the Spurs defence had an argument.

The catalogue of errors continued and Clemence had to dive full-length to hold a fierce, ill-directed back-pass from Roberts.

But Spurs looked more their normal self in the second half although Clemence had to finger-tip away a 25-yard shot from Brian Duff.

And that old defensive haphazardness reared its head again after Crooks had scored.

They should never have lost that lead – good European teams would never have presented such openings at the back.

And unless Spurs can cure this basic fault, they will not win a thing.

Last word from Spurs' manager Keith Burkinshaw: "I worry more about matches like that than playing Manchester United at Old Trafford.

"People say we should win them easily but they are always the most difficult.

"All the same is was a silly goal that we conceded."

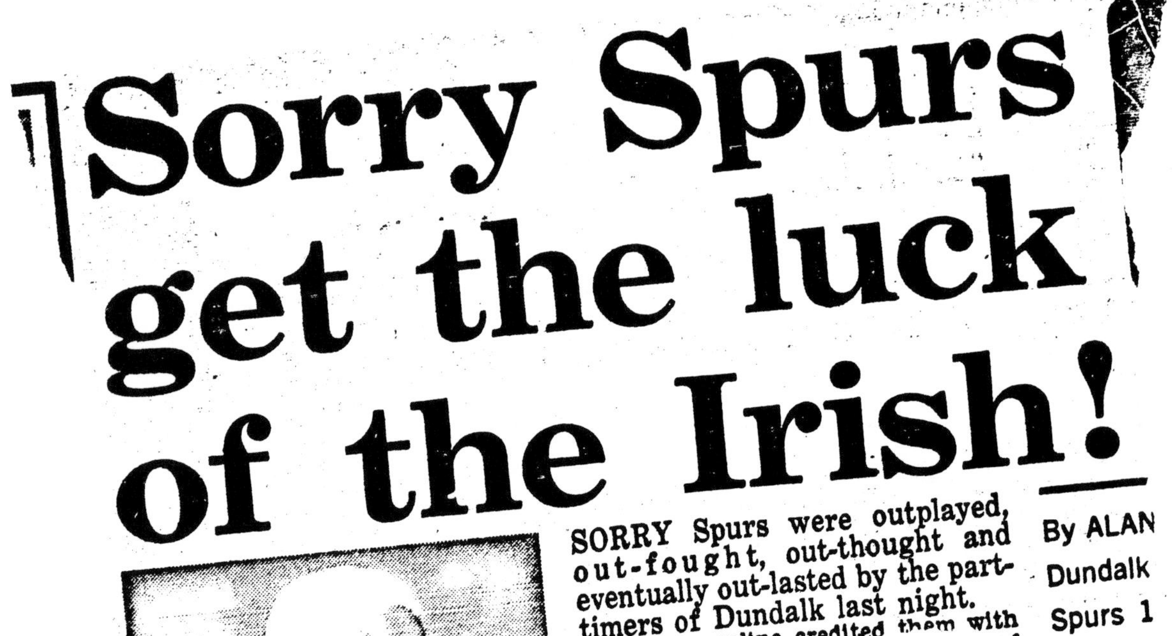

Sorry Spurs get the luck of the Irish!

SORRY Spurs were outplayed, out-fought, out-thought and eventually out-lasted by the part-timers of Dundalk last night.

The scoreline credited them with

By ALAN

Dundalk

Spurs 1

GUARDIAN, Thursday, November 5, 1981

SPURS . . . 1 DUNDALK . . . 0

AGGREGATE 2-1

CROOKS STEALS WIN FOR SLACK SPURS

By ROBERT ARMSTRONG

Tottenham Hotspur laboured like semi-skilled artisans to defeat the Irish part-timers of Dundalk with a scrambled goal in the second round of the European Cup Winners' Cup last night. The League of Ireland side defended with impressive organisation and covering and seriously exposed Spurs' lack of ingenuity when defenders crowd the path to the goal.

Garth Crooks gave Spurs a 2-1 aggregate victory with an opportunist goal in the second half of this second leg tie, thus ensuring a place in the draw for the quarter-final next March. However, the night was one that Tottenham will want to forget soon, with Hoddle sadly anonymous for long periods and Archibald still bereft of the sharpness that often punished defences last season.

Though there was a substantial gap in quality between the sides, the tie remained tense and nerve-ridden the longer that Spurs failed to score. They lost no time in setting up a continuous bombardment of the Irish goal but Archibald, Crooks and Galvin were so eager to score, all from good positions, that they showed more ambition than accuracy at the vital moment.

No doubt the knowledge that their supporters are not best known for unlimited patience played its part in the lack of composure when the strikers were required to apply the killing touch. While the crowd awaited the hoped-for deluge of goals, some of their number amused themselves by chanting "Bobby Sands, Bobby Sands." But it was unclear whether the reference to the dead hunger striker came from English or Irish supporters.

Certainly Dundalk displayed much of the tenacity and self discipline that earned them a creditable draw in the first leg and, if their centre backs did not exactly keep a tight rein on the Spurs' strikers, both Dunning and McConville were adept at blocking avenues of approach inside the penalty area.

By the interval it was clear that Ardiles' habit of running directly at defenders could become crucial. The Spurs defence was far from overstretched but occasionally alarming situations did develop, largely of their own making and caused by a lack of co-ordination between their back four and their goalkeeper, Clemence, who appeared uncertain whether to come off his line. A couple of needless corners were given away but these came to nothing.

When the murmurs of discontent were beginning to rumble Spurs took the lead in the 63rd minute. Soon after Blackmoor made a brave close-range save from Archibald, Spurs won a corner on the right which Hoddle floated into the goalmouth. Dundalk failed to clear a bobbling ball and Crooks darted in to stab his shot over the line from six yards.

Tottenham's best effort in the later stages was a crashing drive from 15 yards by Archibald, which rebounded from the cross-bar. For their part Dundalk might have equalised through Fairclough but the striker's header from a raking 35-yard pass flew high and wide.

Archibald's effort is saved by Blackmoor

Crooks steals win for slack Spurs

Tottenham Hotspur laboured like semi-skilled artisans to defeat the Irish part-timers of Dundalk with a scrambled goal in the second round of the European Cup Winners' Cup at White Hart Lane last night. The League of Ireland side de-ended with impressive organi-ation and covering and seri-isly exposed Spurs' lack of genuity when defenders owd the path to the goal.

Garth Crooks gave Spurs a 2-1 gregate victory with an oppor-nist goal in the second half this second-leg tie, thus en-ing a place in the draw for quarter-final next March. wever, the night was one that tenham will want to forget n, with Hoddle sadly anony-is for long periods and hibald still bereft

hunger striker came from English or Irish supporters.

Certainly Dundalk displayed much of the tenacity and self discipline that earned them a creditable draw in the first leg and if, their centre-backs did not exactly keep a tight rein on the Spurs' strikers, both Dunning and McConville were adept at blocking avenues of approach inside the penalty area.

By the interval it was clear that Ardiles's habit of running directly at defenders could become crucial. The Spurs defence was far from overstretched but occasionally alarming situations did develop, largely of their own making and caused by a lack of co-ordination between their back four and their goalkeeper, Clemence, who appeared uncer-tain whther to

DAILY MAIL, Thursday, March 4, 1982

TOTTENHAM . . . 2 EINTRACHT FRANKFURT . . . 0

TWO FOR THE ROAD

By JEFF POWELL

Tottenham's laboured erosion of a moderate West German side last night kept their ambitions alive on all four fronts.

It would require a drastic collapse of teamwork and temperament in Frankfurt in a fortnight for Spurs to fail now to reach their European semi-final.

Eintracht are among the least distinguished West German teams to have appeared in even the Cup Winners' Cup, traditionally the easiest of the European competitions to win.

Their version of Germany's renowned defensive system was more strained than disciplined. It does not say too much for Spurs that they had to wait almost an hour before Paul Miller and Mike Hazard scored the spectacular goals which put the seal on their superiority.

It was lucky for Tottenham that their latest team's first exposure to German technique was not against more distinguished representatives of the Bundesliga.

For even against Eintracht they needed an alert save by Ray Clemence to prevent this tie becoming uncomfortably close right at the end of this first leg.

Although Eintracht kept a close watch on Steve Archibald and Garth Crooks the marking was not especially oppressive in mid-field. Yet it still took Glenn Hoddle and the even more widely experienced Osvaldo Ardiles a long time to make decisive inroads into their defence.

Still, their performance eventually was good enough, especially since they are committed also to challenging for the League Championship, FA Cup and League Cup. Not every match can be a thriller in those circumstances.

Manager Keith Burkinshaw talked of "how difficult it is when teams keep so many players back against you . . . the need for patience . . . the fascination of the tactical battle of wits."

Yet had his forwards been functioning as incisively as usual, Burkinshaw might have watched them run up a decisive lead in the first quarter of an hour.

Hazard, sent clear by Archibald's header in only the second minute, was frustrated by the swift advance of Joachim Juriens.

When Juriens fell quickly to his right to divert Hughton's shot from the resulting half-cleared corner, Spurs realised this was not a night for the exploitation of a young reserve goalkeeper.

Archibald should have beaten Juriens when Hoddle's pass and Perryman's low cross left him in inviting space. But his shot hit the goalkeeper's leg.

Hoddle's chip floated over the crossbar and then, when he came sweetly on to a magnificent long ball from Miller, the same England forward volleyed wide.

As Spurs increased the pressure in the second half, Juriens reacted hysterically to every challenge. He was booked for simulating agony after a gentle brush with Crooks . . . but so was Archibald for complaining too persistently to the Rumanian referee.

Increasingly, Miller was coming forward from defence into workable space. And when an Ardiles shot from Hazard's pass was blocked, Miller rendered the appeals for handball redundant by firing Spurs ahead from 20 yards.

In need of at least one more goal, Burkinshaw replaced Crooks with Falco for the last half-hour and Price had a header cleared off the line by star Austrian sweeper Bruno Pezzey before Hazard's 83rd-minute run past two defenders was climaxed by another unstoppable 20-yard shot.

That goal would have done no harm to Hazard's personal campaign to hold on to his place at Wembley in the approaching League Cup final even if Ricardo Villa regains fitness next week.

Clemence unoccupied for most of the preceding 86 minutes was still wide awake when Nachtweih, the East German defector, broke clear.

That save should keep Spurs safe in Frankfurt where Burkinshaw expects Eintracht to come at us and perhaps give us a little more space in which to attack ourselves.

The odds on a German revival lengthens still further with the second half booking of Korbel who now misses the second leg.

Two for the road

BY JEFF POWELL

Tottenham 2
Eintracht Frankfurt 0

TOTTENHAM'S laboured erosion of a moderate West German side last night kept their ambitions alive on all four fronts.

Strained

Steve Archibald celebrates Paul Miller's goal

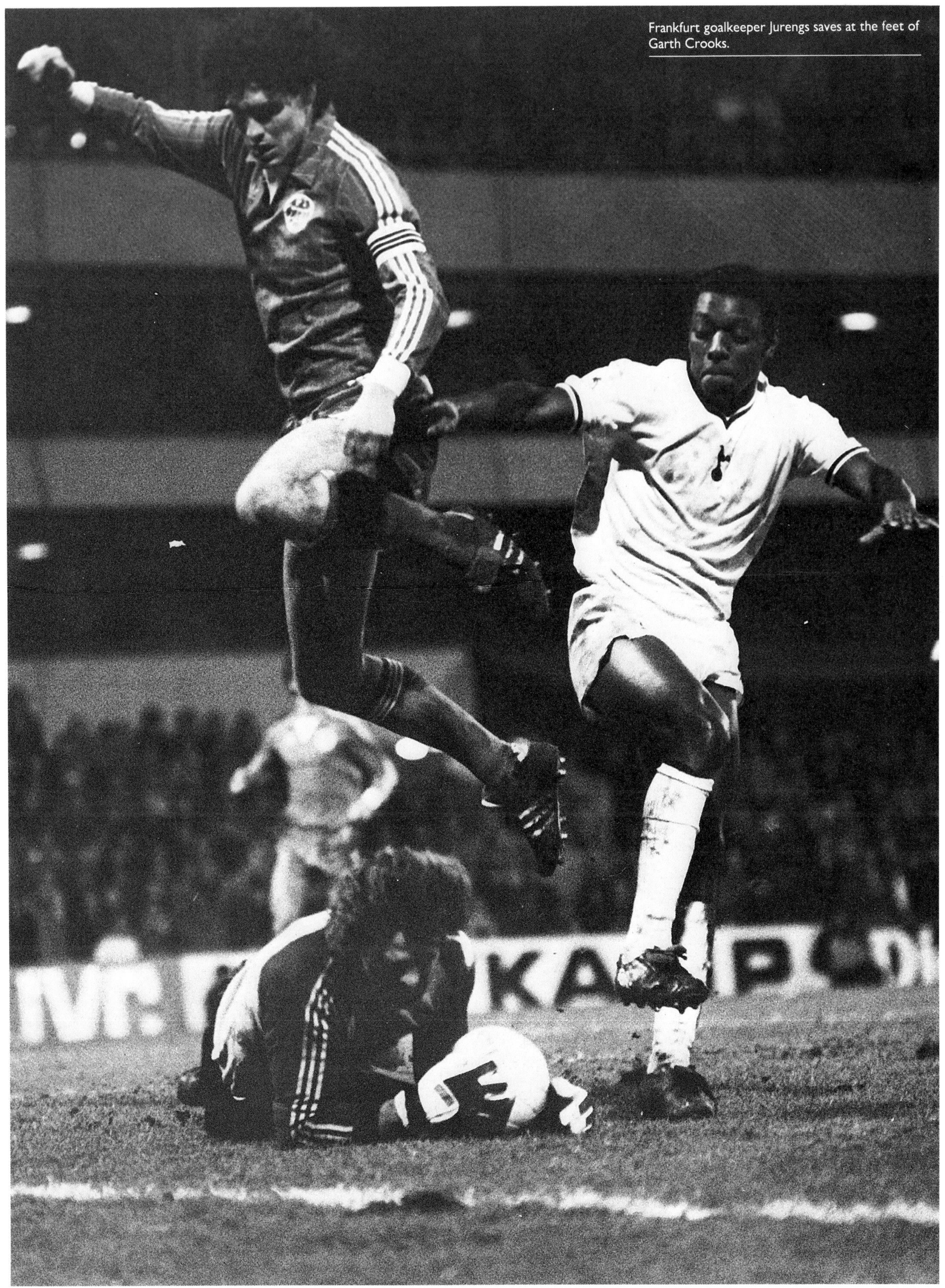

Frankfurt goalkeeper Jurengs saves at the feet of Garth Crooks.

SUN, March 17, 1982

EINTRACHT FRANKFURT . . . 2 SPURS . . . 1

HODDLES A GOLDEN WINNER

By BRIAN WOOLNOUGH

Glenn Hoddle scored the most important goal of his career last night to claw Spurs back from European disaster and send them into the semi-finals of the Cup Winners' Cup.

The brilliant England international struck just when it seemed that Tottenham's season had collapsed with a second demoralising defeat in five days.

Still smarting from Saturday's Milk Cup Final defeat by Liverpool, they looked like crashing out of Europe as well after surrendering a 2-0 first leg lead in 15 crazy opening minutes.

But they reorganised superbly in the second half and refused to die.

With 10 minutes left, Hoddle scored the vital goal that puts Spurs into the last four.

Substitute Ricky Villa sent on for Mark Falco, upset the Eintracht side with his strength and in the 80th minute fought his way through on the left to create the goal that mattered.

He slipped the ball to Chris Hughton, who rolled it quickly into Hoddle's patch. The England star took careful aim and his left foot sent the ball into the bottom of the Eintracht net.

"The most important goal I have scored," Hoddle said in a relieved Spurs dressing room. "I decided to side foot the ball instead of driving it and perhaps that deceived the goalkeeper."

But the night began disastrously for Spurs and Ossie Ardiles.

Ardiles, who injured ribs in practise a few hours before kick off, gave the ball to Norbert Nachweih after two minutes and Ronald Borchers went on to score.

And Eintracht couldn't believe it when Paul Price missed a deflected cross from the left and Bum Kun Cha made the aggregate score 2-2.

Sport

Thursday, March 18, 1982
Telephone: 01-353 3030

HODDLE'S A GOLDEN WINNER!

Spurs battle to semi

From BRIAN WOOLNOUGH: Eintracht Frankfurt 0, Spurs 1
(Spurs win 3-2 on agg)

GLENN HODDLE scored the most important goal of his career last night to claw Spurs back from European disaster and send them into the semi-finals of the Cup-Winners' Cup.

The brilliant England international struck just when it seemed that Tottenham's season had collapsed with a second demoralising defeat in five days.

Still smarting from Saturday's Milk Cup Final defeat by Liverpool, they looked like crashing out of Europe as well after surrendering a 2-0 first leg lead in 15 crazy opening minutes.

But they reorganised superbly in the second-half and refused to die.

With 10 minutes left, Hoddle scored the vital goal that puts Spurs into the last four.

Substitute Ricky Villa, sent on for Mark Falco, upset the Eintracht side with his strength and

VILLA GO THROUGH, LIVERPOOL OUT—Page 31

Hoddle said in a relieved Spurs dressing-room. "I decided to side-foot the ball instead of driving it and perhaps that deceived the goalkeeper."

But the night began disastrously for Spurs and Ossie Ardiles.

GLENN HODDLE . . . saved Spurs

"IT'S NOT THE MONEY IT'S THE

SUN, Thursday, April 8, 1982

SPURS . . . 1 BARCELONA . . . 1

ANIMALS

The Butchers of Barcelona shake battling Spurs

By BRIAN WOOLNOUGH

The Butchers of Barcelona last night dragged Tottenham down into the gutter of European football.

Bitter chants of "animals, animals," echoed around White Hart Lane as the Spaniards kicked and hacked their way through an X-certificate Cup Winners' Cup semi-final.

For 25 sickening second half minutes it seemed that Barcelona – down to 10 men when one of their hatchet men, Juan Estella, was sent off – were going to laugh all the way home.

England goalkeeper Ray Clemence sank to his knees in despair as he let a 40-yard speculative drive from Antonio Olmo slip through his fingers.

For a spell, Spurs lost their heads and it must be said that Graham Roberts was lucky to stay on the pitch as he raced into the thick of every punch-up.

Then with five minutes left, Roberts scored to give Spurs hope in the second leg in two weeks' time.

But that match is in danger of becoming a bloodbath. Last night a 41,000 crowd didn't see a football match – they witnessed a craze kicking contest.

In an early foresight into what the rest of the world can expect in the World Cup, Barcelona were brutes.

In the closing minutes we witnessed the incredible sight of a London policeman flinging himself around Barcelona's huge centre half, Martinez Manolo, as he went for Roberts behind the goal.

Spurs' manager, Keith Burkinshaw said: "If we play in Spain like Barcelona did there would be a revolution.

"And I fear it will be worse out there. We will go out there to win it fairly.

"Their goal was a present from Clemence but that was his first mistake for months and I bet he makes up for it out there."

Barcelona manager Udo Lattek said: "I don't think teams like Spurs and Barcelona should do things like that to each other."

April 8, 1982
Telephone: 01-353 3030

Galvin feels the crunch

DOWN but not out . . . Tor Galvin lies in a crumple heap but he carried on. different story for Jua Estella, who was sent o for a bad tackle on Galvi in another incident.

ANIMALS!

The butchers of Barcelona shake battling Spurs

Spurs 1, Barcelona 1

THE BUTCHERS of Barcelona last night dragged Tottenham down into the gutter of European football.

Bitter chants of "animals, animals," echoed around White Hart Lane as the Spaniards kicked and hacked their way through an X certificate Cup-Winners' Cup semi-final.

By BRIAN WOOLNOUGH

Hope

● Turn to Page 31

Spanish brawl

FLASHPOINT . . . Garth Crooks (left) and Graham Roberts (far right) are caught up in the brawling tactics of the Barcelona Butchers, but Roberts got his revenge with the equaliser. Picture: PETER JAY

HAGAR THE HORRIBLE By DIK BROWNE

Hoddle looks on as Roberts accuses Manolo

YELLOW CARD. The referee books yet another Barcelona player

Paul Price wins the ball from Alan Simonsen

Barcelona scramble the ball away

Steve Perryman's patience finally ran out and the Spurs captain was booked for a lunge at substitute Jose Moratalla.

Dutch referee Egbert Mulder must shoulder a lot of the blame for what went on. He was too weak and allowed Barcelona to dictate the match with their bar-room tactics.

Manolo's kick at Roberts began the fueding and it never stopped. They squared up to each other again moments later then Estella was booked for a foul on Roberts.

Tony Galvin took a revenge tackle on Jose Sanchez and throughout the first half we only had Mike Hazard's dribbling and a Glenn Hoddle shot that went just wide.

Estella was dismissed in the 57th minute and two minutes later Olmo's shot somehow deceived Clemence.

Tottenham threw themselves at Barcelona, who used every tactic to defend their precious away goal.

Chris Jones came on for Paul Miller and as the pressure mounted Moratalla was booked for a kick at Galvin.

Then with five minutes left, Hoddle somehow found space in a clustered Barcelona penalty area with a free kick.

The Spaniards were so busy kicking anything that moved that this time they didn't spot Roberts stealing in at the far post to score with a side foot.

It will need a very strong referee to keep the teams apart in the next clash.

Graham Roberts shows his delight at scoring Spurs' equaliser

DAILY MAIL, Thursday, April 22, 1982

BARCELONA . . . 1 SPURS . . . 0

BARCELONA WIN 2-1 ON AGGREGATE

POWER FAILURE!

By JEFF POWELL

The lights went out on Europe's finest stadium and Tottenham's Grand Slam season here last night.

The match, advertised as Bloodbath II, subsided into twilight despair for Spurs. With the Cup Winners' Cup now gone the way of the League Cup and with the championship mountain growing steeper from match to match, the FA Cup final now offers Tottenham's last realistic chance of glory.

When half the fuses blew in Barcelona's stupendous Nou Camp Stadium, it seemed that the electric circuits were collapsing in sympathy with a team exhausted by the marathon demands of the English season.

Like Leeds, Arsenal and Ipswich before them, Spurs are the victims of a programme which would tax the physical resources of Superman and which leaves little energy to spare for a sustained campaign in Europe.

When it came to the crunch, with Barcelona scoring in the first minute of the second half, Spurs tried so gallantly to step up the pace that manager Keith Burkinshaw was moved to say: "Our heads did not go down. If this is failure I want more of it. We had to play like the home team and we gave them a game."

Power failure!

GOALKEEPER Javier Urruti saves from Spurs Graham Roberts in Barcelona last night.

Barcelona ....1 Spurs 0

Barcelona win 2-1 on agg.

THE LIGHTS went out on Europe's finest stadium and Tottenham's Grand Slam season here last night.

The match, advertised as Bloodbath II, subsided into twilit despair for Spurs. With the Cup-winner's Cup now gone the way of the League Cup and with the championship mountain growing steeper from match to match, the FA Cup Final now offers Tottenham's last realistic chance of glory.

When half the fuses blew in Barcelona's stupendous Nou Camp Stadium, it seemed that the electric circuits were collapsing in sympathy with a team exhausted by the marathon demands of the English season.

Like Leeds, Arsenal and Ipswich before them Spurs are the victims of a programme which would tax the physical resources of Superman and which leaves little energy to spare for a sustained campaign in Europe.

Proud

When it came to the crunch, with Barcelona scoring in the first minute of the second half, Spurs tried so gallantly to step up the pace that manager Keith Burkinshaw was moved to say: 'Our heads did not go down. I was proud of our lads. It's been a great season and still is. If this is failure I want more of it. We had to play like the home team and we gave them a game.'

Weary S… say goo… to anot…

From JEFF POWELL in

In desperate truth, however, the spark was missing, even from Glenn Hoddle in his fitful endeavour to convince the watching Ron Greenwood that he might stimulate England's World Cup challenge back here in Spain this summer.

Not even an unscheduled five-minute rest during the first half gave Spurs enough breathing space to survive this troubled semi-final.

The lights dimmed sufficiently for East German referee Siegfried Kirschen to call a halt and hold talks with players and officials of both teams before allowing this second leg to continue its strained and laboured progress.

The tension was hardly surprising with both teams as well as the stadium, under heavy armed guard against terrorists, and hooligans and with UEFA officials going into both dressing rooms before the game to demand restraint after the brutality of the fir…

—Coppell blow for England—

STEVE COPPELL, the Manchester United winger … missed Tuesday's defeat at Ipswich and has now … up by Northern Ireland for their match with Scotland in

Urruti saves from Graham Roberts

10
DEL

In desperate truth, however, the spark was missing, even from Glenn Hoddle in his fitful endeavour to convince the watching Ron Greenwood that he might stimulate England's World Cup challenge back here in Spain this summer.

Not even an unscheduled five-minute rest during the first half gave Spurs enough breathing space to survive this troubled semi-final.

The lights dimmed sufficiently for East German referee Siegried Kitchen to call a halt and hold talks with players and officials of both teams before allowing this second leg to continue its strained and laboured progress.

The tension was hardly surprising with both teams, as well as the stadium, under heavy armed guard against terrorists and hooligans and with UEFA officials going into both dressing rooms before the game to demand restraint after the brutality of the first leg.

Barcelona's 80,000 fans subjected Spurs to a fearful ear battering and the bitterness carried over from the brutal first leg spread to the public ramparts as the crowd taunted Tottenham with chants of "Argentins, Argentins."

UEFA's appeals for football rather than fighting had less effect on the Spaniards in the first few minutes and Steve Perryman, Hoddle and Garth Crooks were all felled the first time they touched the ball.

The greatest genuine threat was presented by Allen Simonsen, the tiny Danish star who put Barcelona ahead on aggregate.

Alexanco launched a long pass from the centre circle which Quini sent looping towards Tottenham's goal with a huge header.

Paul Price, the Wales captain, failed to control the ball and Simonsen nipped to stab it past the sprawling Ray Clemence.

Spurs, required now to score one goal even to force extra time, pressed forward but were caught on the break twice again and relieved when Quini headed over both chances.

Burkinshaw replaced Price, a downcast defender, with Mark Falco for the last eight minutes. But the seconds ticked away and what began so bitterly in London a fortnight earlier ended with jubilant Barcelona reaching a European final in their own stadium next month and Tottenham shaking hands and exchanging shirts in weary resignation.

WE'VE DONE IT AGAIN

By BRIAN WOOLNOUGH

SPURS' marathon season finally ended in glory last night when a Glenn Hoddle penalty kept the FA Cup at White Hart Lane.

Hoddle's penalty makes it a Spurs double

SUN, Friday, May 28, 1982

SPURS . . . 1 Q.P.R. . . . 0

WE'VE DONE IT AGAIN

Hoddle's penalty makes it a Spurs double

By BRIAN WOOLNOUGH

Spurs' marathon season finally ended in glory last night when a Glenn Hoddle penalty kept the FA Cup at White Hart Lane.

Skipper Steve Perryman, the only ever-present in all 66 matches, hugged the Cup at Wembley and said: "It would have been a crime if we hadn't won anything."

Perryman added: "This is reward for the football we have played all season."

Nobody can deny Tottenham a trophy at the end of a winter that once promised football's first Grand Slam, but every heart went out to Second Division QPR after this final replay.

Rangers fought back superbly in the second half and manager Terry Venables said: "It was a moral victory and I feel very unlucky. But I'm proud.

"We were the better side. Spurs were cracking. I couldn't see us losing. For the rest of my life I will see John Gregory's shot hit the bar."

There were emotional moments when Argentine international Ricky Villa was given a standing ovation before the game, at half-time and at the end.

Manager Keith Burkinshaw, who is about to sign a three-year contract, revealed that he is resisting world-wide offers for Villa and Ossie Ardiles.

Burkinshaw said: "I hope and pray that I can get the little fella back with the big man.

"I hope everything can be sorted out because everyone in the world wants to sign them and I've had offers from the Continent and the Middle East.

"I thought the crowd's reaction to Ricky was fantastic. War or no war, the British are fair-minded."

Burkinshaw was not as elated as last year, but added: "The record books will show that Spurs won and QPR lost it.

I thought Rangers were brilliant and I felt sorry for them. They played their hearts out."

Hoddle said: "I was the only one who didn't practise penalties.

"The penalty did come a bit early and I was nervous."

With the FA Cup firmly under their belts, Spurs continued their domestic rise and carried on into Europe.

DAILY STAR, Thursday, September 16, 1982

COLERAINE . . . 0 SPURS . . . 3

IT'S KIDS STUFF FOR SPURS

By KEN LAWRENCE

Spurs' expected win over the pauper part-timers of Coleraine yesterday was pure kids stuff. Their European Cup Winners' Cup first round leg victory was little more than a game of taf.

While the little Irish League side – half of them players unemployed – chased and puffed their way around Spurs did just enough to keep them at arms length when it mattered most.

And after this catch as catch can win the second leg at White Hart Lane in a fortnight, is nothing more than a formality.

With Argentinian Ricky Villa looking like he came from a different planet to anything the Irish side could offer Spurs went ahead in the 12th minute when Steve Archibald tapped home an early goal after Gary Mabbutt hit the post with a header.

Spurs stretched themselves again and in the 49th minute Garth Crooks made it two with a fine header from Brooke's cross.

And six minutes from time a truer reflection of the huge gap between the sides arrived when Crooks tapped home his second after Brooke's shot was blocked by goalkeeper Vince Magee.

Burkinshaw occasionally erupted from his bench in the second half to hurl directions at his players – but more out of professionalism than panic.

And afterwards he said: "We've got to be happy with the win even though these games often lack pattern and the polish you might hope for.

"We were a little bit wary of them but we believed they would tire in the second half, which in fact they did.

"However it was a good start to our European campaign. I might have looked a bit agitated but I'm just always looking for perfection."

It's kids stuff for Spurs

With Argentinian Ricky Villa looking like he came from a different planet to anything the rish side could offer Spurs went head in the 12th minute when teve Archibald tapped home an arly goal after Gary Mabbutt hit e post with a header.

Spurs stretched themselves ain and in the 49th minute arth Crooks made it two with fine header from Brooke's

And six minutes from time a truer reflection of the huge gap between the sides arrived when Crooks tapped home his second after Brooke's shot was blocked by goalkeeper Vince Magee.

Erupted

Burkinshaw occasionally erupted from his bench in the second half to hurl directions at

And afterwards he said: "We've got to be happy with the win even though these games often lack pattern and the polish you might hope for.

"We were a little bit wary of them but we believed they would tire in the second half, which in fact they did.

"However it was a good start to our European campaign. I might have looked a bit agitated but I'm just always looking for

Ricky Villa being challenged by the Coleraine defence

SUN, Wednesday, September 29, 1982

SPURS . . . 4 COLERAINE . . . 0

SPURS WIN 7-0 ON AGGREGATE

EURO STROLL FOR SPURS

Keith's men cruise home

By IAN GIBB

Ray Clemence knew the moment that Tottenham were through this Cup Winners' Cup battle.

The England 'keeper was taken off with 25 minutes still remaining at White Hart Lane last night.

But the Irish part-timers of Coleraine weren't hurt by such brazen confidence. They had kept the lid on the expected Volcano of Spurs goals.

In fact, only a late double burst enabled Tottenham to improve on their 3-0 first leg win in Ireland.

That was down to a mixture of carelessness – Steve Archibald could have had five – a couple of sparkling saves by Vince Magee, and an effective sandbagging job by the Irish defence.

The Tottenham management had urged their team to lay on a goal bonanza for the North London faithful, with a surprisingly large crowd of 20,925 turning up.

But after Garth Crooks had accelerated away from his Irish shadow to score with a 14th-minute shot, it was hard for Spurs to raise their game.

Spurs' boss Keith Burkinshaw moaned: "We made a lot of chances but we wouldn't have hit a barn door from ten yards on some occasions."

The all-action Gary Mabbutt increased the Spurs lead in the 54th minute when he curled a 20-yard shot away into the right corner of the net from John Lacy's knockdown.

Clemence then departed for sub 'keeper Tony Parks to make his European debut in the 65th minute – and soon after Terry Gibson came on for Crooks.

It was a smart move as Parks did have one fine save to make from World Cup star Felix Hely – and Gibson grabbed his first European goal.

That came in the 86th minute following a Mabbutt shot that rebounded. Garry Brooke had already hit Spurs' third of the night in the 83rd minute.

Archibald did manage to get his name in the referee's book – but only for dissent. That is something Spurs could have done without.

"He would deserve having to face a suspension, for chatting back to the referee," said Burkinshaw.

The Scotland striker is just one caution away from an automatic European one-match ban.

Garth Crooks opens the scoring against Coleraine

EURO STROLL FOR SPURS

GARY MABBUTT ... hit the second for Spurs

Keith's men cruise home

By IAN GIBB: Spurs 4, Coleraine 0
(Spurs win 7-0 on aggregate)

RAY CLEMENCE knew the moment that Tottenham were through this Cup Winners Cup battle.

The England keeper was taken off with 25 minutes still remaining at White Hart Lane last night.

But the Irish part-timers of Coleraine weren't hurt by such brazen confidence. They had kept the lid on the expected volcano of Spurs' goals.

In fact, only a late double burst enabled Tottenham to improve on their 3-0 first leg win in Ireland.

That was down to a mixture of carelessness — Steve Archibald could have had five — a couple of sparkling saves by Vince Magee, and an effective sandbagging job by the Irish defence.

Urged

Tottenham manage- had urged their ... lay on a goal ... the North ... ul, with a ... crowd

from his Irish shadow to score with a 14th-minute shot. It was hard for Spurs to raise their game.

Spurs boss Keith Burkinshaw moaned: "We made a lot of chances but we wouldn't have hit a barn door from ten yards on some occasions."

The all-action Gary Mabbutt increased the Spurs lead in the 54th minute when he curled a 20-yard shot away into ... right corner of the John Lacy's

Clemence then departed for sub keeper Tony Parks to make his European debut in the 65th minute — and soon after Terry Gibson came on for Crooks.

Debut

It was a smart move as Parks did have one fine save to make from World Cup star Felix Hely — and Gibson grabbed his first European goal.

That came in the 86th minute following a Mabbutt shot that rebounded. Garry Brooke had already hit Spurs' third of the night in the 83rd minute.

Archibald did manage to get his name in the referee's book — but only for dissent. That is something Spurs could have done without.

"He would deserve having to face a suspension for chatting back to the referee," said Burkinshaw.

The Scotland striker is just one caution away from an automatic European one-match ban.

HOT-SHOT . . . that's Hotspur Garth Crooks as he fires home the first last night
Picture: PETER JAY

Coleraine goalkeeper Vince Magee seems to be asking his defenders for more cover

GUARDIAN, Thursday, October 21, 1982

TOTTENHAM . . . . 1 BAYERN MUNICH . . . 1

TOTTENHAM RUN ON RESERVE

By DAVID LACEY

Tottenham Hotspur's reserves were not quite up to the task of defeating Bayern Munich at White Hart Lane last night in the opening leg of the their Cup Winners' Cup second round tie. Deprived by injuries of half their regular team, Spurs made a bold attempt to establish some sort of lead but in the end could not beat their overriding handicap and were held to a 1-1 draw.

When Archibald put Spurs in front after only three minutes Bayern, their defence on the point of collapse, looked eminently beatable. Had it not been for a combination of the crossbar and the excellence of Pfaff, who kept goal for Belgium in the World Cup, the Bavarian team would have been four goals down by half-time.

Pfaff thwarted Spurs to the last. Eight minutes from the end a shot from Brooke hit him in the chest and rebounded into the path of Crooks, who seemed certain to score with the goalkeeper lying helpless on the ground. But Pfaff raised an arm and managed to deflect the shot wide.

The agility of the Bayern goalkeeper and the fact that strong appeals for penalties after Mabbutt and Crooks had been sent tumbling by clumsy tackles were rejected by the Italian referee, Luigi Agnoli, gave Tottenham and their supporters a prima facie case for believing they should have been going to Munich in a fortnight's time with a handsome lead. In fact the overall pattern of the match suggested that ultimately the result was just.

Bayern, having drawn level early in the second half, controlled the rest of the match in an imperious manner reminiscent of the way West Germany had beaten England at Wembley seven days earlier.

Rummenigge almost made it 2-1 with five minutes to go when he was left with only Clemence to beat after Lacey had given the ball away to Dremmler near the right hand touchline, a mistake which rather summed up Spurs' performance in the latter half of the game. Bayern, having wilted at the start, emerged after half-time looking as though they had been revived with the beer that refreshes parts other beers cannot reach. Tottenham, so ebullient earlier, appeared to be waiting for their bench to shout "Mackeson".

With Perryman, Hoddle, Roberts, Hughton and Galvin all missing, it seemed Spurs were being tested more for their depth of strength than their obvious talent.

In the second minute Pfaff tipped a header from Crooks over the bar. In the third Archibald ducked in to head past Pfaff after Lacy had nodded on a corner from Brooke and in the fourth Brooke ran on to a short free kick from Villa and produced a thunderous 25-yard shot that rebounded from the underside of the bar. This move was repeated twice before half-time and on each occasion Pfaff had to make urgent saves.

Mid-way through the first half Spurs lost Archibald with a pulled muscle and while his replacement, Falco, showed a sufficient sense of purpose to join O'Reilly in being cautioned for fouling Dremmler, Tottenham's attack lost something of its incisiveness.

At the start of the game the entire Bayern team, apart from Rummenigge, were huddled nervously in their goalmouth as if sheltering from the rain. But as the match progressed Breitner began to organise some sort of resistance in mid-field and Rummenigge's runs into space became increasing dangerous.

Nevertheless they only created one clear chance before half-time. Then, in the 53rd minute, a badly-sliced clearance by O'Reilly put Tottenham's defence in all kinds of trouble. Clemence stayed on his line as Lacy and Rummenigge challenged for the dropping ball, Hoeness completely missed his kick, and Breitner followed up powerfully to put the ball into the roof of the net.

Tottenham run on reserve

Tottenham Hotspurs' reserves ,ere not quite up to the task ,f defeating Bayern Munich at Vhite Hart Lane last night in ıe opening leg of their Cup 'inners' Cup second round tie. eprived by injuries of half eir regular team, Spurs made ›old attempt to establish some ·t of lead but in the end ıld not beat their overriding ıdicap and were held to a 1-1 ν.

'hen Archibald put Spurs in t after only three minutes ·rn, their defence on the ' of collapse, looked emi- y beatable. Had it not been combination of the cross- ıd the excellence of Pfaff,

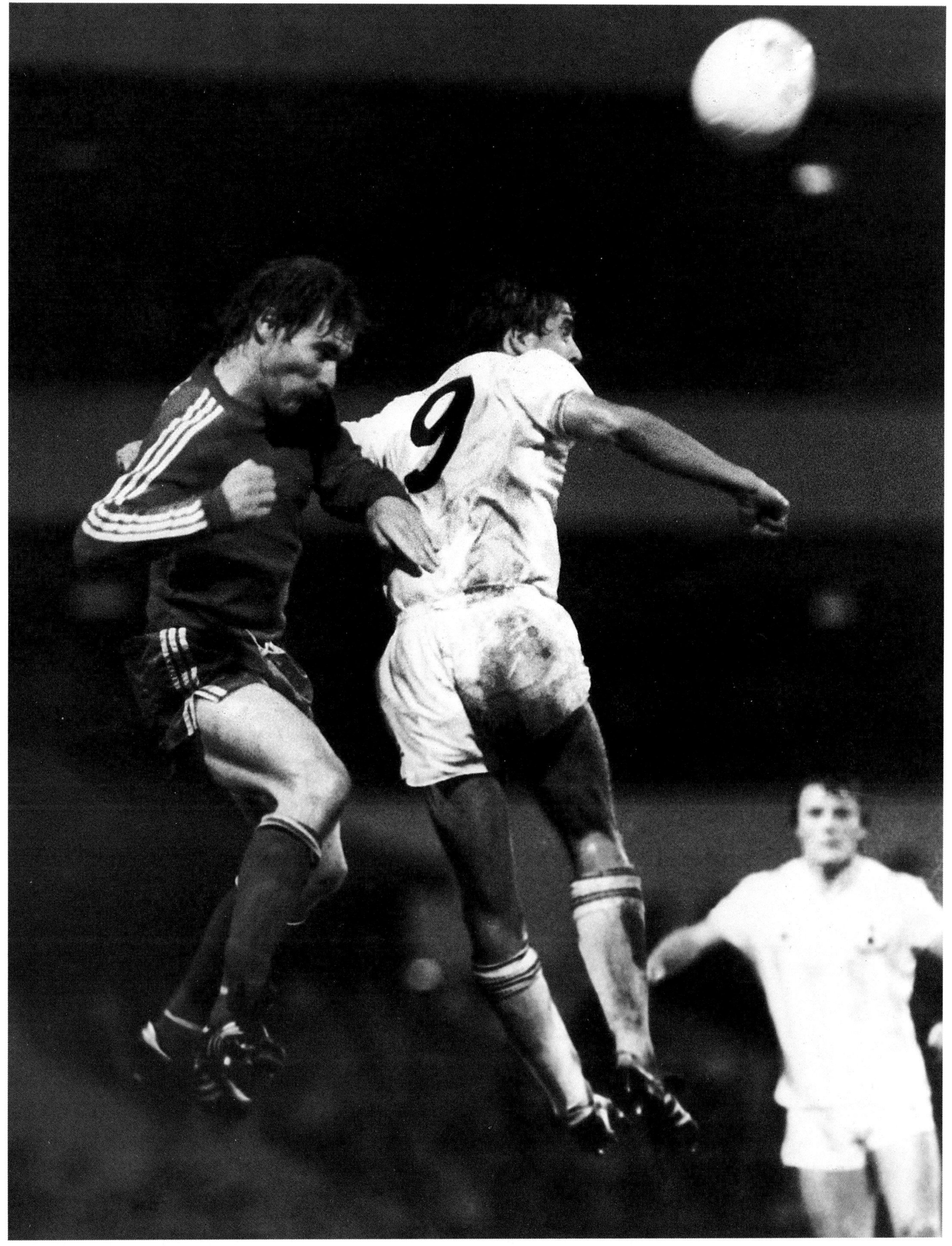

Gary Mabbutt beats Wolfgang Grobe to the ball

Tottenham are the victims of execution in the fog

From Stuart Jones, Football Correspondent, Munich

Bayern Munich....................4
Tottenham H.......................1

(Bayern win 5-2 on agg)

Tottenham Hotspur were delayed by mist at Luton airport on Monday afternoon and they lost their way in even thicker fog here last night. The only time they have gone down by such a heavy margin in a European tie was in the first round of the same competition, the Cup Winners' Cup, against Manchester United, 19 years ago.

Although Hoddle and Perryman came on as substitutes, Tottenham's hopes of holding Bayern Munich in the second leg of the second round were never bright. Yet when they arrived here yesterday evening, the was dismally gloomy. To clear the floodlights were

decade ago, is so spacious, the game became less than a spectator sport. The pass of the ball was often to be traced only through the noise of the crowd nearest to it. With delayed stereophonic sound, the reactions spread to the viewers hidden at the opposite end.

The identity of the scorer of Bayern's first goal, after 18 minutes, would have remained as much a mystery as to the way in which he scored it, had it not been for the electronic scoreboard. Helpfully it spelt out Honess and almost everybody had to take its word. Bayern's manager, Uli Honess, had complained to a linesman about the appalling conditions but, appeased by his younger brother's effort, he then sat down.

His counterpart, Keith Burkinshaw, and Crooks

seen, but once they approached the penalty area their confidence dwindled away in the swirling mist.

Hoddle, absent since the beginning of September and Perryman, missing since the beginning of October, came on to replace Brooke and Miller respectively on the hour and suddenly the sky began to open up. The fog lifted; so, too, were Bayern and they repeated their deadly closing strike at White Hart Lane a fortnight ago.

Breitner emphatically drove home the third a quarter of an hour from the end and, after Hughton had pulled one back five minutes later, Rummenigge at last broke free to add the fourth. It was over that last relatively clear half hour ironically, that Tottenham

Ray Clemence saves at the feet of Dieter Hoeness during the fog at Munich

TIMES, Thursday, November 4, 1982

BAYERN MUNICH . . . 4 TOTTENHAM H . . . 1

BAYERN WIN 5-2 ON AGGREGATE

TOTTENHAM ARE THE VICTIMS OF EXECUTION IN THE FOG

From STUART JONES

MUNICH

For entry into Europe, a team must either win a domestic trophy or have a sufficiently high League position to be considered viable contenders. This season (1982/83), Spurs had a poor domestic run but, as the teams ahead of them in the League had also won other honours and thereby already qualified, Spurs moved into Europe as the highest non-victorious League club.

Despite internal problems, this campaign was to prove their most stirring yet.

Tottenham Hotspur were delayed by mist at Luton airport on Monday afternoon and they lost their way in even thicker fog here last night. The only time they have gone down by such a heavy margin in a European tie was in the first round of the same competition, the Cup Winners' Cup, against Manchester United, 19 years ago.

Although Hoddle and Perryman came on as substitutes, Tottenham's hopes of holding Bayern Munich in the second leg of the second round were never bright. Yet, when they arrived here yesterday evening, the sight was dismally gloomy. To clear the air, the floodlights were switched on early to generate heat but the elements, like Bayern, refused to be beaten.

The eerie scenery could have been a perfect backdrop for an Alfred Hitchcock production. As though tons of dried ice was falling from the network of roofs suspended above the audience, visibility was sometimes reduced to such a short distance that at least one television cameraman was seen to concede defeat.

Since the spectacular stadium, built to stage the Olympic Games a decade ago, is so spacious, the game became less than a spectacular sport. The pass of the ball was often to be traced only through the noise of the crowd nearest to it. With delayed stereophonic sound, the reactions spread to the viewers hidden at the opposite end.

The identity of the scorer of Bayern's first goal, after 18 minutes, would have remained as much a mystery as to the way in which he scored it, had it not been for the electronic scoreboard. Helpfully it spelt out Honess and almost everybody had to take its word. Bayern's manager, Uli Hoeness, had complained to a linesman about the appalling conditions but, appeased by his younger brother's effort, he then sat down.

His counterpart, Keith Burkinshaw, and Crooks spoke to the referee in similar terms as they walked to the dressing room for the interval, and, with a heavy white shroud covering the ground, there was a strong suspicion that the event might be abandoned. The referee's decision to continue was later vindicated, though the scorer of Bayern's second goal after 53 minutes was also clouded from view.

The 25-yard shot was credited to Horsmann and it effectively ended Tottenham's European ambitions. As in the first leg their approach, particularly in the first half, was full of promise, at least as far as could be seen, but once they approached the penalty area their confidence dwindled away in the swirling mist.

Hoddle, absent since the beginning of September and Perryman, missing since the beginning of October, came on to replace Brooke and Miller respectively on the hour and suddenly the sky began to open up. The fog lifted, so, too, were Bayern and they repeated their deadly closing strike at White Hart Lane a fortnight ago.

Breitner emphatically drove home the third a quarter of an hour from the end and, after Hughton had pulled one back five minutes later, Rummenigge at last broke free to add the fourth. It was over that last relatively clear half hour, ironically, that Tottenham would most wish to have drawn a thick veil.

Burkinshaw commented: "We were beaten by a good side. In England we would not have played as it was, but the referee is the final adjudicator, and there will be no complaints. But most of the crowd could not have seen it and that is a pity. At up to £10 a ticket it was expensive, especially for those who had travelled from England."

FOOTBALL LEAGUE FINAL TABLES

DIVISION 1

		Home					Away					
	P	W	D	L	F	A	W	D	L	F	A	Pts
1. Liverpool	42	16	4	1	55	16	8	6	7	32	21	82
2. Watford	42	16	2	3	49	20	6	3	12	25	37	71
3. Manchester U	42	14	7	0	39	10	5	6	10	17	28	70
4. Tottenham H	42	15	4	2	50	15	5	5	11	15	35	69
5. Nottingham F	42	12	5	4	34	18	8	4	9	28	32	69
6. Aston Villa	42	17	2	2	47	15	4	3	14	15	35	68
7. Everton	42	13	6	2	43	19	5	4	12	23	29	6
8. West Ham U	42	13	3	5	41	23	7	1	13	27	39	6
9. Ipswich T	42	11	3	7	39	23	4	10	7	25	27	5
10. Arsenal	42	11	6	4	36	19	5	4	12	22	37	
11. WBA	42	11	5	5	35	20	4	7	10	16	29	
12. Southampton	42	11	5	5	36	22	4	7	10	18	36	
13. Stoke C	42	13	4	4	34	21	3	5	13	19	43	
14. Norwich C	42	10	6	5	30	18	4	6	11	22	40	
15. Notts Co	42	12	4	5	37	25	3	3	15	18	46	

DAILY MAIL, Thursday, September 15, 1983

DROGHEDA . . . 0 SPURS . . . 6

SPURS SPREE

Irish swamped as Falco sparkles in the rain

By HARRY HARRIS

Spurs shrugged off their disappointing start to the League season to score their best-ever away win in European soccer at rain-soaked Drogheda last night.

They hit the Irish side for six in the UEFA Cup tie – and they did it without big-buys Steve Archibald and Alan Brazil or England man Glenn Hoddle.

Mark Falco, drafted in only because of manager Keith Burkinshaw's row with Archibald, scored twice and also hit the woodwork three times. Gary Mabbutt was another two-goal man, and Garth Crooks and Tony Galvin scored the others.

Burkinshaw said: "I thought about putting Hoddle or Brazil on in the second half but the kids were doing so well and I felt they needed the experience."

With better finishing Spurs would have had double figures, but in the second leg in two weeks' time they could still top their 15-1 aggregate against Iceland's Keflavik 12 years ago.

There were no more casulties in this match and Spurs can now put their early season setbacks behind them.

Spurs won comfortably because they responded to manager Burkinshaw's warning not to underestimate the no-hopers and part-timers from Ireland.

It turned out to be a goal jamboree for Spurs and a dampener for Drogheda's first match in European football, played in an incessant downpour before a 7,000 crowd.

Burkinshaw said: "We played with so much discipline. The players showed such a great attitude. Yet we'll probably get little credit for this win.

"Only two years ago we went to Dundalk and came away with only a 1-1 draw. That proves it's not easy. However, it looks as though things are starting to turn for the better over the last week with a win at Leicester and a draw at West Bromwich."

Last night they came up against a goalkeeper who was an amazing mixture of world-class saves and suicidal errors. But Brendan Flynn could take no blame for the Spurs opener in the fifth minute, headed in by Falco after a flowing five-man move.

Flynn allowed a weak shot from Crooks to slip under his body and crawl over the line, and the third goal, a minute before half-time, was even more bizarre,

Flynn raced ten yards out of his area to hit the ball away but it went straight to Galvin whose 40-yard chip sailed into the empty net.

Galvin, Steve Perryman and Garry Brooke combined for Mabbutt to head the fourth in the 52nd minute, and Falco snapped up number five after another Flynn fumble.

Mabbutt made it six with a 20-yard ground shot nine minutes from the end.

Drogheda's consolation is a £65,000 payday and a couple of nights out in London in a fortnight.

Spurs spree

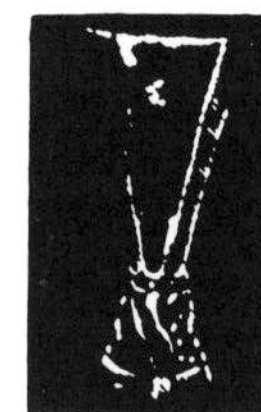

Irish swamped as Falco sparkles in the rain

Drogheda......0 Spurs......6: By HARRY HARRIS

SPURS shrugged off their disappointing start to the League season to score their best-ever away win in European soccer at rain-soaked Drogheda last night.

They hit the Irish side for six in the UEFA Cup-tie—and they did it without big-buys Steve Archibald and Alan Brazil or England man Glen Hoddle.

Mark Falco, drafted in only because of manager Keith Burkinshaw's row with Archibald, scored twice and also hit the woodwork three times. Gary Mabbutt was another two-goal man, and Garth Crooks and Tony Galvin scored the others.

Burkinshaw said: 'I thought about putting Hoddle or Brazil on in the second half but the kids were doing so well and I felt they needed the experience.'

With better finishing Spurs would have had double figures, but in the second leg in two weeks' time they could still top their 15-1 aggregate against Ireland's Keflavik 12 years ago.

There were no mo[illegible] ties in this ma[illegible] can now put [illegible]

Co[illegible] ... goal. [illegible]

DAILY EXPRESS, Thursday, September 29, 1983

SPURS . . . 8   DROGHEDA . . . 0

SPURS WIN 14-0 ON AGGREGATE

GLORY NIGHT FOR SPURS

By COLIN BATEMAN

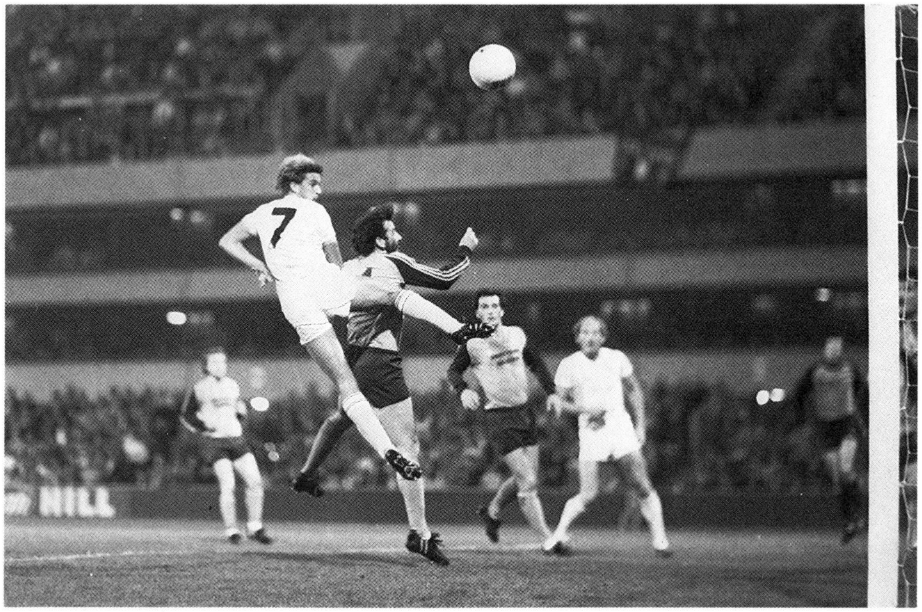

Gary Mabbutt goes close for Spurs

Tottenham showed no mercy to the part-timers of Drogheda as they cruised into the second round of the UEFA Cup.

Irish defenders were like sitting ducks in a shooting gallery as Spurs got the boost of confidence manager Keith Burkinshaw had demanded with a 14-0 aggregate win.

The only thing Tottenham missed was their record European score of 15-1 set 12 years ago against Keflavik of Iceland.

The score last night could easily have been double as Spurs pushed forward against tiring Drogheda and almost fell over each other in their anxiety to get in on the act.

The match almost reached ridiculous proportions when Tony Galvin was penalised for pushing team mate Chris Hughton off the ball.

But the fun night at White Hart Lane was just what Tottenham wanted to convince the supporters that they should return on Sunday to see the First Division clash with Nottingham Forest instead of watching it at home on TV.

Said manager Burkinshaw: "I was pleased. We kept going forward throughout the 90 minutes and goals give you confidence."

Mark Falco and Graham Roberts grabbed two apiece in the first half.

Falco's first after 17 minutes broke the deadlock and his second ten minutes before half-time was the best of the night.

The biggest cheer of the night, however, went to Alan Brazil.

Brazil, without a goal this season, missed a hatful of chances before the 50th minute when he blasted in number five and saluted the crowd from the penalty spot.

Drogheda's defence disintegrated during the next 10 minutes as first Steve Archibald and then Chris Hughton burst through to add their names to the score sheet.

When Brazil dived in to head home Galvin's cross 15 minutes from time it looked certain the European record would go.

Spurs with Glenn Hoddle in mid-field, keying up the chances, took it in turns to have pot shots but somehow Drogheda's defence got foot, leg or backside in the way to stop Tottenham going one over the eight.

Glory night for Spurs

By COLIN BATEMAN
Spurs 8 Drogheda 0
(Spurs win 14—0 on aggregate)

TENHAM showed no mercy to the part-...s of Drogheda as they cruised into the ...nd round of the UEFA Cup.

...rish defenders were like sitting ducks in a ...ing gallery as Spurs got the boost of confidence ...ger Keith Burkinshaw had demanded with a 14—0 aggregate win.

The only thing Tottenham missed was their record European score of 15—1 set 12 years ago against Keflavik of Iceland.

The score last night could easily have been doubled as Spurs pushed forward against tiring Drogheda and almost fell over each other in their anxiety to get in on the act.

The match almost reached ridiculous proportions when Tony Galvin was penalised for pushing team mate Chris Hughton off the ball.

Fun

But the fun night at White Hart Lane was just what Tottenham wanted to convince the supporters that they should return on Sunday to see the First Division clash with Nottingham Forest instead of watching it at home on TV.

Said manager Burkinshaw: "I was pleased. We kept going forward throughout the 90 minutes and goals give you confidence."

Mark Falco and Graham Roberts grabbed two apiece in the first half.

Falco's first after 17 minutes broke the deadlock and his second ten minutes before half time was the best of the night.

The biggest cheer of the night, however, went to Alan Brazil.

Brazil, without a goal this season, missed a hatful of chances before the 50th minute when he blasted in number five and saluted the crowd from the penalty spot.

Drogheda's defence disintegrated during the next 10 minutes as first Steve Archibald and then Chris Hughton burst through to add their names to the score sheet.

When Brazil dived in to head home Galvin's cross 15 minutes from time it looked certain the European record would go.

Spurs with Glenn Hoddle in midfield, keying up the chances, took it in turns to have pot shots but somehow Drogheda's defence got foot, leg or backside in the way to stop Tottenham going one over the eight.

Graham Roberts . . . scored two

Oxford in goal rush

Oxford 6 Walsall 3

OXFORD went goal cra... night, going four up af... minutes and then, six m... after the restart GEO... LAWRENCE gave them fifth.

ANDY THOMAS hit first in four minutes although ALLY BR... levelled for Walsall, O... raced away with goals ... GARY BARNETT, LAWR... and BOBBY McDONALD.

Walsall hit back thr... CRAIG SHAKESPEARE a... BROWN penalty, but Ox... had the final say with a ... from THOMAS.

The win gave Oxford ... Canon League Third Div... £300 prize as top goalsco...

Steve Archibald turns away having put Spurs' into the lead

TIMES, Thursday, October 20, 1983

TOTTENHAM HOTSPUR . . . 4 FEYENOORD . . . 2

HODDLE TAKES FEYENOORD'S BREATH AWAY

By CLIVE WHITE

It had to happen one day, I suppose: Johan Cruyff placed in the wings by an opposing number ten. But who better to take over the mantle from the great but aging champion than our own darling, Glenn Hoddle. Determined that the word "greatness" should be stamped upon his game as permanently as a silver mark he grabbed hold of this game yesterday evening at White Hart Lane and never let go – even if his defence did. His subtle, creative touch plucked four first half goals from out of the cold night air that fairly took Feyenoord's breath away. But the Dutchmen are nothing if not resilient and countered to such effect in the second half that they are still breathing in this UEFA Cup competition.

Much better if your colours happen to be blue and white to remember the first half when Tottenham Hotspur crowned a glorious evening of family-style entertainment (sky-diving, marching bands etc) with a four-goal pounding of the famous Dutchmen.

Spurs were sharp and eager to do them an early mischief. And so it proved after just eight minutes when Hughton seized greedily upon a through pass by the alert Hoddle, Hughton's cross leaving Archibald with an easy finish.

Hoddle's painful, penetrating forward balls gave the Dutch defence no respite. In the 18th minute, Hoddle crossed to perfection from the wing and Galvin sprinted unseen through a thin line of defence to head in.

Five minutes later another through pass from Hoddle ripped through Feyenoord. Falco turned on it with great agility but his shot was parried to apparent safety when Mabbutt arrived like a whippet to pull the ball back from the byline and leave Archibald with another economical finish. Six minutes before half-time the Dutch were left speechless by the audacious Hoddle. He struck a pass from 40 yards at the galloping Galvin who ran on past mesmerized defenders for another simple score.

The great man himself, Cruyff, still showed us glimpses of his past: the soft shoe shuffle of the right-footed feint and the left-footed cross. Less obviously he showed us a fighting spirit when defenders like Roberts attempted to baulk him unfairly. He obviously enjoyed his goal, neatly taken in the 70th minute after a one-two with Duut. But this must have seemed no more than a consolation until the close range goal by Neilsen in the 81st minute which may have changed the whole face of the second round tie.

Pointer for Spurs: Archibald salutes his first and Mabbutt beats Hiele to set up the Scot's second (Photographs: Ian Stewart)

Hoddle takes Feyenoord's breath away

By Clive White

ttenham Hotspur 4
yenoord 2

never let go – even if his defence did. His subtle, creative touch plucked four first-half goals from out of the cold night air that fairly took Feyenoord's breath away. But the Dutchmen are nothing if not resilient and countered to such

Spurs were sharp and eager to do them an early mischief. And so it proved after just eight minutes when Hughton seized greedily upon a through pass by the alert Hoddle. Hughton's cross leaving Archibald with an easy finish.

Hoddle's painful, penetrating forward balls gave the Dutch defence no respite. In the 18th

parried to apparent safety when Mabbutt arrived like a whippet to pull the ball back from the byline and leave Archibald with another economical finish. Six minutes before half-time the Dutch were left speechless by the audacious Hoddle. He struck a pass from 40 yards at the galloping Galvin who ran on past mesmerized defenders for another simple score

Roberts attempted to baulk him unfairly. He obviously enjoyed his goal, neatly taken in the 70th minute after a one-two with Duut. But this must have seemed no more than a consolation until the close range goal by Nielsen in the 81st minute which may have changed the whole face of the second round tie

TOTTENHAM HOTSPUR: R Clemence, C Hughton, A Galvin, G Roberts, G Stevens, S Perryman, G Mabbutt, S Archibald, M Falco, G Hoddle, G Brooke (sub: I Crook)

THE NEW MASTER BEATS THE OLD. Hoddle beats Cruyff to cross for Tony Galvin to head home Spurs' second goal

DAILY MIRROR, Thursday, November 3, 1983

FEYENOORD . . . 0 TOTTENHAM . . . 2

REAL CLASS

Tottenham's quality show masters the Dutch

From HARRY MILLER

IN HOLLAND

The chant "Super Tottenham" rang out round Rotterdam last night as Keith Burkinshaw's star-studded side asked to be remembered for the quality of their football rather than the fury of their fans.

For once, the club's collection of strikers – some in form, some out of favour – had to give way in the glory stakes to a defender.

Tottenham had pledged to throttle the UEFA Cup life out of the Dutch league leaders in the first 20 minutes.

They were only five minutes behind schedule when full back Chris Hughton, outstanding throughout, shot the goal that put this tie beyond Feyenoord's reach.

Tony Galvin scored five minutes from the finish and Tottenham's marvellous night – at least on the football front – was complete.

We have become used to outstanding performances by Spurs on the foreign front. This one, controlled and exciting, came close to comparison with the best.

Feyenoord knew that nothing less than an all-out offensive would enable them to pull back from their 4-2 first leg deficit.

They played two men wide and pushed the indifferent Johan Cruyff forward, but found themselves vulnerable to every swift Tottenham thrust.

Energetic Mark Falco was unlucky not to be on the score-sheet. He chased willingly and three times went agonisingly close before Tottenham hit the front.

Glenn Hoddle, who had another fine game, was heavily involved in that 25th-minute goal.

So were skipper Steve Perryman and striker Steve Archibald before Hughton kept cool to shoot low past Joop Hiele.

Twice in the first half Ray Clemence, who had been doubtful with a thigh injury, made brave saves.

Early on he flung himself to the left to turn away a 30-yard Wim Van Til thunderbolt. Later he turned an Andre Jeliazkov header over the bar.

Feyenoord's cause was not helped when they had to substitute Pierre Vermeulen after the forward's father had suffered a heart attack sitting in the stand.

Falco kept up his one-man shooting war in the second half.

He put one drive narrowly wide of the far post and had another scoring shot ruled out for offside.

Feyenoord plugged away, and in one raid Jeliazkov hit the top of the bar.

The goal that buried Feyenoord came in the 85th minute when Galvin hit a crisp drive from Gary Mabbutt's pass.

One black spot for Tottenham was that Hoddle and Archibald were booked for dissent.

Manager Burkinshaw was later: "It was a very professional performance and we got the result we came for. What pleased me more than anything was that everyone ran for each other."

Perryman said: "Feyenoord tried a lot of different things tactically, but at the end they ran out of ideas.

"All credit to Hughton. He loves to go forward and his goal was similar to one we got against Barcelona."

Tottenham's quality show masters the Dutch

REAL CLASS

Feyenoord 0, Tottenham 2 (agg: 2—6)

THE chant "Super Tottenham" rang out round Rotterdam last night as Keith Burkinshaw's star-studded side asked to be remembered for the quality of their football rather than the fury of their fans.

For once, the club's collection of strikers—some in form, some out of favour—had to give way in the glory stakes to a defender.

Tottenham had pledged to throttle the UEFA Cup life out of the Dutch league leaders in the first 20 minutes.

They were only five minutes behind schedule when full-back Chris Hughton, outstanding throughout, shot the goal that put this tie beyond Feyenoord's reach.

Tony Galvin scored five minutes from the finish and Tottenham's marvel- ... at least on ... front—was

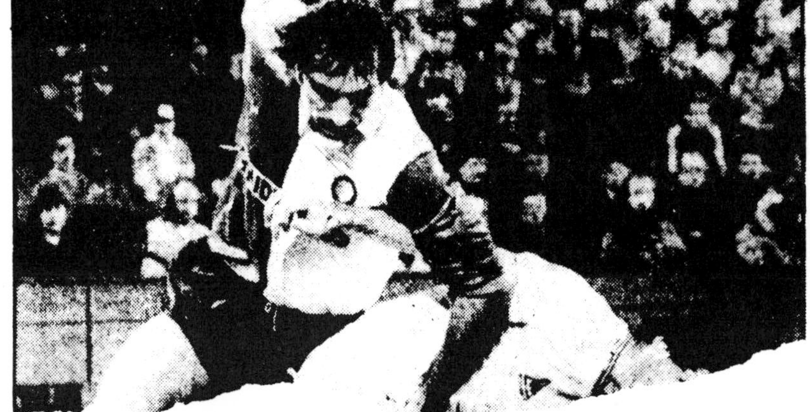

Archibald challenges Feyenoord's Ivan Nielsen

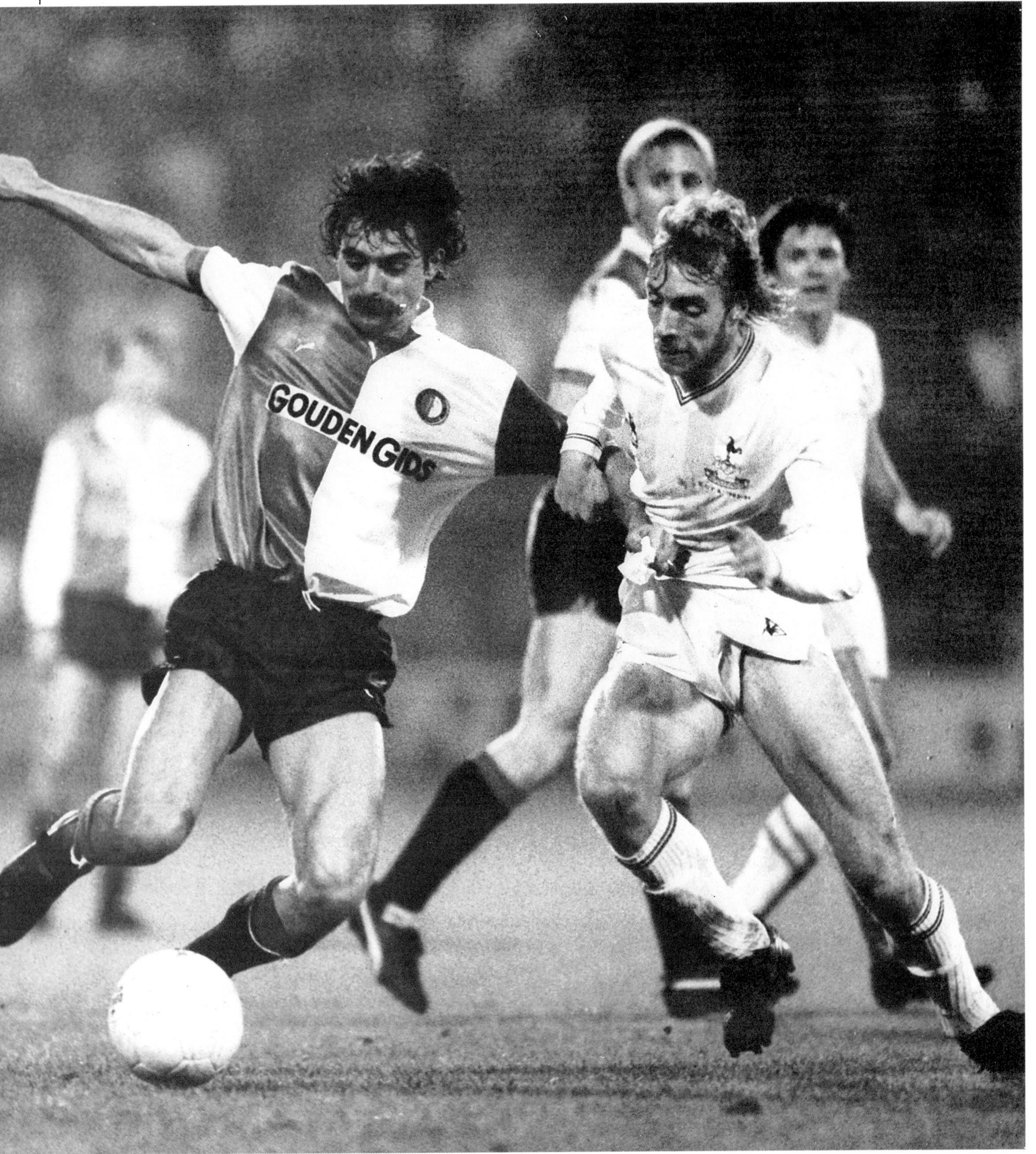

Johan Cruyff tries to organise the Feyenoord defence as Glenn Hoddle shapes up to take a Spurs free kick

LOOKING BACK WITH JOHAN CRUYFF

Johan Cruyff did not make too many mistakes in his glittering career but he certainly made one at White Hart Lane in October 1984.

For the Dutch master, the man who had led Ajax and Holland to the peak of European and World football, wanted to make one more point.

The place he decided to make the great stand was against Tottenham at White Hart Lane. The occasion, a UEFA Cup second round tie. The result: defeat by 4 goals to 2.

For weeks before the tie, Cruyff had been fascinated with the prospect of playing against Glenn Hoddle, the midfield star who was making a name for himself in European terms.

Cruyff said: "I wanted to test myself against the young star of the present. I knew I could play. I wanted to see what level I was at.

"Glenn Hoddle was a great player in my book. He played football the way that I wanted to see it played. He could make great passes and was the best player for Tottenham."

That almost incredible attraction to the Hoddle skill was to prove Feyenoord's downfall. A technical director of the club as well as a player Cruyff made a fatal decision.

Despite the pleas of the Feyenoord boss Thijs Libreghts to rethink, Cruyff insisted that he marked Glenn Hoddle. It was an error from which Feyenoord could not recover.

Within 20 minutes, Feyenoord were in trouble, and not until Cruyff was finally released from his self-imposed torture did the Dutch side pose a threat.

Cruyff admitted: "It was a bad error of judgement. I thought that I could mark him and keep him quiet. The result shows that I could not.

"He was a player that I had liked but it was only on the pitch that I realised how good he really was. I was a shadow without any presence.

"We slipped away into the night and I had to admit to the other players that it was all down to me. We had a glimmer of hope but that was to disappear in the second leg."

Roberts is foiled by Lerby and goalkeeper Pfaff on a freezing night in Munich.

DAILY EXPRESS, Thursday, November 24, 1983

BAYERN MUNICH . . . 1 SPURS . . . 0

SPURS DOWN – BUT NOT OUT!

From STEVE CURRY

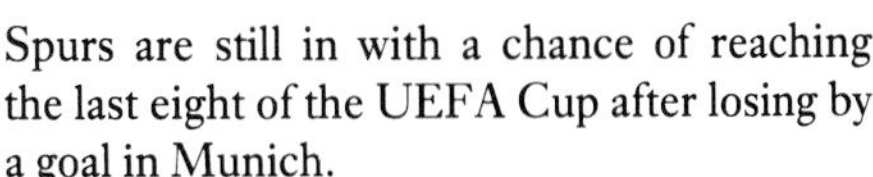

Spurs are still in with a chance of reaching the last eight of the UEFA Cup after losing by a goal in Munich.

Michael Rummenigge, brother of famous West German skipper Karl-Heinz, denied Spurs the merit of a goalless draw against Bayern with five minutes to go in the freezing cold of Munich's Olympic stadium.

But the slender victory margin provides Spurs with a marvellous incentive for a charging comeback at White Hart Lane on December 7.

It was certainly a far more rewarding result than Spurs could manage on their last visit here in the Cup Winners' Cup last season when they were walloped 4-1. But a match that started full of promise for Tottenham turned, in the second half, into a ragged and occasionally bad-tempered affair.

The temperature on the terraces was a chest-searing five degrees below zero but out on the pitch, with its sub-soil heating, it threatened to reach boiling point. Dutch referee Jan Keizer punished Spurs' 'keeper Ray Clemence with a yellow card for dashing out of his area to challenge Calle Del Haye in the 64th minute.

Danny Thomas was also booked in the 74th minute when he almost came to blows with Hans Pfluger after a brawling tackle out on the left.

It seemed the Spurs defence might hold out until Rummenigge collected a long ball out on the left, cut inside and smashed a shot past Clemence.

The relief among the 20,000 fans scattered across this vast stadium echoed into the Bavarian night.

Spurs had begun encouragingly with young Mark Falco shooting just wide in the third minute and Steve Archibald hitting the side netting when he really ought to have done better with Glenn Hoddle's through ball.

But signs that Bayern were settling down came with a swerving centre from Karl-Heinz Rummenigge in the 20th minute which Pfluger snatched at and put wide of the mark.

Despite losing skipper Karl-Heinz Rummenigge with injury at the start of the second half, Bayern began to apply serious pressure, with Spurs having to resort to tactics more associated with Hackney Marshes than White Hart Lane.

Danish international Soren Lerby was narrowly off target with two free kicks and Bayern had a penalty claim turned down after Gary Stevens had collided heavily with Michael Rummenigge.

Mike Hazard and Dick were substituted in the 72nd minute by Alan Brazil and Gary Brooke as Spurs strove to hold on.

They failed to do so by only five minutes but should still have the confidence to pull back their goal deficit and head for victory in the second leg.

Said Spurs' manager Keith Burkinshaw: "It is now an intriguing situation. But we always feel we can score goals, particularly at home, and whatever way you look at it we feel sure we are still in with a good chance."

Bayern's Udo Lattek said: "Before the game we agreed we would need to win 2-0 to be safe. Now a 1-0 win might just be enough. Spurs need two goals in London but we will be looking to hit them on the break. Frankly I don't envy Mr Burkinshaw."

TIMES, Thursday, December 8, 1983

TOTTENHAM . . . 2 BAYERN MUNICH . . 0

TOTTENHAM WIN 2-1 ON AGGREGATE

TOTTENHAM'S GLORY DAYS RETURN

By STUART JONES

The glory days returned to White Hart Lane last night. Tottenham Hotspur, like the majestic team of old, showed that they are learning the continental lesson of combining natural attacking flair with defensive patience to claim a place in the last eight of the UEFA Cup. They will know their quarter-final opponents tomorrow.

Hoddle, at times showing peerless artistry, was responsible for both goals, scored by Archibald and Falco, which put them through 2-1 on aggregate. Bayern Munich, the leaders of the Bundesliga and the last remaining West German representatives in Europe, later admitted they feel the English representatives can go on to win the trophy.

Hoddle, not surprisingly, started it all. The England international, who Uli Hoeness would not buy for Bayern and who Bechenbauer would not include in his all-star side of 40-year olds, brought both wings into play before opening a path for Falco with a glorious pass that fell neatly into his stride.

Falco's ferocious drive ricocheted off the outside of the right hand post with a sharp crack and even though the tie was a mere 12 minutes old, there was an ominous suspicion that Tottenham's hopes might also have been splintered. The Germans may be pale red shadows of the giants they once were but their defence was rugged and disciplined.

They had to be. With little Cook pulling them wide to the right and the equally young Dick stretching them on the left, Bayern suffered pressure that continued almost unabated until the interval. Even the loss of Hughton and later of Dick failed to halt Tottenham's keen search for goals.

Opportunities emerged first in a dribble and then in a torrent. Falco's toe poke was tipped away by Pfaff, Perryman's back-header was cleared off the line, Hoddle's free kick was almost deflected, Archibald's volley dipped just over the bar, Steven's half-volley from five yards was blocked and Hoddle's delightful lob was pushed over. Yet when there seemed no limit to Bayern's resistance, it was suddenly broken in the 50th minute. Hoddle floated a free kick towards Roberts whose precise downward header dropped in front of six white socks. Archibald, brushing aside his colleagues, drilled it home for his 14th goal in his last 17 games.

Having found what they had sought, Tottenham inevitably lost their rhythm and composure, particularly when Brooke came on for the injured Dick. But their resolve was stiffened by two explosions from the Rummenigge brothers, lurking dangerously on the periphery like fireworks that have been lit and forgotten.

Karl-Heinz stung Clemence's fingers with a typically crisp shot and Michael rejected a chance given to him by Thomas's error by lifting the loose ball deep into the terraces from close range. With a mere four minutes to go, Tottenham completed their courageous recovery and Hoddle completed his answer to his German critics.

Falco seized on his astute through ball as he ran inside the area and fired diagonally across Pfaff's body towards the far post. It hit the woodwork again, this time with a dull thud, and then rolled under the guidance of the eager Archibald into the back of the net. As it did so, 42,000 roared in appreciation for the last time.

THE TIMES THURSDAY DECEMBER

IES AFTER WORLD CUP DRAW-FUTURE PERFECT FOR TOTTENHAM AND FOREST IN UEFA

Hoddle fends off the challenges of Lerby (left) and Augenthaler (Photograph: Chris Cole)

Tottenham's glory days return

By Stuart Jones

Tottenham	**2**
Bayern Munich	**0**

(Tottenham win 2-1 on agg)

The glory days returned to White Hart Lane last night. Tottenham Hotspur, like the majestic team of old, showed that they are learning the continental lesson of combining natural attacking flair with defensive patience to claim a place in the last eight of the UEFA Cup. They will know their quarter-final opponents tomorrow.

Hoddle, at times showing peerless artistry, was responsible for both goals, scored [illegible]hibald and Falco [illegible] 2-1

Falco's ferocious drive ricocheted off the outside of the right hand post with a sharp crack and even though the tie was a mere 12 minutes old, there was an ominous suspicion that Tottenham's hopes might also have been splintered. The Germans may be pale red shadows of the giants they once were but their defence was rugged and disciplined.

They had to be. With little Cook pulling them wide to the right and the equally young Dick stretching them on the left. Bayern suffered pressure that continued almost unabated until the interval. Even the loss of Hughton and later of Dick failed to halt Tottenham's keen search for goals.

Opportunities emerged first in a dribble and then in a torrent. Falco's toe poke was tipped away by Pfaff, [illegible]man's back header was cleared

Having found what they had sought, Tottenham inevitably lost their rhythm and composure, particularly when Brooke came on for the injured Dick. But their resolve was stiffened by two explosions from the Rummenigge brothers, lurking dangerously on the periphery like fireworks that have been lit and forgotten.

Karl-Heinz stung Clemence's fingers with a typically crisp shot and Michael rejected a chance given to him by Thomas's error by lifting the loose ball deep into the terraces from close range. With a mere four minutes to go, Tottenham completed their courageous recovery and Hoddle completed his answer to his German critics.

Falco seized on his astute through ball as he ran inside the area and

Sturm Graz lose but go through

Sturm Graz, of Austria, moved into the quarter-final round of the UEFA Cup yesterday despite a second-leg 1-0 defeat by **FC Leipzig**, of East Germany. The Austrians had beaten Leipzig 2-0 in the first leg.

About 20,000 people watched in the Rudolf Plache Stadium as Zoetsche scored from twenty yards in the 12th minute. The East Germans kept attacking throughout the match played in windy weather on a field partly covered with snow.

Sturm Graz prevented further scoring with a fine performance by the goalkeeper, Saria.

Moscow Spartak defeated **Sparta** [illegible] foiling a last-minute [illegible] the quarter-

Karl-Heinz Rummenigge gets away from Mike Hazard.

SPURS V BAYERN MUNICH: Falco in control (see match report p.194)

Gifts from some of Spurs' European Opponents

1962/63 European Cup Winners' Cup replica

Locomotive Leipzig

1971/72 UEFA Cup replica

Aberdeen

Eintracht Frankfurt

Grasshoppers Zurich

Gifts and pennants from some of Spurs' European oppenents

Feyenoord

Real Madrid

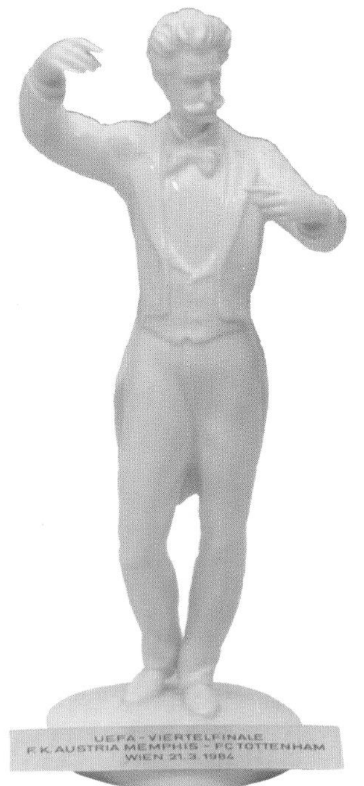

Austria Vienna

Anderlecht

Bohemians Prague

1983/84 UEFA Cup replica

Coleraine

Drogheda

Hadjuk Split

Bruges

Feyenoord

Austria Vienna

Bohemians Prague

DAILY MAIL, Thursday, March 8, 1984

TOTTENHAM . . . 2 AUSTRIA VIENNA . . 0

TOTTENHAM WIN 2-1 ON AGGREGATE

STEVE THE BOLD

Striker shrugs off injury to set up Spurs

Report By HARRY HARRIS

Steve Archibald, watched last night by the Italian agent hoping to set up a £1 million deal for Verona, provided the goals that could help Tottenham win the UEFA Cup in his farewell season.

Transfer-listed Archibald, involved in a personal feud with manager Keith Burkinshaw since September when his willingness to play through an injury was seriously questioned, declared himself fit just hours before this quarter-final first leg.

And he obliged with his 23rd goal of the season, taking his first real chance against a meticulously organised defence in the 58th minute. He also struck the bar with a header a little later and supplied an intricate pass that helped Alan Brazil to the second goal, assisted past goalkeeper Friere Koncilia by captain Robert Sara.

Burkinshaw, although unable to settle his dispute with his Scotland striker, praised him for his bravery in playing through the knee ligament injury that kept him out of Saturday's match against Stoke.

The Tottenham manager said: "Steve was a bit dubious. He had an ice-pack on his knee at half-time. I asked him whether he wanted to come off. He went white and said he wanted to stop out there. He was feeling the knee, but it didn't seem to inhibit him."

Graham Roberts, like Archibald, epitomised the spirit that eventually shook the Austrian sophisticates out of their silky stride.

Roberts's aggression terrorised players of enormous talent like Hungarian star Tibor Nyilasi and Austrian international Herbert Prohaska, but skipper Sara was the one who literally felt the physical presence of a player described by Burkinshaw as 'the Duncan Edwards type.'

Burkinshaw, although wanting a third goal to take to Vienna, was happy that they were denied a vital away goal.

He said: "My one wish is that there is no crowd trouble in Austria.

"Although it was nice for the crowd to produce a highly-charged atmosphere here, I hope no-one travels at all to Vienna."

Burkinshaw said: "When he's in that mood, he sees the ball and goes for it . . . and gets it. I'd like to see him use that sort of spirit and strength when he plays for England."

Austria Vienna coach Vaclav Halama admitted he was surprised by Tottenham's 60 per cent improvement on Saturday's performance. He said: "The aggressive game Tottenham launched against us was very difficult to cope with because we're not used to it. This defeat was very painful, but our chances are still alive."

Sara was more basic in his appraisal of his confrontation with Roberts. He said: "He elbowed me in the face, then nearly took my legs off."

Istvan Magyar, the Vienna mid-fielder, said: "As for Miller and Roberts, they are both wrong in the head!"

In fact, the only player seriously hurt was Tottenham's young stand-in goalkeeper Tony Parks. He had stitches in a deep cut across his knee after a lunging tackle by Magyar. Ray Clemence could be recalled on Saturday against his old club, Liverpool.

Roberts' tackling was dynamic but fair. Steve Perryman was the only player booked, and he also received a severe warning from Yugoslav referee Edvard Sostaric for a subsequent foul. It was clear one more indiscretion would have ended the Spurs skipper's participation in the match.

Although Brazil, as the video evidence clearly showed, had not got the final touch to the second goal in the 67th minute, Burkinshaw awarded the former Ipswich striker his fourth goal of the season.

"He was looking his old self and was a little unlucky that a goal by him was ruled out in the first half for handball," said Burkinshaw.

Ossie Ardiles was more involved than for a long time, taking more command in mid-field with Glenn Hoddle able to play only the last 20 minutes because of an achilles injury.

Daily Mail,

SPORTSMAIL SOCCER

Striker shrugs off injury to set up Spurs

Steve the bold

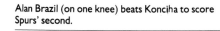

Tottenham ....2 Austria Vienna 0

Report By HARRY HARRIS

STEVE ARCHIBALD, watched last night by the Italian agent hoping to set up a £1 million deal for Verona, provided the goals that could help Tottenham win the UEFA Cup in his farewell season.

Transfer-listed Archibald, involved in a personal feud with manager Keith Burkinshaw since September when his willingness to play through an injury was seriously questioned, declared himself fit just hours before this quarter-final first-leg.

And he obliged with his 23rd goal of the season, taking his first real chance against a meticulously organised defence in the 58th minute. He also struck the bar with a header a little later and supplied an intricate pass that helped Alan Brazil to the second goal, assisted past goalkeeper Friere Koncilia by captain Robert Sara.

Bravery

Burkinshaw, although unable to settle his dispute with his Scotland striker, praised him for his bravery in playing through the knee ligament injury that kept him out of Saturday's match against Stoke.

The Tottenham manager said: 'Steve was a bit dubious. He had an ice-pack on his knee at half-time. I asked him whether he wanted to come off. He went white and said he wanted to stop out there. He was feeling the knee, but it didn't seem to inhibit him.'

Graham Roberts, like Archibald, epitomised the spirit that eventually shook the Austrian sophisticates out of their silky stride.

Roberts's aggression terrorised players of enormous talent like Hungarian star Tibor Nyilasi and Austrian international Herbert Prohaska, but skipper Sara was the one who literally felt the physical presence of a player described by Burkinshaw as 'the Duncan Edwards type'.

Burkinshaw said: 'When he's in that mood, he sees the ball and goes for it . . . and gets it. I'd like to see him use that sort of spirit and strength when he plays for England.'

Austria Vienna coach Vaclav Halama admitted he was surprised by Tottenham's 60 per cent. impovement on Saturday's performance.' He said: 'The aggressive game Tottenham launched against us was very difficult to cope with because we're not used to it. This defeat was very painful, but our chances are still alive.'

Sara was more basic in his appraisal of his confrontation with Roberts. He said: 'He elbowed me in the face, then nearly took my legs off.'

Istvan Magyar, the Vienna midfielder, said: 'As for Miller and Roberts they are both wrong in the head!'

ALAN BRAZIL celebrates Spurs's second goal. Picture: MALCOLM CLARKE

In fact, the only player seriously hurt was Tottenham's young stand-in goalkeeper Tony Parks. He had stitches in a deep cut across his knee after a lunging tackle by Magyar. Ray Clemence could be recalled on Saturday against his old club, Liverpool.

Dynamic

Roberts's tackling was dynamic but fair. Steve Perryman was the only player booked, and he also received a severe warning from Yugoslav referee Edvard Sostaric for a subsequent foul. It was clear one more indiscretion would have ended the Spurs skipper's participation in the match.

Although Brazil, as the video evidence clearly showed, had not got the final touch to the second goal in the 67th minute, Burkinshaw awarded the former Ipswich striker his fourth goal of the season.

'He was looking his old self and was a little unlucky that a goal by him was ruled out in the first half for handball,' said Burkinshaw.

Ossie Ardiles was more involved than for a long time, taking more command in midfield with Glenn Hoddle able to play only the last 20 minutes because of an achilles injury.

Burkinshaw, although wanting a third goal to take to Vienna, was happy that they were denied a vital away goal.

He said: 'My one wish is that there is no crowd trouble in Austria.

Although it was nice for the crowd to produce a highly-charged atmosphere here, I hope no one travels at all to Vienna.'

• UNITED'S LAST-MINUTE BLOW—PAGE 39

Mahood

BUS STOP

WIMBLEDON PRIZE MONEY UP 49%

'It's probably index-linked to the price of their strawberries!'

• MALCOLM FOLLEY — Page 38

Alan Brazil (on one knee) beats Konciha to score Spurs' second.

SUN, Thursday, March 22, 1984

FK AUSTRIA . . . 2 SPURS . . . 2

SPURS WIN 4-2 ON AGG

SPUR-FECT!

Ardiles and Brazil are goal-den heroes

From BRIAN WOOLNOUGH

Ossie Ardiles and Alan Brazil last night repaired Tottenham's season of despair as the London club waltzed into the UEFA Cup semi-final.

The Argentinian and the Scottish interntional scored the goals to steal the limelight in Spurs' night of glory against FK Austria here at the Prater stadium.

Ardiles grabbed his first of the season and Brazil his fifth – and fourth in Europe – in the middle of a confident, composed performance.

It was Tottenham's last chance of glory and this was not so much a Viennese waltz, but a Sunday afternoon stroll. And Spurs were as confident as they have been disappointing in their Jekyll and Hyde season.

Manager Keith Burkinshaw said: "It was our last chance and the players responded perfectly. I was proud of them and it just shows what we can do when we put our minds to it."

At the heart of this performance were the goals by Ardiles, struggling for so long against injury and Brazil, who recently asked for a transfer.

Brazil's goal came after 15 minutes.

Gary Stevens found Steve Archibald, and he quickly spotted Brazil who drove the shot low into the net.

Brazil said: "My goal killed the tie and the Austrians knew then that it was all over."

Then after 82 minutes Ardiles got the goal which Burkinshaw described as a "cracker".

Stevens' corner was only half-cleared and Ardiles pounced to smash in his shot off the bar.

The only disappointment for Spurs was a booking for Stevens that puts him out of the first leg of the semi-final.

Spurs lost their composure twice. First when Stevens pushed Nyilasi and Proshaska scored the penalty.

Then in a frantic last 10 minutes Paul Miller appeared to divert Nyilasi's effort over Ray Clemence into his own net.

But those two Austrian goals didn't detract from one of Spurs' best performances of the season.

SPUR-FECT!

Ardiles and Brazil are goal-den heroes

From BRIAN WOOLNOUGH: FK Austria 2 Spurs 2

OSSIE ARDILES and Alan Brazil last night repaired Tottenham's season of despair as the London club waltzed into the UEFA Cup semi-final.

The Argentinian and the Scottish international scored the goals to steal the limelight in Spurs' night of glory against FK Austria here at the Prater Stadium.

Ardiles grabbed his first of the season and Brazil his fifth—and fourth in Europe—in the middle of a confident, composed performance.

It was Tottenham's last chance of glory and this was not so much a Viennese waltz, but a Sunday afternoon stroll. And Spurs were as confident as they have been disappointing in their Jekyll and Hyde season.

Manager Keith Burkinshaw said: "It was our [illegible] chance and the players responded per- [illegible] was proud of [illegible]

EUROPE SOCCER SPECIAL

GOAL AHEAD . . . Ossie [illegible] second Spurs goal and [illegible]

Alan Brazil putting Spurs ahead 1-0 in Vienna.

DAILY MIRROR, Thursday, April 12, 1984

HADJUK SPLIT . . . 2   TOTTENHAM . . . 1

THE NEARLY MEN

Spurs are poised to give Keith final fling

HARRY MILLER

IN YUGOSLAVIA

Tottenham headed for home last night knowing their determination to give manager Keith Burkinshaw the farewell gift he most wants is still in the balance.

The odds, inevitably, will heavily favour Spurs when the bid for a place in this season's UEFA Cup final is completed at White Hart Lane in two weeks' time.

As the rain slanted across one of Europe's most picturesque stadiums and the smoke from a stream of multicoloured fire crackers finally dispersed, Spurs were happy enough.

Yet they knew, after a gritty performance that only lost its composure for ten fatal second half minutes, that it could have been even better.

Tottenham scored first, through Mark Falco, and that away goal may yet hold the key.

And until Hadjuk lifted their dispirited fans with goals in the 67th and 77th minutes Spurs looked like leaving this Yugoslav port city with a semi-final first leg win.

But Burkinshaw, who is leaving the club at the end of this eventful season on a wave of public sympathy, wasn't complaining.

Tottenham became the first team to score a European goal in Split this season.

And the quality of their football, with Graham Roberts and Mike Hazard outstanding, had Hadjuk's fanatical fans whistling and jeering in derision at their own players.

Spurs soaked up the early pressure, then scored after 17 minutes. It was a goal you couldn't call anything other than lucky.

When Falco crossed from the left Ivan Gudelj, under no pressure, needlessly handled. He had to compete with the crowd in a show of total disgust.

Falco took the penalty that followed and put it straight at keeper Zoran Simovic. Yugoslavia's Player of the Year couldn't hold the ball and it came back to Falco. Again he shot – again Simovic blocked, but couldn't keep possession.

This time the ball ran to Tony Galvin. He pulled it back and Falco – at the third attempt – scrambled the ball over the line.

Tottenham's troubles started in the 67th minute. Hadjuk rose like men from the dead to claim an unexpected equaliser.

Tottenham couldn't clear a corner and Gudelj atoned for his earlier handling offence with a low shot that was helped past Tony Parks by a slight deflection.

Ten minutes later Hadjuk scored again when a left wing corner by Sliskovic was nodded on by the busy Gudelj and Dusran Pesic beat Parks with a neat header.

Manager Burkinshaw said later: "When Split come to White Hart Lane they will find out what noise is all about."

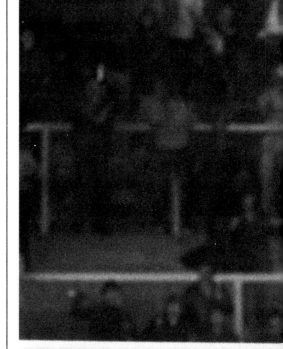

Mirror Sport

Thursday, April 12, 1984 No 24,927
Telephone (STD Code 01) — 353 0246

BATTLE IN EUROPE

The hit men.. It's hard, me

ENGLAND'S hopefuls found it tough going in ... bid to reach European finals last night.

Liverpool managed a narrow 1-0 European Cup victory over the hardmen of Dinamo Bucharest, whose tough tackling brought four bookings and angered the Anfield crowd.

In the Cup-Winners Cup injury-hit Manchester United were held 1-1 at home by Juventus. But Brian Clough's Nottingham Forest grabbed a glorious 2-0 victory over holders Anderlecht.

See pages 30 and 31

THE NEARLY MEN

Spurs are poised to give Keith

HARRY MILLER in Yugoslavia

Hajduk Split 2, Tottenham 1

TOTTENHAM headed for home last night knowing their determination to give manager Keith Burkinshaw the farewell gift he most wants is still in the balance.

The odds, inevitably, will heavily favour Spurs when the bid for a place in this season's UEFA Cup final is completed at White Hart Lane in two weeks time.

As the rain slanted across one of Europe's most picturesque stadiums and the smoke from a stream of ... fire crackers finally ... happy enough.

Yugoslav port city with a semi-final first-leg win.

But Burkinshaw, who is leaving the club at the end of this eventful season on a wave of public sympathy, wasn't complaining.

Spurs soaked up the early pressure, then scored after 17 minutes. It was a goal you couldn't call anything other than lucky.

When Falco crossed from the left Ivan Gudelj, under no pressure, needlessly handled. He had to compete with the crowd ... of total disgust.

Tony Parks is beaten as Hadjuk take the lead after 77 minutes.

Gary Stevens in the thick of the action.

DAILY EXPRESS, Thursday, April 26, 1984

TOTTENHAM . . . 1 HADJUK SPLIT . . . 0

AGG. 2-2. SPURS WIN ON AWAY GOALS

SPURS EARN KEITH GLORY

By COLIN BATEMAN

The emotion and glory at White Hart Lane last night was for manager Keith Burkinshaw.

His Tottenham team provided him with a place in the UEFA Cup final against Anderlecht to climax his eight-year reign at the club.

Mike Hazard scored the goal that beat Hadjuk Split and gave Spurs semi-final victory by virtue of an away goal scored in Yugoslavia a fortnight ago.

Hazard's first European goal of the season came after only six minutes and was as simple as it was precious for Tottenham.

He stroked the ball past the Yugoslav defensive wall from 25 yards and it nestled just inside the post.

Hazard said: "There was a definite mood in the dressing room of winning for Keith. I particularly owe him a lot for the way he and his assistant Peter Shreeve have helped me."

Burkinshaw, who has taken Spurs to their first European final for 10 years, said: "The tension was unbearable. It was as emotional a night as I can remember.

"We were desperate to get through. It's the icing on the cake and if we win the trophy it won't have been such a disastrous season."

Hazard, with his mop of blond, bubbly hair, was given his early chance when defender Nikica Cukrov needlessly handled.

Before the wall had settled the ball was in the net, but Hazard did not see much of the celebrations – one of his contact lenses was knocked out and he had to leave the field for five minutes for treatment.

The goal ended any thoughts Hadjuk might have had of hanging on to their 2-1 first leg lead and that gave Spurs all the space they needed as all the crowd roared them forward.

Somehow Steve Archibald failed to mark an excellent performance with the goal he deserved but his colleagues were also guilty of failing to wrap up the tie.

day April 26 1984

BOLD BID FOR THE BIG FINAL HAT-TRICK

Spurs earn Keith glory

Spurs' Mark Falco (right) wins

By COLIN BATEMAN

Tottenham 1 Hajduk Split 0

(Agg 2—2. Spurs win on away goals)

THE emotion and glory at White Hart Lane last night was for manager Keith Burkinshaw.

His Tottenham team provided him with a place in the UEFA Cup final against Anderlecht to climax his eight-year reign at the club.

Mike Hazard scored the goal that beat Hajduk Split and gave Spurs semi-final victory … away goal scored … fortnight ago.

Hazard's first Eur… season came after … and was as simple … for Tottenham.

He stroked the b… slav defensive wall … it nestled …

Mike Hazard lets fly to score and Spurs are in the final

Winner Zola in tears

From back page

and three benign policemen watched Budd destroy all her opponents. She won the race, running in bare feet, by almost 18 seconds.

She had recovered and was jogging out of the stadium with her guards while others were still finishing the race, looking exhausted.

That she can really run is beyond all reasonable doubt. She settled into fourth place and, when she wanted to after 300 metres, vanished into an evening turned chilly, all on her own, bare feet slapping the track as she went.

She raced herself, raced the clock and qualified by 14 seconds for the U.K. Championships.

She will run the 1,500 there, but wants to go for 3,000 in the Olympics—if she is accepted by the International Olympics Committee and picked by our own selectors.

It does not seem to be logical but then in a situation like this, what is?

Certainly what happened at Crystal Palace last night was a freak event which left a sour note in the mouth and nothing but pity for a superb young athlete surrounded, trapped — and maybe exploited beyond her knowledge.

…NES AND REST OF SPORT IN SHORT…

HAWKEYE'S FANCIES

EUROPEAN CUP Semi-Final: Second Leg

UEFA CUP Semi-Final: Second Leg

CUP WINNERS' CUP Semi-Final: Second Leg

CANON LEAGUE DIVISION II

FULHAM FINISH ON A HIGH NOTE

Steve Archibald is tackled by a Split defender.

STANDARD, Tuesday, April 3, 1984

How The Gates Shut On Sad Burkinshaw

The Spurs bombshell: PETER BLACKMAN'S inside story at White Hart Lane

When a member of the Royal Family has a baby or an illness they usually post a bulletin on the gates of Buckingham Palace or on the wall of some remote country lodge.

But when a football manager resigns or gets the sack, the gates at the ground are slammed shut and locked, as if pointedly suggesting it's not a public issue despite the game's mass appeal.

That happened at Tottenham yesterday as news of Keith Burkinshaw's resignation filtered down from within the tinted-glass stand that looks like a five-star hotel.

It was a pity that the news was so bad. The sun was out and Tottenham High Road was alive with the people who sleep and eat in the shadow of the floodlights, and have probably watched the team since they were kids.

But I was on the other side of those gates yesterday, watching the tension build and the frowns on foreheads deepened as it became apparent that Burkinshaw's eight-year reign was almost over.

There were the gleaming players' cars on the forecourt; the Cortinas and Vivas of the young men who dream of fame; the Mercedes sports cars and Rovers belonging to players who have cost a Pool's win in transfer fees.

In the stand foyer – yes, the best clubs have carpeted foyers these days – sat blazered security men, while ground staff swept stairways and office girls with Woolwich Building Society smiles worked in air-conditioned offices.

Burkinshaw took the training, checked on the players receiving treatment, answered the phone, made coffee, considered ringing his wife, Joyce, who knew the big sports story was about to break in The Standard.

I've never seen Burkinshaw look so drained. The usually affable man was in a daze, his eyes were red-rimmed. He knew all of London, including his family, friends and other managers, would know about his decision at 3.30pm when the board issued a statement.

As he tried to cope with the normal workload the odd director arrived: in a luxury car, impeccably dressed and with briefcase in hand. There were polite nods, thin smiles to the waiting Press outside those high gates.

Now the gatemen realised something big was about to happen. Suddenly they were alive to every sound and every new arrival on the other side of the barrier. "Sorry mate, you'll have to wait 'til I'm told to let you in," they said.

Inside the injured players limped, the fit ones signed footballs for fetes and funfairs and only rarely joked among themselves.

The anatomy of a manager's resignation was slowly unfolding. Nothing could stop it . . . and those gates stayed shut.

There are many separate scenarios in football at this level: there is this one, the other when a manager just quits and walks out in a huff: the hiring of a manager or a star player when gin and tonics are served in celebration along with cheese and cucumber sandwiches handed out by waitresses.

Then it's laughter and talk of ambition – a new page being turned in an old book. For Burkinshaw, it was the day when a full stop appeared in his particular managerial chapter.

Burkinshaw will win some more matches before he finally picks up his coat, takes the family photographs off the shelf and leaves his office and Spurs for the last time.

Then the fanfares will start again for the new man. The show rolls on . . .

Only the gates of heaven open and shut so often.

THE STANDARD, TUESDAY, APRIL 3, 1984 — 39

THE SPURS BOMBSHELL: PETER BLACKMAN'S INSIDE STORY AT WHITE HART LANE

How the gates shut on sad Burkinshaw

WHEN a member of the Royal Family has a baby or an illness they usually post a bulletin on the gates of Buckingham Palace or on the wall of some remote country lodge.

But when a football manager resigns or gets the sack, the gates at the ground are slammed shut and locked, as if pointedly suggesting it's not a public issue despite the game's mass appeal.

That happened at Tottenham yesterday as news of Keith Burkinshaw's resignation filtered down from within the tinted-glass stand that looks like a five-star hotel.

It was a pity that the news was so bad. The sun was out and Tottenham High Road was alive with the people who sleep and eat in the shadow of the floodlights, and have probably watched the team since they were kids.

But I was on the other side of those gates yesterday, watching the tension build and the frowns on foreheads deepen as it became apparent that Burkinshaw's eight-year reign was almost over.

There were the gleaming players' cars on the forecourt; the Cortinas and Vivas of the young men who dream of fame; the Mercedes sports cars and Rovers belonging to players who have cost a Pool's win in transfer fees.

In the stand foyer—yes, the best clubs have carpeted foyers these days—sat blazered security men, while ground staff swept stairways and office girls with Woolwich Building Society smiles worked in air-conditioned offices.

Burkinshaw took the training, checked on the players receiving treatment, answered the phone, made coffee, considered ringing his wife, Joyce, who knew the big sports story was about to break in The Standard.

THIN SMILES

I've never seen Burkinshaw look so drained. The usually affable man was in a daze, his eyes were red-rimmed. He knew all of London, including his family, friends and other managers, would know about his decision at 3.30 pm when the board issued a statement.

As he tried to cope with the normal workload the odd director arrived: In a luxury car, impeccably dressed and with briefcase in hand. There were polite nods, thin smiles to the waiting Press outside those high gates.

Now the gatemen realised something big was about to happen. Suddenly they were alive to every sound and every new arrival on the other side of the barrier. "Sorry mate, you'll have to wait 'til I'm told to let you in," they said.

Inside the injured players limped, the fit ones signed footballs for fetes and funfairs and only rarely joked among themselves.

The anatomy of a manager's resignation was slowly unfolding. Nothing could stop it . . . and those gates stayed shut.

There are many separate scenarios in football at this level: there is this one, the other when a manager just quits and walks out in a huff; the hiring of a manager or a star player when gin and tonics are served in celebration along with cheese and cucumber sandwiches handed out by waitresses.

Then it's laughter and talk of ambition—a new page being turned in an old book. For Burkinshaw, it was the day when a full stop appeared in his particular managerial chapter.

Burkinshaw will win some more matches before he finally picks up his coat, takes the family photographs off the shelf and leaves his office and Spurs for the last time.

Then the fanfares will start again for the new man. The show rolls on. . . .

Only the gates of Heaven open and shut so often.

BURKINSHAW . . . his eyes were red-rimmed as he tried to cope with the normal workload.

DAILY STAR, Thursday, May 10, 1984

ANDERLECHT . . . 1 TOTTENHAM . . . 1

THIS ONE'S FOR KEITH

Golden Miller sets up a Spurs joy day

From BOB DRISCOLL

IN BRUSSELS

Spurs closed one fist on the UEFA Cup last night with a battling performance over Anderlecht in Brussels.

And the man who set them up for a glittering White Hart Lane farewell to manager Keith Burkinshaw was defender Paul Miller.

His second half header brought the precious away goal. And even though Anderlecht equalised with five minutes to go, Spurs are now strong favourites to take the trophy in the second leg.

Having risked the wrath of the League authorities by fielding a team of reserves on Monday, Spurs were under terrific pressure to produce a great performance with all their stars re-assembled.

And it was plain from the opening minutes that they were determined to make their point by coming home from Brussels with the kind of result to set up victory in the second leg.

In Anderlecht's compact stadium, it was easy to see how Forest had relinquished a 2-0 lead here in the semi-final.

Spurs knew they would have to survive an onslaught. But with their own bank of supporters at their backs in the first half, they held firm.

And inevitably, it was the trojan Graham Roberts who was the inspiration in their defence.

It was a typically courageous tackle inside the penalty box in the fifth minute which got Spurs off the hook when Roberts slid the ball away as Hofkens broke clear.

Spurs made no pretence of their intention to absorb whatever Anderlecht could throw at them.

The tackling was robust, to say the least.

But Swiss referee Bruno Galler clearly believed that football was a man's game.

And, as the first half continued with Spurs denying the Belgians, there were signs of frustration in the Anderlecht team.

In fact, had Mark Falco done better with a far post header from Galvin's 19th-minute centre, Spurs would have really dismayed the Belgians.

Minutes later, however, Falco was heading out from under his own crossbar as Anderlecht charged onto a free kick.

As the first half came to a close, Anderlecht went off with heads bowed, clearly worried that home advantage was slipping away.

They mounted a terrific offensive in the opening minutes of the second half.

But it was that vulnerability to crosses which dramatically turned the match Spurs' way in the 58th minute.

From the second of two successive corners by Mike Hazard, Miller connected with a booming header which hit the roof of the net after hitting a defender.

But their joy was quelled somewhat in the 68th minute when skipper Steve Perryman collected a booking which will put him out of the return at White Hart Lane.

Five minutes from time, a shot by Arnesen rebounded and Morten Olsen toe poked it in for the equaliser.

Golden Miller sets up a Spurs joy day

THIS ONE'S FOR KEITH

From BOB DRISCOLL in Brussels

Galvin's 19th minute centre, Spurs would have really dismayed the Belgians.

Minutes later, however, Falco was heading out from under his own crossbar as Anderlecht charged onto a free kick.

As the first half came to a close Anderlecht went off with heads bowed, clearly worried that home advantage was slipping away.

They mounted a terrific offensive in the opening minutes of the second half.

But it was that vulnerability to crosses which dramatically turned the match Spurs way in the 58th minute.

Connected

From the second of two successive corners by Mike Hazard, Miller connected with a booming header which hit the roof of the net after hitting a defender.

But their joy was quelled somewhat in the 68th minute when skipper Steve Perryman collected a booking which will put him out of the return at White Hart Lane.

Five minutes from ...

Geordie ace raps board

by KEN GORMAN

TERRY McDermott last night launched a startling attack on Newcastle's directors accusing them of treating manager Arthur Cox in a "shabby way.".

Cox who has taken the Geordies back to the First Division is still waiting to be offered a new contract—his present one ends in September.

Former England star McDermott, who is concerned about his own future on Tyneside, rapped: "The boss has done a tremendous job, given the club everything and deserves a new contract. It should have been automatic.

Disgrace

"How can he be expected to sort out mine and other players' contracts when he doesn't even know his own future ?

"I think it's a disgrace that everyone should be kept hanging about. And I think it is my duty to let the public know."

Many of the promotion squad's present contracts expire this summer.

"The players are being kept in the dark. But that is nothing compared to the shabby way the ... has been treated."

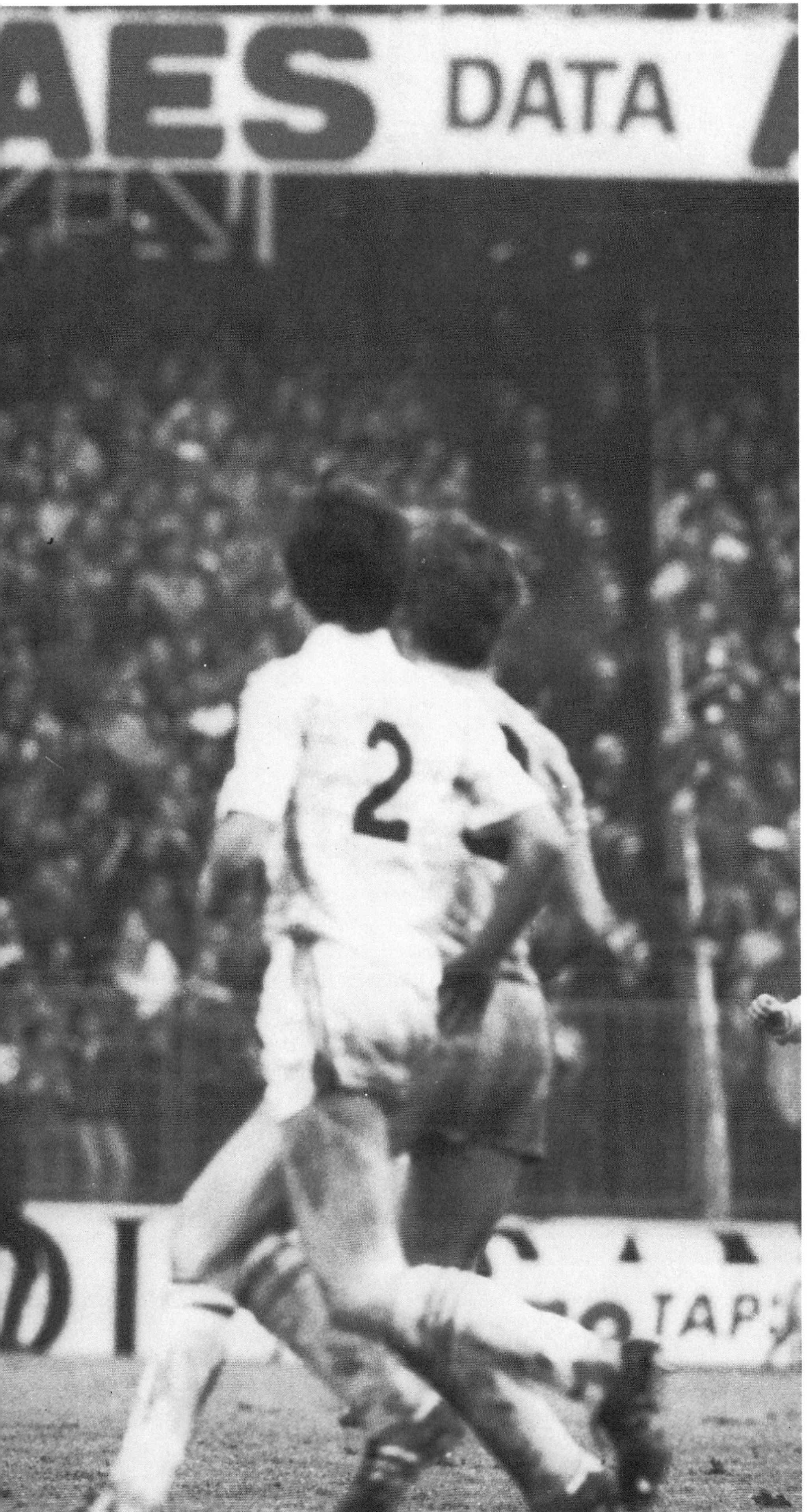

Archibald challenged by the Anderlecht defence as the referee blows for a free kick

Archibald and Galvin tussle for the ball as Scifo (left) looks at the referee

DAILY STAR, Thursday, May 10, 1984

GOLDEN MILLER!

Maxie hits a real gem

By BOB DRISCOLL

Paul Miller, called "Maxie" like the music hall comedian, sent Spurs laughing all the way towards the UEFA Cup last night.

With all the impeccable timing of his legendary namesake, the defender chose last night's UEFA Cup final first leg to score his only goal of the season.

But if Miller's crucial strike justifiably inspired a wave of joy and optimism for the second leg, there was one other moment which brought sadness.

For Spurs' long-serving skipper Steve Perryman will be sitting it out when they use last night's great performances to launch themselves towards final victory.

Perryman collected his second booking of the tournament and now automatically misses out on the big occasion back in London.

Yet, sad though he was personally, he joined in the exuberant delight of the Spurs team when the whistle ended their epic battle.

Miller's goal has Spurs leading with just five minutes left of this rugged battle with the Belgians in Brussels.

Yet, even though Anderlecht snatched an equaliser through Marten Olsen, it was Maxie's marvellous moment which now sets Spurs up for a glittering White Hart Lane farewell to manager Keith Burkinshaw.

And what a thunder-clap of a goal it was, too.

Anderlecht had revealed in the first half that they were not too happy handling centres.

When Mike Hazard swung over the second of two successive corners in the 58th minute, Miller came charging through Anderlecht's grounded defenders to boom a header that flew into the roof of the net.

That precious away goal now means even a goalless draw could win the final for Spurs in the second leg.

The result was one that had to be achieved on pure character and courage.

In the compact Anderlecht Stadium, it was easy to see how Nottingham Forest had relinquished a 2-0 lead in the semi-final.

Spurs supporters being escorted by the Brussels gendarmerie

A near 40,000 crowd were perched so close to the pitch that it seemed the players could feel their hot breath on their necks.

And when the going got rough, the man in the thick of it was again Graham Roberts.

Miller, too, was a stalwart and his overhead clearance from the goalmouth in the ninth minute was a life saver.

Gradually, Spurs began to wear down their opponents.

Anderlecht clearly sensed the chance of lifting the trophy was slipping away.

At the start of the second half they launched a tremendous offensive.

'Keeper Tony Parks, though, was glad to palm away a shot by Czerniatinski for Miller to clear in the 49th minute.

Spurs were still growing in confidence and in the 53rd minute a panicky pass back was intercepted by Falco and his shot was scrambled off the line by Grun.

Then Miller struck to send Spurs' fans into a deafening knees-up behind the goal into which his header flew.

But in the 85th minute a shot from substitute Frank Arnesen rebounded cruelly straight to Olsen inside the penalty area.

And he toe poked the ball home to give Anderlecht at least a fighting chance in the return leg.

But as the Belgians walked off with heads bowed, some turned to look back at Spurs' players dancing their delight at the result.

And those looks suggested that the Belgians themselves know the Cup is on its way to London.

DAILY STAR, Thursday, May 10, 1984

STEVEN'S STUNNER

By STEVE STAMMERS

Steve Perryman last night faced up to the cruel reality that he will miss a potentially glorious finale to Keith Burkinshaw's reign as Spurs' manager.

Perryman was cautioned in the second half of the 1-1 draw in Brussels against Anderlecht – and that puts him out of the second leg at White Hart Lane in a fortnight.

Perryman said: "I am very, very sad. But at least I have the consolation of being part of a very good performance and a very good result.

"I would love to play – but rules are rules and I have to abide by them.

"I suppose it is a little bit ironic that I am likely to be the only player from the squad Keith took over, fit to play in his last game. And that is a game I will now miss.

"I thought it was unfair to be booked tonight. It was my first foul and I think I paid for three or four other things that went on.

"It will be a great night at Tottenham, and the way I am looking at it now is that I have been sent off at half-time in a Cup final."

Burkinshaw was equally distressed at the prospect of Perryman missing his last game as Spurs' boss.

He said: "I would have liked him to pick it up if we win it. But I am delighted with the result."

But Perryman may yet lift the trophy that Spurs took giant strides towards winning – if his replacement as skipper, Graham Roberts, gets his way.

Roberts will send 32-year old Perryman up to get the Cup at White Hart Lane if such a gesture is approved.

Roberts said: "I am quite prepared for Steve to collect the trophy if we win. He is such a good and important player, and we depend on his leadership. I am so upset for him. He has missed only one game this season, and that was at Southampton."

Perryman reflected: "Everyone had great hopes at the start of the season, but we have needed this competition to get us out of trouble."

DAILY EXPRESS, Thursday, May 24, 1984

SUPER SAVERS

Roberts the prize fighter

By BARRY FLATMAN

Tony Parks flung himself into Spurs folklore with his two UEFA Cup-winning saves last night.

Goalkeeper Parks, 21, set White Hart Lane alight as Spurs edged out Anderlecht 4-3 in a penalty shoot-out.

But he recalled: "At the start of the season I wasn't even sure I had a future here.

"I did not think they would be keeping me on, so it's fantastic for something like this to happen.

"It's the sort of thing you read about in comics.

"When I saved that last penalty I immediately saw my wife, Gay, in the crowd and ran straight towards her. She was in tears."

Parks described his two memorable saves: "With the first, the Anderlecht player told where he was going to put it. I could see in his eyes where it was going.

"With the next three I just guessed and got it wrong.

"On the last, I changed my mind and went the other way and got it right."

Parks stressed the players' commitment to departing manager Keith Burkinshaw.

"We all felt so much for him. He has done a great job and we are all very, very disappointed to see him go."

Burkinshaw uncharacteristically showed emotion in his hour of glory.

But he went on: "You don't really want to leave on a night like this. You want it to go on for ever. It is a fairy-tale."

Burkinshaw was full of praise for Parks, admitting: "A lot of people had a lot of doubts about him.

"But he has always given everything and is a better goalkeeper because of what he has learnt from Ray Clemence."

As for stand-in skipper Graham Roberts, Burkinshaw said: "He is a great player, a tremendous captain and a real fighter."

Then Burkinshaw added: "I'm a lucky so-and-so. I must admit it. Somebody up there must like me.

"When we went 1-0 down I thought we had blown it, but we persevered.

"The fighting spirit of the lads was tremendous."

DAILY TELEGRAPH, Thursday, May 24, 1984

TOTTENHAM . . . 1 ANDERLECHT . . . 1

AGG. 2-2 AFTER EXTRA TIME. SPURS WIN 4-3 ON PENALTIES

PARKS CLINCHES UEFA CUP IN CLIFF-HANGER

Triumphant farewell for Burkinshaw

By MICHAEL CALVIN

Tottenham spectacularly survived the emotional torture of a penalty shoot-out last night, when Keith Burkinshaw's fairy-tale farewell to White Hart Lane surpassed even the most extravagant expectations.

The two most important saves of Tony Parks' fledgling career ensured that the UEFA Cup will nestle in Spurs' trophy cabinet as a sparkling reminder of the nerve-shredding climax to Mr Burkinshaw's reign as manager.

The capacity crowd, enthralled by the personal story at the heart of a collective triumph, were unrestrained in their joy and the players forgot the cramp and fatigue which had haunted them through extra time.

Everyone in a ground which eventually resembled a cockpit had suffered on a roller-coaster of emotion which veered between despair, delight and ultimate disbelief.

Anderlecht, the holders, came from Belgium to re-embellish their deserved reputation as one of Europe's most compelling, convincing teams.

They had seemed capable of protecting the 60th-minute goal by Alex Czerniatinski which rewarded their intelligence and industry.

But Graham Roberts, the epitome of Tottenham's unquenchable commitment, dragged the game into extra time with an equaliser seven minutes from the end of normal time.

That set up the unbearable tension of the shoot-out when, at the back of every player's

34 *The Daily Telegraph, Thursday, May 24, 1984*

Triumphant farewell for Burkinshaw

PARKS CLINCHES UEFA CUP IN CLIFF-HANGER

By MICHAEL CALVIN

Tottenham ... 1 Anderlecht ... 1
(Agg. 2-2 after extra time. Spurs win 4-3 on penalties)

Steve Archibald flicks just wide from Tony Galvin's cross in the first-half.

TOTTENHAM spectacularly survived the emotional torture of a penalty shoot-out last night, when Keith Burkinshaw's fairy-tale farewell to White Hart Lane surpassed even the most extravagant expectations.

The two most important saves of Tony Park's fledgling career ensured that the U E F A Cup will nestle in Spurs' trophy cabinet as a sparkling reminder of the nerve-shredding climax to Mr Burkinshaw's reign as manager.

The capacity crowd, enthralled by the personal story at the heart of a collective triumph, were unrestrained in their joy and the players forgot the cramp and fatigue which had haunted them through extra time.

Everyone in a ground which eventually resembled a cockpit had suffered on a roller-coaster of emotion which veered between despair, delight and ultimate disbelief.

Anderlecht, the holders, came from Belgium to re-embellish their deserved reputation as one of Europe's most compelling, convincing teams.

They had seemed capable of protecting the 60th minute goal by Alex Czerniatinski which rewarded their intelligence and industry.

But Graham Roberts, the epitome of Tottenham's unquenchable commitment, dragged the game into extra time with an equaliser seven minutes from the end of normal time.

That set up the unbearable tension of the shoot-out when, at the back of every player's mind, there lurked the potential nightmare of going into the history books as the man who lost the Cup.

It took Graham Rix several months to come to terms with that unjust indignity when he missed the crucial penalty for Arsenal in the shoot-out which ended with Valencia winning the European Cup-Winners' Cup in Brussels in 1980.

Roberts, Falco, Stevens and Archibald all survived their individual ordeal but for an agonising minute it seemed as if Danny Thomas would be saddled with the responsibility of giving Anderlecht a lifeline.

He missed Spurs' fifth penalty at 4-3 when he could have sewn up the Cup but Parks, the understudy whose hopes at the start of the season went little further than the occasional first team game, came to the rescue.

He had saved the first penalty of the shoot-out from Olsen and, when it mattered, kept his nerve and beat away a shot by Gudjohnsen. The Icelandic striker sank to the ground in unconsolable despair while Parks was buried beneath a euphoric posse of team-mates.

As White Hart Lane erupted in a frenzy of celebration Mr Burkinshaw took a poignant bow in the centre-circle. It may seem a churlish comment on one of his greatest nights, but no-one should deny that the Belgians were desperately unlucky to suffer a defeat of such unspeakable cruelty.

Anderlecht looked like cham-

Graham Roberts lifts the Cup

HOLSTEN

mind, there lurked the potential nightmare of going into the history books as the man who lost the Cup.

It took Graham Rix several months to come to terms with that unjust indignity when he missed the crucial penalty for Arsenal in the shoot-out which ended with Valencia winning the European Cup Winners' Cup in Brussels in 1980.

Roberts, Falco, Stevens and Archibald all survived their individual ordeal but for an agonising minute it seemed as if Danny Thomas would be saddled with the responsibility of giving Anderlecht a lifeline.

He missed Spurs' fifth penalty at 4-3 when he could have sewn up the Cup but Parks, the understudy whose hopes at the start of the season went little further than the occasional first team game, came to the rescue.

He had saved the first penalty of the shoot-out from Olsen and, when it mattered, kept his nerve and beat away a shot by Gudjohnsen. The Icelandic striker sank to the ground in unconsolable despair while Parks was buried beneath a euphoric posse of team-mates.

As White Hart Lane erupted in a frenzy of celebration Mr Burkinshaw took a poignant bow in the centre circle. It may seem a churlish comment on one of his greatest nights, but no-one should deny that the Belgians were desperately unlucky to suffer a defeat of such unspeakable cruelty.

Anderlecht looked like champions. They were disciplined in defence, patient and potent in mid-field.

On the hour their ambitions seemed about to be fulfilled. Olsen's through-ball punished a square Spurs defence and Czerniatinski's chipped shot over Parks was composed to perfection.

Tottenham, unbeaten at home in European competition, pushed frantically forward to defend that proud statistic. Time was their enemy, but with only seven minutes until the end of normal time they found a fitting saviour.

Ardiles, a late substitute, prodded the ball against the bar. As the ball broke out Hazard had the presence of mind to cross it back immediately and Roberts surged through a ruck of players to score.

From that emotional high Spurs pushed onto triumph. As the celebrations spilled out on to the streets the name of Mr Burkinshaw echoed around North London. As farewells go this was unsurpassable.

nt flying by a challenge from
›per Graham Roberts.

Galvin.

ANDERLECHT.—Munaron; Grun, De Greef, Czerniatinski, De Groote, Vercauteren, Vandereycken, Hofkens, Scifo, Olsen, Arnesen.

REFEREE: V. Roth (West Germany).

GAMBLE THAT PAID OFF

By COLIN GIBSON

THE greatest gamble of Tony Parks' short first-team career at White Hart Lane won Tottenham the U E F A Cup in a dramatic penalty shoot-out.

Parks, for so long Ray Clemence's understudy, elected to change his tactics for the vital last penalty of the allotted five and he pulled off the match-winning save from Icelandic international Arnor Gudjohnsen.

Tottenham at that stage of the shoot-out were reeling after Danny Thomas's miss with his side's last penalty. But Parks came to the rescue and said: "I had dived to my left for the previous four penalties and I just decided to gamble by going the other way. It paid off."

Parks had saved the first penalty taken by Anderlecht's Danish international Morte nOlsen.

Parks, 21, said: "I could tell his by his eyes that he was aiming to put the ball low to my left. I dived and turned it away."

Contract offered

Parks' reward for his brilliant performance is the offer of a two-year contract from Spurs when his present one-year deal expires, but he is as disappointed as the rest of the Tottenham squad that their manager, Keith Burkinshaw, will not be around to see him serve it.

Mr Burkinshaw, after an emotional farewell in front of a packed White Hart Lane crowd, said: "The king is dead, long live the king. A new man will come in now and if he does well everyone will forget me and that is the way it should be.

"But this was one of those nights which makes you feel lucky to be involved in football. Somebody up there must have taken a liking to me. It was the sort of night you dream about forever."

RESULTS

U E F A CUP-FINAL

Tottenham (0) **1** **Anderlecht** (0) **1**
Roberts Czerniatinski
(After extra time: Aggregate 2-2)
(Tottenham win 4-3 on penalties)

INTERNATIONAL

Eire 0 **Poland 0**
—8,100
(Dublin)

DAILY EXPRESS, Thursday, May 24, 1984

Glorious Goodbye for Burkinshaw

PARKS SPARKS SPURS PARTY!

Penalty hero Tony wins Cup for boss

By STEVE CURRY

Tottenham delivered the UEFA Cup to retiring manager Keith Burkinshaw last night – via the safe hands of a rookie goalkeeper Tony Parks.

Skipper Graham Roberts had rescued Spurs with a late equaliser that forced the game into extra time.

But when the heart-stopping drama reached its climax in a penalty shoot-out, 21-year old Parks became the darling of White Hart Lane with two brilliant saves.

Six months ago, he was the anonymous reserve in the shadow of England's veteran Ray Clemence.

Now here he was facing the five Anderlecht penalties that would not only determine whether Tottenham lifted one of the game's most treasured trophies, but also whether Burkinshaw finished his eight-year reign at Spurs as a winner or loser.

It was a poignant moment that demanded moral courage, intense concentration and the reflexes of a gunfighter.

Young Parks, fresh-faced and a novice in the hard world of professional football, had five eyeball-to-eyeball confrontations with Belgian marksmen in the space of just a few anxious, almost unbearable minutes.

He stopped two of them with saves of remarkable agility – and it was enough.

For Parks' elation saved Danny Thomas, who took the one Spurs kick that was saved, from a nightmare summer.

So the giant UEFA trophy rests at White Hart Lane as a lasting testament to a thrilling night and a postscript to a managerial career that, perhaps, should not be ending, even in glory.

For if ever a night of action portrayed the beliefs and the principles of a manager, then this was it.

Burkinshaw, the Barnsley pit boy, strode off the pitch with the adoration of a crowd of 46,250 thumping in his ears and, for once, the impassive Yorkshire front dissolved into tears.

They have staged many memorable nights in this famous North London stadium and if this one did not reach the peaks of football perfection inspired in the days of Blanchflower and Mackay, then it matched any for its cliff-hanging drama.

Spurs and Anderlecht started level at 1-1 from the first leg, but no shrewd observer was unaware that the Belgians possessed sufficient will, courage and ability to make this night one in which only total commitment would triumph.

It was pulsating action from start to finish. Muscular aggression mixed with delicate skill – the sort of football which makes this a sport to match any at its dramatic best.

There were near misses either way, with Spurs having possibly more of the ball but always vulnerable to Anderlecht's sharp, incisive counter-attacking football.

For an hour there was little to choose, but a stunned silence enveloped the ground after an hour when the heavyweight son of a Polish miner, Alex Czerniatinski, threatened to ruin this North London party.

He collected a ball in space from Anderlecht's marvellous Morten Olsen and thumped the ball past Parks to put the Belgians 2-1 ahead on aggregate.

Spurs seemed doomed, but in the 76th minute Burkinshaw tossed in his final dice.

Ossie Ardiles was thrown in as substitute and it reacted on Spurs like a shot of adrenalin, for with only six minutes remaining, the muscular, aggressive, inspiring Roberts ploughed through to equalise.

Extra time was just a tired stalemate, with both sides dragging their limbs through a punishing period, and it was always inevitable that penalties would eventually decide the issue.

They were taken alternatively – Tottenham striking first, with Roberts thumping home his, and Olsen having his first for Anderlecht brilliantly saved by Parks.

The rest went in sequence – Falco, Stevens and Archibald scoring for Spurs, Brylle, Scifo and Vercauteren for Anderlecht.

Then Spurs' final penalty by Danny Thomas was saved by Jacques Munaron and that left Arnor Gudjohnsen to take the final penalty.

Parks saved it brilliantly. Spurs had won the Cup – and Burkinshaw walked out of White Hart Lane a hero without a job.

UEFA CUP WINNERS

RETROSPECTIVE VIEW BY STEVE PERRYMAN

Steve Perryman missed Keith Burkinshaw's farewell game as manager of Spurs . . . the UEFA Cup final second leg when stand-in skipper Graham Roberts lifted the trophy on an emotionally charged European glory night at White Hart Lane.

For Perryman it was one of his biggest disappointments in his long and distinguished career.

"In all my years in Europe for Spurs, this was the campaign in which I felt I had more command over the direction of the Tottenham team and had done more to keep us in the competition.

"I had played right through the season, and throughout the European campaign, working hard with a young side in Munich and playing alongside Mickey Hazard against Split."

Perryman's annoyance with the decision to book him for an innocuous challenge late in the first leg of the final in Belgium is tempered by the realisation that he deserved his first yellow card of the competition against Austria Vienna.

He recalls: "I fully deserved to get booked in the home tie against Austria Vienna. We were up against some very good footballers and even our crowd were appreciative of their skills.

"And that can be annoying. We would not expect warm applause if we played well away from home!

"We were confronted by a majestic midfield player who burst clear and I felt I had to bring him down.

"Yes, it was a professional foul, which is another word for cheating. I'm not proud of what I did, but I felt it had to be done for the good of the team, and to keep the club in Europe.

"Bill Nick would talk about controlled aggression. We'd learn that away goals are vital. As a player, you build yourself up to do well and progress in Europe.

"You cannot weigh all that up in the split second it takes to commit such an act.

"It's all relevant to how the team is playing at the time. We were struggling. They were stringing good passes together and moving sweetly from one end of the pitch to the other.

"The frustration at not being able to control this team, the tension of the night, and faced by a quality player . . . you live and die by your commitment.

"I tripped him. But there was no intent to hurt him. There have been a lot of cases in Europe where I deserved to get booked and didn't. Here I deserved it, and got it.

"But there was absolutely no way I deserved a booking against Anderlecht.

"We were hanging on at 1-1 and I put my foot up to go for the ball. My only aim was to get the ball as far away from our goal as possible.

"I missed the ball, but I also missed the player. The Swiss referee must have felt it was dangerous play because I went in with my studs showing.

"A player has few opportunities to play in Cup finals. To miss any final is a damper, but it was so disappointing to know I would miss the match at Spurs after such a good performance in Belgium against the UEFA Cup holders.

"The Anderlecht players were delighted that I was booked. They were only too aware that I'd be ruled out of the second leg.

"They boasted that they would now slaughter us at Tottenham. But it didn't quite work out that way, even though I wasn't playing."

LOOKING BACK WITH KEITH BURKINSHAW

It was 12.15 in Tottenham High Road on a wet May Thursday morning. The rain was still falling but it did not bother Keith Burkinshaw.

He was being hailed by the remains of a White Hart Lane full house.

Standing on the balcony of the Tottenham supporters' club he looked down for the last time on the Spurs fans. It was his swan song and what a swan song. The drama of a penalty shoot-out in one of the greatest UEFA Cup finals of all time against the attractive Anderlecht team from Brussels.

Burkinshaw remembers: "It was a wonderful feeling. I had thought from the semi-final stage when we played so well against Hadjuk Split in Yugoslavia that we could win the competition.

"I never lost that feeling until just before Graham Roberts scored his late equaliser for us against Anderlecht at home.

"We had played some magnificent football in Brussels and deserved a lot more than the 1-1 draw with which we came away.

"The team knew that Anderlecht were an outstanding team and that they would come at us in London. They scored a superb goal and for a long time looked as though they would beat us.

"Then Graham scored only the sort of goal that he could score to earn us extra time. Then I knew that it was our Cup again."

But not before the heart stopping drama of a penalty shoot-out. Burkinshaw remembers: "When Tony made his save the place went wild.

"There were people jumping around on the bench. That was not my style though. I just sat calmly through it – well as calmly as I could.

"I thought at the moment the save was made that I was better sitting back and enjoying the moment. Some people found it hard to watch the penalties but I felt better watching them than not.

"It was a very emotional moment when I picked up the trophy and I am not usually an emotional person. There was a great feeling of satisfaction.

"It was a nostalgic moment. It was a wonderful way to finish at White Hart Lane."

Looking back on the response of the crowd, Burkinshaw said: "It was wonderful.

"I had a great affinity with the Tottenham public; they always seemed to appreciate the type of team that I was trying to produce for them.

"I remember standing there thinking how wonderful everything was. Everything had jelled at the right moment."

Burkinshaw was to pack his office up the next day and leave White Hart Lane. It was a decision he does not regret. He said: "At the time I think it was the right thing for both of us.

"When you are leaving a great club even in the wake of such a great triumph there is a feeling of sadness. It was for the best though.

"It had taken three or four years to build that side and I think that is about the time that it takes to put any good side together.

"Leaving it was difficult. It takes new managers a long time to get to terms with everything. That is why Liverpool have been such a shining example to everyone.

"For years they had a continuity of management and that helped them stay ahead of the rest of a changing League.

"It is an example everyone should follow."

LOOKING BACK WITH GRAHAM ROBERTS

Ask Graham Roberts which was the most memorable week in his footballing career and he will tell you immediately. "It was in May 1984."

For in that week Roberts, the tough Tottenham defender, became a television hero for millions of soccer fans up and down the country.

It was in a pulsating UEFA Cup final second leg at White Hart Lane against the Belgian artists of Anderlecht that Roberts' determination reaped its rewards.

"It was an amazing week," said Roberts. "Steve Perryman had been suspended for the second leg after he had been booked in Brussels.

"Immediately after the first leg Steve had told the lads in the dressing room that he was out of the return and I had an inkling that I would be captain.

"It was an honour that I had only dreamt about. I had always wanted to be the captain of a major club and here was the chance in one of the European finals."

Graham was officially told by manager Keith Burkinshaw on the Monday of the game that he was to lead the side. "That was a special moment for me.

"Captaining the side is something really different and I decided to play it the only way I know. I wanted to lead the lads by example.

"At the time I think I was at the peak of my career and I was playing as well as anyone but my game was based on giving all I had.

"With it being Keith Burkinshaw's last match as well there was just as great a determination among the players to do well for him. I don't think that we ever mentioned it as a team but we all knew that we had to make the day special."

Roberts did more than anyone else in the Spurs team to make sure that Burkinshaw's dream of leaving White Hart Lane with a major trophy came true.

There were only a few minutes left when Steve Archibald's shot was turned away for a corner. The cross came in and the ball fell to substitute Ossie Ardiles who shot against the bar.

Roberts takes up the story: "Hazard normally liked to beat a player before crossing but this time he crossed early and the ball cannoned off my chest.

"There were two Anderlecht defenders close by but by taking the ball on the chest, I went away from them.

"That I think was the hard bit. I simply hit the ball then and hoped. It was an incredible feeling of ecstacy and pain. As soon as I ran to the crowd my legs went.

"Hazard jumped on me immediately and he would not let go. The noise was terrific. I was in a total daze."

Roberts also took the responsibility of taking the first penalty for Tottenham in the important penalty shoot-out.

After the victory he admits he was in a quandry. "I desperately wanted Steve Perryman to be a part of the occasion and when it came to collecting the Cup I was thinking of dragging Steve up with me.

"I mentioned it to Keith Burkinshaw but he was not sure if we would get into trouble because Steve was suspended and not supposed to be playing a part in the event.

"Steve also said that he wanted the 11 players who had played in the final to get the final accolade. It was a very emotional moment.

"The whole thing seems a blur now. I had tears in my eyes and I can remember desperately searching the crowd for my wife Anne. It was a wonderful moment."

Even now the man who was snatched from non-League football at Weymouth by Burkinshaw plays tapes of that famous night. "It certainly helps to lift me in the bad times," he said.

RETROSPECTIVE VIEW BY TONY PARKS

Tony Parks saved the first and last penalties in a dramatic penalty shoot-out to decide the fate of the UEFA Cup.

"I just knew I could save those penalties," recalls Parks.

When they handed young Parks the massive UEFA trophy, there was absolutely no chance he would drop it . . . he was on a "high", a hero in the true Roy-of-the-Rovers sporting traditions.

Parks had played in a major final emerging from the obscurity of reserve team football to take over the goalkeeper's jersey from the great Ray Clemence.

"The funny thing was, I was very nervous throughout the whole of the 90 minutes and extra time.

"While the final had been an ordeal of nerves, the penalty shoot-out simply filled me with confidence. I could actually feel the confidence flooding through me, and I knew I could save a penalty . . . or two – and I did.

"I love penalty competitions in training. I'd stay behind with one of my mates and see how many I could save or my mate could score.

"Ian Crook or Mike Hazard were my deadly rivals and I'd usually win quite a few. I just love diving about going for penalties.

"I saved a penalty at QPR against Terry Fenwick and got a hand to Colin Walsh's shot at Nottingham Forest but could only push his penalty into the net.

"I played in the first leg of the UEFA Cup quarter-finals, both legs of the semis and the final against Anderlecht.

"When it came to the penalties in the final, I was overjoyed. I knew if I didn't save any, no-one would say it was my fault. You can't blame the goalkeeper for conceding a penalty.

"When any 'keeper goes for a penalty he must move a little, there's no other way. Wait for the ball to be kicked and you've got no chance.

"Of course I had to move before the ball was kicked otherwise I wouldn't have stood a chance.

"Everyone talks about my second penalty save, which clinched the UEFA Cup.

"But I felt my first save was the more difficult. I watched Morten Olsen when he put the ball on the spot. I watched his eyes. He was looking to the right. That's where I thought he would place the ball.

"I guessed right and pushed the shot around the post. The noise from the crowd was deafening. It sent shivers down my spine. The sensation was terrific.

"It was now up to the lads to score and I was hoping everything would go alright, and it did, until Danny Thomas missed his penalty.

"When it came to the last penalty, I still felt sure I could save it.

"It came at me at the right height, a lovely height to make it look a spectacular save. We all like a bit of glory, and I must admit I made it look a better save than it was . . . I took a leaf out of Bruce Grobbelaar's book."

In fact Parks has copied the Liverpool 'keeper's eccentric antics in more penalty shoot-outs.

"Since I saw Bruce in the European Cup Final wobble around on the goal-line to make the penalty-taker blast the ball over the bar, I've tried the same trick.

"It was at Wembley's indoor arena in the six-a-side tournament. Brian Stein obliged by shooting over the bar. I'm not sure I'd try the Bruce Grobbelaar method in a League game."

Tony Parks' trademark is the penalty saves in the UEFA Cup final. "When youngsters ask for my autograph they ask me about the penalty save, I don't think they know much else about me!"

Parks enjoyed European football when he was a schoolboy . . . at Arsenal.

"My dad was an Arsenal fan and he took me along to Highbury. When I played for Spurs at Arsenal my whole family went. It was a big thrill, but not as big as winning the UEFA Cup!"

Again Spurs went into Europe as victors. Sadly, due to the events at the Heysel Stadium, this was to prove their last European campaign for some time.

DAILY MAIL, Thursday, September 20, 1984

SPORTING BRAGA . . . 0 TOTTENHAM . . . 3

GLORY NIGHT FOR FALCO

By BRIAN SCOVELL

The deadly finishing of Mark Falco gave UEFA Cup holders Tottenham a marvellous start to their bid to become the first club to win the trophy two years running.

Falco had three strikes at goal, and scored twice, bringing his total for the season to seven goals. There is no more modest, unsung hero in the English game.

Three goals in 14 minutes at the end of the first half sank the Portuguese, who supplied Spurs with unintentional motivation by playing in Arsenal colours.

With Southampton and Nottingham Forest threatened with elimination after 0-0 home draws, English football needed this late-night result from Northern Portugal.

Left back Chris Hughton was outstanding for Spurs, and Gary Mabbutt, playing his first full game of the season, worked tirelessly on a night which the Cup holders began in unpopular fashion with their stifling tactics.

Paul Miller was fortunate not to be cautioned after only 15 seconds when he chopped down Jose Abrantes from behind with a ball a yard away. But French referee Gerard Biguet merely warned the Spurs defender.

The 25,000 crowd hooted and whistled as Spurs took their time but it was part of manager Peter Shreeve's plan to take the steam out of the Portuguese in the early stages.

Ray Clemence dived into a cluster of players to hold a shot from Serra after a third-minute corner and a shot from Brazilian striker Jorge Gomes, whose plaited hair made him look like a pop star, flashed past the far post.

Gary Mabbutt became the second Spurs player to be given a stiff warning when he dived into the tackle after Serra and knocked the Portuguese mid-field player flying.

The game changed dramatically in the 31st minute when in their first serious attack, Spurs took the lead.

Tony Galvin put left back Chris Hughton clear down the left and with neither Lito nor sweeper Dio sensing the danger unmarked Mark Falco was allowed to stab in the ball from eight yards.

In the 39th minute the referee finally complied with UEFA's call for strict control when he cautioned Hughton for fouling Zinho.

Then came the two goals just before half time which killed off the Portuguese.

The first, in the 43rd minute, was strongly disputed by Braga. Mike Hazard picked up the ball in the centre circle, and sent Falco clear of every defender. Dito, the last man, raised his arm appealing for offside but Falco went on and side-footed past the goalkeeper Helder. The linesman was mobbed by red shirts to no avail.

Seconds from half-time Hughton served Galvin down the left and the winger was to close in and lob the third goal inside the far post.

The crowd came to life mid-way through the second half when Jorge Gomes twice shot against the bar in a frantic five-minute spell. Then Clemence had to turn shots from Zinho and Dito over the bar as the Portuguese started to play with more determination.

Dito was cautioned ten minutes from time for a foul on Clive Allen.

Glory night for Falco

THE deadly finishing of Mark Falco gave UEFA Cup holders Tottenham a marvellous start to their bid to become the first club to win the trophy two years running.

Falco had three strikes at goal, and scored twice, bring-

Sporting Braga............0, Tottenham............3

FROM BRIAN SCOVELL IN PORTUGAL

full game of the season, worked tirelessly on a night which the Cup holders began in unpopular fashion with their stifling tactics.

Paul Miller was fortunate not to be cautioned after only

Brazilian striker Jorge Gomes, whose plaited hair made him look like a pop star, flashed past the far post.

Gary Mabbutt became the second Spurs player to be given a stiff warning when he dived into the tackle after Serra and

DAILY MAIL, Thursday, October 4, 1984

TOTTENHAM . . . 6 SPORTING BRAGA . . . 0

WE WON'T LET GO

By BRIAN SCOVELL

Tottenham warned Europe last night that they have no intention of relinquishing the UEFA Cup.

There was a freshness and originality about the way they completed the demolition of their Portuguese opponents.

And, on top of some fine goals which included a second hat-trick in a week from Garth Crooks, there was the return of Glenn Hoddle.

Local hero Hoddle came on after half-time for Paul Miller and marked his first senior appearance for six months with the defence-splitting pass which Crooks converted in the 57th minute.

Then the England mid-fielder showed the 22,478 fans what they have been missing all these weeks. As two defenders closed in, he put reverse spin on the ball with a forward chip and ran round them to collect it. The fans loved that.

Braga didn't show the same appetite as in the first leg of this first round tie on their own pitch. They weren't quitters but their defenders had a fatalistic air about them after a series of dreadful early mistakes which soon ruled them out of a contest they began three goals down.

After Mark Falco had accidentally blocked a Graham Roberts shot after a tenth-minute corner, 18-year old defender Carvahal sent a weak clearance towards Gary Stevens and the England under-21 international delivered a powerful shot past goalkeeper Helder.

Peter Shreeve, Tottenham's bluntly honest manager, conceded that the Portuguese had a point when they complained Crooks was offside as Chris Hughton raced through their offside trap to score the second in the 15th minute.

Then Carvahal was at fault again in the 26th minute when he failed to get off the ground to meet Tony Galvin's left wing cross. Crooks, standing behind him, headed down inside the far post.

Crooks then proceeded to take the ball round the hapless goalkeeper from Hoddle's marvellous pass for the fourth goal (57) and leading scorer Falco, no doubt feeling out of things, matched him in the 65th minute with Braga's defenders again unsuccessfully appealing to East German referee Klaus Scheurell for offside.

Richard Cooke came on for Falco in the 70th minute before Dito, Braga's sweeper, with a bad back-pass enabled Crooks to complete his hat-trick eight minutes from time.

Shreeves said: "It was nice to see Garth come back with a bang. His confidence has returned and the crowd have taken to him again.

"Glenn did quite well. His passing was good and I thought he covered the ground pretty well.

"I must admit I thought it would be more difficult for us than it turned out. But I suppose the early goal upset them. We always looked comfortable and overall were far too strong."

Daily Mail, Thursday, October 4, 1984

SPORTSMAIL SOCCER

CHRIS HUGHTON sends 'keeper Helder the wrong way to score Spurs' second goal at White Hart Lane. Picture : MALCOLM CLARKE

Aberdeen out but McGhee marches on

SCOTLAND striker Mark McGhee made his mark in Europe last night — and it was British clubs who suffered.

McGhee struck the goal two minutes from time which helped Hamburg knock Southampton out of the UEFA Cup while Aberdeen, who sold him to Germany, badly missed his skills as they went out of the European Cup at the hands of Dynamo Berlin. Nottingham Forest were also a casualty, but there was good news and plenty of goals for other English and Scottish clubs.

John Wark and Garth Crooks each scored hat-tricks as Liverpool and Tottenham reached the second round of the European and UEFA Cups, Manchester United triumphed while Rangers, Celtic and Dundee United also went through.

Bode Rudwaleit's massive frame came between Aberdeen and a place in the second round. The towering German goalkeeper saved from Willie Miller and Eric Black in a dramatic penalty shoot-out which Dynamo Berlin won 5-4.

It was a miserable night for Miller who gave away the free kick which led to a late Dynamo aggregate equaliser and extra time.

On target

Rangers stepped into the next round of the UEFA Cup with two goals in the last six minutes to defeat Irish part-timers Bohemians, skipper Craig Paterson and Ian Redford scoring.

Frank McGarvey steered Celtic into the second round of the Cup-winners' Cup with two of the three goals which beat Ghent 3-0 at Parkhead and 3-1 overall.

Ralph Milne also hit the target twice as Dundee United beat AIK Stockholm 3-0 (3-1 on aggregate) in the UEFA Cup.

Hearts achieved second leg respectability in their return against Paris St Germain ...

We won't let go

Tottenham .... 6, Sporting Braga 0

BY BRIAN SCOVELL

TOTTENHAM warned Europe last night that they have no intention of relinquishing the UEFA Cup.

There was a freshness and originality about the way they completed the demolition of their portuguese opponents.

And, on top of some fine goals which included a second hat-trick in a week from Garth Crooks, there was the return of Glenn Hoddle.

Local hero Hoddle came on after half-time for Paul Miller and marked his first senior appearance for six months with the defence-splitting pass which Crooks converted in the 57th minute ...

... ceded that the Portuguese had a point when they complained Crooks was offside as Chris Hughton raced through their offside trap to score the second in the 15th minute.

Then Carvahal was at fault again in the 26th minute when he failed to get off the ground to meet Tony Galvin's left wing cross. Crooks, standing behind him headed down ...

... to East German referee Klaus Scheurell for offside.

Richard Cooke came on for Falco in the 70th minute before Dito, Braga's sweeper, with a bad back pass enabled Crooks to complete his hat-trick eight minutes from time.

Shreeves said : 'It was nice to see Garth come back with a bang. His confidence has returned and the crowd have ...

DAILY MAIL, Thursday, October 25 1984

BRUGES . . . 2 TOTTENHAM . . . 1

HODDLE'S FOLLY

JEFF POWELL

Glenn Hoddle was sent off last night as Tottenham's militant tendencies incurred the wrath of even their own manager.

Hoddle, like Clive Allen sent on to try to save the UEFA Cup survived only 23 minutes before his second petulant offence plunged him into international disgrace.

Allen had earlier scored the late, late away goal which gives Spurs hope of extending possession of the European trophy beyond a second leg from which both Hoddle and Chris Hughton will be banned.

Hughton, at least, incurred his second booking in this season's competition in the cause of preventing a potentially fatal Bruges goal, Hoddle and Graham Roberts dismayed manager Peter Shreeve with petty offences committed with the ball dead.

Shreeves said: "Glenn was returning to European football wanting to do his best for the team, but he got a little carried away. His was not the only silly booking. Roberts, again, never seems to learn the lesson.

"We've hammered the message home to the players, but you cannot give referees in Europe any opportunity to book you. Glenn has forgotten that during his time out of the first team."

Tottenham's frustrations were mounting in the face of Bruge's 1-0 lead when Hoddle pushed Belgian goal-scorer Jan Ceulemans over the touchline.

Swiss referee Andre Daina produced the yellow card at once, then followed it with the red card when Hoddle kicked the ball away after a free kick decision.

Roberts, for his part, was booked for a dig at Willy Wellens as they went to collect the ball from behind the Spurs goal-line.

Tottenham's aggression had already inflamed the Belgian crowd of around 30,000, making it doubly fortunate that no more than 300 of their own fans had defied the club's appeal to stay at home.

Tottenham's problem had transferred from the terraces to the pitch as early as the sixth minute when Cuelemans applied the killing touch to one of the many swift, subtle counter-attacks which have become the trademark of Belgian football.

There might have been more first half goals as each team tried to contain the other with off side traps which frequently failed to function.

The second half seemed to be petering out as Spurs made their substutions and Hughton was forced to bring down Wellens with the Belgian in full flight towards goal.

The referee resisted the temptation to send off Hughton but at once placated Bruges by awarding a penalty as Perryman prevented Degryse from reaching the resulting free kick.

Birger Jensen, the Danish international goalkeeper who captains Bruges, trotted the length of the pitch to blast the penalty past Ray Clemence.

There were seven minutes left, time enough for Hoddle to be sent off for the second time in his senior career and for Allen to punish a momentary lapse in Belgian concentration with that priceless away goal, firmly dispatched on the break.

Hoddle misses not only the return match in a fortnight but also the first leg of the third round should Tottenham qualify.

For them to do so, Spurs will need all the support that can be mustered at White Hart Lane by the fans chairman Irving Scholar thanked for staying away last night.

SPORTSMAIL EUROPEAN

Shreeves raps his se

Hoddl

GLENN HODDLE was sent off last night as Tottenham's militant tendencies incurred the wrath of even their own manager.

Hoddle, like Clive Allen sent on to try to save the UEFA Cup, survived only 23 minutes before his second petulant offence plunged him into international disgrace.

Allen had earlier scored the late, late away goal which gives Spurs hope of extending possession of the European trophy beyond a second leg from which both Hoddle and Chris Hughton will be banned.

Dismayed

Hughton, at least, incurred his second booking in this season's competition in the cause of preventing a potentially fatal Bruges goal. Hoddle and Graham Roberts dismayed manager Peter Shreeves with petty offences committed with the ball dead.

Shreeves said : 'Glenn was returning to European football wanting to do his best for the team, but he got a little carried away. His was not the only silly booking. Roberts, again, never seems to learn the lesson.

QPR HIT SIX and other reports—Page 47

Bruges ...... 2 Tottenh

FROM JEFF P

'We've hammered the me
the players, but you cannot
in Europe any opportunity
Glenn has forgotten that d
out of the first team.'
Tottenham's frustrations
ing in the face of Bruges's 1
Hoddle pushed Belgian g
Ceulemans over the touchli
Swiss referee Andre Da
the yellow card at once, th
with the red card when Hod
ball away after a free-kick
Roberts, for his part, w
a dig at Willy Wellens as
collect the ball from behi
goal-line.

Fortunate

Tottenham's aggression
inflamed the Belgian crow
30,000, making it doubly fort
more than 300 of their o
defied the club's appeal to s
Tottenham's problem ha
from the terraces to the pit
the sixth minute when Ceul
the killing touch to one
swift, subtle counter-attack
become the trademark of Be
There might
more first-half
team tried to
other with c
which frequent
function.
The second h
be petering out
their substitutio
ton was forced
Wellens with t
full flight towa
The referee
temptation to s
ton but at o
Bruges by awar
as Perryman
Degryse from
resulting free-k
Birger Jensen
international g
captains Bruges
length of the p
the penalty
Clemence.

WALLAB

ACROSS
1 Under control (11)
7 Buddhist priest (4)
8 Spanish coins (7)
9 Grain crop (3)
10 Abrupt (5)
11 Dangerous (6)
13 Soldiers' quarters (6)
16 Approxi-

PEANUTS

HERE, YOU GOT A

Daily Mail, Th

ER

ff star as Spurs crash

's folly

Man with the knack . . . Ian Rush celebrates his European hat-trick last night

There were seven minutes left, time enough for Hoddle to be sent off for the second time in his senior career and for Allen to punish a momentary lapse in Belgian concentration with that priceless away goal, firmly dispatched on the break.

Hoddle misses not only the return match in a fortnight but also the first leg of the third round should Tottenham qualify.

For them to do so, Spurs will need all the support that can be mustered at White Hart Lane by the fans chairman Irving Scholar thanked for staying away last night.

☐ Eighteen Spurs fans—and six Belgians — were held in jail last night after three bars were wrecked. After being made to pay for the damage the Tottenham supporters were being put on a ferry back to Dover.

EATEN—Page 46

K CROSSWORD

missile (5-6)

DOWN

Churchman (6)

Ancient Greek state (6)

Block (6)

4 Famous composer (5)

5 Unaffected (7)

6 Cut up (7)

11 Defenceless (7)

12 Jilted (5, (5, 2)

13 Part of a gun (6)

14 Lumberjack (6)

15 Cardgame (6)

17 Rubbish (5)

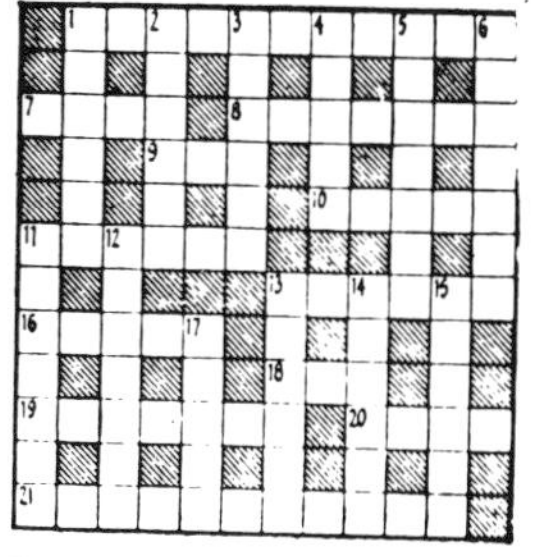

LUTION.—ACROSS: 1 Wizard. 4 Short. 7 9 Risky. 11 Ripples. 13 Rapport. 15 Merit. sed. 20 Expel. 21 Geyser. DOWN: 1 Washer. Super. 5 Owl. 6 Tasty. 7 Proper. 10 Stolid. nor. 15 Moose. 16 Trawl. 17 Defy. 19 Tap.

"DEAR SNOOPY... MY

PAINFUL? WHY WOULD

STANDARD, Thursday, October 25, 1984

OFF NIGHT

Hoddle sets Spurs a fine problem

From MICHAEL HART

Tottenham manager Peter Shreeve is unlikely to discipline Glenn Hoddle for his sending off in the 2-1 UEFA Cup defeat in Bruges.

Spurs have an internal disciplinary procedure for players sent off but Shreeve said today: "I want to think about it before deciding whether to fine him but my initial impulse is to give him the benefit of the doubt. He is very upset and feels he has let the club down.

"In the circumstances I felt he was immature for a player of this experience but I also think he was simply over-enthusiastic."

Hoddle, sent off once previously in a League Cup tie against Crystal Palace in 1980, was cautioned twice by Swiss referee Andre Daina in the space of three minutes. He came on as a 64th-minute substitute and was on the field barely 20 minutes.

The first caution was for pushing an opponent and the second for kicking the ball away at a free kick. Technically the referee was correct but I felt he could have shown a more flexible interpretation of the rules.

"You have to be seen as a holier than holy, when playing in Europe," added Shreeve.

Hoddle is now suspended for two European games – the return leg at White Hart Lane and the first leg of the third round if Spurs get through.

Full back Chris Hughton, booked in the first round against Braga, was also cautioned last night and so misses the second leg.

Graham Roberts, booked along with Mark Falco against Manchester United on Saturday, was also cautioned last night.

The sending off of Hoddle takes the number of Spurs' men dismissed this season to three. Roberts and Clive Allen were sent off at Sunderland.

"I want us to be known for the quality of our football," said Shreeve, "but I don't want a fancy Dan team."

RETROSPECTIVE VIEW BY GLENN HODDLE

Glenn Hoddle admits it was sheer stupidity that got him sent off against Bruges.

He says: "After my achilles operation, I was keyed-up to do well in my comeback game after a frustrating seven months out.

"I came on for Mickey Hazard and straight away Bruges scored from a penalty.

"Somebody brought Tony Galvin down. It's not normally like me to get involved. But I did. I was only on the field for a few minutes and here I was getting booked.

"The referee blew his whistle and as he did the ball rolled to me. I clipped it down the wing.

"The next minute I was sitting in the dressing rooms. I couldn't believe I'd been sent off.

"I'd waited so long for my return. I suppose all the frustration simply built up and spilled over.

"It was such a silly incident. It wasn't as if I'd gone up and kicked someone. Just two very silly incidents, all very harmless, but there I was back in the dressing rooms."

Hoddle had been sent off once before in his career. Once again it was a harmless incident that proved his downfall.

"It was a game against Crystal Palace. I had broken down their offside trap but Jerry Murphy pulled me back by my shirt. To push him off I caught him with my arm. The referee must have thought it was a punch."

TIMES, Thursday, November 8, 1984

TOTTENHAM HOTSPUR . . . 3 BRUGES . . . 0

TOTTENHAM WIN 4-2 ON AGGREGATE

SPURS THROUGH DESPITE MIDDLE MEN

By DAVID MILLER

Tottenham are through to the third round of the UEFA Cup, in which they are the holders, thanks to three goals in the first half last night which owed much to the uncertainty of Bruges' goalkeeper for half an hour in the second half.

Had Bruges not given away the second and third goals in the space of seven minutes last night, it was clear that their superior level of co-ordinated skill might have carried them through, although they were handicapped by the loss of their mainspring, Ceulemans, at half-time with an injury inflicted by Roberts early in the match.

Over the two legs Tottenham undoubtedly created the more chances but there are areas in which their lack of refinement – notably the centre of their defence – suggest they will always be in difficulties against teams capable of attacking them through the middle.

Tottenham could hardly have had a better start, levelling the score at 2-2 on aggregate within five minutes. Falco, working through on the right, had a blistering shot fumbled by Jensen on the near post: Chiedozie pulled his corner back at an angle on the ground to Hazard and, with the entire defence and half of Tottenham's team wondering what was about to happen, Hazard took a stride and a half and clipped a perfect left foot shot over everybody, including the goalkeeper.

Then came one of the moments for which Tottenham make no friends. Roberts jumped in with a two-footed tackle on Ceulemans after the most dangerous of the Belgians had swayed past an earlier tackle and was heading for goal. Verheyen was booked for protesting and Ceulemans was left limping for 10 minutes: from the free kick for the foul Verheyen had swept the ball no more than inches over the crossbar with Clemence beaten.

Yet the early bit of fire in Bruges seemed now to die. Chiedozie and Galvin were regularly and excitingly running past their full backs, the centre of Bruges' defence looked unsure, and Jensen the most uncertain of all.

After 27 minutes Tottenham scored their second, Hazard putting Galvin away, and the winger's beautifully timed sprint and quick cross found Jensen groping and dropping the ball, which was gratefully accepted by Allen. Seven minutes later Frank Van der Elst misjudged a headed back-pass, Jensen only just managing to claw it off the line: a scrambled clearance followed, only for the ball to run straight into the path of Roberts who smashed it into the roof of the net from 30 yards.

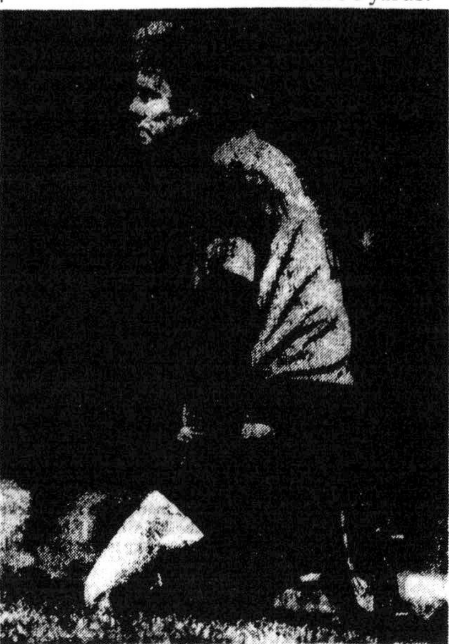

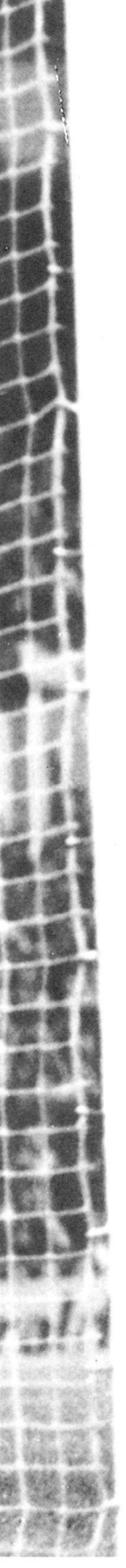

m the heights of ecstasy to the depths of despair. Roberts has just beaten Jensen. (Photographs: Chris Cole)

Spurs through despite middle men

Clive Allen notches Spurs' third goal.

Roberts and Perryman close ranks.

Mark Falco goes close.

DAILY MAIL, Thursday, November 29, 1984

TOTTENHAM . . . 2 BOHEMIANS PRAGUE . . . 0

OUTCLASSED!

Spurs are so lucky to stay in the hunt

By JEFF POWELL

The Tottenham public were treated last night to an exhibition of superlative skills, reminiscent of the glory, glory days of their early European history.

That made all 27,971 of them as hugely fortunate as the 13 Spurs players who clung on somehow to the club's proud record of never losing in 42 home European matches spread across 23 years.

But the performance which took their breath away was given by 11 footballers anonymous this side of the Iron Curtain, with unpronounceable names.

Tottenham were out-thought, out-paced, out-manoeuvred, out-classed and frequently out on their feet.

Yet they finished this third round night celebrating a victory which might just be enough to extend their defence of the UEFA Cup beyond a second leg in Prague on December 12th.

For that, some credit must be given to the durability and persistence fundamental to the character of the English footballer.

That said, Spurs should be thankful for the failure of Prague's Bohemians to take any of their abundance of chances . . . and congratulate themselves on excluding the television cameras.

Nationwide transmission of this first leg would have served only as an embarrassment for Spurs and English football.

Seldom has any club in this country been so lucky to win a European match, rarely have Tottenham been so unflattered by comparison with Continental technique.

The gulf in sheer ability was so wide that Argentinian Osvaldo Ardiles, crippled for so long, may find his craft and experience pressed into service on the ice in Prague.

Had Bohemians been as deadly in their finishing as they were devastating in their build up, we would have been present at the most astonishing European result of many a season . . . something approaching a 7-2 home defeat for the holders of the UEFA trophy.

Only one team was ever going to score the first goal and the pity for Bohemians was that they did so for Tottenham, not themselves.

John Chiedozie's driven cross was sliced into the net by Jiri Ondra to put Spurs in the peculiar position of leading 1-0 after 25 minutes in which they had not mustered a solitary goal attempt worthy of the name.

If there was any justice in the result, it lay with the identity of the scorer of Tottenham's second goal. Gary Stevens had been the outstanding Spurs player for the entire 89 minutes preceding his 25-yard drive.

The Czechs could not believe it. They had filled the rest of the evening with kaleidoscope football culminating in chances too numerous to recount.

As a confirmed admirer of Glenn Hoddle's natural talent, I was as amazed as the crowd to see him looking like an artisan in comparison with the man orchestrating these Bohemians.

Daily Mail, Thursday, November 29, 1984

SPORTSMAIL SOCCER

ggins
se for
replay

atch his way by taking the first frame of the second session. The pair had completed seven sizzling frames in 83 minutes and when they returned, Higgins rattled in a 58 break to level at 4-4.

After that it was all downhill for Thorne as Higgins put him on the rack to win a semi-final spot against Cliff Thorburn or Ray Reardon.

World champion Steve Davis, beaten 16-15 by Higgins in last year's final, hammered Jimmy White 9-4.

Spectacular

It was a spectacular effort, highlighting his skill and consistency and kept him on course for a repeat showdown with Higgins.

'I've always said I'm more consistent than any other player and at the moment I feel very strong,' said Davis. 'It's been a hard draw for me but I'm firing on all cylinders.'

r Thorburn

No way through for Clive Allen . . . blocked by Prokes (left) and Sloup. Picture: TED BLACKBROW

We need Ossie,

TOTTENHAM manager Peter Shreeves is planning a crash course to get Ossie Ardiles fit for the return leg of their UEFA Cup-tie.

Shreeves considers the 32-year-old Argentinian such a key figure that he is arranging a series of games designed to prepare the midfield star for the game in Prague in a fortnight.

Ardiles has played only 13 times in two-and-a-half years since cracking a shin bone and undergoing a cartilage operation.

But Shreeves said last night: 'It is a realistic target for Ossie to play in Czechoslovakia. I plan to confirm tonight or tomorrow a game against Australia at Cheshunt which will be all about Ardiles.

'He is back in full training and his experience out there in the second leg is vital.

'I took him for an hour's training this morning and he looked good, but first he must come through the reserve and trial games.

HARRY HARRIS

Spurs are so lucky to stay in the hunt

Outclassed!

Tottenham 2	Bohemians Prague 0

REPORT BY JEFF POWELL

THE Tottenham public were treated last night to an exhibition of superlative skills reminiscent of the glory, glory days of

of the UEFA Cup beyond a

so wide that Argentinian

they had not mustered a solitary goal attempt worthy of the name.

If there was any justice in the result, it lay with the identity of the scorer of Tottenham's second goal. Gary Stevens had been the outstand-

HOLSTEN

Jiri Sloup, for some unfathomable reason one of two players in this team never to have represented his country, was a revelation. He created chances in double figures, the majority squandered, four of them brilliantly saved by Ray Clemence.

The crowd were bewitched. Except when they were roused to cheer Tottenham's goals, they punctuated an eerie silence only for bursts of instinctive applause for the artistry of the Czechs.

They came out of their trance at the end of the match to voice sympathy for the Bohemians as they stood, incredulous of their failure to achieve an immortal victory.

Bohemians clearly, have done their homework on Spurs in great depth. Even at two up and with the hard men available, Tottenham's survival in Prague will depend on how well they digested last night's lessons.

HARRY HARRIS, Daily Mail writes:
Tottenham manager Peter Shreeve is planning a crash course to get Ossie Ardiles fit for the return leg of their UEFA Cup tie.

Shreeve considers the 32-year old Argentinian such a key figure that he is arranging a series of games designed to prepare the midfield star for the game in Prague in a fortnight.

Ardiles has played only 13 times in two and a half years since cracking a shin bone and undergoing a cartilage operation.

But Shreeve said last night: "It is a realistic target for Ossie to play in Czechoslovakia. I plan to confirm tonight or tomorrow a game against Australis at Cheshunt which will be all about Ardiles.

"He is back in full training and his experience out there in the second leg is vital.

"I took him for an hour's training this morning and he looked good, but first he must come through the reserve and trial games."

Prokes clears from Gary Stevens

RETROSPECTIVE VIEW BY GLENN HODDLE

The 1984/85 season's UEFA Cup campaign was becoming a personal nightmare of Glenn Hoddle.

Sent off in the previous round against Bruges, he was now carried off after one of the ugliest tackles imaginable.

"I've never experienced an incident like it, and I hope I never do again.

"I shouted for the ball from our goalkeeper Ray Clemence, and he threw the ball toward me, at the centre of the pitch.

"I heard Garth Crooks shout, 'He's coming.' In the videos before the game we all knew that Sloup was a little 'naughty' in his tackling. I guessed that Garth meant that this fellow was coming after me.

"I went to flick the ball to one side of him and run around to collect it. I thought he was coming at me from behind. As it turned out he came to my left.

"I flicked the ball and turned and he 'hit' me full on the thigh with his foot, while, at the same time, his elbow caught me on the forehead and caused a massive cut."

Hoddle didn't pass out, but he doesn't remember too much more about the game.

"It was the thigh injury that caused me more concern although my split forehead looked the worst of my injuries."

SUN, Thursday, December 13, 1984

BOHEMIANS PRAGUE . . . 1 TOTTENHAM . . . 1

SPURS WIN 3-1 ON AGGREGATE

SPURS AXE BUTCHERS!

Ace Hoddle is carried off

By BRIAN WOOLNOUGH

Glenn Hoddle was stretchered off with a deep cut over his eye and suffering from concussion as Spurs fought off a bunch of Czechoslovakian brutes to reach the UEFA Cup quarter-finals.

Hoddle, who holders Spurs "feared" could be the target of a hate campaign, was carried off at half-time after being struck down by Sloup, just one of Bohemians' hatchet men.

He needed four stitches and has also a bad thigh strain that is likely to put him out of Saturday's First Division clash at Watford.

The Czechs committed 25 fouls against Spurs' 15 and seven players were booked, four from Bohemians and three from Tottenham – goal hero Mark Falco, Paul Miller, and Graham Roberts.

The caution for Roberts is the only blot on a fine Spurs performance. The England international is now banned from the quarter-final first leg next March.

At the end, Roberts, who held a sponge to a cut head most of the second half, had to be pushed towards the dressing room by manager Peter Shreeve and his assistant John Pratt as he sarcastically applauded the Czech team off.

And Brussels referee Alex Ponnet angrily shoved a Czech fan away as the teams left this little cramped ground.

The Czech side had Jakubec Sloup – for the foul on Hoddle – Kakucha and Hruska all booked, and they deserved to have more punishment handed out.

Shreeve had predicted this would be a game for men and he was proved exactly right. He said: "Bohemians, the fine football team we saw in London, went right to the border-lines of the rules.

"I knew it was going to be physical. I'd seen a tape of how they play at home. We showed our courage and lesser teams could have been frightened."

Spurs made the perfect start with a seventh-minute goal to take the pressure off them.

Crooks began it with great control and a ball wide to Tony Galvin.

He went past Jekubec as if he didn't exist and there was Falco to head Spurs in front. It was his 15th goal of the season.

A bottle was thrown at Chiedozie and keeper Ray Clemence was pelted with fireworks, smoke-bombs and streamers.

In the 50th minute, Tottenham for once lost their defensive concentration.

A cross by Hruska found its way to the far

SPURS AXE BUTCHERS!

Ace Hoddle is carried off

EURO SOCCER SPECIAL

Bohemians Prague 1, Tottenham 1 (Spurs win 3-1 on aggregate)

GLENN HODDLE was stretchered off with a deep cut over his eye and suffering from concussion as Spurs fought off a bunch of Czechoslovakian brutes to reach the UEFA Cup quarter-finals.

Hoddle, who holders Spurs "feared" could be the target of a hate campaign, was carried off at half-time after being struck down by Sloup, just one of Bohemians' hatchet men.

From BRIAN WOOLNOUGH

He needed four stitches and has also a bad thigh strain that is likely to put him

Graham Roberts and Glenn Hoddle with their scars on the flight home

post and skipper Prokes headed his team level.

Spurs now march proudly on and look like maintaining their superb record of never having failed to reach the semi-final stage in the UEFA Cup.

Glenn Hoddle was stretchered off with a cut eye and suffering concussion as Spurs tamed Bohemians' thugs to reach the UEFA Cup quarter-finals.

Hoddle, who holders Spurs feared could be the target of a hate campaign, was carried off at half-time after being struck down by Sloup, just one of Bohemians' hatchet men.

He needed four stitches and has also a bad thigh strain that is likely to put him out of Saturday's First Division clash at Watford.

Hoddle, who returned to Stanstead Airport wearing a bandage round his head, said: "I don't know what he hit me with. I've even got teeth marks in my head.

"But it's my thigh which could keep me out of Saturday's game. I could play with the stitches covered.

"We knew it was going to be hard. We were well warned. We were expecting intimidation and we got it, but we coped."

That was just one ugly incident in a match that saw Spurs suffer some of the worst tackling and provocation seen in European football.

Bohemians were not obvious bullies – they were a nasty dirty team who used every trick they could get away with.

SPURS KO CZECH THUGS

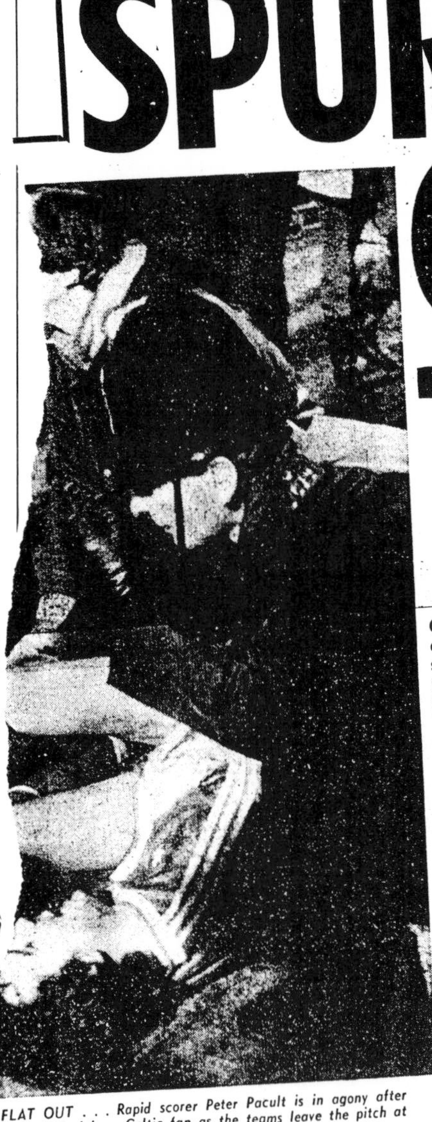

FLAT OUT . . . Rapid scorer Peter Pacult is in agony after being kicked by a Celtic fan as the teams leave the pitch at Old Trafford. More soccer action pages 30-31.

From BRIAN WOOLNOUGH
Bohemians Prague 1, Spurs 1
(Spurs win 3-1 on agg)

Hero Hoddle is carried off in bloodbath

GLENN HODDLE was stretchered off with a cut eye and suffering concussion as Spurs tamed Bohemians' thugs to reach the UEFA Cup quarter-finals.

Hoddle, who holders Spurs feared could be the target of a hate campaign, was carried off at half-time after being struck down by Sloup, just one of Bohemians' hatchet men.

He needed four stitches and has also a bad thigh strain that is likely to put him out of Saturday's First Division clash at Watford.

Hoddle, who returned to Stanstead Airport wearing a bandage round his head, said: "I don't know what he hit me with. I've even got teeth marks in my head.

"But it's my thigh which could keep me out of Saturday's game. I could play with the stitches covered.

"We knew it was going to be hard. We were well warned. We were expecting intimidation and we got it, but we coped."

● Turn to Page 31

Clive Allen tries a shot against Bohemians Prague.
(See match report p.231)

Archibald looks on as Falco's winning goal against
Bayern Munich crosses the line. (See match report p. 194)

Archibald puts Spurs level on aggregate against Bayern Munich. (See match report p. 194)

Hoddle, architect of Spurs' victory, against Bayern Munich holds his hands aloft as the players congratulate Mark Falco who has just put Spurs into the quarter-finals. (See match report p. 194)

Steve Archibald scoring Spurs' first goal against Austria Vienna. (See match report p. 200)

Steve Archibald tries a shot against Austria Vienna. (See match report p. 200)

LOOKING BACK WITH PETER SHREEVE

When Tottenham Hotspur beat Bruges 3-0 in the second leg of the UEFA Cup second round match at White Hart Lane in November 1984 the Belgian coach put his finger on the difference in European football.

Peter Shreeve sat in his office at the club and the Bruges coach shook his hand and said simply: "I wish that we could generate the spirit that English players show."

That match had seen Spurs start 2-1 down after a stormy first leg in Belgium but Shreeve said: "We beat them by sheer heart.

"They looked so confident in that first leg but they could not cope with the blood and thunder type of football that English teams play.

"Even the great teams like Bayern Munich never liked playing English teams because no matter what the score, they knew they could not relax.

"When we played them on the way to the final in 1984 we lost 1-0 on one of the coldest nights I can remember. When a television commentator asked me for my comments on the match I was so cold I could not talk.

"But they thought that they had it all tied up and in the second leg they could not cope either. It was strange that other countries just could not produce that special type of game."

But the match that sticks in Shreeve's memory the most was the battle in Prague that December. They were playing the Bohemians side.

"It showed how deceptive appearances could be. In the first match they came to London, they murdered us playing some delightful football and lost 2-0.

"They looked a gentle little football team. Then I spoke with Aad de Mos the Ajax coach whose team had lost to them in the previous round.

"He told me exactly what we could expect when we got to Prague and to be honest we did not believe it. Then I got a video tape of the match.

"The players watched it after training one day and they were shocked. They did not think that it was the same team they had played."

But the same team it was and in Prague the battle was fierce. Glenn Hoddle came home with a damaged thigh and a cut eye. Other players suffered cuts and bruises.

Shreeve said: "I don't think that I have ever been prouder of a Spurs team. They were intimidated in every way but they stood shoulder to shoulder and fought hard.

"They tried to intimidate us so much but the lads still kept their heads. It reminded me very much of the Barcelona attitude some years before.

"They needed to win at all costs. I will never forget the pre-Terry Venables days at Barcelona. When they played us they fielded eight defenders at home.

"They did not care about the feelings of their fans. They just wanted a result. They had drawn 1-1 in Tottenham and knew 0-0 was good enough.

"The game does not prosper from things like that."

GUARDIAN, Thursday, March 7, 1985

TOTTENHAM . . . 0 REAL MADRID . . . 1

PERRYMAN'S SLIP LETS IN REAL

By DAVID LACEY

The UEFA Cup began to slip from Tottenham's grasp at White Hart Lane last night as they lost the opening leg of their quarter-final 1-0 to Real Madrid, who may be having a bad season in the Spanish League but proved too disciplined and well organised for the holders. It was the first time in 24 years and 44 ties that Spurs had been beaten at home in Europe and the first time they had failed to score, unless one counted the own goal from Perryman that gave Real victory.

The legend of Real Madrid had brought thousands up the Tottenham High Road but present reality suggested that the Spanish team would present Spurs with fewer problems than their previous opponents in the competition, the classy Bohemians Prague. As events were to prove, statistics can be misleading.

Tottenham went into the game all too aware of Real's prolific record in their home legs this season. The two-goal lead usually regarded as a reasonable cushion for the return match now became the barest of necessities. In fact it was not long before Tottenham began to regard any sort of victory as their aim.

As Real's man-to-man marking locked itself on to the Spurs attack, with Stielike sweeping up imperiously behind the defence, the size of the holders' task was thrown into sharper relief. Tottenham needed skill, pace and imagination of course but a fine degree of accuracy in their shots, final passes, and centres was the prime requirement.

Hazard was the first player to worry the Real defence and did so by running headlong at them before shooting a yard wide. Hoddle made space much nearer goal but he too shot past a post. Unable to open up the wings immediately for Chiedozie and Galvin, Tottenham's movements palled and after a quarter of an hour they became less concerned about how many they would score than staying in the tie.

UEFA CUP — QUARTER FINALS

David Lacey—Tottenham 0, Real Madrid 1

Perryman's slip lets in Real

The UEFA Cup began to slip from Tottenham's grasp at White Hart Lane last night as they lost the opening leg of their quarter final 1-0 to Real Madrid, who may be having a bad season in the Spanish League but proved too disciplined and well organised for the holders. It was the first time in 24 years and 44 ties that Spurs had been beaten at home in Europe and the first time they had failed to score, unless one counted the own goal from Perryman that gave Real victory.

The legend of Real Madrid had brought thousands up the Tottenmham High Road but present reality suggested that the Spanish team would present Spurs with fewer problems than their previous opponents in the competition, the classy Bohemians Prague. As events were to prove, statistics can be misleading.

Tottenmham went into the game all too aware of Real's prolific scoring record in their home legs this season. The two-goal lead usually regarded as a reasonable cushion for the return match now became the barest of necessities. In fact the return match now became the barest of necessities. In fact it was not long before Tottenham began to regard any sort of victory as their aim.

As Real's man-to-man marking locked itself on to the Spurs attack, with Stielike sweeping up imperiously behind the defence, the size of the holders' task was thrown into sharper relief. Tottenmham needed skill, pace and imagination of course but a fine degree of accuracy in their shots, final passes, and centres was the prime requirement.

Hazard was the first player to worry the Real defence and did so by running headlong at them before shooting a yard wide. Hoddle made space much nearer goal but he too shot past a post. Unable to open up the wings immediately for Chiedozie and Galvin, Tottenham's movements palled and after a quarter of an hour they became less concerned about how many they would score than staying in the tie.

In a well-timed counter attack Stielike found Michel in space and he sent Butragueno on a race along the right wing with Stevens and Miller. Butragueno won, crossed low and hard from the byline and the hapless Parryman, forcing his way into the goalmouth to stop the pass reaching Valdano, saw Clemence get a slight touch before the ball ricocheted back over the line off the Tottenham captain's knees.

Two minutes later Tottenham were almost out of the competition there and then. Their offside trap clanked shut too late as Butragueno sent Valdano clear on the left. His shot beat the oncoming Clemence but squeezed past the far post.

Tottenham dutifully surged back but their movements remained too frantic and untidy t achieve serious penetration although Hazard's willingness to take opponents on in tight spaces continued to give them some hope.

Hoddle took a long time getting into the game to any serious extent. True he was being stalked in midfield by Angel but he still had the space to create more than he did. As the game wore on Tottenham badly missed the power of the suspended Roberts and especially his ability to carry the play deep and hard into the heart of the opposing defence.

Tottenham Hotspur: Clemence; Stevens, Hughton, Hazard, Miller, Perryman, Chiedozie, Falco, Galvin, Hoddle, Crooks.

Real Madrid: Miguel Angel; Chendo, Camacho, Stielike, Sanchis, Salguero, Angel, Michel, Butraqueno, Gallego, Valdano.

Referee: P. Casarin (Italy)

NICK OF TIME: Steve Nicol, who headed Liverpool's equaliser against Austria Vienna four minutes from time

CAPTAIN'S ERROR . . . Steve Perryman's own goal gave Real Madrid a first-half lead over Spurs

SOCCER IN BRIEF

THE FA have appointed a five-man commission to investi-
-ate the crowd trouble at Chel-
Milk Cup semi-final
against Sun-
The com-

Iran and Iraq, at war since 1980, had been asked to play home matches on neutral ground, along with the Lebanon.

PETER BARNES has agreed
with Coventry City that he
ld leave the club if he
win a regular first
lace. Barnes, 28, had a
with manager Don
fter being dropped
turday's match at
ednesday. Barnes
the reserves last

HERTY revealed
at Walves had
a £160,000 offer
Tim Flowers.
ld Flowers is
attracted Man-
and Everton.
efused to name
ved, said: "I
e is nothing

AGONY. Steve Perryman can do nothing to stop the ball cannoning off him for Real Madrid's winner

In a well-timed counter-attack Stielike found Michel in space and he sent Butragueno on a race along the right wing with Stevens and Miller. Butragueno won, crossed low and hard from the byline and the hapless Perryman, forcing his way into the goalmouth to stop the pass reaching Valdano, saw Clemence get a slight touch before the ball ricocheted back over the line off the Tottenham captain's knees.

Two minutes later Tottenham were almost out of the competition there and then. Their offside trap clanked shut too late as Butra-gueno sent Valdano clear on the left. His shot beat the oncoming Clemence but squeezed past the far post.

Tottenham dutifully surged back but their movements remained too frantic and untidy to achieve serious penetration although Hazard's willingness to take opponents on in tight spaces continued to give them some hope.

Hoddle took a long time getting into the game to any serious extent. True, he was being stalked in mid-field by Angel but he still had the space to create more than he did. As the game wore on Tottenham badly missed the power of the suspended Roberts and especially his ability to carry the play deep and hard into the heart of the opposing defence.

Garth Crooks battles for possession

Mark Falco shoots past Stielike

Mike Hazard beats the wall with a free kick against Hadjuk Split to score the goal that put Spurs in the final against Anderlecht. (See match report p. 207)

Spurs players celebrate Mike Hazard's goal against Hadjuk Split. (See match report p. 207)

HOLSTEN Pils The origi
HOLSTEN
HOLSTEN Pils

Graham Roberts brings the house down as he scores Spurs' equaliser against Anderlecht. (See match report p. 214)

HEROES OF THE NIGHT. Tony Parks and Graham Roberts after the match against Anderlecht. (See match report p. 214)

SPURS v ANDERLECHT. Tony Parks saves the penalty from Gudjohnson.

John Chiedozie goes close with a header against Sporting Braga. (See match report p. 223)

HOLSTEN

Mark Falco scores Spurs' fifth goal against Sporting Braga. (See match report p. 223)

HOLSTEN

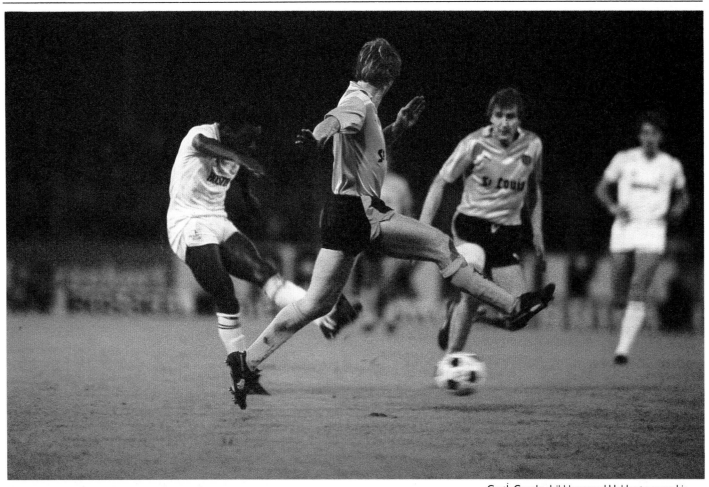

Garth Crooks shoots just wide against Bruges. (See match report p. 226)

Garth Crooks dribbles round Helder to score his second and Spurs' fourth against Sporting Braga. (See match report p. 223)

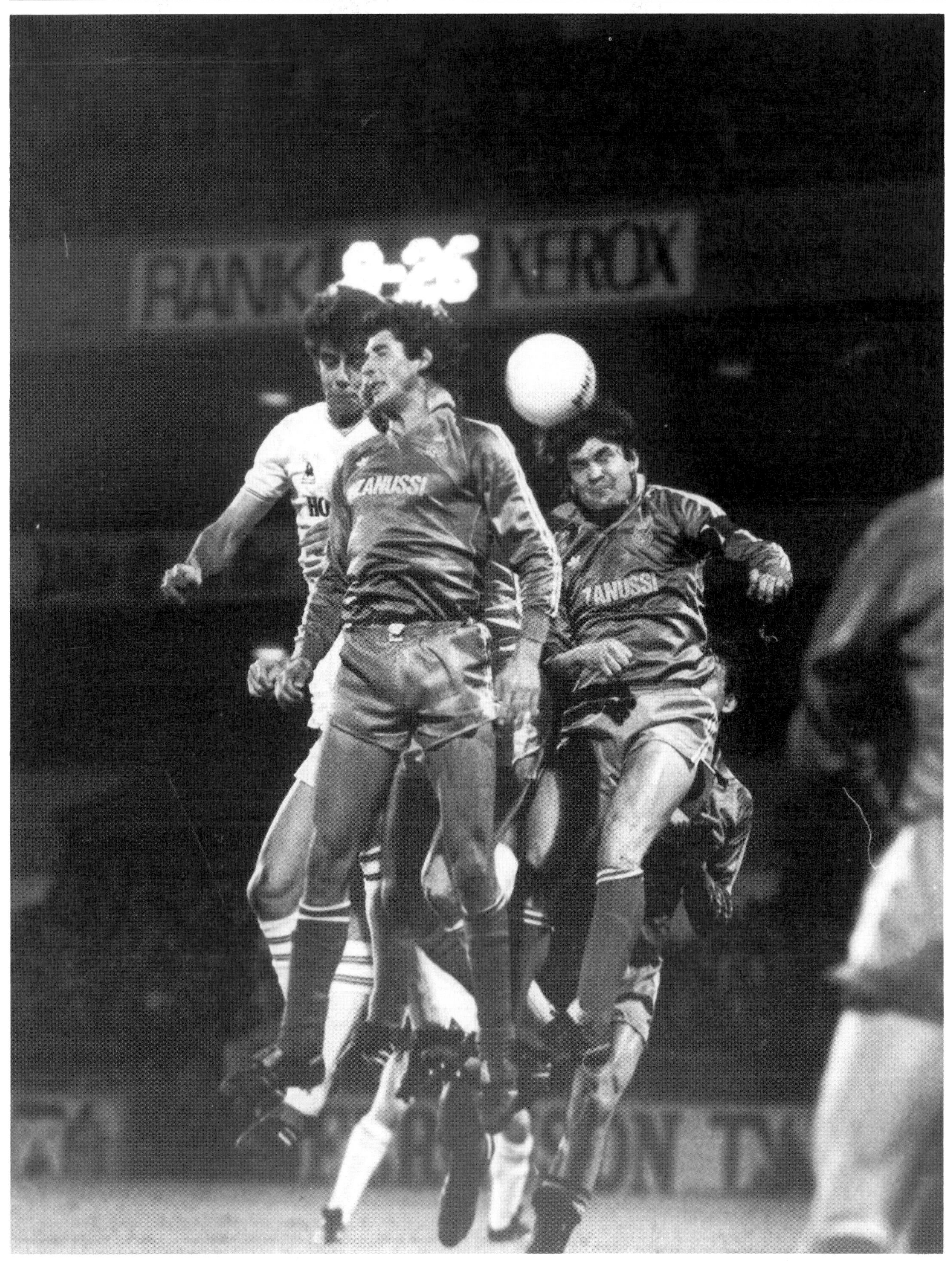

SPURS v REAL MADRID. Gary Stevens is crowded out. (See match report p 242)

DAILY MIRROR, 20th March, 1985

Real Madrid . . . 0 Spurs . . . 0

AGG. 1-0

DOUBLE DESPAIR

HARRY MILLER

Skipper Steve Perryman was sent off in the huge San Bernabeau Stadium last night as Tottenham's latest European adventure ended in despair.

And as the holders lost their grip on the UEFA Cup they won last May, veteran Perryman has more cause than most to look back on his quarter-final with deep disappointment.

It was his own goal in the first leg at White Hart Lane, that proved the difference between Real advancing to the last four and Tottenham being left to concentrate on their championship challenge.

Perryman, a distinguished Spurs servant for 16 years, went in the 79th minute of his 809th game for the club.

Swiss referee Bruno Galler will feel he had no alternative as Perryman sent Real's Jorge Valdano flying as the forward broke clear. But it was Perryman's first bad foul of the match and a booking would have been more appropriate.

It was the third time the 33-year old who played in mid-field last night, has been sent off in his long career.

Spurs contained Real completely for half an hour and were only troubled in the closing minutes of the first half when Manuel Sanchis had a header cleared off the line by Danny Thomas. Then Sanchis and Valdano went agonisingly close.

For much of the time, the match lacked fire and passion.

Ray Clemence, who had performed so superbly at White Hart Lane, was again a hero when he saved courageously at Michel's feet after the Real man had floored Graham Roberts.

Roberts was the player who came closest to keeping alive Tottenham's European bid.

He had a searing 25 yarder saved by Real's keeper Angel and later saw a fine header stopped by Angel at the foot of the post.

Spurs also had a goal disallowed. Mark Falco headed home a long ball forward from Paul Miller only for referee Galler to rule that he had fouled Jose Guero.

Tottenham manager Peter Shreeve said: "We are desperately disappointed to go out. I was particularly sad for Perryman. He was one of our best players on the field.

"We also felt we scored a good goal."

hursday, March 21, 1985 No. 25,217
elephone: (STD Code: 01)—353 0246

DOUBLE DESPAIR

From HARRY MILLER
Real Madrid 0 Spurs 0
(agg 1-0)

SKIPPER Steve Perryman was sent off in the huge San Bernabeau Stadium last night as Tottenham's latest European adventure ended in despair.

Steve is sent off as Spurs tumble

RULED OUT: Mark Falco's goal.

PERRYMAN: Sent off.

Daily Telegraph, Thursday, March 21, 1985

UEFA Cup

PERRYMAN OFF AND SPURS' HOPES DASHED

Real Madrid 0 Tottenham ... 0
(Real win 1-0 on aggregate)

TOTTENHAM'S reign as UEFA Cup holders, which began at White Hart Lane last May, ended sadly at the Bernabeu Stadium in Madrid last night, in the absence of Steve Perryman, their captain.

Perryman, 33, who has served Spurs so nobly for 16 years, was sent off in the 79th minute of the second leg of his quarter final against Real Madrid, for body checking Valdano in the middle of the pitch.

Since 1969, Perryman has played 809 senior games for Spurs. He will not wish to remember the two matches against Real during the past fortnight.

In the first, at White Hart Lane a fortnight ago, he conceded the own goal that ultimately was to allow the Spaniards a passage into the semi-finals.

Receding hopes

Last night, his eagerness to prevent Valdano from breaking upfield, in effect ended Tottenham's already receding hopes of closing the narrow gap.

In my view Perryman was unlucky to be sent off. Certainly he was guilty of a blatant professional foul but Bruno Haller, the Swiss referee, surely could have punished him sufficiently with the yellow card—especially as he had been in no sort of trouble until then.

Be that as it may, I doubt whether Tottenham would have held on to the trophy—even if Perryman had been there right to the end.

Though they enjoyed an encouraging first half-hour, they could not consistently find a way through Real's skilful, well-organised defence.

was not nearly sharp enough to exploit the few chances created.

So, as half time approached, Real began to push forward and Tottenham's defence was in serious trouble as the Spaniards forced a series of corners, three of which could have led to a goal.

Sanchis headed the first of these wide, then had a shot deflected just wide before Valdano drove the easiest of the lot the wrong side of a post from close-range.

The Spaniards continued to push forward menacingly after the interval, and only a brave save by Clemence at the feet of Michel prevented them from increasing the lead.

Still, Tottenham weathered the storm, kept their heads and went back patiently and purposefully to their increasingly difficult task of trying to close that gap.

Eventually, in the 68th minute, Peter Shreeves, Spurs' manager, perhaps sensing that time was running out, pulled off the ineffective Crooks and sent on Brooke, who took over on the right of midfield so that Hazard could join Falco up front.

For a few seconds, in the 74th minute, the switch seemed to have been successful, since Falco headed the ball into the far corner of the net. The referee, however, ruled that Salguero had been fouled and refused a goal.

Then, soon afterwards, disaster struck Tottenham with Perryman's departure. Mr Shreeves responded to this by replacing Galvin, who had not looked fully fit, with the inexperienced young Dick.

A few minutes later, Tottenhar were offered their best and las chance, when Hoddle put Falc clear. The hard-working strike who has scored so many cruci goals in domestic and Europe competitions, this time could n quite manage it.

Real Madrid.—Miguel Angel; Chen Camacho, Salguero, Sanchis, Ang Pineda, Michel, Butragueno, Galle Valdano.

Tottenham. — Clemence; Thon Hughton, Roberts, Miller, Perrym Hazard, Falco, Galvin (Dick, Hoddle, Crooks.

Graham Roberts (left) and M Angel

Real Madrid v Spurs 85 – DISALLOWED! Mark Falco (extreme right) lying on the ground having just headed past the Real Madrid goalkeeper whilst Mike Hazard (extreme left) celebrates a goal. NB, no Real Madrid player is appealing for the foul given by the referee

RETROSPECTIVE VIEW BY STEVE PERRYMAN

For Steve Perryman the nightmare of Spurs' first home defeat in Europe was multiplied by his own peculiar miseries . . . an own goal to contribute to Spurs' downfall in front of their own fans, and then a sending off in the return tie.

"The repercussions of that own goal were immense", recalls Perryman, "it was a piece of history . . . gone – the first home defeat.

"But I've no recriminations. There was absolutely nothing I could have done to avoid that own goal.

"There was a cross from the byline, Ray Clemence got a touch, and as I was coming back to cover, the ball struck me on the knee and flew in.

"It would have required quick silver thinking to have got out of the way of that one."

Spurs, the UEFA Cup holders, crashed out of the competition at the quarter-final stage with a goalless draw in Madrid.

"It was a niggling game. Graham Roberts was having problems with Real's Argentinian player, Valdano.

"I was playing mid-field with Glenn Hoddle and this was one of our better performances although it didn't work out for us on the night.

"They didn't seem to be looking too much for goals, while we played some good football.

"Then, Valdano came across me kicking out and connecting with my calf and achilles, an area of the body I detest being injured.

"The worst injury any athlete can have is an achilles. This tackle made my blood boil. Ossie told me after the match that the guy thought I was Roberts and that's why he made the challenge.

"But I was convinced he was out to get me. I got him first. I really went for him, it was repayment for that tackle 10 minutes earlier.

"There was also a lot of frustration. Mark Falco seemed to score a perfectly good goal but it was disallowed. We watched the replay on Spanish TV but it just confirmed what we thought at the time – there was no foul. The referee must have thought that Mark climbed on the back of the defender to make his far post header."

LOOKING BACK WITH PETER SHREEVE

It was 3 am in a Sydney hotel on May 30, 1985. The Tottenham players were gathering around their sandwiches and beer waiting for the live screening of the European Cup final from Brussels.

They were on a tour of Australia and as Peter Shreeve their manager said: "Suddenly the world was turned upside down. We felt sick to our stomachs."

What had made Shreeve and his squad so upset were the pictures of the carnage in the Heysel stadium. Pictures showing English fans on the rampage, Italian fans dying under the crush of broken stands.

Shreeve said: "I suppose you could say that you had seen it coming. There had been a general decline of standards in society and football reflected it.

"It was a sad, sad day. It hit the clubs dramatically. We turned to each other and saw our season falling apart. We knew that we would be banned from European football.

"Tottenham had qualified and yet we knew from that moment that we were not going to play for a long, long time. In the context of people losing their lives though that was a minor consideration."

Tottenham themselves had been faced in that season with the problems of hooligans in Europe. There had been trouble in the previous seasons in Holland and Belgium itself.

Indeed in Bruges that year they had gone as far as banning their supporters from travelling to the game to prevent trouble. It passed off peacefully.

Shreeve said: "We try to be professional at all times and when our opposition would not listen we asked our fans not to travel.

"We felt that we had almost come to terms with the problem but a lot of the difficulties were making the local club and police face up to the problems.

"We went to Hadjuk Split in the semi final of the UEFA Cup and they seemed shocked when we suggested segregation in the ground.

"They kept telling us they were a Communist nation and that people would not dare cause trouble. We told them that they did not understand the problems.

"We knew that the penalty for any more misbehaviour by the fans would be hard and that is why we were not shocked at the reaction of UEFA in banning the English clubs after the Heysel tragedy.

"It was one of the saddest nights I can ever remember in football."

"Within two weeks English clubs were ordered home and the FIFA ban on friendlies outside Western Europe was to last until December 1985.

The glory nights were over.

STATISTICS

1961/62 – EUROPEAN CUP

September 13, 1961, 60,000

Gornik Zabre 4, Tottenham 2 *(Jones, Dyson)*

TEAM:
Tottenham: Brown, Baker, Henry, Blanchflower, Norman, Mackay, Jones, White, Smith, Allen, Dyson

September 20, 1966, 57,000

Tottenham 8 *(Blanchflower pen, Jones 3, Smith 2, Dyson, White),* **Gornik Zabre 1**

TEAM:
Tottenham: Brown, Baker, Henry, Blanchflower, Norman, Mackay, Jones, White, Smith, Allen, Dyson

SECOND ROUND

November 8, 1961, 64,000

Feyenoord 1, Tottenham 3 *(Dyson, Saul 2)*

TEAM:
Tottenham: Brown, Baker, Henry, Blanchflower, Norman, Marchi, Jones, White, Saul, Clayton, Dyson

November 15th, 1961, 62,144

Tottenham 1 *(Dyson),* **Feyenoord 1**

TEAM:
Tottenham: Brown, Baker, Henry, Blanchflower, Norman, Marchi, Jones, White, Saul, Mackay, Dyson

THIRD ROUND

February 21, 1962, 64,000

Dukla Prague 1, Tottenham 0

TEAM:
Tottenham: Brown, Baker, Henry, Marchi, Norman, Mackay, Medwin, White, Smith, Blanchflower, Jones

February 26, 1962, 60,000

Tottenham 4 *(Smith 2, Mackay 2),* **Dukla Prague 1**

TEAM:
Tottenham: Brown, Baker, Henry, Blanchflower, Norman, Marchi, Medwin, White, Smith, Mackay, Jones

SEMI-FINAL

March 21, 1962, 70,000

Benfica 3, Tottenham 1 *(Smith)*

TEAM:
Tottenham: Brown, Baker, Henry, Marchi, Norman, Mackay, Greaves, White, Smith, Blanchflower, Jones

April 5, 1962, 64,500

Tottenham 2 *(Smith, Blanchflower pen),* **Benfica 1**

TEAM:
Tottenham: Brown, Baker, Henry, Blanchflower, Norman, Mackay, Medwin, White, Smith, Greaves, Jones

1962/63 – ECWC

Bye

SECOND ROUND

October 31, 1962, 58,859

Tottenham 5 *(Norman, White, Allen, Greaves),* **Glasgow Rangers 2**

TEAM:
Tottenham: Brown, Baker, Henry, Blanchflower, Norman, Mackay, Medwin, White, Allen, Greaves, Jones

December 5, 1962, match postponed – fog

December 11, 1962, 80,000

Glasgow Rangers 2, Tottenham 3 *(Greaves, Smith 2)*

TEAM:
Tottenham: Brown, Baker, Henry, Blanchflower, Norman, Mackay, Medwin, White, Smith, Greaves, Jones

THIRD ROUND

March 5, 1963, 15,000

Slovan Bratislava 2, Tottenham 0

TEAM:
Tottenham: Brown, Baker, Henry, Marchi, Norman, Mackay, Saul, White, Smith, Greaves, Jones

March 14, 1963, 61,504

Tottenham 6 *(Mackay, Greaves 2, Smith, Jones, White)* **Slovan Bratislava 0**

TEAM:
Tottenham: Brown, Hopkins, Henry, Marchi, Norman, Mackay, Saul, White, Smith, Greaves, Jones

SEMI-FINAL

April 24, 1963, 60,000

OFK Belgrade 1, Tottenham 2 *(Dyson, White)*

TEAM:
Tottenham: Brown, Baker, Henry, Marchi, Norman, Mackay, Greaves, Smith J, Smith R, White, Dyson

May 1, 1963, 59,736

Tottenham 3 *(Jones, Smith, Mackay),* **OFK Belgrade 1**

TEAM:
Tottenham: Brown, Baker, Henry, Blanchflower, Norman, Marchi, Jones, White, Smith, Mackay, Dyson

FINAL

Feyenoord stadium, Rotterdam
40,000

Atletico Madrid 1, Tottenham 5 *(Greaves 2, White, Dyson 2)*

TEAM:
Tottenham: Brown, Baker, Henry, Blanchflower, Norman, Marchi, Jones, White, Smith, Greaves, Smith

Madrid: Madinabeytia, Rivilla, Rodrigues, Ramiro, Griffa, Glaria, Jones, Adelardo, Chuzo, Mendonca, Collar

1963/64 – ECWC

December 3, 1963, 57,000

Tottenham 2 *(Mackay, Dyson),* **Manchester United 0**

TEAM:
Tottenham: Brown, Baker, Henry, Marchi, Norman, Mackay, Jones, White, Smith, Greaves, Dyson

December 10, 1963, 59,597

Manchester United 4, Spurs 1 *(Greaves)*

TEAM:
Tottenham: Brown, Baker, Henry, Marchi, Norman, Mackay, Jones, White, Smith, Greaves, Dyson

1967/68 – ECWC

September 20, 1967, 25,000

Hadjuk Split 0, Tottenham 2 *(Robertson, Greaves)*

TEAM:
Tottenham: Jennings, Kinnear, Knowles, Mullery, England, Beal, Robertson, Greaves, Gilzean, Venables, Saul

September 27, 1967, 38,623

Tottenham 4, *(Robertson 2, Gilzean, Venables),* **Hadjuk Split 3**

TEAM:
Tottenham: Jennings, Kinnear, Knowles, Mullery, England, Beal, Robertson, Greaves, Gilzean, Venables, Jones

SECOND ROUND

November 29, 1967, 10,997

Olympique Lyonnais 1, Spurs 0

TEAM:
Tottenham: Jennings, Kinnear, Knowles, Mullery, Hoy, Mackay, Robertson, Greaves, Gilzean, Venables, Jones

December 13, 1967, 41,895

Tottenham 4 *(Greaves 2, Venables, Jones),* **Olympique Lyonnais 3**

TEAM:
Tottenham: Jennings, Kinnear, Knowles, Bond, Hoy, Mackay, Robertson, Greaves, Gilzean, Venables, Jones

1971/72 – UEFA CUP

September 14, 1971, 11,000

Keflavik 1, Tottenham 6 *(Gilzean 3, Coates, Mullery 2)*

TEAM:
Tottenham: Jennings, Kinnear, Knowles, Mullery (Souness), England, Beal, Coates (Pearce), Perryman, Chivers, Peters, Gilzean

September 28, 1971, 23,818

Tottenham 9 *(Chivers 3, Perryman, Coates, Knowles, Gilzean 2, Holder),* **Keflavik 0**

TEAM:
Tottenham: Jennings, Evans, Knowles, Mullery (Pearce), England, Beal, Coates, Perryman, Chivers, Peters (Holder), Gilzean

SECOND ROUND

October 20, 1971, 20,033

Nantes 0, Tottenham 0

TEAM:
Tottenham: Jennings, Kinnear, Knowles, Mullery, England, Beal, Neighbour, Perryman, Chivers, Peters, Gilzean (Morgan)

November 2, 1971, 32,630

Tottenham 1 *(Peters),* **Nantes 0**

TEAM:
Tottenham: Jennings, Evans, Knowles, Pratt, England, Beal, Neighbour, Perryman, Chivers, Peters, Gilzean (Pearce)

THIRD ROUND

December 8, 1971, 30,702

Tottenham 3 *(Peters, Chivers 2),* **Rapid Bucharest 0**

TEAM:
Tottenham: Jennings, Evans, Knowles, Coates (Pearce), England, Beal, Gilzean, Perryman, Chivers, Peters, Neighbour

December 15, 1971, 12,000

Rapid Bucharest 0, Tottenham 2 *(Pearce, Chivers)*

TEAM:
Tottenham: Jennings, Evans, Knowles, Coates, Collins, Beal, Pratt, Naylor, Chivers, Peters, Gilzean (Pearce)

QUARTER-FINAL

March 7, 1972, 20,000

UT Arad 0, Spurs 2 *(Morgan, England)*

TEAM:
Tottenham: Jennings, Evans, Knowles, Pratt, England, Beal, Gilzean (Collins), Perryman, Chivers, Peters, Morgan

March 21, 1972, 30,253

Tottenham 1 *(Gilzean),* **UT Arad 1**

TEAM:
Tottenham: Jennings, Evans, Knowles, Coates, England, Naylor, Gilzean, Perryman, Pratt, Peters, Morgan

SEMI-FINAL

April 5, 1972, 42,064

Tottenham 2 *(Perryman 2),* **AC Milan 1**

TEAM:
Tottenham: Jennings, Kinnear, Knowles, Coates (Neighbour), England, Naylor, Gilzean, Perryman, Chivers, Peters, Mullery

April 19, 1972, 68,482

AC Milan 1, Tottenham 1 *(Mullery)*

TEAM:
Tottenham: Jennings, Kinnear, Knowles, Mullery, England, Beal, Coates, Perryman, Chivers, Peters, Pratt (Naylor)

FINAL

May 3, 1972, 38,362

Wolves 1, Tottenham 2 *(Chivers 2)*

TEAM:
Tottenham: Jennings, Kinnear, Knowles, Mullery, England, Beal, Gilzean, Perryman, Chivers, Peters, Coates (Pratt)

May 17, 1972, 54,303

Tottenham 1 *(Mullery),* **Wolves 1**

TEAM:
Tottenham: Jennings, Kinnear, Knowles, Mullery, England, Beal, Coates, Perryman, Chivers, Peters, Gilzean

Wolves: Parkes, Shaw, Taylor, Hegan, Munro, McAlle, McCalliog, Hibbitt (Bailey), Richards, Dougan (Curran), Wagstaffe

1972/73–UEFA CUP

13 September, 1972, 10,770

Lyn Oslo 3, Tottenham 6 *(Pratt, Gilzean 2, Chivers 2, Peters*

TEAM:
Tottenham: Jennings, Evans, Knowles, Pratt, England, Naylor, Gilzean, Perryman, Chivers, Peters, Pearce

27 September, 1972, 21,109

Tottenham 6 *(Chivers 3, Pearce, Coates 2),* **Lyn Oslo 0**

TEAM:
Tottenham: Jennings, Kinnear, Knowles, Pratt, England, Beal, Gilzean, Perryman, Chivers, Pearce, Coates (Naylor)

SECOND ROUND

25 October, 1972, 27,815

Tottenham 4 *(Pearce 2, Chivers, Coates),* **Olympiakos Piraeus 0**

TEAM:
Tottenham: Jennings, Evans, Knowles, Pearce, England, Beal, Gilzean, Perryman, Chivers, Peters, Coates (Neighbour, Naylor)

8 November, 1972, 35,000

Olympiakos Piraeus 1, Tottenham 0

TEAM:
Tottenham: Jennings, Evans, Knowles, Pearce, England, Dillon, Gilzean, Perryman, Chivers, Naylor, Pratt

THIRD ROUND

29 November, 1972, 23,958

Tottenham 2 *(Gilzean, Chivers),* **Red Star Belgrade 0**

TEAM:
Tottenham: Jennings, Evans, Knowles, Pratt, England, Naylor, Gilzean, Perryman, Chivers, Peters, Pearce

13 December 1972, 70,000

Red Star Belgrade 1, Tottenham 0

TEAM:
Tottenham: Jennings, Evans, Knowles, Pratt, England, Kinnear, Coates, Perryman, Chivers, Peters, Pearce

QUARTER-FINAL

7 March, 1973, 30,469

Tottenham 1 *(Evans),* **Vitoria Setubal 0**

TEAM:
Tottenham: Jennings, Kinnear, Knowles, Coates, England, Beal, Gilzean, Perryman, Chivers, Peters, Pearce (Evans)

21 March, 1973, 30,000

Vitoria Setubal 2, Tottenham 1 *(Chivers)*

TEAM:
Tottenham: Jennings, Kinnear, Knowles, Coates, England, Beal, Gilzean, Perryman, Chivers, Peters, Pearce (Naylor)

SEMI-FINAL

10 April, 1973, 42,174

Liverpool 1, Tottenham 0

TEAM:
Tottenham: Jennings, Kinnear, Knowles, Coates, England, Beal, Gilzean, Perryman, Chivers, Peters, Pratt (Evans)

25 April, 1973, 46,919

Tottenham 2 *(Peters 2),* **Liverpool 1**

TEAM:
Tottenham: Jennings, Kinnear, Knowles, Coates, England, Beal, Gilzean, Perryman, Chivers, Peters, Pratt (Pearce, Evans)

1973/74 – UEFA CUP

19 September, 1973, 11,200

Grasshoppers Zurich 1, Tottenham 5 *(Evans, Chivers 2, Gilzean 2)*

TEAM:
Tottenham: Jennings, Evans, Knowles, Coates, England, Beal, Pratt, Perryman, Chivers, Peters, Neighbour (Gilzean, Holder)

3 October, 1973, 18,105

Tottenham 4 *(England, Peters 2, Lador og),* **Grasshoppers Zurich 1**

TEAM:
Tottenham: Daniels, Evans, Knowles, Pratt, England, Beal, Gilzean, Perryman, Chivers, Peters, Coates

SECOND ROUND

24 October, 1973, 30,000

Aberdeen 1, Tottenham 1 *(Coates)*

TEAM:
Tottenham: Daniels, Evans, Kinnear, Pratt, England, Beal, Gilzean, Perryman, McGrath, Peters, Coates (Neighbour, Naylor)

7 November, 1973, 21,785

Tottenham 4 *(Peters, Neighbour, McGrath 2),* **Aberdeen 1**

TEAM:
Tottenham: Jennings, Evans, Knowles, Pratt, England, Beal, Gilzean, Perryman, Chivers, Peters, Neighbour (McGrath)

THIRD ROUND

28 November 1973, 45,000

Dinamo Tblisi 1, Tottenham 1 *(Coates)*

TEAM:
Tottenham: Jennings, Evans, Knowles, Pratt, England, Beal, Naylor, Perryman, Chivers, Peters, Coates

12 December, 1973, 18,602

Tottenham 5 *(McGrath, Chivers 2, Peters 2),* **Dinamo Tblisi 1**

TEAM:
Tottenham: Jennings, Evans, Naylor, Pratt, England, Beal, McGrath, Perryman, Chivers, Peters, Coates

QUARTER-FINAL

6 March, 1974, 28,000

Cologne 1, Tottenham 2 *(McGrath, Peters)*

TEAM:
Tottenham: Jennings, Evans, Naylor, Pratt, England, Beal, McGrath, Perryman, Chivers, Peters, Dillon

20 March, 1974, 40,968

Tottenham 3 *(Chivers, Peters, Coates),* **Cologne 0**

TEAM:
Tottenham: Jennings, Evans, Naylor, Pratt, England, Beal, McGrath, Perryman, Chivers, Peters, Coates

SEMI-FINAL

10 April, 1974, 74,000

Locomotiv Leipzig 1, Tottenham 2 *(Peters, Coates)*

TEAM:
Tottenham: Jennings, Evans, Naylor, Pratt, England, Beal, Neighbour, Perryman, Chivers, Peters, Coates (Holder)

24 April, 1974, 41,280

Tottenham 2 *(McGrath, Chivers),* **Locomotiv Leipzig 0**

TEAM:
Tottenham: Jennings, Kinnear, Naylor, Pratt, England, Beal, McGrath, Perryman, Chivers, Peters, Coates (Holder)

FINAL

21 May, 1974, 46,281

Tottenham 2 *(England, Van Daele og),* **Feyenoord 2**

TEAMS:
Tottenham: Jennings, Evans, Naylor, Pratt, England, Beal, McGrath, Perryman, Chivers, Peters, Coates

29 May, 1974, 68,000

Feyenoord 2, Tottenham 0

TEAMS:
Tottenham: Jennings, Evans, Naylor, Pratt (Holder), England, Beal, McGrath, Perryman, Chivers, Peters, Coates

Feyenoord: Treytel, Rijsbergen, Van Daele, Israel, Vos, Ramljak, Jansen, De Jong, Ressel, Schoenmaker, Kristensen (Boskampx), (Wrey)

1981/82 – ECWC

September 16, 1981, 35,000

Ajax 1, Tottenham 3 *(Villa, Falco 2)*

TEAM:
Tottenham: Clemence, Hughton, Miller, Roberts, Villa, Perryman, Ardiles, Archibald, Galvin, Hoddle, Falco

September 29, 1981, 34,606

Tottenham 3 *(Ardiles, Galvin, Falco),* **Ajax 0**

TEAM:
Tottenham: Clemence, Hughton, Miller, Roberts, Villa, Perryman, Ardiles, Archibald, Galvin, Hoddle, Falco

SECOND ROUND

October 21, 1981, 17,500

Dundalk 1, Tottenham 1 *(Crooks)*

TEAM:
Tottenham: Clemence, Hughton, Miller, Roberts, Hazard, Perryman, Ardiles, Archibald, Galvin (Smith), Hoddle, Crooks

November 4, 1981, 33,455

Tottenham 1 *(Crooks),* **Dundalk 0**

TEAM:
Tottenham: Clemence, Hughton, Miller, Roberts, Hazard, Perryman, Ardiles, Archibald, Galvin, Hoddle, Crooks

THIRD ROUND

March 3, 1982, 38,172

Tottenham 2 *(Miller, Hazard),* **Eintracht Frankfurt 0**

TEAM:
Tottenham: Clemence, Hughton, Miller, Price, Hazard, Perryman, Ardiles, Archibald, Galvin, Hoddle, Crooks (Falco)

March 17, 1982, 44,000

Eintracht Frankfurt 2, *Tottenham 1* **(Hoddle)**

TEAM:
Tottenham: Clemence, Hughton, Miller, Price, Hazard, Perryman, Ardiles (Villa), Archibald, Galvin, Hoddle, Falco (Roberts)

SEMI-FINAL

April 7, 1982, 41,545

Tottenham 1 *(Roberts),* **Barcelona 1**

TEAM:
Tottenham: Clemence, Hughton, Miller (Jones), Price, Hazard, Perryman, Roberts, Villa, Galvin, Hoddle, Crooks

April 21, 1982, 80,000

Barcelona 1, Tottenham 0

TEAM:
Tottenham: Clemence, Hughton, Price (Falco), Roberts, Hazard, Perryman, Villa, Archibald, Galvin, Hoddle, Crooks

1982/83 – ECWC

September 15, 1982, 12,000

Coleraine 0, Tottenham 3 *(Archibald, Crooks 2)*

TEAM:
Tottenham: Clemence, Hughton, Price, Lacy, Brooke, Perryman, Mabbutt, Archibald, Galvin, Villa, Crooks

September 28, 1982, 20,925

Tottenham 4 *(Brooke, Mabbutt, Crooks, Gibson),* **Coleraine 0**

TEAM:
Tottenham: Clemence, Hughton, Price, Lacy, Brooke, Perryman, Mabbutt, Archibald, Hazard, Villa, Crooks

SECOND ROUND

October 20, 1982, 36,488

Tottenham 1 *(Archibald),* **Bayern Munich 1**

TEAM:
Tottenham: Clemence, Price, O'Reilly, Miller, Lacy, Hazard, Brooke, Archibald, Mabbutt, Villa, Crooks

November 3, 1982, 55,000

Bayern Munich 4, Tottenham 1 *(Hughton)*

TEAM:
Tottenham: Clemence, Price, Hughton, Miller, Lacy, Hazard, Mabbutt, Archibald, Brooke, Villa, Crooks

1983/84 – UEFA CUP

September 14, 1983, 70,000

Drogheda 0, Spurs 6 *(Mabbutt 2, Falco 2, Galvin, Crooks)*

TEAM:
Tottenham: Clemence, Hughton, O'Reilly, Roberts, Price, Perryman, Mabbutt, Falco, Galvin, Brooke, Crooks

28 September, 1983, 19,831

Tottenham 8 *(Hughton, Roberts 2, Archibald, Falco 2, Brazil 2),* **Drogheda 0**

TEAM:
Tottenham: Clemence, Hughton, Galvin, Roberts, Price, Perryman, Mabbutt, Archibald, Falco, Hoddle, Brazil (O'Reilly)

SECOND ROUND

19 October, 1983, 35,404

Tottenham 4 *(Galvin 2, Archibald 2),* **Feyenoord 2**

TEAM:
Tottenham: Clemence, Hughton, Galvin, Roberts, Stevens, Perryman, Mabbutt, Archibald, Falco, Hoddle, Brooke (Crook)

2 November 1983, 45,061

Feyenoord 0, Tottenham 2 *(Hughton, Galvin)*

TEAM:
Tottenham: Clemence, Hughton, Thomas, Roberts, Stevens, Perryman, Mabbutt, Archibald, Falco, Hoddle, Galvin (Brazil)

THIRD ROUND

23 November, 1983, 20,000

Bayern Munich 1, Tottenham 0

TEAM:
Tottenham: Clemence, Hughton, Thomas, Roberts, Stevens, Perryman, Hazard, Archibald, Falco, Hoddle, Dick (Brooke, Brazil)

7 December, 1983, 41,977

Tottenham 2 *(Archibald, Falco),* **Bayern Munich 0**

TEAM:
Tottenham: Clemence, Hughton, Thomas, Roberts, Stevens, Perryman, Cooke, Archibald, Falco, Hoddle, Dick (O'Reilly, Brooke)

QUARTER-FINAL

7 March, 1984, 34,069

Tottenham 2 *(Archibald, Brazil),* **Austria Vienna 0**

TEAM:
Tottenham: Parks, Stevens, Hughton, Roberts, Miller, Perryman, Ardiles, Archibald, Brazil, Hazard, Dick (Hoddle)

21 March, 1984, 21,000

Austria Vienna 2, Tottenham 2 *(Ardiles, Brazil)*

TEAM:
Tottenham: Clemence, Stevens, Hughton, Roberts, Miller, Perryman, Ardiles, Archibald, Brazil, Mabbutt, Galvin (Thomas, Falco)

SEMI-FINAL

11 April 1984, 40,000

Hadjuk Split 2, Tottenham 1 *(Falco)*

TEAM:
Tottenham: Parks, Thomas, Hughton, Roberts, Miller, Perryman, Hazard, Archibald, Falco, Mabbutt, Galvin (Crook)

25 April, 1984, 43,969

Tottenham 1 *(Hazard),* **Hadjuk Split 0**

TEAM:
Tottenham: Parks, Thomas, Hughton, Roberts, Miller, Perryman, Hazard, Archibald, Falco, Stevens, Galvin (Mabbutt)

FINAL

9 May, 1984, 40,000

Anderlecht 1, Tottenham 1 *(Miller)*

TEAMS:
Tottenham: Parks, Thomas, Hughton, Roberts, Miller, Perryman, Stevens (Mabbutt), Archibald, Falco, Hazard, Galvin

23 May, 1984, 46,205

Tottenham 1 *(Roberts),* **Anderlecht 1**
Tottenham win 4-3 on penalties

TEAMS:
Tottenham: Parks, Thomas, Hughton, Roberts, Miller (Ardiles), Mabbutt (Dick), Hazard, Archibald, Stevens, Galvin, Falco

Anderlecht: Munaron, Grun, De Greef, Czerniatynski (Brylle), De Groote, Vercautern, Vandereycken, Hofkens, Scifo, Olsen, Arnesen (Gudjohnsen)

1984/85 – UEFA CUP

September 19, 1984, 26,000

Sporting Braga 0, Tottenham 3 *(Falco 2, Galvin)*

TEAM:
Tottenham: Clemence, Stevens, Hughton, Roberts, Miller, Perryman, Cheidozie, Falco, Allen (Crooks), Hazard (Thomas), Galvin

October 3, 1984, 22,478

Tottenham 6 *(Crooks 3, Stevens, Hughton, Falco),* **Sporting Braga 0**

TEAM:
Tottenham: Clemence, Stevens, Hughton, Roberts, Miller (Hoddle), Perryman, Cheidozie, Falco (Cooke), Glavin, Hazard, Crooks

SECOND ROUND

October 24, 1984, 27,000

Bruges 2 , Tottenham 1 *(Allen)*

TEAM:
Tottenham: Clemence, Stevens, Hughton, Roberts, Miller, Perryman, Cheidozie, Falco, Galvin, Hazard (Hoddle), Crooks (Allen)

November 7, 1984, 24,356

Tottenham 3 *(Roberts, Allen, Hazard),* **Bruges 0**

TEAM:
Tottenham: Clemence, Roberts, Stevens, Miller, Mabbutt, Perryman, Cheidozie (Brooke), Falco, Allen (Thomas), Hazard, Galvin

THIRD ROUND

November 28, 1984, 27,971

Tottenham 2 *(Stevens, og),* **Bohemians Prague 0**

TEAM:
Tottenham: Clemence, Stevens, Mabbutt (Hughton), Roberts, Miller, Perryman, Chiedozie, Falco, Allen, Hoddle, Hazard (Thomas)

December 12, 1984, 17,500

Bohemians Prague 1, Tottenham 1 *(Falco)*

TEAM:
Tottenham: Clemence, Stevens, Hughton, Roberts, Miller, Perryman, Cheidozie, Falco, Galvin, Hoddle (Mabbutt), Crooks (Thomas)

QUARTER-FINAL

March 6, 1985, 39,914

Tottenham 0, Real Madrid 1 *(Perryman og)*

TEAM:
Tottenham: Clemence, Stevens, Hughton, Hazard, Miller (Brooke), Perryman, Cheidozie (Dick), Falco, Galvin, Hoddle, Crooks

March 20, 1985, 90,000

Real Madrid 0, Tottenham 0

TEAM:
Tottenham: Clemence, Thomas, Hughton, Roberts, Miller, Perryman, Hazard, Falco, Galvin (Brook), Hoddle, Crooks (Dick)
Real Madrid: Miguel Angel, Schendo, Camacho, Salguero, Sanchis, Angel, Pineda, (San Jose), Michel, Butragueno, (Losano), Gallago, Valdano

PHOTO CREDIT LIST OF ILLUSTRATIONS

p. 128 Ralph Coates seen giving Spurs the lead (Carleton Photographic)

p. 129 Chris McGrath beats Bobby Clark (Monte Fresco, Daily Mirror)

p. 131 The players cross swords at the official banquet (Carleton Photographic)
The players in training (Carleton Photographic)

pp. 132 and **33** Martin Peters heads home Spurs' third (Monte Fresco, Daily Mirror)

p. 134 Chris McGrath beats Cologne goalkeeper Weiz (Carleton Photographic)

p. 136 Martin Peters turns away in triumph (Monte Fresco, Daily Mirror)

p. 137 Martin Chivers scores again for Spurs (Carleton Photographic)

pp. 138 and **139** Coates watches his diving header find the net (Carleton Photographic)

p. 140 Ralph Coates scores Spurs' second goal in Leipzig (Carleton Photographic)

p. 141 Martin Chivers scores Spurs' second goal (Monte Fresco, Daily Mirror)

pp. 142 and **143** Mike England celebrates (Monte Fresco, Daily Mirror)

p. 144 Ralph Coates and Martin Peters look on (Coloursport)

p. 145 Steve Perryman goes close (Coloursport)
Martin Chivers and Martin Peters pressurise a Feyenoord defender (Coloursport)

pp. 146 and **147** Fans run away (Monte Fresco, Daily Mirror)

p. 149 Bill Nicholson receives the OBE (Associated Newspapers Group Limited)

p. 150 John Pratt (Carleton Photographic)

p. 153 Ossie Ardiles and his son (Professional Sport)

p. 155 Triumphant Ardiles lifts the Cup (Tommy Hindley, Professional Sport)

p. 158 Glenn Hoddle in action against Ajax (Coloursport)
Mark Falco celebrates his goal (Coloursport)

pp. 160 and **161** Ossie Ardiles threads his way through the Ajax defence (Monte Fresco, Daily Mirror)

p. 163 Archibald's effort is saved by Blackmoor (Monte Fresco, Daily Mirror)

p. 165 Durens saves at the feet of Garth Crooks (Sport and General)

p. 168 Roberts looks on (Associated Newspapers Group Limited)
Yellow card (Associated Newspapers Group Limited)

pp. 168 and **169** Paul Price wins the ball from Alan Simonsen (Popperfoto)

p. 169 Barcelona scramble the ball away (Coloursport)

pp. 170 and **171** Graham Roberts shows his delight (Coloursport)

pp. 172 and **173** Urruti saves from Graham Roberts (Monte Fresco, Daily Mirror)

p. 175 Ricky Villa being challenged (Mark Jameson, Coleraine Chronicle)

p. 176 Garth Crooks opens the scoring (Associated Newspapers Group Limited)

p. 177 Coleraine goalkeeper Vince Magee (Monte Fresco, Daily Mirror)

p. 179 Gary Mabbutt beats Wolfgang Grobe to the ball (Sport and General)

p. 180 Ray Clemence saves (Popperfoto)

p. 183 Gary Mabbut goes close for Spurs (Monte Fresco, Daily Mirror)

pp. 184 and **185** Steve Archibald turns away (Monte Fresco, Daily Mirror)

pp. 186 and **187** The new master beats the old (Associated Newspapers Group Limited)

p. 189 Archibald challenges Feyenoord's Ivan Nielsen (Monte Fresco, Daily Mirror)

pp. 190 and **191** Johan Cruyff tries to organise the Feyenoord defence (Monte Fresco, Daily Mirror)

pp. 192 and **193** Roberts is foiled by Lerby (Monte Fresco, Daily Mirror)

p. 195 Karl-Heinz Rummenigge gets away from Mike Hazard (Sport and General)

pp. 200 and **201** Alan Brazil beats Koncilia (Monte Fresco, Daily Mirror)

pp. 202 and **203** Alan Brazil putting Spurs ahead 1-0 in Vienna (Monte Fresco, Daily Mirror)

pp. 204 and **205** Tony Parks is beaten (Monte Fresco, Daily Mirror)

p. 206 Gary Stevens in the thick of the action (Coloursport)
Steve Archibald is tackled (Monte Fresco, Daily Mirror)

pp. 210 and **211** Archibald challenged by the Anderlecht defence (Monte Fresco, Daily Mirror)

p. 212 Archibald and Galvin tussle for the ball (Monte Fresco, Daily Mirror)

p. 213 Spurs' supporters being escorted by the Brussels gendarmerie (Monte Fresco, Daily Mirror)

p. 215 Graham Roberts lifts the Cup (Coloursport)

p. 217 UEFA Cup winners (Lawrence Lustig, Global Sports)

p. 218 Steve Perryman (Tommy Hindley, Professional Sport)

pp. 226 and **227** Clive Allen notches Spurs' third goal (Associated Newspapers Group Limited)

pp. 228 and **229** Roberts and Perryman close ranks (Lawrence Lustig, Global Sports)

p. 230 Mark Falco goes close (Monte Fresco, Daily Mirror)

pp. 232 and **233** Prokes clears from Gary Stevens (Lawrence Lustig, Global Sports)

p. 235 Graham Roberts and Mark Falco with their scars (Tommy Hindley, Professional Sport)

p. 237 Clive Allen tries a shot (Lawrence Lustig, Global Sports)

pp. 238 and **239** Archibald looks on (Coloursport)
Archibald puts Spurs level on aggregate (Coloursport)
Hoddle holds his hands aloft (Coloursport)

p. 240 Steve Archibald scores Spurs' first goal (Lawrence Lustig, Global Sports)
Steve Archibald tries a shot (Lawrence Lustig, Global Sports)

p. 243 Agony (Popperfoto)

pp. 244 and **245** Mark Falco shoots past Stieleke (Associated Newspapers Group Limited)
Garth Crooks battles for possession (Associated Newspapers Group Limited)

p. 245 Mike Hazard beats the wall (Coloursport)

pp. 246 and **247** Spurs' players celebrate (Coloursport)

pp. 248 and **249** Graham Roberts brings the house down (Coloursport)

pp. 250 and **251** Heroes of the night (Lawrence Lustig, Global Sports)
Spurs v Anderlecht (Coloursport)

pp. 252 and **253** John Chiedozie goes close (Lawrence Lustig, Global Sports)

pp. 254 and **255** Mark Falco scores Spurs' fifth goal (Lawrence Lustig, Global Sports)

p. 256 Garth Crooks shoots just wide (Lawrence Lustig, Global Sports)
Garth Crooks dribbles round Helder (Lawrence Lustig, Global Sports)

p. 257 Spurs v Real Madrid (Sport and General)

p. 259 Disallowed (Tommy Hindley, Professional Sport)

p. 260 Peter Shreeve (Tommy Hindley, Professional Sport)

Inside back cover Spurs' players stare in amazement (Monte Fresco, Daily Mirror)

Gifts and pennants from some European opponents are from Tottenham Hotspurs' private collection of trophies and were photographed by Carleton Photographic.

Index of Newspapers and reporters

DAILY TELEGRAPH
Byron Butler – Hadjuk Split (1967), p. 72
Michael Calvin – Anderlecht, p. 214
David Miller – Nantes, p. 82
Robert Oxby – Grasshoppers Zurich, p. 127
Donald Saunders – Atletico Madrid (1963), p. 51

EVENING NEWS
John Oakley – Olympique Lyonnaise, p. 74; AC Milan (1972), p. 101

GUARDIAN
Robert Armstrong – Dundalk, p. 163
Frank Keating – Dinamo Tbilisi, p. 132
David Lacey – Olympiakos Piraeus, p. 111; Bayern Munich (1982), p. 178; Real Madrid, p. 242
Eric Todd – Feyenoord (1961), p. 20

MANCHESTER EVENING NEWS
Noel Cantwell – Manchester United, p. 57
David Meek – Manchester United, p. 57

NEWS OF THE WORLD
Frank Butler – Aston Villa, p. 77
Reg Drury – Aston Villa, p. 78; Leicester, p. 151

STANDARD
Peter Blackman – Ajax Amsterdam, p. 156; Keith Burkinshaw, p. 208
Alexander Clyde (Martin Peters interview) – Wolves, p. 106
Michael Hart – Bruges, p. 106
Bernard Joy – Manchester United, p. 59; Wolves, p. 106

SUN
Ian Gibb – Coleraine, p. 176
Brian Woolnough, Eintracht Frankfurt (1982), p. 166; Barcelona, p. 167; Queen's Park Rangers, p. 174; Austria Vienna, p. 202; Bohemians Prague, p. 234

SUNDAY EXPRESS
Alan Hoby – Chelsea, p. 68; Leicester City, p. 10

SUNDAY TIMES
Brian Glanville – Burnley, p. 40; Norwich, p. 124

TIMES
Geoffrey Green – Hadjuk Split (1967), p. 71; Nantes, p. 85; Rapid Bucharest, p. 92; Wolves, p. 103; Red Star Belgrade, p. 113; Cologne, p. 134
Brian James – UT Arad, p. 93
Stuart Jones – Bayern Munich (1982), p. 181; Bayern Munich (1983), p. 194
David Miller – Bruges, p. 226
Clive White – Feyenoord (1983), p. 185
Times Correspondent – Slovan Bratislava, p. 47

THE FUTURE. David Pleat (left) becomes the new manager of Tottenham Hotspur Football Club on 15th May 1986, shaking hands with Club Chairman Irving Scholar.

HOLSTEN
HOLSTEN